St. Thomas Aquinas and Muslim Thought

To Fahad Akbar

St. Thomas Aquinas and Muslim Thought

ZULFIQAR ALI SHAH

CLARITAS
BOOKS

1 2 3 4 5 6 7 8 9 10

CLARITAS BOOKS

Bernard Street, Swansea, United Kingdom
Milpitas, California, United States

CLARITAS
BOOKS

First Published in May 2022

Typeset in Minion Pro 14/11

St. Thomas Aquinas and Muslim Thought
By Zulfiqar Ali Shah

Series Editor: Sharif H. Banna

A CIP catalogue record for this book is available from the British Library

ISBN: 978-1-80011-994-9

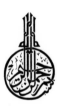

Zulfiqar Ali Shah received his BA and MA (Hons) in Comparative Religions from the International Islamic University in Islamabad, Pakistan and his PhD in Theology and Religious Studies from the University of Wales, UK. He has taught at the International Islamic University in Islamabad, the University of Wales in the UK, the University of North Florida and Cardinal Stritch University in the US. He is the former President of the Islamic Circle of North America and the Shariah Scholars Association of North America. Dr Zulfiqar Shah is currently the Executive Director and Secretary General of the Fiqh Council of North America and Religious Director of the Islamic Society of Milwaukee, USA. He has authored many articles and books including *Anthropomorphic Depictions of God: The Concept of God in the Judaic, Christian and Islamic Traditions*. His forthcoming ground-breaking books include *Islam's Reformation of Christianity, Islam and the English Enlightenment: The Untold Story, Islam and the French Enlightenment* and *Islam and the Founding Fathers of America*.

Zulfiqar Ali Shah is a thorough historian of so much, as well as being an astute theologian – and the way he brings them together is masterful! I learned so much from this study, and found it fascinating as well--given his limpid English. And I found his judgments of matters to be just that: judicious! He has a flair for narrative, so the often disparate topics meld together effectively. So I can only thank him for bringing it all together so seamlessly. The study is a must for those engaged in cross-cultural influences in medieval philosophical-religious thought.

David B. Burrell, C.S.C.
Theodore Hesburgh Professor Emeritus in Philosophy and Theology
University of Notre Dame

St. Thomas Aquinas and Muslim Thought offers an insightful complement to an understanding and appreciation of Thomas Aquinas. Dr. Ali Shah's study shows the impact of Islam on Western Europe, which exposed Aquinas to cultural tensions, political conflicts, and religious (theological and philosophical) controversies. In addressing these, Aquinas was in part directly influenced by, and in part significantly indebted to, Muslim theological and philosophical thought. Despite differences that remain in Aquinas' thought because of his Christian commitments, we are provided with a view that shows Aquinas to be respectful of, and in dialogue with, the religious diversity-Islamic and Jewish-of his time yet instructive to our own.

Joseph A. Buijs
Professor Emeritus (Philosophy)
St. Joseph's College, University of Alberta

Dr. Shah's meticulous exploration of the intellectual relationships between Thomas Aquinas and the rich world of Islamic scholarship of the time is a fascinating study and well worth the time of anyone interested in that field of study. I found this volume a wonderful resource for my own understanding of medieval philosophy and theology.

Bishop Richard J. Sklba
Auxiliary Bishop Emeritus of Milwaukee

Dr. Zulfiqar Ali Shah offers a detailed and well-researched study of the interactions between St Thomas Aquinas and medieval Muslim philosophy.

Paul Badham
Emeritus Professor of Theology and Religious Studies
University of Wales

Contents

Introduction

St. Thomas Aquinas,[1] the most known medieval philosophical theologian and the stalwart of scholasticism, was greatly influenced by Muslim synthetic thought. He quoted widely from Ibn Rushd, Ibn Sina, al-Farabi, al-Ghazali in his writings, acting and reacting to them in a number of ways. He read Latin translations of their works and incorporated many of their ideas, thoughts and arguments into his synthetic project. He was a professional theologian who used philosophy to support his theology, assimilating many philosophical ideas in the process of reconciling theology with philosophy. The Muslim philosophers and some theologians had undertaken the same project centuries before Thomas; consequently, he found a model in them to emulate and benefit from. He mostly preferred Aristotelianism against the Platonism of St. Augustine and other Church Fathers, venturing to reconcile Christian theology with it. He initially studied Aristotle at the University of Naples which was a part of Norman Sicily; Sicily was ruled by Muslims for close to three centuries (831-1072) and countless Muslims stayed behind even after the Norman conquest of it. The Norman rulers, especially Frederick II, had patronised Muslim sciences, encouraging translation of scientific works from Arabic to Latin.[2] Transmission of the Aristotelian philosophy constituted a major bulk of these inter-cultural endeavours. Muslim philosophers such as Abu Nasr al-Farabi, Abu Ali Sina and Abu al-Walid Ibn Rushd and philosophical theologian Abu Hamid al-Ghazali had long studied Aristotle, extensively commenting on and interpreting his philosophy; the Muslim Aristotelian tradition was well established before the times of Thomas. The twelfth century witnessed the peak of translation and transmission of this tradition from Arabic to Latin, as the Spanish and Holy Land crusades increased possibilities of cross cultural assimilations. Thomas was very close to the epicenter of this movement as Southern Italy in general, and Naples in particular was exposed to Muslim philosophical ideas. Gordon Leff suggests that "intellectually, the difference between [the] 12th and 13th century was, at its broadest, the difference between isolation from the Islamic world and contact with it."[3]

Muslim theologians such as Abu Hamid al-Ghazali (1058-111), Muhammad bin Abd al-Karim al-Shahrastani (1086-1158) and Fakhr al-Din al-Razi (1149-1210) had also studied the works of Aristotle and Muslim philosophers with the intention of refuting the parts deemed theologically unsound. Unlike Muslim philosophers, Muslim theologians gave precedent to revelation over reason. They preferred theology and faith over philosophy, and secular knowledge without denying reason and philosophy a secondary place. In the process they created a theologico-philosophical synthesis in accordance with their orthodox understanding of the Muslim religion. The result was partial theistic accommodation of Greek philosophy, though not on par with the pure rationalism of the Muslim philosophers; the rational orientation of the philosophers' theistic paradigm was far more marked than the Muslim theologians. Both parties claimed to remain within the established parameters of Islamic revelation and serve the cause of Muslim faith, though orthodox theologians such as al-Ghazali found faults with some of the philosophers' positions, declaring them altogether un-Islamic.[4]

The medieval Jewish community also witnessed the same sort of struggles. One such struggle was the difficulty of reconciling faith with philosophy, though acuter than in the Muslim tradition. For instance, the Hebrew Bible was inundated with anthropomorphic and, at times, corporeal passages. The problems related to other metaphysical matters were graver than those faced by their Muslim counterparts. For example, unlike the Quran, the Hebrew Bible was a composite work of multiple authors spanning over centuries; polytheism, henotheism and monotheism were all presented in various parts of the Hebrew scripture. Unlike the Quran, transcendental monotheism was not well guarded in the Hebrew Bible.[5] Many such areas were the focus of Muslim ridicule of the Jewish tradition. As a minority among the dominant Muslim majority, the Jews were forced to face these realities and address the perceived problematic areas. Jewish theologians, such a Saadia Gaon (d. 940) and Moses Maimonides, (d. 1204) followed the footsteps of Muslim theologians in reconciling revelation with reason implying almost identical methods and strategies. The medieval Jewish philosophers mostly imitated the Muslim philosophical endeavours in their treatment of the philosophical subjects. Both the medieval Jewish theologians and philosophers were basically a reflection of the dominant Muslim culture and civilisation.

The gulfs between reason and revelation, faith and philosophy or Jesus and Aristotle were wider in Christianity than the other two Semitic traditions.[6] The Christian incarnation theology especially in the pre-scholastic period was mostly Neoplatonic. The Platonic Augustinianism emphasised upon God and salvation more than the utilitarian sphere of here and now. Natural curiosity and rational inquiry were mostly discouraged in the name of faith-based mysteries and divinely-inspired ultimate truths. With the exception of Aristotelian logic, most philosophical and metaphysical works of Aristotle were not available to Latin Christianity from the sixth to the twelfth century; it was in the twelfth century that Latin Christendom was introduced to them through the Muslim medium. The commentaries of Ibn Rushd on Aristotle were so popular by the thirteenth century that he was merely known as the "Commentator". Some works of al-Farabi, Ibn Sina and al-Ghazali were also translated into Latin and were available to the Latin theologians. As Thomas from early on was eagerly engaged in reconciling the Christian theology with Aristotelian philosophy, he was enthusiastic to study the Muslim Aristotelian tradition.

Chapter 1

Muslims in
Aquinas' Horizons

Theology versus Philosophy

Thomas was primarily a theologian. There were certain areas, such as the eternity of the world, where the Aristotelian tradition was in conflict with theology, and Thomas found the Muslim theological treatment of these subjects very helpful especially through the works of Ibn Sina and Maimonides. Therefore, he incorporated Muslim philosophers' arguments wherever no conflict existed between their philosophy and Christian theology. He built upon the Muslim theologians whenever a generic or specific conflict existed between the monotheistic consciousness and Greek philosophy. He differed with Muslim philosophers and theologians alike in areas which were typically Christian, such as the dogmas of Trinity and Incarnation. He was less philosophical in these specifically Christian areas, as he defended most of these doctrines based upon the authority of faith and tradition. The Islamic influence on Thomas was more visible in the philosophical and general theological areas with the exception of specifically Christian theological concepts. Overall, Thomas was less rational than the Muslim philosophers and theologians in matters related to faith.

Muslim philosophers, including the jurist philosopher Ibn Rushd, gave precedence to reason and philosophy over revelation in cases of clear conflict between them. They metaphorically interpreted religious texts to reconcile them with demonstrative knowledge of philosophy. The Muslim theologians also agreed that there could not be a conflict between reason and revelation, and that reason could help in understanding and explaining revelations. They also interpreted many scriptural passages metaphorically, to reconcile them with reason in light of the overall monotheistic and transcendental message of the Quran. But they were less rational than the Muslim philosophers, as they gave an upper hand to the literal meanings of revelation over philosophy in a number of issues, such as the eternity of the world and predestination. The theologians' overall approach guaranteed divine omnipotence and absolute authority over and beyond human and natural autonomy, emphasizing more upon the celestial realms at times at the expense of the terrestrial realms. They never abandoned reason altogether, even in the areas where they preferred revelation over reason. They only limited the scope of rational inquiry in such areas of conflict, and assigned reason a secondary place to revelation.

Thomas considered theology as the crown of all sciences, and employed philosophy in service of theology. He often followed the Muslim Aristotelian tradition wherever it served his theological purposes, such as the arguments for the existence of God. He was most philosophical and rational in these areas of theological discussions. He toed the lines of Muslim theologians in case of apparent conflict between theology and philosophy, such as in issues related to eternity of the world and divine attributes. Thomas was less rational in areas of Christian doctrines, as he mostly depended upon the Christian revelation, faith and tradition to pursue his designs. Thomas's concept of revelation, faith and tradition was quite different than the Muslim philosophers. The Muslim philosophers contended that established demonstrative arguments (universal scientific proofs) could not be refuted or denied based upon the literal meanings of revelation, as the authentic reason was categorical while certain areas of the revelation were probable. They presumed that the authentic revelation supported the rational facts; faith could not create or deny the established rational facts, rather it was supported and substantiated by those facts. Muslim theologians also agreed that faith cannot create rational facts, but is supported by those facts. Thomas, on the other hand, argued that faith could create the facts by itself, because it is founded on the higher authority of revelation and God. Reason could help in determining the authenticity and validity of revelation, but not the content of revelation. Faith is a trust, a willful assent to revelation and its contents; therefore, rational or demonstrative facts were not the original sources of faith. Divine grace was the fundamental source of faith, and the rational facts played second fiddle to it. Thomas was least rational when it came to faith and its contents. Both the Muslim philosophers and theologians were more rational than the mere faith-based theological specifications of Thomas. That is why Thomas's encyclopedic writings, mostly geared towards internal and external mission, could not convince the Muslim population of Spain, Sicily, North Africa and Holy Lands where his Dominican Order was active in evangelism. The Muslim princes, scholars and laity who were actively pursued by the Christian kings, clergy and Mendicant friars could not accept the rhetorical claims of Christian theology's superiority over the Muslim faith merely based on Christian scripture and tradition. They wanted rational arguments and logical proofs for central Christian doctrines, which Aquinas and other friars were at a loss to produce because these dogmas were supra rational mysteries and paradoxes, impossible to be proved by reason and logic.

The main audience of some of Thomas's writings were Muslims, who he intended to convert by means of his philosophical theology. The Jews, Christians and pagans were secondary. His *Summa Contra Gentiles* was geared towards Muslims. Alfred Guillaume observes that "the *Summa contra Gentiles* possesses such enormous value in itself that the primary object of its composition has been lost sight of. Yet the connexion between it and Islam is indissoluble. It was written at the request of the Master-General of the Dominicans, Raymund of Pinnaforte, with the express purpose of convincing the Muslims of Spain of the rational basis of Christianity and the errors of their own religion. In the second chapter of the *Summa* (*quae sit auctoris intentio*) St. Thomas particularly singles out Muhammadans. Jews, he says, can be refuted from the Old Testament; heretics from the New Testament; but *Machomestitae et Pagani* can only be convinced by natural reason. And it is to natural reason that he proceeds to appeal."[7] Thomas made several references to Prophet Muhammad and Muslims in his *Summa*. Guillaume notes that "the first is in I, vi. Here St. Thomas shows that he is acquainted with the Quran (*ut patet eius legem inspicienti*). Presumably his knowledge of it was gained from the version which was completed in 1143. It was a translation in Latin made by "Robertus Retinensis, an Englishman, with the assistance of Hermannus Dalmata, at the request of Peter, abbot of Clugny". St. Thomas makes two important points, one explicit, the other implicit. Muhammad, he says, produced no miracle in support of his claim to be the apostle of God (*signa etiam non adhibuit supernaturaliter facta*) and, to remove in advance Muhammad's claim (of which he seems to be aware) that the Quran itself is a miraculous proof of his divine mission, he prefaces this statement by the words *Documenta etiam veritatis non attulit nisi quae de facili a quolibet mediocriter sapiente, naturali ingenio, cognosci possint.*[8]

Unlike his Christian colleagues, Thomas was not afraid of consulting the Muslim and Jewish authorities. He directly referred to the works of Muslim theologians and philosophers, but claimed that he had known the Muslim theologians mostly through Rabbi Moses Maimonides.[9] He mentioned the Muslims by name only when refuting their ideas, and mostly ignored the references when agreeing or copying from them. In spite of this scheme, his references to the Muslim philosophers and theologians were enormous, and Muslim philosophers and theologians loomed large in the creative synthesis of Thomas. He studied their works, very often acting and reacting in response to them. On the way he integrated many Muslim philosophical and theological ideas, to the extent that sometimes even the vocabulary, sequence, methodology and overall strategies were nothing but copies of his Muslim predecessors. He "moved in the same circle of ideas as his would-be converts."[10] Muslim people, religion, philosophy, theology and spirituality were vital to Thomas's critical synthesis.

David B. Burrell depicts Thomas as an interfaith figure, who liberally interacted with the Jewish and Islamic theologico-philosophical thought. He observes that "The work of Thomas Aquinas may be distinguished from that of many of his contemporaries by his attention to the writings of Moses Maimonides (1135–1204), a Jew, and Ibn Sina [Avicenna] (980–1037), a Muslim [...] So while Aquinas would consult "the commentator" [Averroës] on matters of interpretation of the texts of Aristotle, that very aphorism suggests the limits of his reliance on the philosophical writings of Averroës, the *qadi* from Cordova. With Maimonides and Avicenna his relationship was more akin to that among interlocutors, especially so with "Rabbi Moses", whose extended dialectical conversations with his student Joseph in his *Guide of the Perplexed* closely matched Aquinas' own project; that of using philosophical inquiry to articulate one's received faith, and in the process extending the horizons of that inquiry to include topics unsuspected by those bereft of divine revelation."[11]

It is pertinent to mention here that Maimonides was also a pure product of Islamic culture and civilisation.[12] In fact, the majority of me-

dieval Jewish philosophers and theologians in a sense were the product and reflection of the Muslim civilisation, as will be discussed in the
coming pages. Undoubtedly Islamic civilisation was the dominant culture during most of the Middle Ages. Burrell observes that "it is worth
speculating whether the perspective of Aquinas and his contemporaries
was not less Eurocentric than our own. What we call "the west" was
indeed geopolitically surrounded by Islam, which sat astride the lucrative trade routes to "the east". Moreover, the cultural heritage embodied in notable achievements in medicine, mathematics, astronomy, and
well as the logical, philosophical commentary, translation, and original
work in metaphysics begun in tenth-century Baghdad, represented a
legacy coveted by western medieval thinkers. Marshall Hodgson has
called the culture that informed this epoch and extended from India to
Andalusia "the Islamicate", intending thereby to include within its scope
Jewish thinkers like Maimonides who enjoyed the protected status of
dhimmi and contributed to Muslim civilisation. Christians like John of
Damascus enjoyed a similar status, reserved by Quranic authority for
"people of the book", yet the divisions in Christendom saw to it that
thinkers in Paris were better acquainted with Muslim and Jewish thinkers than with their co-religionist in Islamic regions."[13]

Burrell also notes that Thomas's upbringing in Southern Italy, and
his geographical and intellectual affinity with the Islamic culture and
civilisation, played a role in his intellectual development. "Aquinas'
own geographic and social origins could well have predisposed him
to a closer relationship with thinkers representative of the Islamicate
than his contemporaries could be presumed to have had, in Paris at
least. For his provenance from Aquino in the region of Naples, itself
part of the kingdom of Sicily, reflected a face of Europe turned to the
Islamicate, as evidenced in the first translations commissioned from
Arabic: "Latin, Muslim, and Jewish culture mingled freely in Sicily in
a unique way that was peculiarly Sicilian." Moreover, in his later years,
when his Dominican province asked him to direct a theological *studium*, Aquinas expressly chose Naples (over Rome or Orvieto) for its
location, and that for intellectual reasons; "there was a vitality about
Naples that was absent from Rome or any other city in the Roman
province". So it might be surmised that these dimensions of his own
personal history led him to be more open to thinkers from the Islamicate than his co-workers from Cologne or Paris might have been. In

any case, the number and centrality of the citations from Avicenna and Moses Maimonides leave no doubt as to their place in his intellectual development."[14] Thomas's interfaith approach to theology was unique for his times and valuable for the coming generations.

Thomas and Crusades

Islam, Muslims, Crusades to the Holy Lands, Muslim treatment of philosophy, theology, spirituality and Dominican missions to Spain, North Africa and Middle East loomed large on the horizon of Thomas. Looking at his geographical location in Southern Italy, surrounding countries with large Muslim populations and Latin Christendom's entanglements with them, his cultural milieu, time, academic interests, vocational passions and overall outlook, he seems to be acting and reacting to Muslim related matters throughout his life starting from his very early childhood. Personalities must be understood in their historical contexts as their progress, development and outlooks are very often defined by their contexts. The geopolitical, cultural, religious and intellectual context of thirteenth century Italy, France and Spain was inundated with Muslim related politics, mission, religion, philosophy, culture, people and conflicts. Muslims were indeed an intrinsic part of Thomas's world and concerns.

Thomas's thirteenth century was full of drastic changes, movements and revolutions; on occasion radical changes and conflicts sometimes so violent, extraordinary and powerful that they defined the rest of history. It is impossible to outline the dynamics of the thirteenth-century in this brief introduction, but a number of important historical events, movements and influences must be singled out to understand Aquinas's cultural milieu and thought.

On the international scene crusades were among the most imminent realities of the thirteenth century Christendom.[15] The relatively smaller and culturally backward Christendom[16] was entangled with a far larger and culturally sophisticated Muslim world since 1095, and Thomas's thirteenth century witnessed a crusading zeal unprecedented in the previous centuries. This fanatical vehemence involved leaders both ecclesiastical and imperial along with knights and laymen from Italy, France, Germany, Spain, Hungry, Austria and Byzantine areas. Starting from 1200 to 1272 five crusades (the fourth to ninth) were organised by various segments of Christendom under the leadership of different princes, kings and popes. The epicenter was Rome, just a few hundred miles from Thomas's birthplace, and the peripheries were all over the continent, especially in France. King Louis IX, the most Catholic prince and the most Christian king,[17] was central to this crusading and Christianizing scheme.[18] He, along with early French-leaning and later French national popes, put internal European and external global Christianization squarely at the top of Latin Christendom's agenda. The Church and state were largely merged as they shared a united world view, orientation, strategy and platform.[19] The monarchical and ecclesiastical resources were pooled together to bring about an aspired spiritual revolution and Christian reformation that would usher the millennial Kingdom of God in conformity with the life and teachings of Christ. The newly established Mendicant Orders, especially the Franciscan and Dominican Orders, were an essential part of this ideal construct.[20] This trio of King Louis, French-inspired and leaning popes and French-sponsored Mendicant Orders with their global net of convents, schools, priories[21] and well-trained, disciplined friars, became the heralds of the aspired Christianization.[22] The crusades against various segments of Christian and Muslim populations were the most visible marks of this Christianisation process.[23] Jerusalem and the Holy Land was the pinnacle of all crusading efforts. Crusades against internal distractions such as Emperor Frederick II and heretics such as Cathars were necessary to produce a united front against the arch enemy, the Muslims occupiers of the Holy Lands. This exigency was compounded by the re-conquest of Jerusalem by Saladin in 1187, and the constriction of Latin Kingdom to Acre. The earlier crusading fervor had changed into a crusading fever by the middle of the thirteenth century with King Louis IX at the top.

There had been constant communication between the Latin World and Holy Land Crusade States since the eleventh century; many Franciscans, Dominicans, soldiers and diplomats frequently travelled between the Middle East, North Africa, Sicily, Spain and the Latin centers of culture, education and politics. These communications and travels were enhanced and expedited by the 1240s when King Louis was preparing for his first crusade of 1248 (the Seventh Crusade).[24] The crusade preaching all over France, Germany, Italy and other areas of Europe like Spain (specifically for Spain and not for Holy Lands) involved papal legates, mendicant friars, secular clergy, volunteer preachers and government officials. "Popes called on the Christian faithful throughout Europe to crusade by means of general letters or bulls. These enjoyed wide circulation and were propaganda instruments in their own right. Although Urban II himself did not issue a general letter for the First Crusade, solemn written proclamations were used regularly by popes to authorise later crusades, both to the Near East and within Europe. These letters outlined the reasons for the crusade and elaborated the major themes that crusade preachers would need to employ in their appeals if they were to recruit successfully. They also outlined the various privileges crusaders would enjoy for participation."[25] The entire Latin population was aware of the papal bulls, ecumenical councils' decisions, crusade fundraising and recruiting campaigns.[26] Criticism of Islam and Muslims was central to these propaganda schemes.[27] Islam was introduced to Latin Christendom in extreme negative terms, as the absolute other to be feared and destroyed.[28]

For many crusaders, the military expeditions were a sort of pilgrimage. They returned home with a better knowledge of the so-called barbarian, inhumane Muslim East, including its people, culture and religion. Some of them even converted to Islam. Many of them looked at Christendom and its socioreligious debacles from the new prism of the Muslim East and its culture. The crusaders' proximity and close interactions with eastern Christians also expanded their horizons. The frequent back-and-forth encounters in the Holy Lands, Levant, North Africa, Spain and Sicily facilitated constant communications, increasing the possibility of interreligious transmissions and intercultural assimilations. European expansion through crusades, increased networks of Afro Asian and European trade circuits, close contacts with Muslims, Byzantium and Mongols and consolidation of Latin Christendom's culture and institutions all facilitated Christendom's exposure to and assimilation of other's ideas.[29] The result was a century of exceptional physical, religious, economic and cultural connectivity between Europe, Africa and Asia not seen in recent history before. This Afro-Eurasian supercontinent facilitated movement of important ideas with greater velocity and volume across greater distances.[30]

On the other hand, the many failures, mishaps, manipulations and utter immoralities of the Crusades lead to much Christian soul-searching and many theological conundrums. Throughout his life, from Aquino to Naples, Paris and Rome, Thomas was exposed to these exchanges and curiosities. The Crusades and their cultural and intellectual aftermaths were intrinsic to Thomas's person and thought. His entire life was dominated by the towering figures of King Louis, Popes Urban IV, Clement IV and Gregory X who were absolutely immersed in the crusades, and were the sole patrons of Aquinas and his Dominican order; the realities and figures related to the Crusades were important parts of Aquinas's development as a person. Islam and Muslims in turn were central to the Crusades. Thomas was in the middle of these contending religio-philosophical ideologies and at the forefront of needed appropriations, adjustments and defenses.

Chapter 2

International and Intellectual Struggles

Power Struggles on the Continental Scene

On the continental scene, popes and secular leaders were vying for authority, control and economic resources. The Holy Roman Emperor Frederick II was King of Germany, Sicily, Italy and at times of Jerusalem. The Lombard League was a separate and opposing entity involving the Northern cities of Italy (both Italian and Lombard) and Papacy. France was under the House of Capet and King Louis IX (1214-1270) was a submissive son of the Catholic Church and the most Christian of all the Christian kings of not only the thirteenth century but all times. His total alignment with and absolute loyalties to the papacy and his brother Charles of Anjou's imperial aspirations were of concern to the then Holy Emperor Frederick II.

On the other hand, the initially weak and internally-challenged King Louis was up against a stronger Henry III (1207-1272), the King of England who invaded France in 1228 to reclaim his inheritance, and this costly war continued till 1234. Henry cultivated close relations with Frederick II, inciting him to attack France or encourage his French allies to revolt against Louis. Both Louis and Henri III were devoted Catholics, while Frederick II was perhaps more Saracen in overall outlook than Catholic. Louis was the most Catholic of them all, as his early childhood training and interactions were dominated by the newly established mendicant friars with their focus on poverty and preaching. He looked up to popes and friars for spiritual guidance, and his cordial relationships with papacy and mendicants were cemented in 1245 when Frederick II captured and imprisoned many cardinals, bishops and accompanying friars on their way to the First Council of Lyon, and was subsequently formally excommunicated and deposed by Pope Innocent IV. Louis vowed to crusade in 1245 as Frederick was in no position to wage a war against the Muslims, especially under the auspices of his excommunicator Pope Innocent IV. After three years of financial, political and military preparations Louis sailed to Cyprus in 1248 and then to Egypt in 1249 for the Seventh Crusade. In 1250 Louis' army was annihilated and Louis was captured along with his brothers, with some of his crusaders converting to Islam. He remained in the Muslim Mamluks' jail for a month, until he was ransomed and released. He remained in Acre until 1254 by establishing an alliance with the Muslim Mamluks, who were the rivals of Damascus' Sultan. He returned to Paris in 1254. Meanwhile Frederick II suddenly died in 1250 after a long and costly warfare with papacy, a struggle which his children continued.

With the death of Frederick II in 1250 Henry III of England saw an opportunity to install his son Edmund as the new Sicilian King with the help of Pope Innocent IV.[31] The Pope wanted a more amenable Sicilian king than the irritating Manfred, the illegitimate son and heir of Frederick II, and promised to write off Edmund's military campaign in 1254 by increasing demands for tithe and indulgences. Unfortunately the needed money did not come through as expected, despite King Louis' efforts and support. The next Pope, Alexander IV (pope from 1254-1261), could no longer afford to pay Henry's expenses due to Manfred's unrelenting pressure and instead demanded that Henry pay the 90,000 pounds spent so far on his preparations. Under the pressure of excommunication Henry could raise only 40,000 pounds in 1258, mostly through extortion of the English clergy. Later he tried to influence the elections of the new Holy Roman Emperor, and supported the selection of his brother Richard by bribing Richard's supporters all over the empire. The English were pitched against the French and German in the race for Roman Emperorship, and Rome was the center of these conflicting struggles. Finally, Louis's brother Charles of Anjou was offered the crown of Sicily by the French Pope Clement IV, and convinced by his brother Louis. Charles killed Manfred in the Battle of Benevento, and publicly hanged Frederick's grandson Conardin and his entire entourage in Naples.

During these years, Thomas was in Paris, Rome and Naples, the epicenters of these conflicts. He was engaged with the high echelon of the papal trio- Louis, popes and mendicants- and was well aware of the contending parties' claims and designs. He was in a position to differentiate between Frederick's Oriental adventures and Louis's religious crusades.

Crusading was a popular strategy for gaining papal and mass support during the thirteenth century, and King Louis announced the Seventh Crusade (1248-1254) after receiving papal and English guarantees that France would not be attacked. Thomas was in Paris, which was the epicenter of this mostly French crusade, under the leadership of King Louis, Thomas's patron and friend. Louis' subsequent defeat at al-Mansurah in 1250, resulting in the annihilation of his army and his capture by the Ayyubid Muslims, followed by severe dysentery treated by a Muslim physician, his final release to the price of a hefty 80,000 bezant ransom and his alliance with Muslim Mamluks[32] all must have been discussed by Louis on his return to Paris. These facts were open secrets discussed and lamented by poets and masses in the streets of Paris, and these historical failures left psychological scars all over Latin Christendom.[33] "The thirteenth century undoubtedly represented a most critical stage in the decadence and ultimately the fall of the Crusader Kingdom."[34] Thomas was also privy to the King's personal experiences and their theological ramifications. These experiences caused people to question why God, who graced the crusading Christians in Spain, would humiliate them in the Holy Lands, the most deserving areas of His victorious grace. Why would God grace the impious Muslims, and annihilate in disgrace the most pious crusaders and their most Christian King in their most sublime campaign of freeing the Holy Lands from the perdition of infidels? The Dominican Thomas and his fellow Franciscan Bonaventure were friends and spiritual counselors of the King, and Louis often listened to Bonaventure's sermons; he must have consulted them about his inner agonies and theological concerns. The intensity of the theological soul searching can be gauged from the lamentation of a Templar knight otherwise known for their sobriety and perseverance: "Rage and sorrow are seated in my heart [...] so firmly that I scarce dare to stay alive. It seems that God wishes to support the Turks to our loss [...] ah, lord God [...] alas, the realm of the East has lost so much that it will never be able to rise up again. They will make a Mosque of Holy Mary's convent, and since the theft pleases her Son, who should weep at this, we are forced to comply as well [...] Anyone who wishes to fight the Turks is mad, for Jesus Christ does not fight them anymore. They have conquered, they will conquer. For every day they drive us down, knowing that God, who was awake, sleeps now, and Muhammad waxes powerful."[35] These deep theological conundrums would have not escaped Aquinas, Bonaventure and Louis.

Louis discussed, preached and prepared for the next crusade and Holy Lands from the 1250s until his death in 1270. He launched the Eighth Crusade against Tunis in 1270 with the help of his brother Charles I of Anjou and English prince Edward I, hoping to Christianise Tunis on his way to freeing the Holy Lands. Louis along with a host of his soldiers died in Tunis as a result of an epidemic, without realizing his dream of Christianising Tunis.[36] Thomas was in Paris during this time, and witnessed the preparations, propaganda and preaching as well as the disastrous outcome of the Tunis crusade.

In neighbouring Spain the crusaders were triumphant. The Reconquista crusading expeditions established the Kingdoms of Leon, Castile, Navarre and Aragon and in Portugal the Kingdom of Portugal. "These lands witnessed a remarkable shift in the thirteenth century, as Christian forces gained territory and maritime dominance at the expense of Muslim rulers (the process known somewhat anachronistically as the *reconquista*). The king of Aragon's conquest of Mallorca (1230) and Valencia (1238) were two major milestones; like Castile's seizure of Cordoba (1236) and Seville (1248) these established Christian regimes as leading powers in the region. They also hastened the decline of the Almohad caliphate which had previously dominated western Muslim territories on both sides of the Mediterranean. The result was a virtually unprecedented period in which Christian rulers began to rule over large populations of Muslims as well as Jews."[37] Many Iberian Muslims were killed, deported to North Africa and forcibly converted, but a good size Muslim community remained in these newly established small Iberian Kingdoms. The Dominican Order of preaching friars was introduced there, to preserve the faith of Christians living among the Muslims and to convert the newly possessed Muslims. The thirteenth -century transition "coincided with the creation of the Dominican Order; it thus offers a rather special circumstance in which the first few generations of Iberian Friars Preacher were obliged to find their way and invent their own roles. It was a troubled yet exciting and intriguing time, when all possibilities were open."[38] The Iberian Kings, especially James I of Aragon, were pragmatic and diplomatic in dealing with the Muslim populations of their areas. They allowed the mission-

ary works of Franciscan and Dominican orders, and encouraged dialogue with Muslims and Jews, but initially avoided forced conversions
and persecutions. Thomas's fellow Dominicans were actively engaged
in the missionary works in Spain, North Africa and Holy Lands, with
countless priories, schools and convents all over these areas. Their strategic geographical locations, central organization, unified system of
education and training, collective team mentality, missionary bent, assigned crucial roles, imperial and papal connections made rapid communications a necessity. Thomas was among the main theoretician of
the Mendicants and in touch with the central papal and Dominican
leadership as well as friars in the field. He was the Regent of Studies at
the Studium Generale at Saint Sabina, the international headquarter of
the Dominican Order, and was fully engaged in the Dominican mission through planning, training, correspondence and manual writing.
Among the audiences of his theological works, including the two *Summas,* were Christians living among the Muslims, as well as the Muslims
living among the Christians, in addition to the Christian scholastics
who embraced the ideas of Averroes and, to a lesser extent, Maimonides. Thomas's works were fully aligned with the two global concerns
of the Dominicans. The internal and external soul-savings through
preaching were the cornerstones of Aquinas's writings, and Muslims
wittingly or unwittingly loomed large in these constructs.

Power Struggles on the Italian Scene

Thomas's immediate Italian scene was inundated with warfare between
the Hohenstaufe Dynasty and Papacy, and Muslims were a big part of
the Staufen army. Frederick II (1194-1250) was actively warring against
the papacy and its Northern Lombard clients from 1237 till his death in
1250; these were the formative years of Thomas's life. He witnessed many
of these military struggles and they left a clear mark on his thinking and
life, as will be seen in the coming pages. The Italian division between the
papal camp of Guelphs and the Emperor's Ghibelline allies, as well as the
constant warfare between the Emperor and popes, had fully engulfed
Thomas's family and surroundings. Frederick's children and grandchil-
dren continued this struggle until 1266, when Manfred and Conardin
were killed by the French Charles I of Anjou. Frederick's son Conrad
(King from 1250-1254), his grandson Conradin (from 1254-1258) and
his illegitimate son Manfred (from 1258-1266) aggressively fought the

papal, Lombard and French troops. Thousands of Muslim soldiers and archers were an important part of all these Hohenstaufen long military campaigns against the papacy. The Staufen's Saracen orientation and long lasting alliance was the scandal of the Continent publicly discussed all over Europe by popes, kings and commoners. Thomas's own family alternated between the Emperor and papal armies; his father and two brothers initially served in the Emperor's army against the papal troops, but changed their loyalties in 1245, and Thomas's own brother was charged for treason and executed by Frederick II.

Thomas was earnestly bothered by the chaos, destruction and routine military conflicts between the contending Christian parties; it left indelible marks upon his person and thought. By his discussions of divine law, natural law and human law he would try to strike a balance between the conflicting sovereignties. Thomas was compiling these treatises in the backdrop of papal and imperial juristic reforms and excessive legal tendencies. Both the monarchs and popes were moving towards centralised absolute power structures. The resultant expected common legal framework, practices and legislations were causing confusion to a mostly nationalist Europe with local common practices, norms and traditions. Thomas was writing during these years of religious, political, legal and social uncertainty. Thomas's thoughts were a reflection of these mounting tensions and anxieties. Many of his solutions were often appropriation of others' ideas in accordance with the local needs and his Christian faith; he was a creative synthesist and improviser.

Meanwhile, in spite of centralising monarchical designs, the central Christian institution, the papacy itself was passing through a transitional period, suffering from instability, insecurity and uncertainty.[39] Thomas witnessed nine popes in his lifetime. Popes like Innocent IV had to flee Rome for France in 1244, and from France he convened the First Council of Lyon in 1245 to excommunicate Frederick II. The continental politics took its toll on the papal curia; the cardinals were divided into pro-French and anti-French camps, and this division was exacerbated by the rivalries among the Orsini and the Colonna families of Italy. The papal elections were manipulated, and at times forced upon the cardinals by dint of imperial powers. For instance, in 1250 cardinals were locked up in the ancient Septizonium (Septizodium) Palace with armed guards, to produce a pope. No candidate could win the required two thirds majority and the nightmare was exacerbated by the crippling heat, overflowing lavatories and consequent death of a cardinal.[40] They hastily elected the elderly theologian Celestine V who remained Pope just for 17 days. The terrified cardinals fled Rome, and there was no pope for the next two years. Two years later, the cardinals met at Anagni (and not Rome) to elect the next Pope, Innocent IV, who could not enter Rome, living mostly in Lyon. The popes increasingly depended upon French protection and support against the pressures of Frederick and his successors. The later Urban IV (1261-1264) and Clement IV (1265-1268) were both French citizens and imperial courtiers. They solely depended upon the physical protection of Charles of Anjou and moral and financial support of French King Louis IX. Infighting between the French and Italian cardinals caused the longest papal election in the history of the Catholic Church, which resulted in there being no pope from 1268 to 1271. The new elected Pope Gregory X was also a confidant of King Louis IX and his brother Charles of Anjou, and owed his election to the papal office mostly to the French influences. Later on, Charles I of Anjou, the original savior of papacy from Frederick's children, became a monster of his own.[41] He utterly jeopardised the papal independence and restricted its financial interests in Italy and Sicily. The papacy lost a great deal of its money, and began extorting bishops and lower clergy. By the end of the thirteenth century bishops and abbots were appointed by the papal curia, and were required to pay one third of their first-year income to the pope and cardinals.[42] The second half of the thirteenth century saw a rapid turnover of popes, with thirteen popes between 1252 and 1296. The influx of French cardinals tipped the balance towards French monarchy and the Sicilian King Charles of Anjou at the expense of Italian, Spanish and English interests. Thomas was disturbed by these sad realities of the papal institution, its involvement in secular warfare, its political crusades,[43] its corruptions, extortions and the damage it caused to the material and spiritual life of the Christian community.

Power Struggles on the Academic Scene

On the academic and intellectual scene, the establishment of medieval universities was an important milestone in Thomas's life and upbringing. The University of Paris was chartered in 1200 by King Philip II and recognised by Pope Innocent III in 1215. The University of Naples was founded by Frederick II in 1224, around the time of Thomas's birth. The medieval pre-university period was marked by cathedral schools and abbeys, where little but the Bible was taught.[44] This very literal, fully traditional approach was carried over to the newly established universities. The politics of papacy and empire were transmitted to the academic arena when Frederick II established the University of Naples, to counteract the papal academic institutions such as Bologna, Padua and Paris. The anti-traditional and rational Greek philosophy and logic was introduced in the University of Naples long before their introduction into other universities.[45] The study of Aristotle along with the commentaries of Spanish Muslim jurist and philosopher Ibn Rushd propelled a rational attitude unprecedented in the previous Christian centuries. Rational discourse and philosophy received relative independence and became autonomous of official theology, especially in the circles of Ibn Rushd's Parisian followers. Their insistence that the truth can be reached through two distinct ways - philosophy and religion - diluted the Church claims to absolute propriety of the truth. This was a serious secular breach of the sacred ecclesiastical realm. That is perhaps what Frederick had intended by the introduction of Greek and Muslim philosophy in both the Sicilian court and university of Naples; every action has a reaction, and papal traditionalism was met with the equal force of Aristotelian logic and rationalism. Aristotle's main commentator Averrois (Ib Rushd) was introduced to Parisian scholars by early 1220's when individual masters began reading Ibn Rushd's commentaries on Aristotle. The Aristotelian metaphysics and natural philosophies were later introduced to the university faculty, resulting in a wave of rationalism. The Church's long traditionalism was met with equal rationalism of Latin Averroists all over learning centers of Christendom, especially at Paris from the 1230s to the 1270s. "In 1255, the statutes of the Parisian arts faculty declared all known works of Aristotle mandatory reading for the students – a very influential move, which much contributed to the rise of Averroes' commentaries as the principal secondary literature of Latin university culture."[46] This was the beginning of a long-lasting intellectual warfare between the clerical establishment and academics. Ibn Rushd was a philosophical, political and social progressive, challenging the status quo in religio-secular as well as social realms. He demanded emancipation of philosophy from theology (in fact he found Muslim kalâm not a satisfactory discipline given its being limited to dialectical, not demonstrative knowledge) state from religious establishment and women from the undue restrictions of men. Consequently, his Latin followers spoiled the peace of imperial, ecclesiastical and social conservatives, papal curia being the vanguard of all three.

Latin Averroists such as Siger of Brabant, Boetius of Dacia, John of Dry Town (or Jean de Sécheville), and later on John of Jandun and Marsilius of Padua, followed Ibn Rushd's reconciliation of Aristotle with Muslim faith and politics to their endeavours of reconciling Christian faith and politics with Aristotelian philosophy and political thought. They were called Latin Averroists, radical Aristotelians and heterodox Aristotelians. The traditionalists felt challenged by the so-perceived anti-faith, relatively democratic and rationalist discourse of the Averroists; Mendicants, the apples of imperial and papal eyes,[47] took it upon themselves to confront the new wave of exaggerated rationalism and political activism. They were the vans of establishment, preserving conservative status quo. We will not indulge in the scholarly debate between contemporary Thomists and Rationalists whether the Franciscans or Dominicans were in the forefront of this intellectual war against Latin Averroists. Steenberghen and William Drapers' discussions are well summarised by I. L. Horowitz[48] and are sufficient to show that the mutual Mendicant jealousies and controversies were a later development (in the 1270s), and that in the middle of the thirteenth century both Franciscan and Dominican orders were pitched against some Latin Averroists. We also accept the existence of Latin Averroists as a historical reality and do not indulge in the scholarly nit-picking between Renan and Kristeller as to whether it was an organised ideological movement or individual attitude.[49] We agree with I. L. Horowitz and others that "it must be concluded that Averroism existed as an ideological entity quite apart from philosophic considerations of Aristotelianism in the medieval world; functioning as a defense of philosophy from theological and institutional encroachments."[50] Their organised writings are missing, due to severe persecutions and condemnations of their works by the Church. They were forced out of their academic positions, exiled and killed. For instance, John of Dry Town escaped to England for protection, Boetius of Dacia ran for his life to Italy after the condemnation of 1277 and Siger of Brabant was forced to appear in front of the French Inquisitor Simon du Val but fled to Papal Viterbo to be sentenced and stabbed by his mad secretary there. These are historical realities, and leave no room to doubt that Latin Averroism was a major ideological challenge confronted by the Catholic Church. The Mendicants were in the forefront of this intellectual confrontation.

Chapter 3

Islamic Interactions

Franciscan and Dominican Orders

The Franciscan and Dominican houses were initially established in Paris and elsewhere to guarantee their presence on university campuses. They became the champions of Christian faith and perpetuators of the Church's intellectual and political dominion. They put all their energies and resources to thwart seemingly anti-faith rationalism of the Averroists. Thomas was mostly bogged down with these controversies, both in Paris and Rome. He adopted a middle position between the traditionalists and rationalists; his synthesis allowed partial significance to rational inquiry and philosophy but under the full auspices and authority of faith and revelation. He contended that faith can be defended by reason, but cannot be proven by reason, logic or demonstrative proof. Many of Thomas's mature works were stimulated by these intellectual controversies and in line with the overall Dominican agenda. "Thomas Aquinas was led to write his *Summas* to halt the threatened liquidation of Christian theology by Arabic interpretations of Aristotle [...] indeed, the industry of Aquinas was due not to the love of Aristotle but to fear of Averroes."[51] The Muslim's demand for logical proofs and the Latin Averroists' rational orientations were considered the two sides of the same coin. Both were confronted as arch-enemies, and Aquinas was in the forefront of this intellectual warfare.

On the mission level Dominicans and Franciscans were divided over the mission strategy and priorities; one group insisted upon internal mission while others were enthusiastic about the external. To some, saving Christian souls from the bad influences of Muslims and Jews was fundamental while others wanted to convert Muslims and Jews. Conversion of Muslims and Jews had become the top priority of the mendicants by the time Thomas joined the Dominican Order. Thomas's three consecutive master generals (Raymond of Penyafort, John of Wildeshausen and Humbert of Romans) were bent on converting Muslims and Jews in line with the apocalyptic prophesies of Joachim of Fiore and Pope Innocent III; they expected mass conversions of Muslims and Jews. The Reconquista increased their hopes and strengthened their confidence, while King Louis and the popes' unqualified- and Valencian and Castilian Kings' qualified - support for evangelism emboldened them. Their biggest concern was the Muslims, as the Jewish community was far smaller and mostly local. The Muslims of Spain, Sicily and Levant were part of a larger Muslim world and supported by them. The Muslim conversion constituted the top priority of Thomas's Dominican fellows, especially from the 1230s to the 1270s, almost the entire life span of Aquinas. The mendicant priories from Spain to Antioch, in various capacities, were engaged with the Muslim question. Thomas could not have resisted the top priority of his superiors and ignored external mission to Saracens. His apologetic works from 1265 to his death in 1274 were mostly geared towards the Muslim audience and to Christians living among the Muslims.

The Mendicants also had difference of opinion regarding the appropriate mission methodology. Franciscans such as Roger Bacon and Raymond Llull insisted upon rational approach to Muslims while Raymond Marti, Bonaventure and Thomas believed that reason was not sufficiently equipped to traverse the mysteries of Christian faith. The Christian doctrine was beyond reason, and could only be proven through the authority of scripture. Human reason and philosophy could be used to dispel doubts, but was unable to prove its validity by rational premises. Here again Thomas chose a middle path between the sheer traditionalism of Bonaventure and aspired rationalism of Bacon and Llull. He utilised philosophical arguments and rational discourse in certain areas of the Christian faith such as the existence of God, while denying its authority over Christian paradoxes such as the Incarnation and Trinity. In spite of this very cautious centrist approach, Thomas was condemned in 1277 for overstepping some of the faith areas.

On the pastoral level Thomas faced two polar tendencies of the secular clergy and mendicants. The overarching material propensities of the secular clergies were antithetical to the ultra-spiritual inclinations of some Franciscans and Dominicans.[52] The ultra-spirituals argued that absolute poverty and total lack of material possessions were the cornerstones of Christian mission and faith,[53] strongly criticising the worldly pomp of secular clergy and the material possessions of Franciscan and Dominican orders.[54] The Franciscan Bonaventure and Dominican Thomas would strike a middle ground by allowing possession of basic necessities such as buildings, books, and other material sources needed for institution building and international mission while prohibiting personal possessions and unnecessary exhibition of collective pomp and material possessions.[55] William of Saint Amour's "The Dangers of Our Times" was a bitter harangue against the Mendicants. Thomas jealously defended the Mendicant Orders, their poverty and charity.

Thirteenth-century Latin Christendom was passing through a transitional period, witnessing rapid social and intellectual changes. The Muslim world had gone through similar circumstances in the eighth and ninth centuries. They had faced the cultural invasion of Greek logic and philosophy, the sophisticated Byzantium culture, controversies related to reconciliation of faith and reason, conflicts between the secular and religious authorities, infighting among the academic religious institutions called Madrassahs, disputes between orthodoxy and Muslim mystics and rationalism of Muslim philosophers and speculative theologians (Mu'atazilites) against the legalism and literalism of traditional orthodoxy. The Muslim community had also experienced a synthesis of Ash'arite school, which blended a moderate rationalism with traditionalism of the orthodoxy, putting reason under the command of revelation. Thomas had ample precedents in the Muslim culture and community for his synthetic project. The debates and discussions prevalent in Thomas's thirteenth century were all exhausted by Muslim intellectuals in the 8th and 9th centuries. Many related Muslim philosophical and theological works were translated into Latin during the twelfth-century renaissance, and were available to Thomas and his contemporaries. There was also an oral tradition of partial translations, verbal discussions and transmissions generated by the Dominicans, Franciscans and other missionaries based in the Muslim lands and crusade states. The Dominican apologetic manuals were often the product of team work. The questions, inquiries and suggestions came from all over priories and debated and discussed, and answers were shared with the field workers, especially those involved with the external mission. Thomas's larger works could also have been compiled with the help of other friars; they reflected overall Dominican orientation and methodology, in addition to Thomas's individual genius.

All the above facts, circumstances, factors and realities collectively shaped the person, works and agenda of Thomas Aquinas. The most notable of these were perhaps the Norman conquest of Sicily and the subsequent Christian Muslim interactions in Southern Italy; Fredrick II's rise to power, his co-option of Sicilian Muslims by settling them in Lucera, just a few hundred miles from Aquino in the province of Foggia in the region of Apulia, the heartland of Italy bordering both the Northern Italy and Papal states; constant warfare between secular and papal authorities, especially between Holy Roman Emperor Fredrick II, his son Conrad, illegitimate son Manfred and Popes; European (Northern) Crusades (Spanish, Albigensian, Bosnian), Holy Land Crusades and ensuing evangelism; rise of mendicant orders such as Franciscan and Dominican; spread of mystical, spiritual and prophetic ideas of figures such as Abbot Joachim; translation movements transmitting Greek and Islamic philosophy and sciences to the Latin West; transmission of Platonic, Aristotelian and Islamic ethical and spiritual traditions via Muslim bridge of Spain and Sicily; Scholasticism and establishment of universities and general study schools. Thomas's life mostly revolved around these realities and Muslim related issues were part and parcel of them. Thomas acted and reacted to these realities and on the way accepted, absorbed, borrowed, modified, criticised, refuted and rejected many Muslim ideas, concepts and doctrines. In a sense Thomas was engrossed by the Muslim philosophy, theology, spirituality, politics and Christian mission to Muslims.

Thomas, Lucera and Islam

Thomas was born around 1224-1225 in the castle of Roccasecca, Aquino, in the Kingdom of Sicily. Aquino was roughly 116 miles northwest of Lucera where, according to conservative estimates, some 20,000 Muslims were settled by Fredrick II in 1224. The Muslim exile Ahmad ibn Abi al-Qasim al-Rummani in 1230 told the Caliph "al-Kamil that 170,000 people had been turned out of their homelands, stripped of their wealth and transported to the Italian mainland."[56] Saba Malaspina claimed that there were 40,000 to 50,000 Muslims in Lucera.[57] Graham A. Loud rejects these high numbers as exaggerations and agrees with Taylor, Metcalfe and Abulafia that there were between 15,000 to 20,000 Muslims settled by Frederick in Lucera.[58] Close to 30,000 Muslims were settled in the nearby areas of Apulia, and 10,000 outside Apulia. Lucera was as big as the London of the early thirteenth century.

There was then a huge and conspicuous Muslim presence within 116 miles of Aquino, the birth place of Thomas Aquinas. Apulia virtually became a Muslim commune. David Abulafia notes that Lucera "became a Muslim town. With the arrival of the Saracens, the bishop of Lucera found himself forced to flee the town. Lucera was to be a special Muslim enclave, and the future loyalty of its inhabitants was assured by their isolation from the Islamic world."[59] Lucera then was a sizable Muslim city by thirteenth-century standards. The Emperor did not interfere with the practice of Islam at Lucera; he initially demanded payment of Jizya, the poll tax levied on Muslims, but relaxed that later on in lieu of military service. The implementation and exercise of Islamic Shari'ah was permitted, and Muslim institutions such as mosques, madrassas and courts were given a free hand. "The Muslims of Lucera practiced Islam with relative freedom. People observed Friday prayers in a mosque, perhaps a converted building, in the city. While Frederick's son Manfred was in power, an ambassador of Sultan Baybars of Egypt visited the city. He noted that the inhabitants of the city observed their religion openly. Influential Muslim men were even present at Manfred's court. The Lucerines may have established Quranic schools. Pope Gregory IX stated that there were "*Agarenorum gymnasia*," or schools of the Hagarites there, a Biblical reference to Arabs as the descendants of Hagar. A class of educated persons is known to have lived in the city. The community appears to have had a *qadi* or judge. One Latin source refers to a "bishop of the Saracens.""[60]

Lucera was an example of "rare enlightenment".[61] Karen Armstrong notes that "Here (in Lucera) they were allowed to build their own independent city-state. They had their own amir, their own qadis, sheik and imams. They built mosques and the muezzin sounded loudly and freely. Within the city, Frederick built a scientific institute for the study of all branches of speculative science, and he made the Muslims of Lucera his favoured court officials. "Most of his officials and courtier were Muslims," wrote the Arab historian Jamal ad-Din Ibn Wasil "and in his camp the call to prayer and even the canonic prayer themselves were

openly heard." The Arabs themselves were fanatically loyal to Frederick and called him their sultan."[62]

Frederick really was an innovating paradigm breaker. The pomp-
ous thirteenth-century historian Matthew of Paris labelled Frederick
with the epithet *"Stupor qouque mundi et immutator mirabilis."*[63] To
the papal camp he was the anti-Christ, the sixth or the seventh head of
the terrible dragon envisioned in the revelation of St. John the Divine.[64]

The Emperor had multiple reasons for establishing a thoroughly
Muslim colony in the heart of mainland Italy. He wanted to discon-
nect Muslim rebels from their main North African sources of arms,
connect them with the new land and turn them into loyal taxpayers,
craftsmen and soldiers. He even exempted them from all royal taxes in lieu of imperial services.[65] He intended to use their agricultural
skills to enhance grain, cotton and fruit production, amplify their military skills to produce arrows, bows, swords, shields and other kinds of
specialised weapons, enlist them in his army to fight papal forces and
increase his tax base by levying jizya upon some of them. He greatly
facilitated their settlement at Lucera and provided them with needed
capital and means to enhance their output. The Emperor was pragmatic, diplomatic and accommodative in accordance with his economic,
military and political interests. He developed a special affinity with his
Muslim soldiers due to their skills, loyalty and vigour to fight his arch
enemy, the popes. Unlike his Christian soldiers, the Muslim mercenaries were immune to papal bulls, whispers and religious insinuations.
The papal curia was Frederick's biggest enemy and the Muslim archer
battalion was his most trusted ally against the Curia and its loyal clients, the Lombard League. That is why Frederick greatly invested in the
Muslim colony of Lucera. Julie Ann Taylor states that "Frederick made
an investment in the colony, sending oxen to the Muslim settlers and
making arrangements with local landowners so that the arrivals could
farm land in and around the city. In his lifetime, the Emperor would
demonstrate a certain affinity for the region of Apulia. Frederick built
a castle there, ordering that decorative statues be brought from Naples,
and he imported animals such as camels and leopards to be raised by
Muslim keepers."[66] Metcalfe states that "in 1239–40, Frederick offered
a thousand head of cattle to the Luceran Muslims in order to tie them
to the land, 'as was the case in the time of King William', strengthening
the idea that Lucera was intended as a type of imperial tax farm."[67] He

further notes that "Frederick had also been eager to stimulate the rural economy – and in this respect Lucera certainly prospered. Indeed, the occupations of the Luceran Muslims were almost as wide-ranging as they had been in western Sicily. Many names indicating an involvement in a 'profession', which are found among the population of Monreale in the 1170s and 1180s, are also attested (in much less rich sources) at Lucera. In addition to the various tasks which existed in any south Italian medieval town surrounded by countryside, professions specifically attested in both Monreale and Lucera were: those involved with stock breeding and animal husbandry (including rearers and keepers of pigs, goats, sheep, horses, donkeys and bees), shepherds, butchers, tanners, saddlers, falconers and huntsmen, millers, bakers, potters, stonemasons, cotton growers, vintners and fruit growers, tailors, tentmakers, carpenters, soldiers, guards, castellans and stewards, in addition to a range of smiths and metal-workers, buglers, musicians, bath-house keepers, notaries, minor officials and *qa'id*s – who in the case of Lucera were clearly associated with the military."[68]

Julie Taylor notes that "Most members of the privileged class at Lucera had served the crown as soldiers, but people became influential and prosperous in other ways as well. An Arabic-speaking physician practiced in the city. Muslims served as intermediaries between the local population and crown officials, helping to coordinate major building projects at Lucera. Most of the people who lived at Lucera made their living by farming. They grew wheat and barley, and they planted fruit trees. Honey from the bees raised at Lucera was used to make sweets. Lucerine wine was transported to Rome and other cities. Among the animals kept at Lucera were leopards and camels. People also raised sheep, cows, and goats."[69] Frederick established one of the seven annual fairs in Lucera where people from all over the empire would participate, and the Muslim craftsmen of Lucera were encouraged to participate in other fairs. "With permission, merchants and some skilled craftsmen were able to travel outside the city. Merchants sold their goods to Christians nearby in San Severo and as far away as Salerno. Muslim smiths, carpenters, and animal keepers worked in Canosa and Melfi."[70]

The Muslims of Lucera and greater Apulia province were well assimilated in the larger society. They moved around, travelled within the empire for business and imperial services, mingled, communicated and interacted with their fellow Sicilians and often adopted Latinised names. "Where assimilation into the background culture was attested, it was in the direction of Latinisation – or, rather, south Italianisation. Thus, the limited onomastic evidence available reveals a number of Muslims who had adopted (alternative?) names chosen from Frankish, New Testament or saintly repertoires such as Richard, Roger, Jordan, Matthew, John, Peter, Anthony and Paschal."[71] The Muslims spoke Arabic between themselves, but used various forms of Italian dialects while communicating with the surrounding Christian populations and their army colleagues.

The Sicilian Muslims were reliable soldiers especially against the papal army, the main opposition to Frederick's political designs in Southern Italy. Metcalfe notes that "while farming and agriculture were fundamentally important to the Luceran economy, the population also played vital military roles both as a resource for soldiers (especially light cavalry and archers) and as manufacturers of specialist weaponry such as bows, arrows and shields. Over this formidable arsenal, the Muslims acted as reliable guardians within the walls of the city."[72] There were around 10,000 to 15,000 Muslim men in the special forces of Frederick II; contemporary sources noted that over 10,000 Muslim archers were employed by Frederick in the battlefield of Cortenuova fought on November 27, 1237 against Pope Gregory IX and his Lombard League. The Muslim soldiers constituted the majority of Frederick's army. Abulafia observes that "It has been suggested that about thirty-five thousand men were on the Cortenuova battlefield, about nineteen thousand under imperial banners, the rest fighting for the Lombard League."[73] Fergus Kerr notes that "Thomas's father was one of the officers entrusted with guarding prisoners captured at the battle of Cortenuova [...] when, with up to 10,000 Apulian Muslim archers, Frederick II defeated the city states in Lombardy."[74] The same battalion was part of Frederick's attacks on Viterbo, Benevento, Rome (the papal possessions) as well as Monte Cassino in 1239. Thomas was a teen oblate in the Abbey of Monte Cassino when Emperor's troops including thousands of Muslim soldiers expelled papal troops and monks from the Abbey.

There existed tremendous trust between the Emperor and his Muslim bodyguards and soldiers. The Emperor and his immediate family members often leaned on the Muslims of Lucera in their most difficult times. The Muslims were happy to fight for an Emperor who was relatively secular, enlightened, Muslim friendly and pitched against the popes who hated Muslims, wanted to kill or convert them and were actively engaged in crusades against the Muslim lands. This sense of mutual enemy translated into cordial and trustworthy relations between Frederick and thousands of his Muslim soldiers. Metcalfe observes that "the castle at Lucera, built by the 1240s and probably begun shortly after the earliest Muslim settlement, served not only as a well-appointed palace which Frederick himself had often visited, but also as an armoury, illustrating the considerable extent of mutual trust and understanding that existed between Frederick and the Muslims – a political relationship continued by his son, Manfred, who took refuge in the town in 1254 when fleeing papal forces. Such was the importance of arms-manufacturing at Lucera that at the start of the Wars of the Sicilian Vespers in 1282, some 60,000 arrows were commissioned from there. The established tradition of military service was the principal mechanism open to the Muslims for socio-economic improvement, and families known to have been associated with the army were also attested as landholders. Indeed, given the colony's strategic military role as a fortress and armoury, the Luceran military – subject to Christian command – constituted a prestigious, responsible and privileged group within the community."[75] Thomas's family, including his brothers were also part of Frederick's army and until 1245 fought alongside the Muslim soldiers against the papal armies. They must have made some Muslim friends.

Julie Taylor notes that "the transfer of the Sicilian Muslims resulted in the dislocation and decline of the Christian population at Lucera and in the surrounding area. Bells from at least one church were taken down and placed inside the castle that Frederick had built at Lucera. Unable to levy the tithe on Muslims, the bishop was described as living in poverty in 1296. Frederick's call for the restoration of the Lucerine church in his last will and testament points to the extent to which Christian life had deteriorated."[76] J. P. Lomax explains that Pope Gregory IX charged Frederick of not protecting the churches from destruction and profanity of Muslims. "We excommunicate and anathematize him because in the Kingdom churches consecrated to the Lord are destroyed and profaned."[77]

The popes harboured venomous animosity towards the Emperor,

especially for challenging the political authority of papacy, settling thousands of Muslims in the heartland of Italy just 200 miles away from Rome and enlisting thousands of them into his army.[78] The Emperor had snatched the pope's rich patrimonies of Southern Italy and Sicily, contested their authority to appoint bishops and turned their ideals of crusades and forced conversion upside down. To Lomax "Muslim Lucera served as a metaphor for Frederick's rejection of the papal ideal of crusades."[79] Instead of engaging in crusades against the Muslims and converting them by force to Christianity, the Emperor trained, armed and employed them against the central Christian authority, the popes, and their most reliable clients, the Lombard League. Frederick and his family fought almost all popes from Gregory IX (died in 1241) to Boniface VIII (died in 1303) with the help of their Muslim regiment. To the popes, Frederick had adulterated the Christendom, weakened the Christian commonwealth and community of baptised from within while jeopardising the moral authority and political autonomy of papacy. According to Lomax, "the bitter and inflammatory rhetoric with which the popes consistently assailed the Muslims of Lucera, and often their royal masters, reveals the depth and character of papal animosity."[80] The Muslim colony of Lucera had clearly shaken the papal curia, "Gregory truly feared Frederick's Muslim subjects, who represented a special kind of threat to the well-being of papacy."[81]

Pope Gregory IX urged Frederick to 'shatter' the 'presumptions' of these Muslims so that they would dare not disturb the hearts of God's faithful even a little, especially since particular injury will seem to be done to our Redeemer if the sons of Belial, who are bound by the shackle of perpetual servitude, assail the sons' of light within our borders or damnably imagine themselves to be equal to them in privileges."[82] The Pope established a special Dominican mission to convert Muslims of Lucera.[83] In reality, the mendicant orders owed much to Gregory IX and served his religious and political agendas, especially against Frederick II, to the best of their abilities. They were considered the special protégé of papacy.[84] Thomas would join the Dominican Order later on in his early youth. Gregory IX demanded the Emperor to support the Dominican mission with material sword. He urged him to terrorise the Muslims to absolute servitude and to protect the faith of neighbouring Christians from the Muslim menace. The conspicuous presence of Muslims just 200 miles from Rome, with so much religious freedom and so many privileges, was a thorn in the side of many popes. They were furious that some of the closest and most trusted allies and advisors of the Emperor were either Muslims or ex Muslims. "Uberto Fallamonaca is said to have been of Muslim ancestry, and became one of Frederick's closest advisers."[85]

The Muslims of Lucera were the bone of contention between the two sovereigns. Pope Gregory was as ambitious, fearless and power hungry as Frederick. He believed that his spiritual domain entitled him to the universal political authority, and he hated Frederick for disputing such a Christendom-wide control. To Frederick's historian Ernst Kontorowicz, Gregory was a "tiara-crowned, papal Imperator," "drunk with hate."[86] David Einstein observed that Gregory possessed a "fearless will and dynamic force of immeasurable power."[87] Gregory's universal hegemonic designs were foiled by Frederick with the help of Muslim soldiers, and he demonised them all over the Continent. To Gregory, Frederick and his Muslim soldiers were the epitome of Satan incarnate while the Emperor and his Muslim mercenaries thought otherwise; the Muslims considered the Emperor a secular and nominal Christian.

The nineteenth-century historian Joseph Francois Michaud described Frederick and Gregory as "both animated by boundless ambition, jealous to excess of their power, implacable in their revenge and always ready to employ the arms which the church or fortune placed in their hands."[88] To Frederick, Pope Gregory was an evil manipulator and enemy of true Christianity. After his excommunication, Frederick claimed that, "from him [Gregory IX] in whom all men hope to find salvation of body and soul comes evil example, deceit, and wrongdoing."[89] The Muslim chroniclers described Frederick as a secular ruler, bent on acquiring material gains and not believing much in the Christian faith. He was a cultural Christian defending the Christian faith and gospel whenever it suited his political interests.[90]

Gregory IX died in 1241 and his successor Pope Innocent IV declared a crusade against Frederick in 1245. The infidel Saracens' presence in the heart of Italy and their satanic Jihad against the Pope and Christendom were among the supposed main reasons for the crusade. At the death of Frederick in 1250, the Muslim colony of Lucera and Muslim battalion of Frederick's army were still haunting the papal curia. Thomas, who had joined the Dominican Order by now and had travelled a thousand miles to Paris, could not have been ignorant about the huge Muslim presence in the neighborhood of Aquino and the crucial role Muslims played in the army of the Emperor. Lucera was indeed Frederick's favourite place- David Abulafia well summarises the situation: "There is no doubt that Frederick came to like the place. Later, papal taunts at Lucera's very existence endeared the Saracen colony still more to Frederick. In the 1230s a fine palace was built there, and excavations have revealed the luxurious life of its occupants in the thirteenth century. Whether it was Frederick II or one of his successors who delighted in Chinese celadon ware and other Eastern ceramics it is impossible to say. But it must be assumed that the palace at Lucera was recognisably oriental in style, with its harem, its Muslim sentries and Eastern exotica amid the decor. For Frederick, of course, this was no real departure: the palaces at Palermo in which he had spent his childhood were also modelled on North African examples. What was new at Lucera was the ruler's willingness to accept that the Saracens would stay Muslim; whereas, as has been seen, William the Good discouraged open exhibition of Islam at court, Frederick, was unworried by the devotions of his Saracen servants. In the first place, he knew that they had fought hard for their faith; a hundred and fifty years of Christian rule had not converted them. They were five or ten per cent of a very much larger Muslim population that had been converted or slaughtered, or had left, often voluntarily, for Africa: a hard fighting core, whose military skills he could exploit. In the second place, they were his: serfs of the chamber in the same way as the Jews. They owed no other allegiance, and were at his beck and call. While the Jews, skilled craftsmen and farmers, were encouraged to work in industry and specialist agriculture, the Muslims were also used as soldiers, personal servants, concubines; some attempt was made around 1240 to provide them with oxen so they could resume cultivation of the soil in Apulia. A Saracen bodyguard travelled with Frederick, even to Jerusalem on his crusade! But Saracen bodyguards had protected his Norman predecessors too. The Saracens possessed military skills, as light cavalry and archers, that could not easily be rivalled from other sources. Thus Frederick bonded to himself the most troublesome of his subjects, by a policy extremely tough in the short term — the misery of deportation — but almost generous in the long term."[91] For Muslims the Emperor was not much different than their secular Sultans.

Lucera had a vibrant Muslim community till 1300, and played a crucial role in the imperial court of Fredrick II, his son Conard and his illegitimate son Manfred. All popes (Gregory IX, Alexander IV, Urban IV and Clement IV) issued bulls against the Muslims of Lucera, and Pope Clement IV declared a special crusade against the colony in 1268 when the Muslims supported Conardin, the grandson of Frederick. The Crusade was announced in the general chapter of the Dominican Order in Viterbo, while Thomas was in Viterbo. Cardinal Eudes de Châteauroux, the French royal and Louis's main crusade preacher, was assigned the preaching and recruiting task and the crusade resulted in the success of Charles of Anjou's armies against Conardin and his Muslim soldiers.[92] The Muslims surrendered the city to Charles of Anjou, making peace on mutually agreed terms. They played a major role in the military expeditions of Charles I of Anjou (King of Sicily from 1266 to 1285) especially in his Albanian and Romanian campaigns. The colony was permanently dismantled by Charles II in 1300. In short, Muslims of Sicily, Lucera and Apulia loomed large in the horizons of Thomas whose entire family including his father and two brothers served Frederick's army along with thousands of Muslim soldiers. Thomas witnessed first-hand the struggles between the Emperor's army and papal troops in the Abbey of Monte Cassino.

Thomas's father Landulf was a minor knight. His mother Donna Theodora D'Aquino was from Naples and a very remote cousin of Fredrick II. Aquino was the farthest north-western province of the thirteenth-century Kingdom of Sicily. Sicily was ruled by Muslims for close to three centuries (831-1072). Thomas's brother "Aimo, or Aimone, became a soldier and fought with the army of Frederick II, accompanied him on the fifth crusade, was captured in 1232, was held for ransom on the island of Cyprus, and was eventually released through the intercession of Pope Gregory IX in 1233. From 1233 onward Aimo supported the Pope's cause against Frederick."[93] His other brother "Rinaldo, or Reginaldo, also served in the Emperor's forces until 1245. In 1240 he is mentioned as *valettus imperatoris,* i.e., the Emperor's page, a noble youth attending the sovereign's service and being trained-such at least was the custom at Frederick's court-for responsible office in the realm. In 1245, when Frederick II was deposed by Innocent IV at the Council of Lyons, Rinaldo changed allegiance and fought with the armies of the Pope against Frederick."[94] Frederick ordered Rinaldo's execution in 1246 as a result of assassination attempt at Capaccio. The Aquinas family considered him a martyr in the cause of faith and church. Thomas was well aware of these incidents and indirectly alluded to them in his later works.

Thomas's early education and upbringing was in the Benediction tradition at Monte Cassino, just 110 miles from the Muslim colony of Lucera. "After his fifth birthday," i.e. around 1230 or 1231, his parents brought Thomas to the ancient Benedictine Abbey of Monte Cassino." As the youngest son in the family, he was brought as an oblate *(oblntus)*; that is to say, he was offered to God in the Benedictine way of life for elementary training, in the practice of the rules and basic education. Landulf and Theodora had made careful plans for the future of the family; Thomas, it was hoped, would become abbot of Monte Cassino."[95] During his decade-long stay at Mont Cassino, Thomas witnessed constant warfare between the papacy and the imperial forces of Fredrick II. Their troops continuously fought at various fronts. The popes repeatedly commanded Fredrick to fulfil his vow of crusade to the Holy Land, but the Emperor was afraid that papacy would misuse his absence from Italy to consolidate its powers in the neighbouring Sicilian areas. "Monte Cassino had been held by imperial troops from about1225 onward. When Frederick II finally fulfilled his vow to go on a crusade to the Holy Land, a papal army under the command of a cardinal invaded the abbey and laid hands upon its valuable treasures to keep them from imperial forces. In 1229, after Frederick's return from the Holy Land, imperial troops with a contingent of Saracens among them invaded Cassinese territory and laid siege to the abbey. The following year, 1230, saw these campaigns ended by the peace of San Germano (present-day Cassino at the foot of the Cassino Mountain), concluded on July 23."[96] The decade between 1230 and 1239 witnessed relative calm in the Abbey, but not without simmering tensions. In 1236 the abbot Landulfo Sinnibaldo, a distant relative of the Aquino family, who originally received Thomas at Monte Cassino, died. The Abbey did not receive the replacement for the next three years due to power struggle between papacy and Fredrick II. "It was not until February 1239 that the abbey obtained a new abbot. The excommunication of Frederick in March of that same year was the signal for another outbreak of hostilities between the Pope and Emperor. In April the abbey was occupied and fortified by imperial troops. Some of the monks were expelled. In June of 1239 an edict of Frederick's banished from the kingdom all religious born outside its· territory. Only eight monks remained at Monte Cassino. It is obvious that in such circumstances there was no room for young oblates at the abbey."[97] Thomas came back to his house in Aquino. The abbot encouraged his father to enrol him in the University of Naples to study liberal arts and philosophy. Naples was just 75 miles west of the Muslim colony of Lucera. Thomas's father was not shy from training his son in the anti-papal camp of Frederick II.

The early childhood experiences had lasting effects upon the life and thoughts of Thomas. "This situation is reflected in the life and writings of Thomas, who has given us two answers to this unfortunate confusion into which the Christian world was plunged. One was doctrinal, the other personal. The doctrinal answer was to be given in one of his earliest works, the *Scriptum super Sententias* II, dist. 44, in which Thomas states that the Pope, in virtue of his canonical office, is the spiritual head of the Church and nothing else; every other political or worldly accretion to this essentially spiritual authority is a historical accident, which may or may not be there without in any way diminishing the Church's inner spiritual nature. Thomas's personal answer to this problem, the one which surely grew out of his experiences with his own family, was to refuse any position in the Church that would have involved him in temporal transactions, which the Popes and ecclesiastics of his time, especially Innocent IV, considered to be their ordinary and natural business. This is the most likely reason why Thomas refused the offer of the Pope to make him abbot of Monte Cassino, even when allowed to remain a Dominican Friar and wear his habit,' as well as the offer to promote him to archbishop of Naples with the addition of funds from the monastery of St Peter ad Aram," and finally his firm intention to remain a Friar even if he were to be offered a cardinal's hat."[98] Likewise, the long presence of Fredrick's troops, including thousands of Muslims in Monte Cassino and then their reoccupation of the Abbey by expulsion of papal forces and monks, would have been traumatically noticed by Thomas.

At Naples (1239-1244) Thomas witnessed Muslim philosophical tradition in the garb of Aristotle's philosophy and Greek logic. The university was also known for its anti-papal tendencies due to Fredrick's patronage. "The studium at Naples was founded by Frederick II in 1224 to rival the papal studium at Bologna in particular. In the foundation charter of Frederick II explicitly stated that the first 1224 function of the studium was to train shrewd and intelligent men for the imperial service [...] it had clearly two fighting fronts, one toward the Church, the other toward Bologna."[99] Its anti-papal orientation can be gauged by its reactions to the papal anti-imperial decisions and policies. Lectures in the university were "suspended from 1229 to 1235 because pontifical troops invaded the Puglia. There was a temporary suspension of lectures in 1239 in retaliation for Frederick's second excommunication, but the professors of the studium pleaded with him not to close the studium altogether. When Frederick's anger abated, classes resumed on November 4, 1239, when Thomas entered the studium with other young nobles who were also oblates. In 1252 King Conrad moved the studium to Salerno, where there was already a school of medicine that dated back for centuries. In 1258 King Manfred returned it to Naples."[100]

Thomas did not study theology at Naples but liberal arts and philosophy; He was interested in Aristotelian natural philosophy and metaphysics at a time when students at Paris and other universities were forbidden by papal bulls to study them. Aristotelian philosophy was initially considered antithetical to the Christian faith and a tool of Muslim polemics against Christianity- that could have been one of the reasons that Fredrick encouraged translation of Aristotelian philosophy, along with Muslim commentaries, to undermine papal bulls and overly orthodox traditional tendencies. Aristotle was understood through the commentaries of the Muslim jurist, theologian and philosopher Ibn Rushd commonly known as "commentator" in the Latin West. "Aristotle's natural philosophy into the schools in southern universities was the culture prevailing in Frederick's court in Palermo [...] The commentaries of Averroes were the most important single project of the early thirteenth-century translators. We do not know exactly who translated the rest of the Averroist corpus, but parts of it were in circulation by 1220 or by 1230, and these came from the pen of Michael Scot."[101] Muslim philosophers such as Abu Nasr al-Farabi, Abu Ali Sina and theologians such as Abu Hamid al-Ghazali had closely studied Greek philosophy and acted and reacted to it. Ibn Rushd (Averrois) was heir to this long Muslim tradition and an expositor of Greco Islamic philosophical symbioses. Fredrick enthusiastically patronised Averrois' commentaries and other Muslim scientific works. "The whole breadth of Aristotelian science, Arabic astronomy, and Greek medicine flourished in Palermo, Salerno, and Naples prior to their assimilation in northern universities."[102] Therefore Thomas's early exposure to Aristotelian and Islamic philosophy was at Naples and not at Paris as commonly contended. Albert the Great and Paris university settings enhanced that experience but did not initiate it. The twelfth century Latin Renaissance was centred in Spain and Sicily far before reaching to the academic centres of France, Germany and England.

The European transition from the so-called Dark Ages to the Medieval Renaissance began in the twelfth century, partly due to the translation of countless philosophical and scientific Arabic manuscripts to Latin. Charles Homer Haskins, the Harvard historian of the Middle Ages, and advisor to U.S. President Woodrow Wilson, noted that in Europe "A library of ca. 1100 would have little beyond the Bible and the Latin Fathers, with their Carolingian commentators, the service books of the church and various lives of saints, the textbooks of Boethius and some others, bits of local history, and perhaps certain of the Latin classics, too often covered with dust."[103] But the twelfth century witnessed a Latin campaign to translate books of "philosophy, mathematics, and astronomy unknown to the earlier mediaeval tradition and recovered from the Greeks and Arabs in the course of the twelfth century," ushering in the "Twelfth Century Renaissance."[104] Haskins stated that the "Renaissance of the twelfth century, like its Italian successor three hundred years later, drew its life from two principal sources. Each was based in part upon the knowledge and ideas already present in the Latin West, in part upon an influx of new learning and literature from the East. But whereas the Renaissance of the fifteenth century was concerned primarily with literature, that of the twelfth century was concerned even more with philosophy and science. And while in the Quattrocento the foreign source was wholly Greek, in the twelfth century it was also Arabic, derived from Spain and Sicily and Syria and Africa as well as from Constantinople."[105]

Muslim Philosophy, Spain and Sicily
Early Muslims were heir to the Greek scientific and philosophical tradition, thanks to Nestorian Christian translators, long lost in the Western world. They also absorbed the Egyptian, Persian, Chinese and Indian traditions of knowledge, and created an Islamic synthesis in conformity with the fundamental principles of their faith. Steven P. Marrone stated that "taken in its entirety, the evolution of speculative

thought in the Muslim world marked a considerable enrichment of the philosophical heritage of late Antiquity. And Arabic achievements in mathematics and natural philosophy, especially astronomy, laid the foundations for later medieval science in the West and ultimately set the stage for the Scientific Revolution of the seventeenth century."[106] E. J. Holymard observed that "during the twelfth and thirteenth centuries there was a scientific renaissance in Europe, and scholars from Christian countries journeyed to Muslim universities in Spain, Egypt, Syria and even Morocco in order to acquire knowledge from their foes in religion but friends in learning. Arabic science soon began to filter through, and by the middle of the thirteenth century the trickle had become a river."[107]

England's 'first scientist,' Adelard of Bath, explained what he had learned from his Arab masters in these words: "From the Arab masters I have learned one thing, led by reason, while you are caught by the image of authority, and led by another halter. For what is an authority to be called, but a halter? As the brute beasts, indeed, are led anywhere by the halter, and have no idea by what they are led or why, but only follow the rope that holds them, so the authority of writers leads not a few of you into danger, tied and bound by brutish credulity."[108] Haskins observed that the Muslims "with no native philosophy and science of their own, but with a marvellous power of assimilating the culture of others, quickly absorbed whatever they found in Western Asia, while in course of time they added much from their own observation and from the peoples farther to the East. Arabic translations were made directly from the Greek, as in the case of Ptolemy's Almagest (A.D. 827), as well as from Syriac and Hebrew. Certain of the caliphs especially favoured learning, while the universal diffusion of the Arabic language made communication easy and spread a common culture throughout Islam, regardless of political divisions. The most vigorous scientific and philosophical activity of the early Middle Ages lay in the lands of the Prophet, whether in the fields of medicine and mathematics or in those of astronomy, astrology, and alchemy. To their Greek inheritance the Arabs added something of their own: observation of disease sufficiently accurate to permit of identification; large advances in arithmetic, algebra, and trigonometry, where we must also take account of Hindu contributions; and the standard astronomical tables of the Middle Ages. The reception of this science in Western Europe marks a turning-point in the history of European intelligence. Until the twelfth century the intellectual contacts between Christian Europe and the Arab world were few and unimportant."[109]

The Muslim Spain played a major role in this transmission process.[110] "Spain's part was to serve as the chief link with the learning of the Mohammedan world; the very names of the translators who worked there illustrate the European character of the new search for learning: John of Seville, Hugh of Santalla, Plato of Tivoli, Gerard of Cremona, Hermann of Carinthia, Rudolf of Bruges, Robert of Chester, and the rest. Christian Spain was merely a transmitter to the North."[111] Haskins further observed that "when, in the twelfth century, the Latin world began to absorb this Oriental lore, the pioneers of the new learning turned chiefly to Spain, where one after another sought the key to knowledge in the mathematics and astronomy, the astrology and medicine and philosophy which were there stored up; and throughout the twelfth and thirteenth centuries Spain remained the land of mystery, of the unknown yet knowable, for inquiring minds beyond the Pyrenees. The great adventure of the European scholar lay in the Peninsula [...] the lure of Spain began to act only in the twelfth century, and the active impulse toward the spread of Arabic learning came from beyond the Pyrenees and from men of diverse origins. The chief names are Adelard of Bath, Plato of Tivoli, Robert of Chester, Hermann of Carinthia, with his pupil Rudolf of Bruges, and Gerard of Cremona, while in Spain itself we have Dominicus Gondisalvi, Hugh of Santalla, and a group of Jewish scholars, Petrus Alphonsi, John of Seville, Savasorda, and Abraham ben Ezra. Much in their biography and relations with one another is still obscure. Their work was at first confined to no single place, but translation was carried on at Barcelona, Tarazona, Segovia, Leon, Pampiona, as well as beyond the Pyrenees at Toulouse, Beziers, Narbonne, and Marseilles. Later, however, the chief centre became Toledo."[112]

The European pursuit of Arabic and Islamic knowledge continued for the next few centuries, culminating in an insatiable philosophical and scientific curiosity in France, Italy and many other areas of Northern Europe.[113] Haskins notes that "This Spanish tide flowed over the Pyrenees into Southern France, to centres like Narbonne, Beziers, Toulouse, Montpellier, and Marseilles, where the new astronomy appears as early as 1139 and traces can also be found of the astrology, philosophy, and medicine of the Arabs on into the fourteenth century."[114]

In Italy, the cultural and philosophical revival first started in the South. Sicily had been under the Muslim rule from 902 to 1091.[115] Additionally, Italian city states such as Amalfi, Venice, Milan, Genoa and Florence were in constant close relations with the Muslim Spain, Sicily, North Africa, Syria and Egypt. Their lucrative international trade with the Middle East was on going long before the Crusades; it flourished during the two centuries of Crusader presence in the Holy Land and continued afterwards. The Italian merchants transmitted a host of skills, sciences, arts and values to the Italian Peninsula. For instance, "Leonard of Pisa, son of a Pisan customs official in North Africa, acquired there a familiarity with Arabic mathematics which made him the leading European mathematician of the thirteenth century."[116]

The Sicilian contributions to the translation and transmission movement were far greater than any other Italian state. The process was not impeded by the Norman conquest of Sicily. In fact, the opposite was true; the Norman conquest of Sicily greatly enhanced and facilitated the transmission process. Haskins states that there was "one Italian land which took more direct part in the movement, namely Sicily. Midway between Europe and Africa, Sicily had been under Arab rule from 902 to 1091, and under the Normans who followed it retained a large Mohammedan element in its population. Moreover, it had many commercial relations with Mohammedan countries, while King Roger conducted campaigns in Northern Africa and Frederick II made an expedition to Palestine. Arabian physicians and astrologers were employed at the Sicilian court, and one of the great works of Arabic learning, the Geography of Edrisi, was composed at King Roger's command. A contemporary scholar, Eugene the Emir, translated the Optics of Ptolemy, while under Frederick II Michael Scot and Theodore of Antioch made versions of Arabic works on zoology for the Emperor's use. Frederick also maintained a correspondence on scientific topics with many sovereigns and scholars of Mohammedan lands, and the work of translation went on under his son and successor Manfred, while we should probably refer to this Sicilian centre some of the versions by unknown authors."[117]

The Western Europe learned, understood and digested much Greco-Roman science through the Muslim medium. It does not make sense that Europe, which for centuries had no or minimal contact with the Greco-Roman sciences and philosophy, suddenly woke up to understand, digest, master and apply these sophisticated philosophical concept and scientific precincts. The Europeans needed a continuous philosophical and scientific tradition with relevant contemporary vocabulary, concepts, explanations and understandings to make sense of an old philosophical legacy and scientific heritage. This legacy was well preserved, explained, adapted and synthesised by Muslim cultures and traditions, as George Saliba very well demonstrates.[118] The Latin Europe received a well-preserved and cooked scientific tradition from the East, initially absorbing it as it was and then expanding upon it with the passage of time. The assimilation and expansion process left its indelible imprint upon the ultimate outcome; Haskins states that the "indebtedness of the Western world to the Arabs is well illustrated in the scientific and commercial terms which its various languages have borrowed untranslated from the Arabic. Words like algebra, zero, cipher tell their own tale, as do 'Arabic' numerals and the word algorism which long distinguished their use as taught by al-Khwarizmi. In astronomy the same process is exemplified in almanac, zenith, nadir, and azimuth. From the Arabic we get alchemy, and perhaps chemistry, as well as alcohol, alkali, elixir, alembic, not to mention pharmaceutical terms like syrup and gum arabic. In the field of trade and navigation we have hazar and tariff, admiral and arsenal, and products of Mohammedan lands such as sugar and cotton, the muslin of Mosul and the damask of Damascus, the leather of Cordova and Morocco. Such fossils of our vocabulary reveal whole chapters of human intercourse in the Mediterranean. If Arabic learning reached Latin Christendom at many points, direct translation from the Greek was in the twelfth century almost wholly confined to Italy, where the most important meeting-point of Greek and Latin culture was the Norman kingdom of Southern Italy and Sicily."[119]

The Italian peninsula was too close to Muslim Sicily and Spain to escape Islamic influences. The Islamic bridge did help in transmitting many sciences, technologies, ideas and institutions to Italy. Transmission of Arabic manuscripts from Spain and Sicily to Southern Italy was quite easy, and "it was through Spain and Sicily that Muslim learning penetrated Latin Christendom and helped stimulate the cultural awakening of the twelfth and thirteenth centuries."[120]

Muslim presence in Sicily (827–1091) had rippling intellectual effects on Italian cities. Even the Norman conquest of Sicily and rule

(1030–1198) did not eliminate the Muslim influences. During the early Norman rule of Rogers I, as Alax Metcalfe observes, "the Muslim leaders were able to take a robust stance, particularly over the inter-related questions of religious continuity and leadership of their own communities. By and large, the same people who appeared to rule the towns led both the fighting and the post-conflict resolutions. In most cases, these leaders were maintained in their positions, thereby reducing the risk of rebellion since they had personally sworn to be bound by the treaty in the first instance."[121] He further observes that the "basis of interfaith diplomacy to guarantee peace and security was made *on* terms imposed by the Normans, but *in* terms proposed by the Muslims because the treaties, such as that at Malta, were specifically drawn up 'according to their own [Islamic] law.' The Muslims paid the *tributum* or the *censum*, equivalent to that of the *jizya*, while the term 'subjects' (*confoederati*) which the Maltese Muslims agreed to become in relation to Count Roger, can be taken as the counterpart for the *ahl al-dhimma* ('people of the protection'). In effect, what emerged was a type of indirect rule, not inconsistent with the constitutional and fiscal regulation of government of the Muslim *dhimmi* system under which the island's Christians and Jews had been permitted to continue to worship freely, to use their own laws within their own communities, and to pay tribute in return for such guarantees."[122] Muslim settlements remained in Sicily for almost five centuries. Both Alfonso VI (d. 1109), the king of Leon-Castile, and his son in law Norman King Roger I (1031–1101) were admirers of Islamic culture, civilisation and sciences. They were patrons of Islamic sciences and facilitated their translation to Latin, even at the expense of Pope's wrath. Metcalfe notices that the "kingdom of Sicily, with its Muslim majority population on the island, played a central role in the formation of medieval Europe during the twelfth and thirteenth centuries."[123] Muslim population was "vital to the island's economy, in both rural agricultural and urban trades and manufacturing, as well as providing skilled craftsmen, merchants and products for export. During the period of Norman state-building, Muslims maintained their roles as naval officers, foot soldiers and as bureaucrats charged with the management of the royal fiscal administration and palaces. Arab-Muslim influence made significant impressions on palace life, art and administration as well as on the outlook and lifestyles of the kings themselves. Above all, an Arab- Islamic facet was adopted as an element within the self-consciously tripartite, authoritarian and sacral kingship of Roger II. Protocols, ceremonies, clothes and the evolution of courtly behavioural codes complemented the art, architecture and recreational pursuits around the palaces. Moreover, royal patronage of scholars made Sicily a key link in the transfer of knowledge between the lands of Islam and Christian Europe."[124] It was Roger II who asked the known Muslim scholar Abu Abdullah Muhammad al-Idrisi to compile the book on geography.[125] This Muslim Norman collaborated work of geography was completed in 1154 AD. Al-Idrisi worked for William I after his father's death but returned to his homeland Morocco to die there in 1165.

Frederick II: the Islamophile
Sicily remained a major centre of Norman Muslim collaborations in the coming centuries. The Holy Roman Emperor Frederick II (1194-1250), the grandson of Roger II, was a thorough Sicilian in his approach to Islam and Muslims. Frederick enjoyed a multicultural outlook; we need to return to him as he was among the main factors of transmission of Muslim sciences and discourse to medieval Christendom.

Frederick, according to Donald Detwiler, was "a man of extraordinary culture, energy, and ability – called by a contemporary chronicler *stupor mundi* (the wonder of the world), by Nietzsche the first European, and by many historians the first modern ruler – Frederick established in Sicily and southern Italy something very much like a modern, centrally governed kingdom with an efficient bureaucracy."[126] He was proficient in Arabic, in addition to five other languages; Arabic was an important part of his Sicilian School of poetry, which played a vital role in the development of modern Italian language. Joseph Schacht calls him "the Islamophile Arabist" who "discussed philosophy, logic, medicine, and mathematics with Muslims, was influenced by their Islamic ways and established at Lucera a colony of Saracens in his service, with its own mosque and all the amenities of eastern life."[127] He wore an Arabic mantle at his coronation ceremony; this red silk mantle was crafted during the reign of his grandfather King Roger II[128] by Arab workers[129], and bore an Arabic inscription specifying that the robe was made in the Islamic year of 528 A. H. The robe had an Islamic benediction written in Arabic language, wishing its wearer prosperity, generosity, splendor, fame and magnificence. This coronation robe can be found today in the *Schatz-kammer* of the Kunsthistorisches Museum in Vienna.[130]

Frederick II enlisted Muslims in his army and many of his personal bodyguards were Muslims, as discussed above. He did not mind his bodyguards prostrating and offering prayers at the time of five Muslim daily prayers, and his personal Arabic tutor was a Muslim.[131] He, like his Muslim friends, kept his wives secluded. The frequent daily ins and outs of fully covered Saracen ladies from his palace caused countless rumours of various kinds. He also tolerated Jews and included them in the court. His attitude towards Muslims was really different than his contemporaries, "that he was able to see Muslims as normal and often admirable human beings was a great achievement, for he was living in a period of great intolerance."[132] He was more at home with Muslims than his contemporary Christian princes.[133]

Initially he did not heed papal orders to crusade against Muslims. Later on, when he besieged Jerusalem, he did not enter the city for almost five months and negotiated the peace treaty with Egyptian Ayyubid Caliph al-Malik al-Kamil Naser ad-Din Abu al-Ma'ali Muhammad (1177-1238). It has been noticed that the "lslamophile Frederick was perhaps never personally eager to pursue a crusade against the Muslims. Instead he preferred to end the war without blood and listening to the muezzin in the holiest city of Christendom."[134] It is reported that the Caliph al-Kamil dispatched spies to Sicily to find out more about Frederick before his trip to Jerusalem. "The reports he was getting back from his informants in Sicily seemed astonishing: here was a Christian Emperor who allowed the muezzin to summon Muslims to prayer, whose most powerful officers and court officials were Muslims, and who spoke fluent Arabic. When he heard of Frederick's marriage to Yolanda, he felt that it was time to look into the matter more closely and he sent the learned Emir Fakhr ad-Din al-Shaykh to Palermo. The Emir reported back in astonishment that all the rumors were true. Frederick spoke Arabic fluently, his courtiers and bodyguards were all Arabs, and the muezzin sounded freely in Palermo. The Emperor was full of contempt for the barbarous Europeans, especially for the Pope of Rome. This sounded very reassuring and al-Kamil began to correspond with Frederick. They discussed Aristotle, jurisprudence, the immortality of the soul and astronomy, and the Sultan sent animals as gifts for the menagerie. It transpired that neither Frederick nor the Sultan had any time for the useless and fanatical practice of the holy war and in 1227 the Sultan suggested that Frederick come out to the East."[135] The Pope called him the anti-Christ because he took Muslim soldiers on a supposed crusade to Jerusalem, making a mockery of the crusade concept itself.[136]

The treaty of Jaffa in 1229 allowed Muslims full access to the Muslim holy sites with full control of the facilities. Al-Kamil wrote to his followers that "we have only conceded to them some churches and some ruined houses. The sacred precincts, the venerated Rock and all the other sanctuaries to which we make our pilgrimages remain ours as they were; Muslim rites continue to flourish as they did before, and the Muslims have their own governor of the rural provinces and districts."[137] The Emperor, who would fight the popes and their Christian troops for decades, had wonderful diplomatic skills in dealing with the Muslim enemy. It was not the traditional religiosity but the high culture of science and philosophy that attracted the Emperor. "The treaty must be one of the most extraordinary diplomatic achievements of all time. Without fighting a single Muslim, Frederick had managed to win back Jerusalem; by means of peaceful cooperation he had achieved what no other Western Crusader had managed with mighty armies. There would be a truce between Muslims and Christians for ten years and the Christians would take back Jerusalem, Bethlehem and Nazareth, together with the western part of Galilee that adjoined Acre. The Muslims would evacuate Jerusalem, but they would keep the Dome of the Rock and al-Aqsa and a small group of imams and ulema would remain there. Muslims would be able to pray at these shrines and visit the city as unarmed pilgrims. Frederick and al-Kamil were offering the solution of peaceful coexistence."[138]

It is argued that Frederick's overall kind treatment of Muslims was a product of his diplomatic political disposition. Indeed, diplomacy cannot be discounted, but given his appreciations for Muslim sciences, language and culture his sympathetic tendencies towards Muslims can neither be slighted. There was a genuine affinity that existed between the early Norman kings and the Muslim civilisation. Frederick's mother was Norman Sicilian and he had spent his childhood around the Muslims of Palermo; he was truly at home with Muslims. Of course, Frederick was not very diplomatic during his struggles with Popes and many European princes, and his antagonistic approach to the ecclesiastical hierarchy in and of itself spells a secularist rather than conservative Christian propensity. The Popes identified Frederick's antagonism of the Church with his love for Islamic ways and Muslim manners. Frederick had amply displayed the Renaissance penchant of Christian indifference and subtle appreciation for Muslim ways and was amply scolded for such a non-traditional bent.

While Muslims had good opinion of Frederick II, the Pope excommunicated him for four times due to a number of reasons, one being his cordial relationships with and appreciation of Muslim religion. Abulafia notices that "the papal propagandists also accused Frederick of being too friendly to one of the religions he was said to condemn, Islam."[139] The Emperor was genuinely sceptical about certain aspects of the Christian tradition, especially its incarnational and Trinitarian bent. The Pope's solo right of salvation and governance, an unintended offshoot of the Trinitarian outlook, was unacceptable to the Emperor. He had problem with papal authority throughout his time as Emperor of the Holy Roman Empire; Dorothea Weltecke notes that "Frederick's dramatic life and reign were affected by many conflicts, notably overshadowed by his long struggle with Popes Gregory IX (1227-1241) and Innocentius IV (1243- 1254), primarily concerning rule in Italy. His demand for universal ruler ship as Christian Roman Emperor collided with the same claim by the popes. This is the time when the papal claim to real power in European politics approached its climax in theory and practice. In 1245 a council in the city of Lyon officially pronounced the emperor deposed."[140] Thomas was then in Paris, and well acquainted with the Council proceedings, as well as King Louis's vow to take up the Cross, arrange for the real Christian Crusades against the Muslim infidels, and free the Holy Land from the impious Saracens. Thomas's brother was also executed by Frederick in 1245 after his excommunication in the Council of Lyon. The Pope's excommunication bulls were publicised all over Europe, especially in Louis' France and the University of Paris. The Mendicant friars were the bulwark of the imperial and papal propaganda machine.

Pope Gregory's toxic bulls declared Frederick the "forerunner of Antichrist', a monstrous Leviathan roaring blasphemy from a lion's mouth, formed like a panther but with the feet of a bear [...] Metaphor was heaped on metaphor: the panther was also a 'wolf in sheep's clothing' [...] a scorpion."[141] The Pope sent him a stream of invective letters that "portrayed him in blood-curdling apocalyptic language as the fourth beast in the vision of the prophet Daniel, a destroyer and devourer, iron-toothed and brazen clawed, believing himself able to transform those things that are set, to direct the course of history away from its path. The atheistic emperor was seen as a new Herod, a Saddu-cee, and much else."[142] Abulafia notices that in "Gregory IX, certainly, we do see a passionate commitment to the destruction of Frederick, that is carried through to his successor Innocent IV."[143] The Pope pub-licly called him a "Saracen lover", "a destroyer of churches" and "the denier of God."[144] The defiant Frederick cared less about the Pope and his decision of deposing the Emperor. Frederick took out a crown and "with his eyes blazing, placed it on the head where it belonged, roaring: 'I have not yet lost my crown, neither will pope or council take it from me without a bloody war!'"[145] Frederick thought of introducing a new civil religion tolerant of various religious groups, a religion without bloody popes, persecutions, distortions and manipulations.

The Emperor's scepticism regarding some Christian dogmas em-bodied by Papal authority and office might have played a role in Aqui-nas' efforts to rationalise Christian theology and political thought. Aquinas' political theories, embodied by his discussions of divine law, natural law and positive law and his ambivalence towards absolute pa-pal political authority, are less reflective of the universal papal monar-chical theory envisaged by the popes of his time and more reflective of Frederick's relative theories of state. As mentioned above, Thomas was born in Aquino county of Sicily and was a graduate of Naples University which was founded by Frederick II in 1224. It was here that Thomas was introduced to Aristotle, Averroes and Maimonides. Aristotelian ethics were thoroughly discussed, debated and interpreted by Muslim philosophers such as al-Farabi, Ibn Sina, Ibn Rushd and al-Ghazali. Al-Farabi's "Perfect or Ideal State" was an amalgamation of Platonic, Aristotelian and Islamic political ideals. Al-Farabi's political philosophy of limited government and qualified monarchy had lasting influence upon the Spanish Muslim philosophers such as Ibn Bajja, Ibn Tufayl and his student Ibn Rushd. Maimonides was thoroughly influenced by al-Farabi, and that influenced stretched all the way to Aquinas. Al-Fara-bi's insistence upon an accomplished philosopher, prophet and lawgiver as the ideal ruler of an ideal city excluded and depreciated the signifi-cance of absolutely orthodox religiosity in terms of rulership. Al-Farabi had faced identical political tensions in the tenth century of Abbasid Muslim caliphate, which Aquinas was to face in the thirteenth century Christendom. Ibn Rushd's Andalus and times were not far from Aquinas's Sicily and Italy. Their sense of religious depreciation and inclusion of philosophical wisdom in matters of authority and rulership, were absolutely opposed to the papal claims of absolute, universal and monarchical authority based upon religious office. Religion was needed for socio-communal coherence, but was not the ultimate source of political authority; philosophical wisdom and morality along with a host of other qualifications were needed for qualified government besides religion.[146] Aquinas stood at the crossroads between the Christian Gospel and Aristotelian political doctrine; unlike the popes, he contended that the Gospel and the Christian faith can flourish in any political regime as long as believers were allowed to practice their faith. Unlike Islam and Judaism, there was no religious law in Christianity. The Gospel principle of "render unto Caesar the things that are Caesars'" drew a demarcation line between the secular and spiritual dominions. Even though Jesus claimed to be the King, his kingdom was spiritual. Thomas never wrote a systematic treatise on the subject, but his partial treatment of the subject was more anti-papal than anti-emperor. He, like Aristotle, al-Farabi and Ibn Rushd insisted upon natural law, virtues- especially the virtue of justice, common law or common good, fair distribution of economic resources- and morality as fundamental to rulership.[147] He maintained that the papacy could be invested with political authority due to circumstances and not as an essential part of the spiritual package. This was markedly in contrast with the popes' theories of universal monarchy as the vicars of Christ. In the end, in 1277 Thomas, like Frederick, was also condemned by the Church authorities.

Frederick was well acquainted with the Muslim models of governance; Jacob Burckhardt states that Emperor Frederick II "early accustomed himself to a thoroughly objective treatment of affairs, the first modern man to sit upon a throne. His acquaintance with the internal condition and administration of the Saracenic States was close and intimate; and the mortal struggle in which he was engaged with the Papacy compelled him, no less than his adversaries, to bring into the field all the resources at his command."[148] He collected "taxes, based on a comprehensive assessment and in accordance with Mohammedan practice,"[149] and "it was after genuine Mohammedan fashion that

Frederick traded on his own account in all parts of the Mediterranean, reserving to himself the monopoly of many commodities and restricting the commerce of his subjects."[150] According to Burckhardt it was during such times and under such Sicilian leadership that "St. Thomas Aquinas, a born subject of Frederick, developed the theory of a constitutional monarchy in which the prince would be assisted by an upper house named by himself and a representative body elected by the people."[151] This concept was close to the Muslim doctrine of *Shura* or consultative body and limited monarchy bound by the Islamic law.

Frederick's court was an important centre, not only of Aristotelian studies but especially of Averroistic studies. The translations made in this court were of Aristotelian Greek and Arabic authors, the most important of whom was Ibn Rushd, translated in part at Toledo and at the court in Palermo. The "works of Averroes slowly penetrated into Latin scholasticism after 1230 and their channels were the court in Palermo and the studium in Naples."[152] It seems that Frederick's Sicily, with its multiple intellectual, political, cultural and theological upheavals, went deeper into making the person and overall thought of Thomas; in the end he was a pure Sicilian.

Chapter 4

The Dominican Order

Thomas and the Dominican Order

It was at Naples in 1244 that Thomas joined the Dominican Order, the Order of Friar Preachers, against his family's will. "The prior who received Thomas into the Order was Friar Thomas Agni da Lentini (Sicily), an eminent man who later became provincial of the Roman Province in 1252, bishop of Cosenza in 1267, and finally patriarch of Jerusalem in 1272."[153] Agni de Lentini remained an important figure in the Dominican Order throughout his life. "Thomas, who had earlier headed the Roman province of the Dominican order, arrived in the Levant in the spring of 1259 as the bishop of Bethlehem and papal legate, and held these offices there till shortly before February 1264. He reached Outremer again in October 1272, now as the patriarch of Jerusalem, the bishop of Acre and papal legate, and remained there until his death in September 1277."[154] Agni brought a different approach to the Oriental Christians; in spite of being an original Dominican inquisitor he initiated theological and liturgical dialogues with the heretic denominations. He used to have inter-denominational assemblies in his house at Acre where members of the Oriental Christians such as Coptics, Maronites, Armenians, Syrians and Greeks would present their theological and liturgical positions and Agni would present the Latin rebuttals of them. "In 1262 Agni convened an assembly which, according to its only extant description, was attended by Geoffrey, the 'commander of the city' (k'ałak'apetn), the masters of both the Templar and the Hospitaller orders, all of the princes of the shores of Syria except the prince of Antioch and all of the advocates (avukat'k'). At the heart of this event was an Armenian theologian named Mxit'ar, who was to express the Armenian position on various subjects in this forum."[155] He strictly followed the two pronged mission strategy of the Dominican Order and convened assemblies for internal as well as external mission; "the assemblies initiated by Thomas were intended not only to confront 'the other' – in this case, Eastern Christians – but also to fortify the belief of the Catholic audience [...] Thomas were unhappy with the level of Frankish religious observance and, perhaps, specifically with what they would have perceived as local influence on Outremer's Catholic society."[156] Throughout his life Aquinas remained in touch with his Sicilian Dominican mentor.

Thomas was to go to Paris but his brother Renaldo, who at that time was part of Frederick army, violently separated him from Agni with the help of his army comrades, including the Luceran Muslims. Frederick was aware of this incident. Thomas was brought back to Aquino and confined to the castle of Roccasecca for a year. Frederick was excommunicated in 1245, and Thomas's family's fortunes were turned upside down. Consequently, Thomas's family allowed him to join the Dominican Order and study at Paris.

Thomas at Paris and Cologne

At Paris and Cologne (1245-1259) Thomas studied with Albert the Great. Thirteenth-century Paris was a city of philosophers, and Muslim, Jewish and Greek teachings were flooding the academic market. Albert was thoroughly influenced by Muslim philosophers such as al- Farabi, Ibn Sina, Ibn Rushd and the philosophical theologian-mystic Abu Hamid al-Ghazali.[157] He extensively quoted these Muslim sages in his writings while accepting and rejecting their views. "Albert's paraphrase on the *Metaphysics*, written immediately after his preaching of a crusade in the German speaking countries (1263–64) by order of Pope Urban IV, bears no sign of animosity against Islam. On the contrary, as in the case of all of Albert's Aristotelian paraphrases, as well as his previous and later theological works, the *Metaphysica* contains frequent references to a wide array of Muslim philosophers and astronomers, foremost among whom are the authors of the two major Arabic treatments of metaphysics, namely Avicenna (Ibn-Sīnā, d. 1037) and Averroes (Ibn-Ruśd, d. 1198)."[158] Albert interacted with Aristotle through the lenses, analysis and commentaries of Ibn Sina and Ibn Rushd; "they are, after Aristotle, the authorities to whom Albert most often refers. Since they are cited not only by name, but also occasionally in an explicitly indeterminate way ('aliqui,' 'nonnulli,' etc.), and often—what is most significant—silently, they represent the two real 'sources,' together with the *Metaphysics*, of the paraphrase."[159] Thomas was one of Albert's favourite students and inherited his teacher's tendencies. Together, they produced works of tremendous significance. "The four years during which Thomas studied under Albert *(1245-52)* were the most propitious years both in Albert's life and in the life of young Thomas."[160] Like Albert, crusades, Aristotelian philosophy through the prism of Muslim philosophers, and mission to Muslims were fundamental parts of Aquinas's life and works.

Latin Averroism and Dominican Order

Latin Averroism was rampant in Paris during Thomas's first (1245-1248) and second term (1269-1272) there. Centering on Boetius of Dacia and Siger of Brabant (1240-1284), Ibn Rushd's commentaries and views exerted tremendous influence in the academic circles of Paris. Ibn Rushd's philosophical views were considered anti-Christian and anti-faith, "the reception of Aristotle and his Arab commentators created bitter divisions between 'radical' Aristotelians in the arts faculty and 'traditional' theologians who remained wedded to Augustine."[161] Traditional theologians like the Franciscan Master General Bonaventure played down the significance of reason while emphasising the primary role of Holy Scripture; "Some wish to be all-wise and all-knowing, but it happens to them just as to the woman: 'And the woman saw that the tree was good to eat, and fair to the eyes' (Genesis 3.6). They see the beauty of transitory science and being delighted, they linger, they savour, and they are [deceived]. We do not belong to the party of their companions, the disciples of Solomon, but to that of David his father, who preferred the study of sanctity and wisdom to that of science."[162] He categorically preferred the Bible over all kinds of learning, including philosophy and rational discourse; "Thus, let him who wishes to learn, seek science at its source, namely, in Holy Scripture, since 'the knowledge of salvation given for the remission of our sins' (Luke 1.77) is not found among the philosophers, nor among the *summas* of the masters, since they draw from the originals of the saints. But certain science cannot be taken from the originals beyond what the saints draw from Holy Scripture, since the saints could be deceived."[163]

To him, philosophical reasoning and rational inquiry was full of dangers; "Thus there is danger in descending to the originals; there is more danger in descending to the *summas* of the masters; but the greatest danger lies in descending to philosophy."[164]

The Averroists, on the other hand, in conformity with Ibn Rushd's pure rationalism, insisted that rational inquiry was the foundation of authentic knowledge and could never be discarded. They insinuated that demonstrative philosophical rational proofs were scientific and hence categorical while the faith-based arguments were imprecise, probable and tentative. To them rational and scientific inquiry was higher than faith-based prepositions, but they could not publicly state that due to fears of persecution. The rational Averroists thought highly of their philosophical methodology while considering the traditional theologians' ways as primitive, persuasive but irrational, meant for popular mass consumption. They developed a theory of double truth to strike a balance between their aspired philosophical truths and traditionally propagated religious truths. They contended that there was only one truth, but two ways to reach it- through religion and through philosophy. They, like Ibn Rushd, gave autonomy and independence to reason, separating its realms from the realms of religion and faith. This was a real challenge to the Church's intellectual domination; Siger assigned the hard truth of philosophy and reason a higher place over and beyond soft religious truth gained through revelation. That was alarming to the Church leaders. To Albert, Bonaventure and Thomas, they were heretical hypocrites, who placed reason over faith, philosophy over theology and Aristotle over Christ. Will Durant notes that "the 12th and 13th centuries brought to the West the revelation and challenge of Greek and Muslim philosophies so different from the Christian that they threatened to sweep away the whole theology of Christendom unless Christianity could construct a counter-philosophy."[165] Albert and Thomas just did that. They saved the Christian Church and faith by declaring theology as the crown of knowledge and authenticity; the pagan Aristotelian and Islamic philosophical traditions were to be used in explaining and understanding the Christian biblical theology, and not to undermine or supersede the Christian faith. The Christian revelation was divine and hence authoritative, while the Greek and Muslim philosophy was manmade and probable. The probable was to be rejected when confronted by the authoritative revelation. This way they thwarted the utter rational challenges caused by Ibn Rushd's revolutionary commentaries with some caveats. "To begin with, the success of Ibn Rushd's commentaries had caused orthodox revulsions everywhere—first among the Muslims of Spain, soon afterward among the Talmudists, and finally in Christendom. Aristotle and Ibn Rushd reached the Christian schoolmen at about the same time, and during the first period of reaction they were treated as a single evil: in 1210, they were both forbidden by a provincial council at Paris; in 1215 the prohibition was confirmed with special reference to the Metaphysics; in 1231 a papal injunction interdicted the reading of their works until their complete expurgation."[166] Orthodox extreme reactions caused Averroism to go underground but with subversive zeal. "Meanwhile Averroism, being ostracised, became necessarily more subversive, Thomas Aquinas' immense effort was essentially a part of the general reaction against the heterodox doctrines which had gradually gathered under the Averroistic banner of revolt. By the year 1277 the bishop of Paris was able to condemn specifically 219 errors in the teachings of these troublemakers. Thus Ibn Rushd came to be regarded as the arch-infidel, and the greatest enemy of the faith. This was absolutely wrong; he was neither better nor worse than St. Thomas himself; his creed was different, but his intellectual purpose was essentially the same, and his honesty and good-will not inferior. As shown by Renan, the history of Averroism is nothing but a series of misunderstandings."[167]

The Averroists also insisted that all humans shared a single universal intellect; that true happiness in this world could be attained through pursuit of rational truth; that dead would not be resurrected and that the world was eternal. These ideas were antithetical to the Christian religion, tradition and faith. The "Latin Averroists' embrace of Aristotle included Averroes' interpretation of him. This position entailed two conclusions for them. First, they shared Averroes' conviction that it was possible, and appropriate, to study philosophy as an end in itself, ignoring any theological issues that this enterprise might provoke. Second, they adhered to Averroes' reading of Aristotle in all particulars, including the agent intellect and eternity of matter doctrines. These proved fully as vexatious to the Latin Averroists' Christian colleagues as they had to Averroes' Muslim critics, and for the same reasons. For the first of these doctrines denies the immortality of the individual soul, while the second opposes divine creation out of nothing."[168] The

Aristotelian materialism was eroding the very foundations of Christian scripturalism, spiritualism and Church authority.

Both the Franciscans and Dominicans went full force against the Latin Averroists and their ultra–rationalist views, whom they thought misunderstood both Aristotle and Ibn Rushd. Therefore, discussions about Muslim philosophy, theology, spirituality and ethics were an intrinsic part of Thomas's career in Paris, as his main mission was to reconcile the Christian faith with Aristotle without jeopardising the Christian faith, theology and Church. He, like his teacher Albert the Great, believed that the apparent conflict between the Christian faith and Aristotle was due to misinterpretations and misunderstandings of Aristotle's works; proper explanation and commentary were needed to bridge the gap between Christian faith and Aristotelian philosophy.

In 1270, Aquinas compiled his treatise "*On the Unity of the Intellect against the Averroists.*" Explaining the context at the start of the treatise he wrote: "For a long time now there has been spreading among many people an error concerning the intellect, arising from the words of Averroes. He tries to assert that the intellect that Aristotle calls the possible intellect, but that he himself calls by the unsuitable name 'material', is a substance separate in its being from the body and not united to it in some way as its form, and furthermore that this possible intellect is one for all men. Against these views we have already written many things in the past. But because the boldness of those who err has not ceased to strive against the truth, we will try again to write something against this same error to refute it clearly."[169]

Thomas was concerned that Latin Averroists' monopsychism eliminated the need for Day of Judgment, when individuals would be judged by God for reward or punishment. He explained: "if we deny to men a diversity of the intellect, which alone among the parts of the soul seems to be incorruptible and immortal, it follows that after death nothing of the souls of men would remain except that single substance of intellect; and so the recompense of rewards and punishments and also their diversity would be destroyed."[170] Thomas also contended that the claims of attainment of true happiness through rational discourse would eliminate the need for God, afterlife or revelation while the true happiness was possible only in the life to come. The eternity of the world discarded the need for a creator, and the double truth theory ridiculed the authenticity of revelation. Thomas had ample precedents in the Muslim and Jewish theological traditions.

Muslim and Jewish philosophers and theologians had preceded Thomas in dealing with these issues at length. George Sarton notes that "In fact, St. Thomas made considerable use of the writings of Muslim philosophers, chiefly al-Ghazali and Ibn Rushd, and of Jewish ones, chiefly Ibn Gabirol and Maimonides. His attitude was essentially one of moderation, comparable to al-Ghazali's, between the extreme Aristotelianism of Averroism on the one hand and the extreme anti-Aristotelianism of Scotism on the other."[171] Al-Ghazali, al-Razi and al-Shahristani had extensively analysed, rebutted and refuted these materialistic philosophical claims. Therefore, Thomas was occupied with Muslim philosophers and theologians' interpretations and analysis of true happiness, creation of the world *ex nihilo*, and reconciliation of faith with reason. These intellectual pursuits were an integral part of his Dominican mission and training. Albertus Magnus and his pupil Aquinas made it "the goal of their lives to reconcile Aristotelian and Moslem philosophy with Christian theology.[172] In the way they assimilated ideas from both Muslim philosophers and theologians in accordance with their synthetic needs. For instance Thomas agreed with Ibn Rushd in the "idea of a single Truth [...] the independence of philosophic discourse from theological edict [...] epistemological naturalism [...] and the religious character of universal wisdom [...] Although there exist wide disparities in social approaches between the two, they held in common the idea that the central aim of secular society is to provide man with temporal happiness."[173] On the other hand, he agreed with Ibn Rushd's theological opponents in the creation of the world *ex nihilo*, multiplicity of souls and ultimate happiness in beatific vision. Thomas was not a mere follower but the influence of Muslim discussions, debates, ideas and concepts was really marked on him and his Dominican order.

Muslim Faced Dominican Order

The Dominican Order was founded by the Spanish priest St. Dominic of Caleruega and approved by Pope Honorius III in 1216.[174] Pope Gregory IX (Pope from 1227-1241), in his struggles of 1220's against Emperor Frederick II, used the Order effectively as loyal preachers, propagandists, spies and negotiators. By 1227, the friars were adept executors of papal agenda.[175]

The Order's mission was preaching and salvation of souls. Preaching was geared towards the Christians to make them better Christians, but the salvation of souls was mostly directed to heretical Christians and non-believers, "for the purpose of stamping out the perversion of heresy, uprooting vice, teaching the rule of faith, and instructing the people [*homines*] in sound morals. They propose to travel on foot and to preach the word of the Gospel in evangelical poverty as religious."[176] Confirming the Order's privileges in 1217, Pope Honorius III wrote of his expectation that the friars would "zealously spread the word of God, whether welcomed or not, and so laudably complete the work of the evangelist."[177] The Jews and Muslims of Spain, Sicily, North Africa and Middle East and Oriental and heretical Christians of various denominations were the eventual major recipients of the friars' evangelism.

Their zeal to preach the Gospel with professional preparations and confront heresy with informed tools soon propelled Dominican preachers to the forefront of intellectual life, and of medieval scholasticism. The orders' focus upon systematic education, skilful training, informed preaching in vernacular languages and intellectual treatment of religious problems of burgeoning populations of cities made the order quite relevant to and popular among the urban Christians of the thirteenth century. The friars' insistence upon poverty, learning, contemplation, virtue and spirituality earned them respect and veneration of those who were appalled by the pomp and ceremonial extravagances of the secular clergy. The Dominican begging, utter poverty and state of self- denial was quite appealing to even the so-called heretics such as the Cathars or Albigensians, who were dismayed by the worldly tendencies and extreme material propensities of bishops and cardinals.[178] Even though the Dominicans had little success in converting Cathars to the Catholic Church, they earned the respect and support of papacy, kings and Christian community at large and grew rapidly. They became royal and papal friends, counsellors, employees, servants, diplomates, missionaries, political theorists and propagandists, constant companions and especial trusted friends.[179] For instance the two biographers of King Louis IX, Geoffrey of Beaulieu and William of Charters, were friars. The Dominican Geoffrey was Louis' constant companion and confessor who stayed with Louis for twenty years from Egypt to Tunis. He was entrusted with King's almsgiving, and shared some of Louis' darkest moments in the Egyptian captivity as well as his painful death in Tunis. He officiated the last Church rites for Louis.[180] During his life Louis used to attend mendicant special services at their churches and their chapter, provincial and general meetings. The friars dined with the King, stayed overnight and discussed religion and mission in a cordial environment. Aquinas recorded several of these personal encounters with Louis. The mendicants in 1250 created a special office of procurator at Rome to protect their interests at the papal curia. The friars were outspoken at the Council of Lyon in 1245 and their views were heard by the imperial and papal leaders.

R. F. Bennet estimates that between 1221 and 1277 the number of Dominican convents grew from 60 to 404 and continued to multiply at a steady pace into the early fourteenth century, boasting 582 communities by 1303.[181] Some Dominican scholars have offered rough estimates of the number of friars active in the order by the end of the thirteenth century. Hinnebusch has noted that a minimum of 12 friars were required to be in any given canonical priory, including a *lector* and a prior. Hinnebusch estimates that by the year 1300 the averages of each convent probably ranged from 28-51 to 250-300 friars depending upon the region.[182] Bennett cites Pierre Mandonnet's estimate of between 7-10,000 Dominican clerics overall serving from between 1256 and 1300.[183] Hinnebusch, on the other hand, gives the much greater estimate of 13,000 total friars in the Dominican Order by 1256, and 20,650 by 1303."[184] This was a huge growth in such a short span of time- the secular clergy was obviously envious and irritated.[185]

The Dominicans were independent of the local bishops and answerable only to the pope. The friars preached, took confessions and performed last rites anywhere they deemed fit; this autonomy had financial repercussions for the secular clergy, who despised the competing friars. Additionally, an anonymously distributed book "Introduction to the Eternal Gospel" widely known to be written by Franciscan friar Gerard of Borgo San Donnino argued that soon, in the age of true gospel, the barefoot mendicants would replace the worldly bishops and other church leaders. Pope Innocent IV was understandably alarmed, and revoked this autonomy in 1254 by abolishing their privileges of open preaching, confession and burying. Innocent IV died just sixteen days after the revocation, and the new pope's election was highly influenced by the mendicant interventions. The friar-friendly Pope Alexander IV was elected in December 12, 1254, and immediately overturned Innocent's bull on December 22, 1254.[186] This shows the level of influence these friars had in the Catholic society. The pope authorised them to preach universally. Thomas was an integral part of these controversies.[187]

The Dominican house or *priory* was established in the university centre of Paris in 1217, with the Convent of St. Jacques becoming the order's first *studium generale*. The Franciscans followed suit.[188] Soon after the other university centres had their Dominican priories: Bologna in 1218, Montpellier in 1220 and Oxford in 1221.[189] In 1219, Pope Honorius allotted the ancient Roman basilica of Santa Sabina to be the order's international headquarter. In the thirteenth century, Dominican missions were visible all over Europe and many parts of North Africa, Middle East and Asia. From Spain to Acre, mendicant convents were active in education and mission. "Acre's Dominican convent, arguably the largest in the Latin East, was founded during 1228–9."[190] Each priory was required to have its own *studium conventuale* or learning institute with focus on scripture, theology and mission thus initiating a long-lasting tradition of Dominican learning, education and missionary works.[191] The provincial centres were equipped with more qualified staff and better facilities. Thomas would establish the first provincial study centre in Santa Sabina. "In 1265, Thomas was assigned by the Order to establish a study house at Santa Sabina on the Aventine hill, the splendid 5th-century basilica given to Saint Dominic in 1221 and still the headquarters of the Dominican Order. Thomas began to write his greatest work, the *Summa Theologiae*. In July 1268, however, Conradin, Frederick II's grandson, invaded Rome: Santa Sabina was sacked by his troops."[192] The ghost of Hohenstaufen dynasty- and its battalion of Muslim archers- followed Thomas all the way to Santa Sabina.

The Dominicans had a systematic curriculum, from elementary to master levels. Lectures, studies and libraries became the hallmarks of the Order. Doctrinal training and apologetics were prized. Master General Jordan of Saxony's *Encyclical Letter* (1233) highly emphasised concentrated studies for the purpose of saving souls.[193] Studies were, like charity, beneficial to others. The study of philosophy was prioritised for the defence of Christian faith, but only for chosen elites,[194] though the Dominican ascetic life style was required of all friars. The Bible was taught along with the works of St. Bernard, St. Anslem and St. Augustine; education, preaching, spirituality and evangelism were merged together. Being able to preach using the priory pulpit was the aspired goal of every friar, and adequate sermon preparations as well as professional communicative skills were highly emphasised. Recitation, repetition, dialogue and debate were part of daily routine, and critical thinking, analytical skills and argumentative methodology and scheme were an integral part of the syllabus.[195] The in-house proficiency would lead to outside assignments. Theological, doctrinal and philosophical training, along with professional communicative skills, made the friars respected preachers capable of drawing attention and crowds.[196] This was a higher level achieved by the brilliant through hard work, studies and practice. Theological training was the rule and philosophical education was an exception for the elites. Daily and weekly reviews, debate preparations, well planned and supervised topical debates prepared the friars for their ultimate goal of confronting the heretics and infidels. Preaching and evangelism (saving souls) was the aspired goal, and the elite friars were to keep themselves abreast of the contemporary trends in Europe and abroad. They were trained at the Dominican general houses, the order's own houses of higher learning. They were a sort of Dominican universities. *Studia generale* was for the selected elite, a "small and jealous aristocracy of learning."[197] Aquinas was among the top intellectual elites, the new prestigious academic class, top-notch Dominican intellectual evangelists.

Under the orders of Dominican leadership, Thomas in Orvieto, Rome and Naples (1259-1268) compiled his works such as *Summa Contra Gentiles* and *Summa Theologiae* directed partially both to the Muslim audience and Christians living among the Muslims. Thousands of Christians were settled in the areas of Spain and Sicily re-conquered by the Christian crusaders. Countless Muslims stayed in the newly established Christian kingdoms of Sicily, Aragon, Castile and Valencia, and the Dominican friars were fully engaged with them in different capacities and at various levels. From "Christian Toulouse, Montpellier and Barcelona to newly colonised Valencia and Mallorca, and even in Muslim-ruled cities like Marrakesh and Tunis with their small Christian minorities, the Friars Preacher adapted their methods to local circumstances."[198]

The Christian leadership was afraid that the advance of Muslim culture and philosophical theology would threaten the traditional faith of Christian settlers. Thomas and other Dominicans' writings were mostly geared towards preservation of the Catholic faith of those Christians living among the Muslims. They were also directed towards converting Muslims to Christianity, as the missionary works of Dominicans and Franciscans to Muslims and Jews were at their peak during the early and middle of the thirteenth century. The Dominican and Franciscan missionary zeal went hand in hand with the crusades, Reconquista and papal claims of universal authority. "By the time of the Dominican Order's foundation in the thirteenth century, however, Church reforms had combined with new political realities to make a renewed consideration of "outsiders" unavoidable. In an age of crusade and *reconquista*, Christians could no longer ignore the fact that they lived in a world largely populated by unbelievers. Furthermore, one of the central arguments of the Gregorian reform was that the pope's status as heir to Peter and hence vicar of Christ on earth made him subject to none and master of all – Christians and non-Christians alike. It was a bold claim which would be fully elaborated only after decades of legal, political and theological wrangling."[199]

Chapter 5

A New Kind of Crusade

The call for intellectual and philosophical crusade against the Muslims was made, particularly by those Christian intellectuals who witnessed many failures of the military crusades and their minimal impact on the conversion of Muslims and Jews. Roger Bacon was among the open critics of crusades- John Tolan notes that "Far from diplomatic, Bacon was a vocal critic of many of the intellectual and political tendencies in the church: notably the Crusades and the missionary strategies of his fellow friars. He develops his ideas in his various works, particularly the *Opus maius,* which he composed at the bidding of pope Clement IV in 1266–68. For Bacon, the fruits of centuries of crusade and mission were scant: 'there are few Christians; the whole breadth of the world is occupied by unbelievers, and there is no one to show them the truth.' No one, that is, until Roger Bacon came along. War does not win converts; it kills infidels and sends them to hell, making the survivors all the more hostile to Christianity. More often than not, crusades fail to meet their military goals, as the expedition of Louis IX so painfully illustrated [...] But it is preaching and philosophical argument, not war, that will win converts to Christianity."[200]

The dissent against armed violence grew by the end of the twelfth century. The renowned medievalist Robert I. Burn notes that "in the thirteenth century 'the overall strategy of Christendom underwent modification'; the battle now was 'not only military but doctrinal, through a dialogue of controversy.' Nowhere does this spirit of combative dialogue appear more visibly than in the realms of Arago-Catalonia, which subdued and attached to itself in the thirteenth century an Islamic kingdom roughly the size of the crusader kingdom of Jerusalem during its earlier, palmy days. Thrusting into a sophisticated commercial region belonging to Islam's heartland, the Aragonese crusade had persisted stubbornly for almost a quarter century. Preceded by an abortive foray in 1225 its central victories fell between 1232 and 1245. In 1243 Murcia, the Islamic principality south of Valencia, had affiliated itself with Castile as a tributary state under colonial garrison. Murcia's actual conquest, largely by Aragon's armies, came only in 1266. For nearly forty years after the Valencian crusade a series of revolts and crises threatened to loosen Christendom's grip on the kingdom of Valencia and demonstrated that region's residually Islamic character. The Christian fever for converting Muslims can be charted, in its ups and downs, both in precrusade and crusader Valencia."[201] The pre-crusade evangelism prepared the ground for military attacks, and the post crusade evangelism helped in maintaining the control. The kings fully supported such an evangelising strategy.

The Christian missionary fervour can be traced back to the eleventh century, taking on strength by the middle of the twelfth century when the influential Peter the Venerable (1094-1156),[202] the ninth Abbot of Cluny, completed the first Quran translation by 1141 and commissioned a number of scholars such as Robert of Ketton, Herman of Dalmatia, Peter of Toledo, and an otherwise anonymous Mohammed, to translate four books of Mohammedan teaching and the *Apologia Alquindi*, a Christian-Islamic polemical work from Arabic into Latin. He wanted Christian missionaries trained in Muslim doctrine and apologetics.[203] The Abbot personally visited the Spanish areas to witness the missionary work and its potentials. He emphasised upon the use of relative reason in dialogue with Jews and Muslims. "Peter decided to move away from his assessment of the Bible and to move into the realm of reason."[204] Peter harboured enthusiasm for both the internal and external mission. "Internal and external missionary objectives were intertwined in Peter's Cluniac concept of mission, with the former ultimately emerging as his top priority. A century later, the Dominicans would follow a similar course."[205]

The archbishop of Toledo Roderick Jimenez of Rada ordered Mark of Toledo to render another Quranic translation in 1213. The two-pronged French and Spanish mission schemes were in line with the overall papal strategy of winning souls. "Pope Lucius III, promulgating regulations for the crusading Order of Santiago in 1184, sounded the same note as Urban a century before: he 'stringently commanded that they aim at one thing alone in their fighting against the Sar-acens-not love of worldly praise, not desire of shedding blood, not greed over land acquisition-but either that they defend Christians from their onslaught or else that they may be able to draw these [Sara-cens] to practice the Christian faith.' Less than a decade later, in 1192, Pope Celestine III asked the Toledo archbishop to dispatch a bilingual missionary for preaching to Christians in 'Morocco, Seville, and other cities of the Saracens.' Presumably such a missioner also served the dreams of conversion."[206]

Berthold Altaner has observed that early generations of Domin-icans were thoroughly missionary, having "ambitious missionary idea. They crossed the borders of Latin Christianity and approached Christian non-catholic groups in the Balkans, travelled to countries and peoples still pagan: the Baltic countries, Prussia, Finland, parts of Eastern Europe (Tartars, Kumans, etcetera). They created mission posts in the Christian commercial quarters of North-African cities (for example in Tunis) and preached among Muslims in Southern Europe (Sicily and Spain) and the Holy Land. Where possible they established convents."[207] B. Kedar agrees. "In the early years of their existence, the Franciscan and Dominican orders dedicated consider-able energy to the furthering of Saracen conversion. The memory of Francis's attempts to go to the Saracens and of Dominic's plan to do so was still fresh. The Aragonese conquest of Majorca (1229-35) and the kingdom of Valencia (1229-45) and the Castilian push to Cordova (1236) and Seville (1248) made large Muslim populations accessible to Catholic missionizing, while the spectacle of an erstwhile ruler of Muslim Valencia becoming Catholic and assisting the crusaders of Jaume I of Aragon in the conquest of his former possessions boded well for further conversions. The fact that the ruler, Abu Zayd, con-verted to Christianity not long after ordering the execution of two Italian Franciscans who had attempted to assail Islam publicly in Va-lencia city must have fortified Franciscan enthusiasts in their belief in the efficacy of the practice of preaching even unto martyrdom."[208] He further states that "recurring prophecies of the impending end of Islam—like the one about the speedy destruction of Mecca and Bagh-dad, the spread of doubt and uncertainty among the Saracens, and the abandonment of their mosques, which was attributed *to* Master John of Toledo and widely diffused after 1229—might have beguiled some

Mendicants into seriously underestimating the durability of Muslim resistance to Christianisation." [209]

The Order highly encouraged friars to learn the local languages of mission recipients. "Already in 1236, at the General Chapter of Paris, master-general Jordan of Saxony ordered: 'We demand that in all provinces and convents friars learn the languages of their neighbours.'"[210] The Holy Land priories responded immediately. "In 1237 Philip, the prior of the Dominicans in the Holy Land, informed Pope Gregory IX that he had ordered the study of Oriental languages in the convents of his province, and that his friars were already capable of conversing and preaching in the newly acquired languages, 'and especially in Arabic, which is the more common among the people.' Besides reporting to the pope on activities among Oriental Christians, Philip writes that he sent three friars to preach to the Saracens who had witnessed the miracles that occurred near the spot where the Dominican master general, Jordan of Saxony, had drowned a short time before."[211] The western priories followed the suit. "In the western Mediterranean, the Dominicans, under the leadership of Ramon of Penyaforte, established schools where friars were trained to engage in polemics with Muslims. The first of these schools was set up in Tunis in the early 1240s; others soon followed in Muslim cities recently conquered by the Aragonese and Castilians."[212] Arabic and other Muslim languages were enthusiastically learned by the friars.

Raymond of Penyafort
Raymond of Penyafort (1175-1275), the Dominican Master General in 1238, became the leading soul of this unrelenting missionary campaign with proper language, religious and cultural training. "Historians agree that Raymond of Peñafort (1185-1275) was probably the main initiator behind this enterprise, as he was of other missionary initiatives directed towards Muslims in Spain and North Africa in the period 1240-1270. According to Peter Marsilius, Peñafort constituted Dominican language schools in Tunis and Murcia, and was involved in the selection and mission of Catalan friars to these schools. Another chronicler, Gerard of Fracheto, called him a *zelator fidei propagandae inter saracenos*, an advocate for the spread of the faith among the Saracens."[213]

Raymond was a very influential and well-connected ecclesiastical leader. He was the central juristic figure in papal ideological, theological and legal fight for universal authority and monarchical power. He was the main jurist of inquisition providing legal, institutional and manual framework to the institution of inquisition. "In 1230 the jurist Peñafort was commissioned by Pope Gregory IX (1227-1241) to edit the *Decretales*. This collection of papal bulls – in fact, papal *responsa* to questions – which had the force of law, was promulgated in 1234. During this period Peñafort would become a confidant of the pope, being one of his confessors. In 1238, he was elected master-general of the Dominicans."[214] He was the confessor and confidant of both Pope Gregory IX and King James I of Aragon rendering tremendous influence upon the Pope and King.[215]

He was a missionary enthusiast, even before taking up the leadership of the Dominican Order. In his *Summa de paenitentia*, composed in stages between 1225 and 1235, we find a rudiment of a missionary strategy concerning Jews and Muslims: "According to the words of [Pope] Gregory [the Great], Jews as well as Saracens should be invited again and again to embrace the Christian faith, through [biblical] *auctoritates* and *rationes*, and mildly rather than harshly. They should not be compelled, since forced servitude does not please God."[216] The Order's master generalship granted him additional resources, and opportunities to speed up his missionary designs. "Already passionately concerned with converting Muslims, he was now able to channel the energies of the young order in that direction. The central part of his life's work in the missionary movement, however, came after his resignation from the general-ate; there is reason to think he resigned precisely to concentrate on the promising areas of Tunis, Murcia, and conquered Valencia. From headquarters set up at the Barcelona friary he managed a far-flung program for the conversion of Jew and Muslim in which the Valencian kingdom figured prominently."[217] King James I responded to Penyafort's call for forcing the Jews and Muslims to listen to Christian sermons in their synagogues and mosques. King Louis also heeded the advice. Jews and Muslims were compelled to listen to the friars' preaching and sermons. Robin Vose somehow plays down the effectiveness of such a forced missionary vision.[218]

Penyafort strongly pushed for Arabic institutes of higher learning to prepare selected friars in Arabic language, Muslim history, philosophy and apologetics; Hebrew and Greek were later added, and by 1237 Oriental languages were taught in all Dominican convents of the Holy

Lands.[219] By the end of the thirteenth century there were at least five Dominican language schools of higher education. "Equally important as a convert-making technique was the institution of schools of Arabic studies to train specialists in controversy, especially with Muslim academics. These centers applied to the Valencian and North African situation a long-standing Dominican policy. As early as 1235 the master-general, writing from Milan to all the order, called for men 'prepared to learn Arabic, Hebrew, Greek, or some other outlandish language.' Penyafort transformed the Arabic schools into something special. They did not aim to instruct in the elements of Arabic; students undoubtedly knew the language before arriving. The mass of Dominican missioners from whom they came learned their Arabic without counting it anything special, probably working under veteran colleagues in the Near East. Relatively few 'selected Catalan friars' plus later volunteers profited from these advanced centers designed to give facility in polemical conversation. The ideal graduate was a man like Raymond Marti, described shortly after his death as 'philosophus in arabico.'"[220] Later we will see that Raymond Marti was an expert in Arabic language, well versed in the Muslim scripture (Quran), prophetic tradition (Hadith) and adept in Muslim history, philosophy, mysticism and apologetics. The teachers at these Arabic language schools were mostly former Muslims or Muslim Arabs though help of Christian Arabs was at times sought.

Penyafort's initiatives bore fruits. He, with the imperial support of kings of Castile and Aragon, trained hundreds of friars in the Arabic schools who converted thousands of Muslims to Christianity. "More than ten thousand Saracens were converted by the friars who preached to them, and among the Saracens of Spain and even in Africa the truth of the Christian faith was spread and already approved in such a way that especially many of their wise men were ready to accept the truth of the Christian faith, and almost every one of the teachers of the friars who taught them the Arabic language were converted by their efforts."[221]

Robin Vose considers this narrative problematic, and insists that one should not exaggerate the importance of language schools and higher learning in the Dominican Order, as such facilities were available only to the elites. "Higher studies of all sorts were controversial within the Order and generally restricted to a minority of friars. Also, Hebrew and Arabic language studies were quite rare and never comprised more than a fraction of the friars' educational program in any region. Their pursuit by a select few should be understood within the overall context of Dominican learning."[222] Vose does not deny the existence of such institutions of higher learning and their missionary bent, especially from 1230 to 1270. He contends that usually the Dominican external mission to convert Muslims was secondary to the primary internal mission of converting Christian heretics and preserving the faith of those Christians who were exposed to the Muslims.

Berthold Altaner, Robert Burn, John Tolan, Benjamin Kedar and many others absolutely disagree with Vose's take on the mission priorities of the Dominican Order, especially in the middle of the thirteenth century. They insist that Dominican missionary zeal to convert Muslims of Spain, Sicily, North Africa and Middle East constituted the top priority of the Dominican Order from the late 1220s to the early 1270s, covering almost the entire life span of Thomas. Their position is substantiated by the historical and contextual facts. The increased enthusiasm for Muslim mission in the early part of the thirteenth century was fuelled by two historical realities: the success of crusades in Spain and failures in the Holy Lands and internal Christian fiasco. The Christian crusades in Spain were gaining grounds in the early thirteenth century, while the crusade states in the Holy Lands were losing significantly. Internally, the papacy was threatened by the imperial claims of Frederick II. The Spanish kings were more amenable to the popes than the frantic Frederick. The popes highlighted the Spanish crusade's successes to emphasise the need for Christian internal cooperation and coordination, and to blame Frederick for the failures in the Holy Lands; he did not fulfil his crusade vow and disrupted Christian unity by challenging and fighting papacy. The papacy had to attend to Frederick's menace instead of pooling resources together to fight the Muslim enemy in the Holy Lands. The popes encouraged mendicants to closely work with the Spanish kings and help in their internal and external missions. They also pushed the newly established energetic orders to fill the vacuum in the Holy Lands and North Africa created by Frederick's peril.[223] The trio of Spanish successes and ensuing confidence, catastrophic Holy Land failures, and the resultant urgency and constant internal warfare between the Holy Roman Emperor and popes, along with apocalyptic prophecies, were the imminent realities which funnelled the missionary zeal and energy. Mendicants were central to both the post-crusade mission in the Spanish areas and pre-crusade mission in North Africa and Holy Lands. They constituted the major bulk of the thirteenth-century papal political crusades and external missions in terms of logistic preparations, preaching, fundraising, recruiting, counselling, communications and diplomacy.[224] The French inclusion in the political and ecclesiastical equation and Louis' categorical Church submission, crusade, evangelical and mendicant bent expedited these pre-crusade and post-crusade mission fervours. Both Dominicans and Franciscans, the apples of papal and Louis' eyes and their main evangelical conduits, and the University of Paris were in the forefront of these missionary campaigns. They were faced to Muslims both westward in Spain and eastward in North Africa and Holy Lands. It was essential that the friars be trained in Arabic language, Muslim history, theology, philosophy and apologetics to the best of their abilities. The need was fulfilled by the higher institutes of Arabic learning established from Spain to Antioch by the Dominicans.

Franciscans and Arabic Learning

The Franciscans also emphasised Arabic language and Muslim learning as tools for conversion. It is true that the initial top leadership such as the Master General Bonaventure (1257–74), Aquinas'ss friend and fellow Parisian, insisted that "reason alone is not sufficient to prove the truth of Christianity, that miracles are sometimes necessary to incline the hearts of infidels to the True Religion."[225] There were some Franciscans who insisted upon an alternate methodology of rational discourse in mission works to Muslims. Roger Bacon (1219-1292) was such a Franciscan; he was an intriguing figure of unique vision and insight. Amanda Power states that "Roger Bacon occupies a prominent, if ambiguous, position in the history of the medieval period. He is widely regarded as a significant figure in the development of modern scientific thought, playing an important role in the assimilation of Graeco-Arabic learning into the Latin world. He was one of the first to teach Aristotle's natural philosophy in Paris, and his later investigations were imaginative and diverse. In particular, he explored controversial fields such as astrology, alchemy and magic, which sought to harness the power of nature at the very boundaries of the licit. Although he was one of a number of scholars who were involved in the process of adapting this material for Christian use, he was unique in producing a series of treatises for the papal curia in which he offered pungent analyses of his society and its intellectual life. These, together with his programme for its reform, have brought him lasting attention and repute. Displaced from their original setting, his ideas have been valued as a remarkable early statement of a set of aspirations central to Western secular identity: the rejection of prejudice and superstition and the continuing advance of science."[226] Bacon insisted that Muslims of Holy Lands in general and Muslims of Spain and Sicily in particular have a philosophical leaning. They do not respond to biblical arguments, rhetorical claims and miracle-based proofs of the Christian missionaries but engage in rational and philosophical discussions. "Like Abelard, friar Roger was convinced that rational argumentation was a universally intelligible and effective means of communication – particularly well suited to the philosophically minded peoples of Islam."[227] Bacon observed that "persuasion of the truth as alone contained in the Christian religion is a twofold matter, since we may appeal to miracles which are beyond us and beyond unbelievers, a method in regard to which no man can presume; or we may employ a method familiar to them and to us, which lies within our power and which they cannot deny, because the approach is along the paths of human reason and along those of philosophy [...] We are not able to argue in this matter by quoting our law nor the authorities of the Saints, because unbelievers deny Christ the Lord and his law and the Saints. Wherefore we must seek for reasons in another way which is common to us and to unbelievers, namely, philosophy."[228] John Tolan comments that Bacon's ambition was "to create a science of religion: a rational basis for Christian truth and a scientific way of understanding the different religions of the world. He affirms that the only two ways to bring infidels to the faith are through miracles or through human reason; since we cannot count on miracles, rational argumentation is the only real alternative."[229] The literary Arabic language was a must for such a rational and philosophical training. "Arabic serves little use for theological study, but for philosophy and for conversion of infidels much."[230] Bacon noticed that countless Western Christians knew how to speak and communicate in Arabic, Hebrew and Greek but very few were equipped with literary tools to decipher the philosophico-rational underpinnings of the written corpus.[231] He stated that "many men can be found among western Christians, who know how to speak Greek or Arabic or Hebrew, but very few who know the literary structure [*orationem grammaticae ipsius*] or how to teach it- I've put many of them to the test."[232] Bacon was himself proficient in Arabic language and many Muslim sciences. [233]

The focus on Arabic language, history, religion and philosophy found a sympathetic influential leader in Bacon's friend Pope Clement IV, who in 1265 agreed that "the best strategy for a campaign of mass proselytism would be to train multilingual missionaries in philosophical argumentation."[234] The same Pope Clement IV was the patron of Thomas and assigned him the Cathedral of Santa Sabina to initiate the Dominican school of higher learning and training. Aquinas's works, such as *Summa Contra Gentiles* and *Summa Theologiae,* completed at Rome, should be reflected through the prism of this broader philosophical missionary orientation towards Muslims.

Bacon insisted that his rational discourse and intellectual methodology was much needed in the apocalyptic times. He argued that "the current situation was dire: a divided, apathetic, unphilosophical Christendom was surrounded by numerous infidel peoples, against which it sent ineffectual crusading armies and poorly prepared missionaries. Yet there was cause for hope: the predictions of the Apocalypse, confirmed by the scientific calculations of Saracen astrologers and by the Mongol sack of Baghdad, showed that Islam had at most thirty years ahead of it. The need to educate Franciscan missionaries in Bacon's intellectual system was urgent, but the hopes for success were good."[235] He prepared his works for Pope Clement IV, but the pope died before being able to implement Bacon's vision.

Bacon's fellow Parisian Franciscan Rymond Llull (1232-1315), a former seneschal to Prince James (later James II of Mallorca) also highlighted the importance of Arabic language and rational discourse. He learned Arabic language from an Arab slave and encouraged the kings, popes, princes, teachers and ecumenical councils to open higher institutes of Arabic learning, to adequately prepare Christian missionaries working in the Muslim majority as well as minority settings. "Like Bacon, Llull became convinced that the best means for bringing unbelievers to conversion universally was for missionaries to be trained in foreign languages and the techniques of philosophical disputation. On the advice of fellow Catalan and former Dominican master-general

Raymond Penyafort, he gave up an initial impulse to attend the university in Paris and devoted himself instead to Arabic studies with the help of a Muslim slave at home in Mallorca."[236] The contemporary Llullian authority and translator Anthony Bonner observes that "it then occurred to him that he should go to the pope, to kings, and to Christian princes to incite them to institute, in whatever kingdoms and provinces might be appropriate, monasteries in which selected monks and others fit for the task would be brought together to learn the languages of the Saracens and other unbelievers, so that, from among those properly instructed in such a place, one could always find the right people ready to be sent out to preach and demonstrate to the Saracens and other unbelievers the holy truth of the Catholic faith, which is that of Christ."[237] King James granted Llull the means necessary to fulfil his vision of Arabic schools of language and philosophy. "His former employer, king James II of Mallorca, granted land and funding for the establishment of an Arabic school at Miramar on the coast of the island, where thirteen Franciscans at a time were to be trained in the language and arguments necessary to fulfil Raymond's evangelical vision.[238]"

Both Franciscans and Dominicans were granted lands, buildings and other kinds of trust funds to support their learning and missionary works among Muslims and Jews. For instance, in 1231 King James wrote: "Desiring that the new tree of the Order of Preachers should thrive and flourish, thrusting and spreading strong roots into the earth, so that in time a most plentiful harvest of souls might be gathered in, especially in these parts where the pagans and the Mallorcan Saracens have been defeated and made captives, and their kingdom happily obtained through their submission and the power of our rule, We, James [...] for the remedy of our soul and that of our parents, freely give and concede this place in the Almudayna of the City of Mallorca [...] in perpetuity to our lord God and to his most blessed mother Mary and to saint Dominic and to his Order of Preachers [...] for the building and construction of a monastery and church of the said Order of Preachers."[239] The outlandish imperial and papal support for Dominican and Franciscan language, philosophical and apologetical institutes of higher learning and informed missionary endeavours continued throughout the thirteenth century, fading only at the end of the thirteenth century. Robert Burn notes that "Most of the records for these schools have disappeared, though minutes from Dominican general and provincial chapters, along with references from the lives of leaders, supply some information. A converted Moor, the Dominican Michael of Benazar (Ibn Nasr), may have created the first such philosophy and language school shortly after the fall of Majorca; if so, it soon foundered. The Dominicans placed their central schools for work with western Muslims at those spots within the area that combined density of Muslim population with maximum opportunity-Tunis for a while, then Jativa, Murcia, and Valencia city, with Barcelona as the base back home. Tunis was the first center established from Barcelona. It dates from the early 1240s, at the latest from 1245. An assignment of eight friars in 1250, often mistaken as the founding, shows it in full career."[240]

Higher Institutes of Arabic Learning

There were multiple higher institutes of Arabic learning *studia linguarum* and *Arabic studium* in Spain, Sicily, France, Tunis and the Middle East. "The order founded such schools in some of their convents in Spain, North Africa, Greece, the Holy Land, Syria, and probably also elsewhere in the Orient."[241] Many such Dominican schools were in operation by the end of the thirteenth century. "From 1248 at least, and probably earlier, Paris boasted a college of Arabic and other Near Eastern languages that instructed relays of ten young clerics from overseas, but we know nothing about the establishment beyond that bare fact."[242]

The Spanish, Sicilian, Tunisian and Oriental Arabic schools earned the respect of Dominican leaders. For instance the Dominican Master General Humbert of Romans praised "the friars in the region of Spain who for many years already have studied in Arabic among Saracens land] are wonderfully proficient in the language."[243] Nicholas Eymeric, the contemporary of Raymond Penyafort recorded that "with the help of the lord king of Castile and the lord king of Aragon (Penyafort) saw to the establishment of a school of Arabic language" at Murcia."[244] In addition to the missionary schools of higher learning, some secular institutes of Arabic language and learning were founded for scientific and cultural purposes. For instance, King Alfonso X (1221-1284)[245] inaugurated "his famous *studium generaile* or university of Arabic and Latin studies at Seville in 1254, it was by no means a missionary but an academic enterprise, springing from the king's fascination with Arabic culture and university learning; its charter bore the confirmatory signatures of three Islamic kings."[246] Consequently there were hundreds of Dominican and Franciscan friars, along with a host of secular academics, who were trained in these Arabic institutes having ample training in Arabic language, Muslim doctrines, scriptures, history, philosophy, mysticism and apologetics.[247] They helped in translating, disseminating and assimilating many Muslim works, ideas and concepts into the Latin Christendom, and their efforts expanded the intellectual capacities and horizons of the Latin World just coming out of the intellectual slumber often labelled as the Dark Ages. The Dominican Thomas played a major role in this transition.

Millennial and Missionary Fervor
The opening decades of the thirteenth century witnessed flourishing of end time prophecies and millennial hopes.[248] The Italian theologian and mystic Joachim of Fiore (1135-1202) preached that the world would end between 1200 and 1260.[249] Joachim was very popular, and many Franciscans, especially the spiritualists, considered him a prophet.[250] Richard the Lionheart wanted to meet him before embarking upon the Third Crusade of 1189 to 1192. "Innocent III came to the papal throne in 1198 and was to make his mark as the most powerful and influential Pope of the Middle Ages. Innocent was anxious to recoup Christian losses in the East. Jerusalem had fallen to Saladin in 1187, and the third Crusade, led by Kings Richard the Lionhearted of England and Philip Augustus of France, was unable to wrest it back. Joachim of Fiore, the Calabrian abbot and mystic that Richard had stopped to visit on his way East, identified Muhammad and Saladin with key elements in the Apocalypse and predicted that Christendom would be devastated by an alliance between Saracen armies and Cathar heretics. This devastation would be followed by a final Christian victory to be won not by crusading armies but by humble, pious missionaries."[251] Raymond Llull and Roger Bacon embraced Joachim's scheme of history. After the initial failure the Joachimites rescheduled the end times to 1290.[252] Thomas would later analyse and refute these claims in his *Summa Theologica*.[253]

Pope Innocent III, who died in 1216, thought that the world would end around 1284. He predicted that the world would end 666 years after the rise of Islam. He "envisioned a final crusade effort in East and West to prepare the mass conversion both of Jews and Muslims." Jacques de Vitry, preaching and baptising converts in the crusader Holy Land, informed Europe from 1217 to 1221 that "many" Muslims, "if they heard sound doctrine, would easily be converted"; "many" already had their children baptised out of superstitious hope for health; "frequently a number of Saracens cross over" into Christianity."[254] This dream of mass conversion reached its climax by the middle of the thirteenth century, when the hopes of conversion of Sultan of Tunis, Morocco, Syria and other Muslim lands were high. "Thirteenth-century crusading popes like Honorius III, Gregory IX, and Innocent IV encouraged conversion of Muslims by persuasion; from time to time the program tended to focus on a promising princely candidate."[255] The Dominican friars were leading this missionary campaign during the so-perceived apocalyptic times in Spain, Sicily, North Africa and the Middle East. "Spanish Dominicans were instructed [...] to direct their attentions "to the lands of the Spanish Saracens, throughout all the kingdom of Tunis, and to any other infidel nations."[256]

The missionary campaign reached its climax between 1230 and 1270. The height came under the master generalship of Humbert of Romans (1254-1263) who put proselytisation of Muslims squarely at the top of the agenda of the Order.[257] "Preaching is also indispensable to the infidels; for without it they could not arrive at faith, a necessary condition for salvation [...] 'How,' said St. Paul, 'are they to believe him whom they have not heard? And how are they to hear if no-one preaches?' (Rom. 10:14.) Our Lord gave the gift of tongues to His Disciples so that they would be understood by all, and that they might lead to the faith many nations who evidently would not have been converted to Christ without their preaching."[258] He commanded the Dominicans including the Arabic translator Yves le Breton to accompany King Louis on his failed crusade against Egypt. Yves le Breton proved to be a professional translator, skillful negotiator and trusted ambassador.[259] Humbert stated that "among the many heartfelt desires aroused within me because of the leadership I have undertaken, there is one which is of no small importance: that is, that the ministry of our Order should both recall schismatic Christians to the unity of the Church and bring the name of the lord Jesus Christ to the perfidious Jews, the Saracens who have for so long been so deceived by their pseudo-prophet, to the idolatrous pagans, to all the barbarians and peoples of the world (*barbaris et gentibus universis*), so that we might be its witnesses, and

the salvation of all to the very ends of the earth."[260] He encouraged
the friars to learn foreign languages and take the word of God to all
corners of the world. "If anyone, inspired by the grace of God, should
find within his heart that he is prepared (in accordance with the will
of the leadership) to learn the Arabic, Hebrew, Greek or other barbaric languages, through which he might acquire rewards for himself in
undertaking the work of salvation in a timely manner; or indeed if he
should find himself disposed to depart the fortress of his own nation,
passing over to the Province of the Holy Land or of Greece or to other [Provinces] bordering infidel regions, which without doubt greatly
lack in friars prepared to suffer for the Order, for the faith, for the salvation of souls and for the name of our lord Jesus Christ – I admonish
him not to refrain from writing to me concerning the disposition of his
soul on this matter."[261]

Humbert believed that the gift of preaching must be polished with
the knowledge of Muslim and Jewish languages, doctrines, history,
philosophy and whatever else was needed for friars to succeed in their
mission works. He insisted upon adequate training in Arabic language
and Muslim doctrine in addition to biblical and Catholic studies. "One
must never engage in debate with heretics or infidels without thorough
knowledge of his opponents' position, as well as the answers they give
to orthodox beliefs, or the devices they employ in disputation. Ignorance of opposing claims invites disaster."[262] He commanded the friars to prepare manuals of philosophical and doctrinal natures to fully
equip themselves with the infidels' religion and culture. "Although the
order should care about promoting the spiritual well-being of all souls,
it should have even more special concern and fervent zeal regarding
barbarian nations, and the pagans, Saracens, Jews, heretics, schismatics, etc., [...]. They are outside the Church and they should be directed
to the road of salvation by the labour and care of the order, so that the
glory of Christ will be disseminated in them. Thus, we need to take
care that the order always has treatises against their errors, by which
the friars are able to train themselves adequately, and that at proper
places eligible friars labour to learn Arabic, Hebrew, Greek, or barbaric
languages."[263] Aquinas's multiple *Summas* were the outcomes of such
official encouragements and policies.

Focusing upon the Dominican universal mission, Humbert challenged the friars to leave their comfort zones and travel around the

globe for reversion of souls to Lord Jesus Christ. "Another thing is the love for the native soil, of which the sweetness traps many. Nature in them is not yet transformed by grace, so that they do not want to leave their land and relatives, nor forget their people. They want to live and stay among family and friends, not troubled by the fact that the Saviour was even untraceable for his own mother [...] If we want to be preachers, we also should depart from the footsteps of such preachers."[264]

In 1256 Humbert issued a new encyclical letter to publicise the fact that many friars heeded to his instructions of learning foreign languages, which had resulted in countless conversions among the heretic Christians, Muslims and pagans. "A great multitude of the Cumans, concerning whom the friars had been solicitous, were baptised. The Maronite people, who for a long time were schismatics and subversives, are said to have offered up their books to be corrected in all things according to the will of the brothers of the Province of the Holy Land, who had been very concerned about their rectification [...] In the regions of Spain the friars, who have now for many years been studying Arabic among the Saracens, have not only laudably progressed in the language; even more to be praised, their cohabitation has yielded (*cedit*) these same Saracens up to salvation. This can be seen in the many who have now received the grace of baptism. [Concerning] the most grand nation of the Prussians, newly submitted to the dominion of Christians, many of them have abandoned the rite of the pagans and are rushing to the grace of baptism"[265] Such optimistic claims were hailed by Pope Alexander IV (Pope from 1254-1261), who wrote "to congratulate and encourage the Spanish Dominicans in particular for their efforts in Tunis and elsewhere among the Muslims."[266] The Dominicans reported a great success in converting countless Muslims and Oriental Christians of various denominations like Maronites, Syrian Melkites, Jacobites, Coptics, Greeks and Armenians.

In the wake of such historical proofs, it becomes difficult to fully endorse Robin Vose's claims that the external mission was not the priority of the Dominican Order. It is an undeniable historical fact that the Dominican Order harboured full enthusiasm for external mission, especially to the Muslims from the late 1220s to the late 1270s. It faded away only after the mission works rendered far less than the expected fruits, and that only happened by the end of the thirteenth century. We conclude this section with Wiersma, who stated that "preaching was an essential element of the Dominican enterprise, and in order to accomplish successful preaching, an integral, regular, and systematic study program was created. The study of languages was considered to be inevitable for the non-Christian side of the Dominican mission, as modest and restricted as this part of the Dominican apostolic mission may have been. At several convents at the borders of Latin Europe, or possibly even among the unbelievers, *studia linguarum* were founded, probably also among the Muslims of southern Spain and northern Africa. Almost all evidence for these language *studia* comes from Catalan-dominated regions of the Spanish (later Aragonese) Province, which was apparently seen as the most propitious place for providing friars with access to qualified teachers of Arabic and Hebrew."[267]

Humbert's external missionary optimism faded after the mission to the Muslims of Spain, Sicily, North Africa and Middle East mostly failed. The crusade states were mostly lost and the Latin Christians were pushed back to Europe. Humbert turned his attention to crusades to support the dying Latin Kingdoms in the Holy Lands, and to help King Louis' last crusade against Tunis. "Ever the educator, Humbert did advise friars to inform themselves about the Holy Land and about Islam before undertaking crusade-related preaching campaigns."[268] Therefore, it is only logical to conclude that many thirteenth-century elite Dominican friars were well versed in Arabic language, history, religious sciences, philosophy, culture and apologetics.

Raymond Marti and Islamic Sciences

Let us look at Raymond Marti, a fine graduate of these foreign language schools and a thirteenth-century model of Dominican mission to Muslims and Jews.[269] Marti was a fellow Catalan of Raymond Penyafort, who spotted this talented friar, perhaps in 1241 in Barcelona, and encouraged him to study Arabic, Hebrew, theology and philosophy. Marti was one of the first eight friars assigned to the Arabic school. "Marti was not only educated in Arabic and Hebrew but also studied the Talmud and works of Arabic philosophy: al-Ghazali, Ibn Sina, al-Razi, and others."[270] He extensively quoted Ibn Sina, Ibn Rushd, al-Ghazali and al-Razi in his writings, especially in his *Pugio fidei adversus Mauros et Judaeos.*[271] Later on we will see that Marti became the main source of Aquinas's possible access to the works of Muslim philosophers and theologians such as Ibn Rushd, al-Ghazali and al-Razi, which were not yet officially translated into Latin. Marti thoroughly quoted these Muslim philosophical theologians and reformers in his multiple writings and became perhaps the main source, along with a host of other Dominican Arabists, of Aquinas's acquaintance with the non-translated works of Ibn Rushd, al-Ghazali and Al-Razi.

Marti was an influential Dominican involved in a number of different capacities in the ecclesiastical and imperial affairs related to Spain, France, Italy and North Africa. "From the 1260s Raymond became an influential Dominican, certainly in Spain and perhaps in France as well. The fact that he appears in two of the three extant Acts written down during the years of his active career, makes it probable that the lost Acts would have shed more light on his life and activities. Other texts in which he is mentioned are: the autobiography of King James I, the chronicle of Peter Marsilius on the king's life, and Arnold of Villanova's *Allocutio super significatione nominis Tetragrammaton*. Finally, in a story of Raymond Lull, about a Dominican friar who debated with the emir of Tunis, the friar is identified by some historians as Raymond Martin."[272] He dedicated his life to the study of Islam and Judaism, and mostly led the Dominican mission to them. He taught Arabic and Hebrew to other friars, censored rabbinic literature especially Talmud, served as a royal diplomate to the courts of King Louis and Amir of Tunis, and enjoyed friendship of many popes and princes such as James I of Aragon.

He wrote two apologetic works against Islam in the 1250s: *De seta Machometi* (ca. 1257), *the Explanatio* (ca. 1257), followed by *Capistrum* in 1267.[273] In these books he quoted the Quran and Hadith, as well as many Muslim philosophers and theologians. Unlike the other Christian apologetics of his time, Marti treated Muhammad as a prophet and Islam as a religion, venturing to answer genuine Muslim criticisms of Christianity in a detailed systematic fashion.

Marti was a colleague of Thomas. He possibly studied with Albert the Great along with Thomas in Paris. "Raymond joined the Dominicans between 1235 and 1240 [...] and he studied seven to eight years in his home-convent, he could have arrived in Paris between 1242 and 1248, where the *studium generale* lasted for about three years. It is therefore likely that he was a student of Albert the Great, and very well possible that he studied together with Thomas Aquinas, who was a young student at St. Jacques 1248. between 1245 and Albert left Paris in 1248 in view of his teaching at the new *studium generale* in Cologne, and Thomas followed him. In his editorial introduction to the second edition of the *Pugio fidei* (1687), Johann Benedict Carpzov included a letter from Yvo Pinsart, then prior of St. Jacques, to Joseph de Voisin, the first editor of the *Pugio* (1651). It seems that Pinsart presents Raymond and Thomas as students of Albert the Great, and he calls Raymond a *sodalis* of Thomas, that is, his comrade or companion."[274]

Some historians, such as J. Saranyana, doubt the authenticity of this account, but the majority validate it.[275] For instance, John Tolan confirms this historical possibility in the following strong words: "Thomas and Ramon Marti had together been students of Albert the Great, and it is apparently Marti who transmits (in 1269?) the request from Ramon de Penyafort, that Thomas compose a *Summa* to serve as another weapon in the Dominican arsenal of philosophical polemics and apologetics against Islam. Aquinas incorporates into his *Summa*, arguments from Marti's *Capistrum Iudaeorum* (1267); Marti, in turn, employs arguments from the *Summa contra gentiles* in his *Pugio fidei* (composed in 1278). There is some debate over whether Thomas's 'gentile' adversaries are meant to be Muslims, generic non-Christian philosophers, or even Averroists in Paris; indeed Thomas may have thought his work appropriate to all three groups."[276] Marti and Thomas had ample opportunities of exchanges in Rome, Paris and Sicily. There is a possibility that Marti's friendship with Thomas was enhanced during his second visit to Paris, when King Louis was planning a crusade against Tunis in 1270 and might have invited Marti for consultation.

Marti had lived in Tunis for over twelve years where the Dominican mission was initiated in the 1220s. There was a sizeable Christian community and Christian preaching was permitted under certain guidelines. "The commercial relationship with Europe expanded under Abu Zakariya's rule, generating much wealth in Ifriqiya. Tunis knew a sophisticated urban life. Commercial treaties with important Italian cities, such as Venice (1231), Pisa (1234), Genoa (1236), permitted nationals of these cities to settle and trade in the Hafsid ports. A treaty of peace and commerce with the kingdom of Aragon was signed at the end of the 1240s, shortly before the Spanish Dominicans appear to have (re)initiated an Arabic language school in Tunis. Aragon had its own ambassador in Tunis, and its subjects their own fondaco, a compound where their shops, taverns and consulate were located. Christian merchants were allowed to practise their religion freely, to build churches, to appoint priests, and to lay out cemeteries. King James of Aragon had even been 'busy securing papal guarantees that Tunis would not be attacked by any crusade ventures.'"[277] Abu Zakariya's son, al-Mustansir who ruled between 1249-1277, largely comprised the period of Raymond Martin's active career in Tunis and North Africa. Marti travelled throughout Tunis and North Africa, engaged in active debates with Muslims including the Amir of Tunis and was well respected by the Amir. King Louis might have invited Marti to Paris to consult him about the crusade.

Bertheir contends that Marti, after long years of failing to convert Muslims through mission works, finally concluded that crusade and forced conversion were the only option.[278] Raymond Penyafort and Raymond Marti both persuaded King Louis to wage war on Tunis. Peter Marc extended Bertheir's thesis to state that Marti conveyed Penyafort's request for a systematic treatise against the Muslims to Thomas Aquinas during his visit to Paris. "Marc's findings are part of his thesis that Thomas Aquinas did not write the *Summa contra gentiles* until his second Parisian period (1269-1272). According to Marc, Penafort sent Raymond Martin to Paris in order to ask Thomas to write a *summa* against the infidels. During his stay, Marc maintains, Raymond not only conferred with Thomas, but was also consulted by Louis on the situation in Tunis."[279] Thomas was in Paris during 1269-1272 as the Dominican Master of Theology. "Marc assumes Raymond to have travelled to Paris at the end of the 1260s to request Thomas Aquinas on behalf of Raymond of Peñafort to write a *summa* against the errors of different groups of non-Christians. According to Marc, among the many sources Thomas used for this *summa* was Raymond's *Capistrum Iudaeorum*, which was completed around 1267. Marc argues that when, in Chapter 6 of the *Contra gentiles,* Thomas contrasts Muhammed's ways to the miracles performed by Christ, he quotes from *Ratio 7* of the *Capistrum Iudaeorum*. All this contributes to his main thesis that the *Contra gentiles* was composed during Thomas's second Parisian *magisterium* (1268-1272)."[280]

Many scholars, such as R. A. Guthrie,[281] disagree with this late date of *Summa*'s compilation. They argue that Thomas started parts of his *Summa* during his first magisterium in Paris and completed it later in the 1260s, or even in Naples in the 1270s. "Robles Carcedo held that the composition of the work took Thomas more than a decade. According to him it was written in different stages. He agrees with Gauthier that it was started during Thomas's first *magisterium* in Paris, but argues that it continued evolving until the late 1260s and that Thomas was still working on it even in Naples (1272-1273). Robles Carcedo's view opens a way of integrating the facts provided by Marc's indicating a late composition with the traditional chronology (1258-1265) defended by Gauthier et al."[282]

It is beyond the scope of this enterprise to delve deeper into the *Summa Contra Gentiles'* compilation date controversy. This brief incursion was needed to highlight the fact that there are many literal parallels between Marti and Thomas's writings. The question is who quoted whom? This issue has been hotly debated by scholars of many fields, including Thomism, Medievalism, Muslim Christian and Jewish Christian relations. For us it is relevant to decode many non-referenced parallels between Thomas's writings and some Muslim philosophers and theologians. There are many possible parallels between Ibn Rushd, al-Ghazali and al-Razi's yet non-translated works and Aquinas's *Summas*. Marti and other Dominican Arabists are considered the missing links and possible translators and transmitters of some of these ideas, concepts and passages.[283]

Three scholars have directly attended to the issue of who quoted whom. They are Miguel Asín Palacios, Petrus Marc, and Laureano Robles Carcedo. The first (Asin) opened the discussion "at the beginning of the twentieth century by presenting the radical new view that it was not Raymond who quoted Thomas but vice versa. The second presented a new and surprising thesis on the dating of the *Summa contra gentiles*, using the parallel passages between the *Capistrum Iudaeorum* and the *Contra gentiles* as important evidence. And the third summarised the state of the question in the 1970s and did valuable additional research on the matter. Since the 1970s no serious study on the parallel texts has appeared."[284]

The famous Spanish Arabist Palacios argued that Thomas benefitted from Ibn Rushd's discussion about faith and reason, and that Marti transmitted to Thomas passages of Ibn Rushd's works which were not translated into Latin yet. He also claimed that Thomas copied them from *Pugio*, which were originally thought to be written by Marti after Thomas's death. Palacios contended that Marti wrote the first part of his *Pugio* in 1250's when he was occupied with Islam. He compiled the second part of *Pugio* in 1278 where he mentioned the date. Palacios argued that Marti could not have depended upon Thomas in an area of his speciali-sation. Islam and Muslim philosophy were Marti's areas of expertise and Thomas depended upon him regarding Muslim philosophical sources. Secondly, in *Pugio* Marti treated the issue of one universal intellect, in conformity with Ibn Rushd's theory and through the translation of one of Ibn Rushd's passages on the subject. This could not have been possi-ble when Latin Averroism played havoc in Paris during the 1270s, and the Church and Mendicant Orders were actively fighting the idea of one universal intellect. Thirdly, the thirteenth century contemporaries usual-ly quoted Albert the Great and Thomas by name out of respect for their works. In spite of many parallels with *Summa Contra Gentiles* Marti nev-er mentioned Thomas by name. Therefore, it was Thomas who quoted Marti and not the other way around.[285]

Robles Carcedo concluded otherwise. He observed that, generally, "Raymond's texts are longer than those of Thomas. In most of the cas-es this is either due to the fact that Raymond identifies the origin of sources not revealed by Thomas or that Raymond adduces additional sources to further corroborate Thomas's arguments. For the rest, the texts are literally almost the same. This observation makes it rather obvious that Raymond quoted Thomas, and that, where he could, he specified unidentified sources and underpinned Thomas's arguments by adducing quotations from several Arabic philosophers."[286] Carce-do conceded that even though Marti quoted from Thomas's *Summa*, it was Marti who initially provided Thomas with Muslim and Jewish ideas and doctrines in 1250's when he was fully engaged with Islam. Carcedo identified an important aspect of overall Dominican process of education, mission and transmission. "'The large works of Thomas Aquinas are not exclusively his own. They are the fruit of a group of men who worked together, passing notes to one another, facilitating others with facts.' In such a process, the exact relation between parallel texts and the priority of one over the other is hard to determine. Ray-mond and Thomas may have exchanged facts and texts during many years, the last stage of which was, then, Raymond quoting and amplify-ing passages from the *Contra gentiles* in the *Pugio*. In any case, it makes clear that the *Contra gentiles* very soon circulated among the Cata-lan Dominicans, making Raymond one of the first to employ Thom-as Aquinas's writings."[287] We already had the opportunity to discuss

Marc's take on the subject.

We will conclude this discussion with Wiersm who puts the point in a nutshell. "It is very well possible that, during the composition of the *Contra gentiles*, Raymond provided Thomas with innovative translations. In the late 1250s, and early 1260s, Raymond may have provided Thomas with information which he used to compose ScG I, c. 6. Around 1267 Raymond may have taken this chapter as a starting-point to compose CI, r. 7, ns. 19-22. Such a procedure would suppose a companionship between Thomas and Raymond, the possibility of which was posed in the previous chapters. However, such material might equally well have originated from other Dominican specialists in Arabic philosophy. After all, the Dominican *studia arabica* and the *negotium arabicum* flourished by the end of the 1250s, as Penafort wrote to his superiors."[288]

The above detailed discussion highlights the fact that the Dominicans had well-organised priories all over Europe including Spain, France, Italy, Sicily; North Africa and also a few in the Holy Lands.[289] The friars closely coordinated in matters related to mission. They collectively studied Christian, Islamic and Jewish theology, prepared manuals for mission, compiled material, books and apologetics. Islam and Muslims, especially from 1220 to 1270, were their main audience, targets and focus. They had the needed imperial and papal backing, financial and academic resources, religious fervour, missionary bent and intellectual tools. They served in multiple capacities as preachers, confessors, teachers, ambassadors, spies, notaries, military chaplains[290] and inquisitors.[291] The Spanish, French and Sicilian inquisitions were initiated by and officiated through them.[292] The Dominican Master General Raymond of Penyafort played a large part in the development of inquisition.[293] He had "the greatest long-term influence on the development of the institution's procedures."[294] Fighting heresy was part of their original mission of evangelism, "the order stated succinctly its sense of a unique evangelical foundation and purpose: 'our order was especially founded from the beginning for preaching and salvation of souls.'" This evangelical charge most boldly establishes the Christian potentialities of heresy inquisitions."[295] Theirs was a "sincerely persecuting Christianity."[296]

The Dominicans had a set system of education, training and mission methodology. The intellectual treatises and manuals were an important part of their internal and external mission. The genius friars were spotted early, commanded to grow further into education, training and apologetics, assigned certain specific areas of specialisation in accordance with their personal interests and calibre, were well supported in their intellectual endeavours and well facilitated in their collective coordinated efforts. Their collective works were disseminated to the relevant priories and training centres. The central leadership, such as Raymond Penyafort and Humbert of Romans, assigned, facilitated and oversaw the projects, coordinating their proper dissemination and application with the help of papacy and kings.

French Leaning Papacy

There was a well-knit system of patronage. The popes and kings served as the patrons of individual Dominican stars. For instance, King Louis was the patron of Pope Urban IV, Pope Clement IV, Gregory X, Thomas Aquinas, Bonaventure and Raymond Marti. Popes Urban and Clement in turn became the patrons of Dominican and Franciscan friars such as Thomas Aquinas, Raymond Marti, Roger Bacon, Raymond Llull and William of Tripoli. The imperial hands and support of King Louis and his Paris University played a major role in this global network of coordinated intellectual work. Many trained mendicant theologians, preachers, philosophers and apologetics of the thirteenth century were either directly or indirectly connected with University of Paris. The French contributions to the thirteenth-century intellectual landscape of Latin Christendom were huge.

The thirteenth century was marred by the struggles between Papacy and Staufen Dynasty as discussed above. The papacy leaned towards French King Louis and his brother Charles of Anjou for support, and the French in turn pushed for their loyal popes and cardinals. By the middle of the thirteenth century, the College of Cardinals and Papal Curia became a tug of war between the French, Italian and German interests, in which the French were the winners in most parts of the thirteenth century. "The French orientation can be illustrated by the papal predilection for appointing Frenchmen as cardinals and the preference for Frenchmen in filling vacant curial posts."[297] The son of a French cobbler from Troyes, Pope Urban IV, studied theology and law at Paris and graduated when Thomas was a student at Paris. In 1255 Pope Alexander IV made him Patriarch of Jerusalem. He was never a cardinal, but was unexpectedly chosen pope in 1261 when on a business visit to the Viterbo papal palace. The French influence upon the college of eight cardinals was imminent. Urban IV brought Charles of Anjou into Sicily to fight King Manfred and take over the thrown of Sicily.[298] "His presence near Rome divided the cardinals into pro-French and anti-French camps, a division further exacerbated by rivalries among the great Roman families, especially the Orsini and the Colonna."[299] Philip Schaff summarised the situation in the following words: "Urban IV., 1261–1264, was consecrated at Viterbo and did not enter Rome during his pontificate. He was a shoemaker's son and the first Frenchman for one hundred and sixty years to occupy the papal throne. With him the papacy came under French control, where it remained, with brief intervals, for more than a century. Urban displayed his strong national partisanship by his appointment of seven French cardinals in a conclave of seventeen. The French influence was greatly strengthened by his invitation to Charles of Anjou, youngest brother of Louis IX of France, to occupy the Sicilian throne, claiming the right to do so on the basis of the inherent authority of the papacy and on the ground that Sicily was a papal fief. For centuries the house of Anjou, with Naples as its capital, was destined to be a disturbing element in the affairs, not only of Italy, but of all Europe [...] Charles of Anjou became dictator of its policy and master of the political situation in Italy."[300]

Urban's successor Pope Clement IV (pope from 1265 to 1268) was also a Paris lawyer and theologian who worked as the secretary of King Louis. Louis pushed for his cardinalship. His election to papacy was marred by the military pressures of Charles of Anjou, whose name was often mentioned in the cardinals' French conclave in Perugia which continued for four months in dire human and political conditions. Clement was accused of overly protecting French interests. He crowned Charles of Anjou as King of Sicily in January of 1266, giving him huge financial support from papal funds, and Charles killed Pope's archenemy King Manfred in the battle of Benevento in 1266. "The Bishop of Cosenza, Bartolomeo Pignatelli, was allegedly sent afterwards by the pope to have Manfred's corpse exhumed from the (papal) soil of Benevento and deposited in a distant river."[301] Staufen King Conardin, barely 16 years old, along with his entourage was publicly executed in Naples by Charles in 1268. Conardin's pleas to Pope Clement for help went unheeded. This sheer dependence upon Charles backfired and the later popes were to fight Charles for authority in Southern and Northern Italy. "Charles of Anjou and his immediate successors cared less for papal and ecclesiastical rights than the Staufens did. But through his connexions Charles knew how to influence at least some of the cardinals, a fact which accounted for the inability of the College of Cardinals to reach a two-thirds majority after the death of Clement IV: the vacancy lasted nearly three years."[302]

Clement IV was the patron of Thomas, Raymond Marti and Roger Bacon. Both Urban and Clement pushed for the French crusades in the Holy lands and levied special tithes and indulgences to support French principalities in Acre and elsewhere. The French and Italian friars were encouraged by the French and papal authorities to choose the near East, and were made a big part of these papal and French political crusades. The Dominican historian William Hinnebusch has shown that the majority of French friars in the thirteenth century were in Palestine.[303] Charles of Anjou meddled in the papal elections to get his ways around. After the death of Clement IV in 1268 the "cardinals who assembled at Viterbo took three years to elect a successor, Gregory X. As public resentment against them mounted, the civic authorities of Viterbo finally locked them in the papal palace, then removed the roof, and finally threatened to cut off their food supply if they did not come to a decision. The learned and devout Gregory, not a cardinal and elected in absentia, was as scandalised as everybody else by the long interregnum and as pope decreed that henceforth the cardinals would be sequestered until they elected a pope and suffer a carefully calculated reduction of food and drink as the deliberations dragged on."[304] Gregory X also had French leaning and was a confidant of King Louis. He studied theology in Paris from 1248-1252, when Dominican Thomas and Franciscan Bonaventure were beginning their teaching careers there. His nephew Bishop Vice-domino de Vicedomini was an advisor of Charles of Anjou. His election took place while he was engaged in the Ninth Crusade in Acre. Gregory had known Thomas, Bonaventure and other friars since the Council of Lyon in 1245. Throughout his rein he pushed for a crusade to protect the French enclaves in the Holy Lands and to free Jerusalem but in vain.

In short, throughout Aquinas's life he was entangled between the Staufen dynasty and French interests. Originally his family supported the Staufen dynasty till 1245 turning against Frederick II only after the Pope excommunicated the emperor. From 1245 to his death in 1274, Thomas was fully occupied by study and mission work (both internal and external) under the patronage of King Louis and French-leaning popes. This period of Aquinas' life was filled with crusade narratives, both at Paris and in Italy. His University of Paris was leading the intellectual, missionary, outreach, pastoral, logistical and fundraising fronts for the crusades and his papal curia in Viterbo was the universal cover and face of the crusade preaching, ideology and implementation. His Dominican Order was among the main facilitators and coordinators of the entire scheme. His Christendom from Spain to Jerusalem was fully engaged in crusades against Muslims, whether physical or intellectual. The leading forces of the thirteenth-century crusade, from King Louis to popes Gregory IX, Innocent IV, Alexander IV, Urban IV, Clement IV and Gregory X, were all absorbed in the crusades at various levels and capacities. Many of them had physically participated in the crusades or crusade preparations and preaching, or had lived in the Holy Lands as patriarchs, and had countless encounters with Muslims in various capacities. The mendicant orders were central to these Christian ventures of expansion and mission, and were fully engaged with Muslims, Jews and Oriental Christians. Dominicans were the intellectual wing of the Latin Christianity in addition to their multiple other hats. They studied Arabic language, read Muslim primary and secondary sources, including various sciences (especially theology and philosophy), discussed and debated Muslim ideas, concepts, criticisms to refute them, translating and transmitting the same to their Dominican fellows and superiors at home so that elaborate and systematic manuals could be prepared for wider dissemination and benefit. The central leadership such as Penyafort and Humbert of Romans directed their stars- such as Aquinas- to lead the theoretical work and produce theological philosophical manuals to train and facilitate the friars at home and abroad. Therefore, Aquinas's major works, such as the two *Summas,* could have been a sort of collective works facilitated by a host of friars in various capacities. This is not to take anything away from the genius and creativity of Aquinas himself; he was the main theoretician behind these projects, and an heir to longstanding Dominican policies, strategies, systems and traditions. He understood the verbal, literal and academic Dominican traditions, which helped him in serving the Dominican mission to the best of his abilities. In the end, his major works can be seen as an amalgamation of Eastern, Muslim, Christian and Jewish ideas and their Latin appropriations in accordance with the local and external needs. It is appropriate to situate Aquinas and his thought into the historical context of crusades, internal and external Christian mission and struggles, and the on-slaught of Aristotelian philosophy through the Muslim bridge of Sicily and Spain. France stands out as the major contributor to Thomas's academic upbringing, education, intellectual formation, production and overall mission orientation. The crusades to the Holy Lands, and their theological antecedents, were perhaps the most incisive factors in the making of Aquinas' thought. Thomas was a citizen of the super Afro-Eurasian continent, where people were connected from Spain to Jerusalem to China through trade, crusades and missionary activities. This French led international circuit of connectivity expanded Aquinas's horizons and outlook, making him an interfaith global citizen.

Mendicants and Christianisation

The crusades were mostly a French enterprise from the beginning to end, and the French-leaning popes and cardinals played a major role in them. The French King Louis, his brother Charles of Anjou, his patronised university of Paris, mendicant orders and papal curia served the French grand design of Christendom's internal unity and external expansion into the Holy Lands and North Africa. The mendicant orders and the University of Paris served as the intellectual and missionary wing, the popes provided the needed universal religious cover and theological foundations, and the princes and kings led the financial and military campaigns. Thirteenth-century Christendom was waking up to the world realities and carving its place on the world stage. Thomas was an integral part of this new global role and consciousness of the Latin Christendom; he took upon the challenge of reconciling the newly discovered Aristotle with the Christian faith, aiming to diminish the internal Christian and external Muslim and Jewish challenges. He adopted a middle way between the mere traditionalism of secular clergy and some Franciscans such as Bonaventure and the rationalism of Latin Averroists and some Franciscans such as Roger Bacon and Raymond Llull. He accepted the role of reason in certain aspects of faith such as the existence of God while denying its role in certain other areas such as Christology, Trinity and Incarnation. Unlike Bacon and Llull, he contended that rational discourse with Muslims on these specifically Christian doctrines was not constructive but destructive. Faith can be defended but not proved by reason. These specifically Christian doctrines must be preached via the scripture and not reason, though the Muslim criticisms of them could be thwarted by possible rational arguments. He was totally in line with the overall Dominican mission strategy.[305] His writings were geared both to the Christians and non-Christians in conformity with the Dominican mission of saving souls through preaching. The Muslims of Sicily, Spain, North Africa and Holy Lands constituted a major part of his missionary designs. The Muslim world and population were central to the Christendom of his century. The Christian leadership was fully entangled with the Muslims in Sicily, Spain, North Africa and the Holy Lands, and these physical encounters produced theological and intellectual confrontations. The thirteenth-century Muslim civilisation was central to Christendom and far sophisticated than the Latin West in terms of population, politics, economy, theology, philosophy and mysticism. The giant of Europe was just waking up to take its right place in the leadership of the then known world. Thomas was in the highest echelons of such a Christian team; his Dominican Order was at the climax of its internal and external missionary fervour during the middle of the thirteenth century. They had priories, schools and convents from Spain to Acre and Antioch, and were a major part of the crusades in the Middle East. As seen above, the papal, imperial and orders leadership from top to bottom was obsessed with crusades and mission. They had first-hand knowledge of the Holy Lands, Levant, North Africa, Sicily and Spain. King Louis, his queen and his brothers spent years in the Holy Lands. The King had three of his children there, had continuous communications with Muslim rulers and princes, was given personal dress (black samite lined with squirrel fur, adorned with a lot of gold buttons)[306] by the Muslim Sultan Turan Shah, and a ship to go to Acre from Egypt, and made alliances with some Muslim princes against the others. While living in the East he tried to unite the Eastern Christians under the banner and purpose of freeing Jerusalem from the Muslims infidels. The great chronicler of France Jean de Joinville (1224-1317) "recalled the kindness of an old Muslim soldier who used to carry one of the sick Crusaders to the latrines every day on his back; he remembered the kindness of the emir with whom he was billeted: Joinville had eaten meat on Friday by mistake and the emir was at pains to reassure him that God would not punish him for this accident."[307]

Pope Urban IV was a patriarch of Jerusalem and knew the Christian (Eastern) and Muslim leadership in Acre and surrounding areas. Pope Clement IV was fully engaged with the Muslim world especially the Holy Lands. Pope Gregory X participated in the Ninth Crusade and stayed in the Holy Lands for a long time. The mendicant friars especially the Italians and French were in the forefront of these multifaceted encounters with Eastern Christians and Muslims in Palestine. They learned Arabic, Muslim history, doctrines, rituals and practices. They read Muslim books and debated religious and political matters with Muslim leaders and laymen. They translated Muslim works for their fellow friars in France, Italy and Spain, wrote treatises to explain Muslim religion and culture to the popes, kings and theologians, advised them on political, economic, military and social matters and worked as spies, ambassadors and diplomate in the Muslim areas. The thirteenth-century Latin Christendom was obsessed with Muslim-related matters, and Thomas was no exception. His works, especially the two *Summas,* should be understood in this historical context. As mentioned earlier, these large *Summas* were a collective Dominican work. Many Arabist friars supplied him with questions, information, ideas, concepts, criticisms and translations from the Muslim areas. He supplied them with intellectual tools and manuals to face these realities with confidence. His "*Summa Contra Gentiles*" and "*On the Reasons of the Faith against the Saracens, Greeks and Armenians, to the Cantor of Antioch*" substantiates the point. The mendicants also used the external Muslim ideas to counteract some of their internal challenges, such as against the Latin Averroists, extreme spiritual Franciscans and secular clergy.

The Dominican friars regularly met on the conventual, provincial and general levels, collectively studied materials, discussed, debated and sorted out arguments and finalised responses. These discussions were turned into written manuals for broader use and consumption. Thomas's *Summa Theologiae* was also a Dominican manual, to be used in priories instead of Peter Lombard's Sentences. Thomas O'Meara O. P. observes that "the Crusades led to a variety of contacts with the world of the Muslims. While the first Crusaders appeared full of prejudice about an idolatrous religion, the next generation more and more changed their viewpoint, noting that the way their opponents thought and lived was quite different from what they had previously believed. In the later time of the Crusades information came from diplomatic contacts between Muslim rulers and Christian kings and the pope. Also the new mendicant orders of Franciscans and Dominicans, whose missionaries were in daily contact with non-Christians and who traveled far into Islamic areas contributed to an improvement of European knowledge of Islam."[308] He further notes that the "Dominicans had been in the Latin Kingdom since 1226, and a central organizational meeting, the general chapter held in Paris in 1228, added four more provinces to the eight instituted by Dominic: Greece, Poland, Dacia, and the Holy Land. The Holy Land remained a small province with six or seven priories Dominicans from Jerusalem, Tripoli, and Antioch sought to convert Muslims and to evangelise Jews and members of schismatic Eastern Christian churches."[309]

The mendicant friars had ample communications and contacts with Syrian Jacobites and Melkites, Lebanese Maronites, Egyptian Coptics and Armenian, Greek and Eastern Orthodox Christians. Christopher MacEvitt in his book *The Crusades and the Christian World of East: Rough Tolerance* amply shows that the crusade communities were neither isolated nor segregated. They were a mix of various kinds and levels, "we should imagine societies in which a religious community was only one of a number of groups or associations in which a person might participate. Others were based on professional identity (doctors, for example, came from all religious communities) or regional, urban, or even neighbourhood identities. Middle Eastern cities were not segregated by religious community, although some might have quarters identified with certain groups (a Christian or Jewish quarter, for example). The establishment of the Frankish principality simply added another community, language, and religious identity to the mix." [310] He further states that "although theoretically separated by belief and practice, Frankish, Armenian and Syrian laity found churches and monasteries, priests, and monks to be conduits of divine grace irrespective of theology. On a daily basis, in rural churches, in pilgrimage shrines, on building sites, and in scriptoria, local Christians, resident Franks and pilgrims, met, rubbed shoulders, swapped stories, and shared in the common Christian heritage of the Holy Land and Syria."[311]

The Greek, Syrian, Lebanese, Armenian, Egyptian and Latin laity and monks often studied, worshipped and celebrated together. The Latin friars were missionary oriented; they often preached to Oriental Christians to convert them to Roman Catholicism. The Armenians, Syrians, Egyptians and Ethiopians were Monophysites, while some

Persian Christians and others were Nestorians. "Among certain sectors of Oriental Christianity there appeared at this period a disposition to some sort of union with the west."[312] The Lebanese Maronites, Syrian Melkites and Egyptian Coptic leaders were reported by Dominicans to have submitted to the authority of Rome and ecclesiastical unity- only the Greek remained hostile.[313] Some friars learned Syriac and Armenian in addition to Arabic; for instance, the Italian friar Ricoldo of Monte Croce[314] (1243-1320) spoke Greek, Hebrew and Syriac.[315] They transmitted knowledge about the Oriental Christians, their liturgy and practices, their books, knowledge about the Holy Lands and pilgrimage to their Latin compatriots.

The mendicant friars regularly communicated with their local, provincial and general leadership. Some of them communicated directly with the papal curia and popes; for instance, the Dominican friar William of Tripoli[316] regularly communicated with Pope Urban IV, Clement IV and Gregory X. William was born and raised in Latin Acre, preached in Arabic[317] and Latin and wrote multiple books on Prophet Muhammad, Islamic history, doctrines, practices and rituals directly for pope's information. As noted above, Urban IV had been Latin Patriarch of Jerusalem and knew William very well. Urban mentioned William in three of his bulls issued from his papal court in Orvieto in 1264. "A first bull issued on January 7, 1264, to Louis IX, says that William has informed the pope concerning the attacks of Sultan Baybars and urges the King to send the money collected for strengthening the fortification of Haifa. The bull also says that William would travel to France and report directly to the King on the situation of the Holy Land. 'Moreover, this William works ceaselessly for the Holy Land, exposing himself to the dangers of travel on land and sea.' On the same day Urban wrote to Archbishop Giles of Tyre and John of Valenciennes, Lord of Haifa, about the needed funds. Six months later the pope wrote again to the archbishop of Tyre (who was still in France) about William, his 'nuntius' for the faithful in the Holy Land, concerning the fortifications of Acre and the need for money; the pope implied that the three would meet in Europe."[318] Pope Urban was the dot connector, the go between Louis, Dominican friars and local French officials in the Levant. "Thomas Aquinas was residing in Orvieto at the time when the pope dispatched letters about William's efforts. He was the 'lector of the priory,' the director of that Dominican community's intellectual life. During his first months in Orvieto he completed his *Summa contra Gentiles.*"³¹⁹ Therefore, like William's writings, Aquinas's *Summa* also attended mainly to the Muslim question.

William knew Pope Gregory X very well, and frequently communicated with him. "In 1270, in the aftermath of Louis IX's crusade to Tunis, several small contingents of crusaders sailed on to Acre; accompanying them was Tedaldo (Theobaldo) Visconti, Archdeacon of Liege, who upon his return to Rome in 1271 was elected Pope Gregory X. While in the East, Tedaldo met William, friar at the Dominican convent of Tripoli, who wrote for the future Pope a treatise, *Notitia de Machometo,* describing the life of Muhammad, the rise of Islam, the contents of the Koran, and the main rituals of Islam [....] William provides a detailed description of Muslim doctrine and ritual, some of which he presents in a positive light."³²⁰

William was far more knowledgeable of Islamic sciences and practices than Raymond Marti, and was among the most knowledgeable Dominicans about Islam and Muslims. "Marti's fellow Dominicans, Riccoldo da Monte di Croce and William of Tripoli, were both much more widely read on matters Islamic."³²¹ He directly quoted from primary and secondary Islamic sources related to a variety of Islamic sciences. "William of Tripoli, also quoted widely from the Quran and at least periodically from Quran commentaries and the Hadith, we get some picture of the impressive range of Arabic books that circulated among these learned Dominican missionary-Arabists."³²² It was perhaps due to his sheer expertise on Islam and Muslims that Pope Gregory X asked William to prepare a detailed report about what was expected to be achieved from the Council of Lyon in 1274. The other Churchmen selected for this purpose were two Franciscans- Gilbert of Tournai,³²³ and Fidenzio of Padua³²⁴- and two Donincans- Humbert of Romans and Thomas Aquinas. William's tract "On the State of the Saracens" was prepared in two years; one can just imagine the enormity of influence these Dominican and Franciscan friars yielded in papal and imperial courts of the thirteenth century. It also demonstrates the fact that King Louis, Pope Gregory X, and the highest echelons of Franciscans and Dominicans were all captivated by the fate of Latin Christians in the Holy Lands and overall Church mission to the Oriental Christians (including union with Byzantium) and Muslims. This fact, combined with the friars' occupation with Muslims of Spain, Sicily and

North Africa, leaves little room to doubt that the religious and imperial leadership of the thirteenth century Latin Christendom was highly occupied with Muslim related matters at home and abroad. Thomas, the main theoretician of the thirteenth century Latin Christianity, could not have escaped this mounting concern.

The Dominicans regularly communicated and shared their works, ideas and experiences with their fellow friars, and the overall mission strategy incorporated these shared ideas into the grand scheme of Dominican Order. The manuals were refreshed, adjusted and modified based upon new information, ideas and strategies; for instance, Thomas modified some of his theological positions based upon the information he got from friars in the Holy Land. Thomas O'Meara O. P. shows how Aquinas adjusted and improved some of his theological views about Islam after reading the treatises and reports of the friars based in the Holy Lands.[325] Let us not forget that Thomas Agni of Lentini (fl.1220-1272), who originally received Aquinas in the Dominican Order in Naples, was the Patriarch of Jerusalem in 1272 and lived in Acre from 1272 until his death in 1277. As mentioned earlier, he was a man of his kind in creating mission opportunities. The late thirteenth-century Acre was a unique Latin city of global concerns, communications and exchanges. Rubin amply shows that "the thirteenth-century [...] Acre housed a considerable number of learned men, some of whom possessed knowledge that was unique and rare. While in Acre, many of these scholars engaged in the accumulation, development and distribution of knowledge in a range of fields such as theology, jurisprudence and geography; some of them composed an impressive number of still-extant texts."[326] Agni's Acre was a multi-denominational city: "The city certainly hosted numerous Orthodox churches; the Armenians had a hospital in the city at least during 1190-1192; Acre had a Jacobite bishop; there was a Nestorian community in the city; and the Maronites may have had a church there."[327] There were some Muslims also[328]: "Among these were, for example, Oriental Christian and Muslim peasants who would bring daily basic victuals to the city, as well as Venetians returning from Damascus with high-quality silk textiles, or Tuscans leaving to Egypt with cloth."[329]

Acre hosted many of the renowned theologians, crusade preachers, philosophers and cardinals; for instance, Jordan of Saxony, the Master General of Dominican Order, lived and preached there. Cardinal Eudes de Chateauroux, the chancellor of Thomas's Paris University from 1238 to 1244, a known theologian, philosopher and powerful crusade preacher, as well as a confidant of Pope Urban IV and King Louis, lived and preached in Acre. He spent decades at the papal curia when Thomas was there. He died in 1273 in the papal palace of Orveito. He preached crusade against the Muslim colony of Lucera in 1268-69 and was close to Aquinas.[330] The Franciscan Guillaume de Cordelle,[331] another powerful crusade preacher,[332] lived and preached in Acre. Rubin confirms that "Jordan of Saxony, Eudes de Châteauroux and Guillaume de Cordelle all preached in the city."[333] The clergy, theologians, preachers (including Jordan and Agni) and secular officials wrote regular reports to popes, kings and superiors in their orders. Transmission of religious and secular knowledge was an important part of these constant communications between the Latin States and Christendom. The Dominicans were especially keen to transmit theological and intellectual information to their superiors for mission purposes. "Acre's clergy to gain knowledge concerning Oriental Christianity were often made with the intention of transmitting the newly acquired information to colleagues in the West."[334] The friars coming from the West brought new tools, ideas, concepts and instructions, while the friars returning home transmitted new ideas, materials, questions and concerns from the East. The mendicants were central to the intellectual transmission from the East to the West. "That members of the mendicant orders played a central role in the city's intellectual arena is hardly surprising given the very nature of these institutions. Both the Dominicans and the Franciscans viewed learning as a significant part of their activities and included highly learned members among their ranks. Additionally, both organisations viewed communication with non-Catholic groups and the accumulation of knowledge concerning them as central aspects of their activity. Furthermore, as both communities formed international networks, whatever knowledge they developed in Acre could have easily made its way to Western centres of knowledge and vice versa."[335]

We are also aware of particularly learned friars who were active in Acre through the thirteenth century. To give some examples: "François Balme has shown that the Dominican Robertus Normannus, who was prior of the Acre convent in 1277, as well as his superior, Berengarius Provincialis, were both either masters of theology or general preachers. More surprising perhaps is that the Franciscan Elias of Cortona was known for his wide knowledge not only in Roman law but also in the natural sciences [...] The Dominican Yves the Breton was known for his expertise in Arabic (and probably in additional languages as well) and was also responsible for introducing into the city pieces of information with regard to Islam. It is noteworthy that he was a prominent figure within the order, in all likelihood serving as the provincial prior of the Holy Land and, at least in one case, examining the details of a miracle taking place in Tripoli and putting them into writing."[336] The names of William of Rubruck, Fidenzio of Padua, David of Ashby, Peter of Boreth, Burchard of Mount Sion and many others can be added to the list. Rubin shows that in addition to clergy and friars, there were members of nobility, merchants and burgesses, Christian, Muslim and Jewish scribes and notaries, physicians, envoys, travellers and pilgrims who wrote reports, treatises and conveyed ideas through verbal interactions. "We have seen that numerous individuals, belonging to different social groups, were involved, in various manners, in intellectual pursuits in Acre."[337] For a century, from 1192 to 1291, the Latin Kingdom was confined to Acre. The city served as the last hope of Jerusalem Reconquista and re-establishment of the lost Levant principalities. This was the main hub of all crusade activities throughout the thirteenth century. The kings, nobility, envoys, legates, leaders of various Orders, mendicant friars, preachers, missionaries, notaries, jurists, scribes and new converts all lived in and moved through this city. There was tremendous turnover of visitors, pilgrims, merchants and officials and "the range of fields in which residents engaged was extremely wide, and included theology, jurisprudence, history, poetry and geography. Additionally, Acre's intellectuals paid much attention to the accumulation, development and dissemination of knowledge concerning Oriental Christianity and the Muslim and Mongol worlds. As many of the involved agents were prominent figures, one must conclude that the impact of these intellectual pursuits was considerable. Thus, Acre should be seen as a significant intellectual centre on the eastern shores of the Mediterranean."[338]

In conclusion, we state that Thomas did not live in an isolated Paris, Rome or Naples, but in a closely connected supercontinent. He was fully involved with the highest echelons of leadership in France, Italy, Spain, North Africa and Holy Lands. He was the main theoretician of his globally active and well-connected Dominican Order. He received information, ideas, questions and concerns from Spain to Antioch as the main theologian of the papal curia and Parisian theologian and crafted answers and solutions accordingly. His major works were perhaps the outcome of these collective efforts and struggles. He was fully engaged with the larger Muslim question as his Christendom and Catholic faith were absorbed by the conflicts in Spain, Sicily, North Africa and Holy Lands. The anti-papal forces on various levels and capacities pushed for the Aristotelian logic and philosophy in the garb of Muslim commentaries and interpretations to weaken the intellectual dominion of the Church. The Muslim version of Aristotelian rationalism and accompanying Muslim theological, political, spiritual and ethical discussions were detrimental to the scripture and tradition based supernatural, Trinitarian, hierarchical and absolute faith of the Church. Thomas and his elite mendicant fellows had no choice but to study the new material, partly to refute and partly to assimilate. In the end, Aquinas's works incorporated, assimilated, appropriated, accepted and rejected many Muslim ideas, concepts and works. We will quote Juan Casciaro to gauge the tremendous influences which Muslim philosophers, theologians and moralists had upon Thomas. A study by Juan Casciaro, *El dialogo teologico de Santo Tomas con musulmanes y judios: El tema de la profecia y la revelacion* (The Theological Dialogue of Saint Thomas with Muslims and Jews: The Theme of Prophecy and Revelation), Juan "surveys the questions of the *Summa's Secunda Secundae* (Second Part of the Second Part) on prophecy with a view to assessing the influence of Muslim thought (and that of Maimonides specifically among Jewish scholars). The study categorises Thomas's conclusions variously as largely borrowed, borrowed and partly refuted, profoundly influenced, influenced to a lesser but still measurable degree, or independent. Casciaro observes that about two-thirds of Thomas's material relates directly or indirectly to earlier speculations of Muslims and Jews. Quantitatively speaking, more than half of Thomas's texts on this subject find important correspondences in Islamic and rabbinic literature, much in the form of opinions shared by Maimonides and one or more of the Muslim thinkers. There is much more extensive direct citation in Thomas's earlier works concerning the subject, especially in the *De Veritate* and *Summa Contra Gentiles*."[339]

Therefore, it would not be an exaggeration to state that Thomas

Aquinas was surrounded by the Muslims, riveted by the Muslim related sciences and matters throughout his life, acted and reacted to
Muslim religion, philosophy, theology, spirituality and politics, and
on the way appropriated, absorbed and assimilated a lot of Muslim
ideas and thoughts in accordance with his synthetic project and missionary needs. Thomas was profoundly indebted to Muslim philosophical as well as theological thought. He was a product of Latin
scholasticism, which in turn was influenced by Muslim thought and
philosophy. In the estimation of E. Renan "St. Thomas owes practically everything to Averroes."[340] Al-Farabi, Ibn Sina, al-Ghazali and
Ibn Rushd, for instance, were actively consumed by the scholastic tradition including Thomas had directly or indirectly studied al-Farabi,
Ibn Sina, al-Ghazali, Ibn Rushd and frequently referred to them in his
Summa Theologiae, as they all traversed the same intellectual areas.
Some scholars, such as A. M. Giochon, David Burrell, John Wippel
and Jon McGinnis, argue that Aquinas was indebted more to Ibn Sina
than any other Muslim philosopher, while others such as E. Renan,
E. Gilson, Majid Fakhry and Booth contend that Aquinas was a true
disciple of Ibn Rushd. Rev. Robert Hammond argues that he owed
most of his metaphysics to Abu Nasr al-Farabi. Herbert Davidson,
Alfred Guillaume, Frank Griffel and others show close similarities between Thomas and Ash'arite theologians such as al-Ghazali, al-Razi
and al-Shahrastani. These multifaceted studies of Thomas leave no
room to doubt that Thomas was clearly indebted to the Muslim and
Jewish thought, as the project "Aquinas and Arabs" under the leadership of Richard Taylor highlights[341]. He was not a plagiarist who just
copied material from Ibn Rushd or Maimonides; rather, he picked and
chose ideas in accordance with the nature of his project and created a
unique Christian theological synthesis. A comparative analysis of the
Muslim thought and Thomas's synthetic fusion makes is evident that
he moved in the Muslim philosophical/theological world and was tre-
mendously influenced by it. Let us turn to some parallels between his
thought and Muslim philosophers/theologians starting with Ibn Sina.

Chapter 6

Ibn Sina and Aquinas

Ibn Sina was among the most influential medieval Muslim figures. Many contemporary scholars pinpoint his direct impact upon the medieval Europe especially upon Albert the Great and Thomas. For instance, A. M. Giochon notes that "there is not one thesis on one of our medieval philosophers which does not examine his relations with Avicennan philosophy. And the deeper these examinations go, the more clearly one sees that Avicenna was not only a source from which they all drew liberally, but one of the principal formative influences on their thought".[342]

Thomas, like his Jewish contemporaries, was heavily indebted to Ibn Sina. Parts of important works of Ibn Sina were translated into Latin and were available to Thomas. Fazlur Rahman notes that *"In the history of philosophical thought in the Medieval Ages, the figure of ibn Sina (370/980-428/1037) is, in many respects, unique, while among the Muslim philosophers, it is not only unique but has been paramount right up to modern times. He is the only one among the great philosophers of Islam to build an elaborate and complete system of philosophy—a system which has been dominant in the philosophical tradition of Islam for centuries, in spite of the attacks of al-Ghazali, Fakhr al-Din al-Razi, and others. This ascendancy has been possible, however, not merely because he had a system but because that system had features of remarkable originality displaying a type of genius-like spirit in discovering methods and arguments whereby he sought to reformulate the purely rational and intellectual tradition of Hellenism, to which he was an eminent heir, for and, to an extent, within the religious system of Islam."*[343]

In addition to his numerous scientific works, Ibn Sina had developed a unique and complete metaphysical system in an effort to reconcile Islamic theology with the Aristotelian rational philosophy. He had replaced Aristotle's "First Cause" and "Prime Mover" with the One and Only transcendent God of monotheistic tradition. As the problems of conflict between theology and philosophy, as well as reason and revelation, were common to Judaism, Christianity and Islam, Ibn Sina's synthesis was helpful to theologians of the three Semitic traditions.

Ibn Sina dealt with philosophical arguments regarding God's existence, His necessary and eternal being, creation of nonessential beings through emanation (Intellects) (and seemingly not by direct divine will or action), divine actions and attributes, difference between essence and existence, human psychology, prophecy, universal intellect and many other related topics. He developed a fully-fledged system of metaphysics and human psychology, i. e. God, man and cosmos. God was the only necessary being, the efficient cause who caused everything other than himself. God is eternal while everything other than God is contingent. His essence is the Life, Wisdom, Knowledge and all the other absolute perfections. Man and world are contingent and dependent upon God's actions. The contingent material world is corruptible, mutable and imperfect while God, the First Mover of all contingent motions, is immutable, in-corruptible and perfect. The pure Intellect (God) did not create the material contingent cosmos directly but through the emanative scheme of intermediary lower "Intellects". The utilitarian sublunary sphere of existence had emanated from the lowest and most imperfect of all the pure intellects, the tenth Intellect. Therefore, the contingent world is an indirect product of the efficient cause and not the direct product of God. Ibn Sina utilised the Neoplatonic metaphysics to maintain pure divine transcendence. He endeavoured to create an Aristotelian, Platonic/Islamic synthesis by merging reason with revelation to produce a creative philosophical symbiosis.

He strictly preserved the Quranic God's absolute unity and transcendence with the help of Neoplatonism. He absolutely severed the ties of an absolute, pure, transcendent God from the impure, corrupt material world. The emanative scheme of intermediary intellects was geared towards preservation of divine transcendence. Ibn Sina also tried to resolve the problem of anthropomorphism prevalent in some Muslim sects such as *al-Hashawiyyah* and some traditionalists by absolutely negating the divine attributes. The multiplicity of positive attributes and creations, to Ibn Sina, could lead to multiplicity and change in the divinity. Ibn Sina's overall metaphysics will become clear in the subsequent pages, and the interactions of Thomas and Maimonides with it. Here I will highlight his treatment of divine attributes and the related problem of anthropomorphism. This section will help in understanding his overall approach to philosophy and theology. His overarching transcendental metaphysics will impregnate his theological outlook. He will strip God of all possible attributes, largely in line with the Mu'atazilite view, to strictly maintain his absolute transcendence, perfection and eternity. Many of these discussions will eventually shape Thomas's philosophical theology.

It is pertinent to give a brief synopsis of theological debates regarding divine attributes which took place between various segments of the Muslim community prior to Ibn Sina. That will help in understanding Ibn Sina's metaphysics in its proper historical context.

Muslims and Divine Attributes

In spite of its strong emphasis upon the transcendence, uniqueness, and inaccessibility of God, sometimes even to the point of jealousy, the Quran contains only a few verses with a somewhat picturesque style that, if taken absolutely literally, could seem to ascribe certain human attributes or acts to God. This group of verses is often termed *mutashābih* meaning "ambiguous" verses, in contrast to the verses termed *muḥkam,* whose meanings are firm and clearly established. The Quran says: "He it is Who has sent down to thee the Book: in it are verses basic or fundamental clear (in meaning); they are the foundation of the Book: others are not entirely clear. But those in whose hearts is perversity follow the part thereof that is not entirely clear. Seeking discord, and searching for its interpretation, but no one knows its true meanings except Allah. And those who are firmly grounded in knowledge say: "We believe in it, the whole of it is from our Lord:" and none will grasp the Message except men of understanding." (3:7).

This set of ambiguous verses has been the subject of much exegetical as well as theological dispute in later Islamic theological thought. Although mainstream Muslims have always denied and refuted any anthropomorphic conceptions of God, certain individuals and sects have fallen prey to an anthropomorphic conception of the Deity. The anthropomorphic tendency under discussion is neither crude nor graphic; nor is the problem, in addition, one of absolute corporealism or physical anthropomorphism. What we have rather is a sort of relatively refined anthropomorphism, which crept into the thoughts of certain traditionalists; for instance, Muqatil ibn Sulaymān and some early Shiite figures such as Hishām ibn al-Ḥakam. In spite of his literal disposition, Muqatil metaphorically interpreted many Quranic phrases that could have led to corporeal depictions of God if taken literally. For Binyamin Abrahamov the case of Muqatil's alleged corporealism "needs further examination, because it demonstrates the unreliability of the sources where we learn about his views. His exegesis of the Quran which is now available presents him in a different way. Muqatil had different notions concerning anthropomorphic expressions in the Quran."[344] According to Hishām God had a body, but one unlike other bodies, meaning that no resemblance or likeness exists between the divine body and non-divine ones. Proponents of this line of anthropomorphism rationalised their speculation with the assumption that as all things that exist have bodies, proof that God exists can be done through assigning Him a body, but one of course unlike other bodies.[345] We are hardly in the realms of marked anthropomorphism here, for in no way or form have these theorisers compared God with His creatures or completely blurred the line between the divine and non-divine realms. The only thing they are guilty of is to have seemingly slightly muddied the strict demarcation lines dividing the two realms, and this largely due to their literalism prone disposition and a sense of needing to prove God's existence. The result of this faulty speculation was severe chastisement by mainstream Muslims who dubbed them as corporealists, defending and underscoring with great fervour the well-presented, guarded and uncompromising transcendental nature of the Quranic message.

It is clear though that the Quran and Hadith both contain poetical expressions which, if taken absolutely literally, could lead to anthropomorphism. In the words of I. R. Netton, "Islam too has had a problem of divine 'faces': not in the sense of a single deity divided up among, or represented by, many gods but simply in the fact that Muslims over the ages have regarded their one God in several widely differing ways."[346]

It was the Mu'tazilite school which initially devised and refined a comprehensive system of refuting anthropomorphisms, negating most of the divine attributes and metaphorically interpreting the texts to

meet their ends. The Mu'tazilites utilised, in the first place, Greek logic and rationalism to support Islamic belief and revelation to convince
non-Muslims of their vitality, but then later went to the extremist position of giving priority to reason (*al-'aql*) over revelation (*al-wahy*), as
Z. Jarallah observes,[347] in effect subordinating the latter to the former.
While the Quran, argues Rippin, "had its place in the discussions, it was
not so much a source, when used by Mu'tazila, as a testimony to the
veracity of the claims which they were making. The basic assumptions
of the Greek philosophical system (as understood and transmitted
through Christian scholars) was the fundamental element underlying
the whole position; it was argued that reason, and not only traditional
sources, could be used as a source of reliable knowledge for human
beings."[348] This view of the role of reason, Rippin further argues, "is
significant in terms of the ultimate fate of the Mu'tazila, for it implied
that the legal scholars of Islam had, in fact, no particular claim to sole
possession of the right interpretation of all Muslim dogma."[349] Later on
exactly the same struggle took place in Latin Christianity.

The Mu'tazilite doctrine was founded on five axioms.[350] The first
two i.e., *al-tawhīd* (the unity of God) and *al-'adl* (the justice of God),
were directly related to the nature of God and His actions. Like the
Qadariyyah before them, the Mu'tazilite emphasised the uniqueness,
transcendence, and unicity of God at all costs. If the Orthodoxy believed that the divine attributes were not God but outside divine essence and were eternal, then, to the Mu'tazilites, transcendence could
no longer be maintained. The Mu'tazilites asserted that "Divine
knowledge is either eternal or it is created. If eternal, it is either in God,
outside of God, or nowhere. If in God, then God is a theater where
change takes place. If outside of God, then God is not omniscient and
someone else is. And knowledge cannot be nowhere. It is somewhere
and eternal. But it cannot be outside of God for that involves polytheism. It must therefore be in God and intrinsic to Him."[351]

The founder of Mu'atazilites Wāsil bin Atta, in Macdonald's view,
"reduced God to a vague unity, a kind of eternal oneness."[352] The later
Mu'tazilites, like Abu Hudhayl M. al-'Allaf (d.841/226 A. H.), made
great advances regarding the issue of divine attributes utilising the
rational devices of the ancient philosophy. Al-'Allaf taught that "the
qualities were not *in* His essence, and thus separable from it, thinkable
apart from it, but they *were* His essence. Thus, God was omnipotent

by His omnipotence, but it *was* His essence and not *in* His essence. He was omniscient by His omniscience and it *was* His essence. Further, he held that these qualities must be either negations or relations. Nothing positive can be asserted of them, for that would mean that there was in God the complexity of subject and predicate, being and quality; and God is absolute unity [...] He endeavoured – and in this he was followed by most of the Mu`tazilites – to cut down the number of God's attributes."[353] Ibrahim Al-Nazzām (d. 231 AH/845 AD), on the other hand, was closer to the later Muslim philosophers in denying the attributes absolutely and replacing instead the essence of God itself. Abd al-Karim Al-Shahrastānī observed that "The difference between saying that God is knowing with his essence and not by knowledge, and that he is knowing by knowledge which is his essence, is that the first proposition denies the attributes, while the second affirms either an essence which is identical with his attributes, or an attribute which is identical with the essence."[354] Al-Qādī `Abd al-Jabbār reduced the attributes to only three i.e., knowledge (*al-`ilm*), power (*al-qudrah*), and perception (*al-idrāk*). He insisted, like his predecessors, that these attributes were not other than God's essence.[355]

Ismai'l Al-Faruqi summarises the Mu`tazilite's position on the issue of attributes as follows: "all divine attributes must be declared either negative, denying that their opposites are predicable of God; or positive, affirming a facet of the divine self, not an accident or quality. The Islamic notion that the Quran was the eternal word of God invited the same kind of argument. The Mu`tazilah maintained that the Quran was created by God in time to fulfill a purpose He had for man and creation. The evidence they adduced was that the Quran was composed of language, of sound and meanings established by human custom, that it was kept in ink and paper and memorised completely by humans. It cannot be God. On the other hand, to hold that the Quran is 'outside' of God and eternal is to affirm the existence of another eternal being besides God."[356]

Finally, the Mu`tazilite metaphorically interpreted all verses of the Quran that refer to the face, hands, eye of God etc, and tried to impose such interpretations upon other Muslims. Despite "their several disagreements on points of doctrinal details," observes Netton, "most of the Mu`tazilites were agreed on a non-literal mode of interpretation of much of the anthropomorphic data about God in the Quran."[357] Thus, they interpreted the word "face" in the verse "everything will perish except the face of thy Lord" (28:88) to mean the being of God Himself.[358] God's hand was interpreted as referring to His "favor or bounty"[359], God's eye as referring to His "knowledge", and God's settlement upon the Throne (*istiwà*) as His "dominance", and His coming down in the later part of the night as meaning the closeness of His "mercy".[360] Watt observes, that the Mu'tazilite dealt "with the anthropomorphisms by the method of *ta'wil* or 'metaphorical interpretation'. More precisely, this meant that they claimed they were justified in interpreting single words in the Quranic text according to a secondary or metaphorical meaning found elsewhere in the Quran or in pre-Islamic poetry. Thus, in the phrase (38:75) about God 'creating with his hands' they said that hands meant 'grace' (*ni'ma*), and justified this by a usage roughly parallel to our colloquial phrase 'I'll give you a hand'. Similarly *wajh*, usually 'face', was said to mean 'essence'. Verses which spoke of God being seen in the world to come were interpreted in the light of other verses where 'see' did not mean physical sight. In some ways this method of interpretation is artificial; but at least it keeps thinkers at the 'grass roots' of religious experience and away from an abstract academic discussion of relations between attributes and essence."[361] It is pertinent to note that these metaphorical meanings were from within the established rules of Arabic language and not fabricated or imposed upon the text in the name of allegorical interpretations.

The Mu'tazilites reduced the vivid and living God of Muhammad, as Macdonald puts it, to "a spirit, and a spirit, too, of the vaguest kind."[362] To F. Rahman they "denuded God of all content and rendered Him unsatisfactory for religious consciousness."[363] To I. Netton they "made God more unknowable rather than less, and dug a wider gulf between man and his Creator. A dry hermeneutic intellectualism restricted the former's mental image of his Deity."[364] Their creed, observes Watt, "leads to an abstract, bare and featureless conception of God, which robs the religious consciousness of much that is precious to it."[365] The Mu'tazilite, however, "exercised an influence indirectly. An important role was played by al-Ash'ari who, after being trained as a Mu'tazilite, was 'converted' to a form of Hanbalite view. There were other channels, however, by which [the] Mu'tazilite's ideas entered the main stream [...] It was then left to other men to sift these ideas so as to discover which were genuinely assimilable. In the end a great many ideas were retained, though seldom in precisely the form in which Muʿtazilites had presented them."[366]

A good example of the assimilation process cited was the method of metaphorical interpretation, bequeathed by the Muʿtazilite and later adopted by Sunni theologians such as al-Baghdàdi, al-Juwayni, and al-Ghàzali. Al-Ràzi noted that "all the Islamic sects affirm that metaphorical interpretation (ta'wil) is a must with regards to the few (apparent words) of some Quranic verses and Prophetic reports."[367]

A further development came with religious philosophy and Islamic Hellenistic philosophers, as well as later with the Ismaʿilites, who in the name of God's unity and transcendence, absolutely negated the attributes of God. Religious philosophers for instance like al-Farabi, Ibn Sina, and Ibn Rushd in essence stripped God of all possible attributes ascribed to Him in the Quran.[368] Al-Farabi's First Cause and necessarily existent One is indivisible in His substance and indefinable or ineffable.[369] He is simultaneously Intellect (ʿaql) and the Discernment of the Intellect (maʿqâl). He is eternally the All-Knowledge because He knows His Being (yaʿlamu dhàtahu).[370] I. R. Netton observes that "in his second mode al-Farabi emphasised among other things the different facets of perfection of the Deity, while underlining the fact that all His attributes were subsumed in, and not distinct from, His essence."[371] I. Madkur sees in al-Farabi the origination of all the later theological debates regarding the divine attributes.[372] Al-Farabi, to a large degree, defines God in negative propositions and statements to maintain His absolute transcendence. He renders God to a mere intellect or ʿaql as Netton observes: "The logic of al-Farabi's identification of attribute and essence means that God is intellect in action (ʿaql bi ʿl-fiʿl) as well as wisdom, truth, and life themselves."[373]

Just like al-Farabi, Ibn Sina's "Necessary Being"[374] is essentially one. According to Netton, "Ibn Sina admits that it is possible for God to have a variety of characteristics (Persian: sifat-ha) without there being any kind of resultant multiplicity in His essence (dhat). But this admission implies no desire to indulge in a Muʿtazilite exercise of allegorizing the attributes out of all recognition into something else. The key is rather a very Neoplatonic urge towards negativity, similar to that which was previously encountered in the work of al-Farabi."[375] Ibn Sina argues that "since it is established that God is a Necessary Being, that He is One in every respect, that He is exalted above all causes... since it is further established that His Attributes do not augment His Essence, and that He is qualified by the Attributes of Praise and Perfection; it follows necessarily that we must state that He is Knowing, Living, Willing, Omnipotent, Speaking, Seeing, Hearing, and Possessed of all the other Loveliest Attributes. It is also necessary to recognise that His Attributes are to be classified as negative, positive, and a compound of the two: since His Attributes are of this order, it follows that their multiplicity does not destroy His Unity or contradict the necessary nature of His Being. Pre-eternity for instance is essentially the negation of not-being in the first place, and denial of causality and of primality in the second place; similarly the term One means that He is indivisible in every respect, both verbally and actually. When it is stated that He is a Necessary being, this means that He is a Being without cause, and that He is the Cause of other than Himself: this is a combination of the negative and the positive.[376]

To Muslim philosophers, all these attributes boil down to "nothing but (1) union, where 'union' is an idea in the intelligence rather than in essence, or (2) negation (*nafy*) and denial. In so doing they do not imply existence of many characteristics, but rather an omission of many characteristics."[377] To further emphasise the otherness of God, Ibn Sina insisted upon emanation of the First Intelligence, "Since the first thing to emanate from God was not a body, it follows that it was an abstract substance, namely, the First Intelligence."[378] In short, the Muslim philosophers campaigned for an abstract and absolute divine transcendence which differed markedly to both Mu`atazilite and Orthodox understanding of the deity, being very close, as Madkur observes, "to Aristotle's Metaphysics."[379] The Muslim philosophers such as Ibn Sina fused Islamic theology with Aristotelian metaphysics. Some elements of this metaphysics were assimilated by the Latin West.

Thomas and Divine Attributes
The British philosopher Anthony Kenny has argued that "the most valuable part of Aquinas' philosophy of religion is his examination of the traditional attributes of God, such as eternity, omnipotence, omniscience, benevolence. He takes great trouble with the exposition and resolution of many of the philosophical problems which they raise. In the wider area of philosophy of religion Aquinas' most influential contribution was his account of the relationship between faith and reason,

and his defense of the independence of philosophy from theology."[380] One can see from the above discussion that Thomas had predecessors among the Muslim theologians and philosophers who had handled the topic of divine attributes in great details long before him.

The Harvard philosopher H. A. Wolfson has shown that there was no discussion of divine attributes as predicates (in its ontological sense) in post-Patristic Christian theology. The discussion always revolved around divine names. In the thirteenth century the likes of Albert the Great and Thomas were introduced to the problem of divine attributes and Muslim discussions of them through Moses Maimonides' "Guide for the Perplexed" which was translated to Latin. First Albert and then Thomas discussed them in their works following Maimonides detailed treatment of the subject.[381] "Thus the use of the term attribute and the rise of the problem of attributes in medieval Christian philosophy had their origin in the Latin translation of Maimonides' *Guide of the Perplexed*. This is how the Muslim problem of attributes was introduced into medieval Christian philosophy. From medieval Christian philosophy through Descartes, and through medieval Jewish philosophy through Spinoza it was later introduced into modern philosophy."[382]

Moreover, Thomas's endeavours to reconcile reason with revelation were also preceded by Muslim theologians. Both the Mu'atazilites and Asha'rites, especially the posterity like al-Ghazali and F. al-Razi, thoroughly adopted the method of "*Ta'wi'l*" (non-literal metaphorical interpretations of the religious texts). In fact, F. al-Razi claimed a sort of consensus among the Muslim sects that metaphorical interpretation was a necessity in certain situations. Al-Razi noted that "all the Islamic sects affirm that metaphorical interpretation (*ta'wil*) is a must with regards to the few (apparent words) of some Quranic verses and Prophetic reports."[383] M. Watt notes that the teacher of Abu Hamid al-Ghazali, "al-Juwayni draws the conclusion that the method of *ta'wil* cannot be avoided in some cases, and in particular that God's presence with the believers must mean His knowledge of their secrets. In this he is assuming that there must be harmonious rational interpretation of the Scriptural phrases, and apparently his opponents were not capable of defending the opposite view."[384] Al-Ghazali agreed that God was neither a body nor a contingent and that the literal meanings of the anthropomorphic phrases could not and cannot be attributed to Him, the only option left would be to accept their metaphorical meanings.[385] It is clear that long before Thomas the Muslim philosophers and theologians strove to reconcile reason with revelation by dint of metaphorical interpretations.

What needs mentioning at this juncture is that the nature of these metaphorical interpretations differed markedly from the allegorical interpretations of certain Christian sects, starting from the times of St. Augustine and Origen.[386] The Mu'atazilite and later Ash'arites' metaphorical interpretations, unlike Christian allegorism, were bound by strictly fixed linguistic rules with regards to the language, to which they had to adhere, and their metaphorical interpretations were further limited by the fixed number of linguistic meanings governing each term. In other words, interpretation was controlled by clearly defined linguistic parameters, forcing the Ash'arites to employ one of the already existing linguistic meanings of the term under question as an appropriate or intended meaning, preventing the invention of far-fetched facts or speculative suppositions to fit or prove whatever was wanted proven from the text. Moreover, this fixation was further substantiated by the usage of the same meanings in established Arabic metaphors.[387] Although there was scope to arrive at a number of different yet mutually related interpretations, with different scholars perhaps emphasising different aspects or meanings out of the few commonly used meanings of a phrase, nevertheless this was a far fry cry from free and open speculation, closing the doors to fanciful and absurd interpretations. Watt rightly observes, that "We must be careful, however, not to exaggerate the liberty in interpretation claimed by men like al-Juwayni. The conceptions which they interpreted metaphorically were few in number, and even to these they applied the metaphorical interpretation only in order to bring them in harmony with principles which long discussion had convinced them were thoroughly in accordance with the sacred texts."[388] Therefore, we see a kind of consensus existing among most of the interpreters over the meanings of several of these problematic Quranic expressions. Having said this, the method of metaphorical interpretation, or *ta'wil*, employed by the Asha'rite was in contrast with that of other exponents of the method such as the Mu'tazilite or the *Jahmiyyah*, in the sense that "it was not a rationalism in which reason was set above the revealed Scriptures, but one in which reason was assumed to be competent to understand and interpret the main truths contained in the Scriptures, and with these as basis to fathom the mystery of the Divine nature. That is to say, it was argued that, though the conceptions of religious intuition could not be reached by purely rational procedures yet, once they reached, they were thoroughly rational conceptions, forming harmonious system."[389] The orthodox Muslim theologians did not deny the fact that reason is quite capable of understanding the revealed doctrines; they only denied that reason in itself could not establish the religious facts, and they were initially determined by the revelation but were not in conflict with the human reason.

The Mu'atazilites, especially the later ones, argued for the relative independence of reason from revelation, and the Muslim philosophers argued for a total independence of reason and philosophy for the elite, not for the masses, and not necessarily on practical matters since they cannot be 'demonstated' in a strong sense. Ibn Rushd's treatise *Fasl al-Maqa'l* (Decisive Treatise) was the hallmark of such a struggle while his other works were the implementation of his methodology delineated in the *Fasl*. Thomas had access to some of Ibn Rushd's works and referred to Ibn Rushd about 503 times in his works.[390] Therefore, it will be appropriate to credit the Muslims for their quality works on divine attributes, reconciliation of reason with revelation and independence of philosophy from theology or in the post-Avicennian period, more and more melting of philosophy and theology in certain significant areas. Thomas was an heir to the Muslim contributions in these aspects of philosophical theology and in fact far less liberal than the Mu'azilites and Muslim philosophers *vis a vis* reason versus revelation.

Philosophy to Thomas was not independent of theology, as Kenny argues; philosophy was subservient to theology and revelation. Thomas toed the overall lines of Asha'rites like al-Ghazali and was far from the relative rationalism of the Mu'atazilites and pure rationalism of the Muslim philosophers such as Ibn Rushd. He was less rational even than the orthodox Muslim theologians, as he gave absolute precedence to faith and revelation over reason in matters specific to Christian faith such as Trinity and Incarnation. Thomas argued that "There is a two-fold mode of truth in what we profess about God. Some truths about God exceed all the ability of the human reason. Such is the truth that God is triune. But there are some truths which the natural reason also is able to reach. Such are that God exists, that He is one, and the like. In fact, such truths about God have been proved demonstratively by the philosophers, guided by the light of the natural reason."[391] The rationally unintelligible Christian doctrines must be accepted based on revelation. "Although those things which are beyond man's knowledge may not be sought for by man through his reason, nevertheless, once they are revealed by God, they must be accepted by faith. Hence the sacred text continues, "For many things are shown to thee above the understanding of man" (Ecclus. 3:25). And in this, the sacred science consists."[392] Even though certain parts of Christian theology are beyond rational inquiry, it is still the crown of all sciences as it supposedly proceeds from the knowledge of God. "So it is that sacred doctrine is a science because it proceeds from principles established by the light of a higher science, namely, the science of God and the blessed. Hence, just as the musician accepts on authority the principles taught him by the mathematician, so sacred science is established on principles revealed by God."[393]

Theology is not dependent upon premises of philosophy or other sciences; it just uses them as handmaidens. "This science can in a sense depend upon the philosophical sciences, not as though it stood in need of them, but only in order to make its teaching clearer. For it accepts its principles not from other sciences, but immediately from God, by revelation. Therefore it does not depend upon other sciences as upon the higher, but makes use of them as of the lesser, and as handmaidens: even so the master sciences make use of the sciences that supply their materials, as political of military science. That it thus uses them is not due to its own defect or insufficiency, but to the defect of our intelligence, which is more easily led by what is known through natural reason (from which proceed the other sciences) to that which is above reason, such as are the teachings of this science."[394] The servant cannot overrule the "Queen". Therefore, the servants must be judged and condemned as false whenever they betray the queen or dare to differ with her. "The principles of other sciences either are evident and cannot be proved, or are proved by natural reason through some other science. But the knowledge proper to this science comes through revelation and not through natural reason. Therefore it has no concern to prove the principles of other sciences, but only to judge of them. Whatsoever is found in other sciences contrary to any truth of this science must be condemned as false."[395] It becomes evident that Thomas gave absolute precedence to theology over philosophy and all other human sciences. He did not allow much room for reason and rational inquiry in faith-based matters. He condemned reason and philosophy wherever it differed with faith and revelation. It is here that Thomas was the least rational of all.

Thomas's Synthesis

Thomas's position on the divine names and attributes was a synthesis of Mu'atazilites and Asha'rites' positions with a few excursions to Muslim philosophers, in addition to Pseudo- Dionysius' De Divini Nominibus and De Caelestia Hierarchia.. He was more philosophical and rational in his treatment of this subject than his explanations of Trinity and other specifically Christian doctrines.

He followed the philosophers and Mu'atazilite's position; that the attributes are of God's essence and not contingent upon it. We have already seen above the Mu'atazilite's view that attributes were of God's essence. Al-'Allaf taught, that "the qualities were not *in* His essence, and thus separable from it, thinkable apart from it, but they *were* His essence. Thus, God was omnipotent by His omnipotence, but it *was* His essence and not *in* His essence. He was omniscient by His omniscience and it *was* His essence."[396] As also seen above, Ismai'l al-Faruqi had summarised the Mu'tazilite's position on the issue of attributes as follows: "all divine attributes must be declared either negative, denying that their opposites are predicable of God; or positive, affirming a facet of the divine self, not an accident or quality."[397] Therefore, the attributes are of divine essence and not out of it. Thomas would pretty much say the same thing with some refinements. The Muslim philosophers and theologians were his predecessors.

Majid Fakhry notices that the divine attributes play almost the identical role in al-Farabi's metaphysics. Al-Farabi's divine attributes "have a distinct Quranic ring. He is 'alim (knowing), h'akı̄m (wise), haqq (true) and hayy (living). He is knowing, al-Fa̅ra̅bi explains, in the sense that, in knowing everything including Himself, He does not require the assistance of anything or anybody other than Himself; wise in the sense that His knowledge is the highest and most enduring. He is true insofar as truth is equivalent to existence, of which He has the highest share. Another meaning of 'truth' is the correspondence of knowledge with being, which is a characteristic of the First, who knows Himself as He really is. Finally, He is living in the sense that the living is the 'one who knows the best object of thought [ma'qu-l] in the best manner of thought ['aql]', which, as we have seen, is equivalent to Himself. Another meaning of 'living' refers to any entity that has attained its highest perfection, of which, as the Perfect Being, the First is most deserving"[398] Therefore, the divine attributes unlike the human beings refer to God's essence, being, perfection and eternity. Al-Farabi usually negates rather than affirming the attributes to avoid any possibility of resemblance between God and creatures. The Mu'atazilites also tend to negate the divine attributes. Whenever the attributes are affirmed, they are affirmed in the essence; Thomas also affirms them in the essence.

The Ash'arites differed with the Muslim philosophers,[399] and argued that even though the divine attributes as predicates were in divine essence they were not identical to the essence but were other than it (Dhat), eternally subsisting in the essence, which St. Thomas agreed with. Al-Ghazali argued that the attributes were neither divine essence nor without it, neither identical with it nor different from it. St. Thomas agreed with this positive approach that divine attributes were of divine essence (Muslim philosophers) but not identical with essence, eternally subsisting in the essence (Muslim theologians). However, while he agreed with the Muslim philosophers' argument that attributes were of divine essence, he differed with them in their negating the attributes. He affirmed the attributes like the Ash'arites in essence; even his arguments and phrases regarding divine names and attributes are identical to al-Farabi, Ibn Sina and al-Ghazali. To Aquinas divine attributes are of God's essence. He states that God has knowledge of what is perfect and what is of his essence: "God necessarily knows things other than Himself. For it is manifest that He perfectly understands Himself; otherwise His existence would not be perfect, since His existence is His act of understanding [...] God sees Himself in Himself, because He sees Himself through His essence."[400]

Aquinas argues that God has intellect which is of his essence. "It must be said that the act of God's intellect is His substance. For if His act of understanding were other than His substance, then something else, as the Philosopher says (Metaph. xii), would be the act and perfection of the divine substance, to which the divine substance would be related, as potentiality is to act, which is altogether impossible; because the act of understanding is the perfection and act of the one understanding [...] Thus it follows from all the foregoing that in God, intellect, and the object understood, and the intelligible species, and His act of understanding are entirely one and the same. Hence when God is said to be understanding, no kind of multiplicity is attached to His substance."[401] He further observes that "God has nothing in Him of potentiality, but is pure act, His intellect and its object are altogether the same; so that He neither is without the intelligible species, as is the case with our intellect when it understands potentially; nor does the intelligible species differ from the substance of the divine intellect, as it differs in our intellect when it understands actually; but the intelligible species itself is the divine intellect itself, and thus God understands Himself through Himself."[402] His knowledge, wisdom and intellect are all an integral part of his essence. Here Thomas is in agreement with Aristotle and Theistius as refined and expanded upon by the Muslim philosophers and Mu'atazili theologians.

Thomas identifies his sources when he discusses in details the Muslim philosophers and Maimonides' positions regarding divine names and attributes. He says: "But as regards absolute and affirmative names of God, as "good," "wise," and the like, various and many opinions have been given. For some have said that all such names, although they are applied to God affirmatively, nevertheless have been brought into use more to express some remotion from God, rather than to express anything that exists positively in Him. Hence they assert that when we say that God lives, we mean that God is not like an inanimate thing; and the same in like manner applies to other names; and this was taught by Rabbi Moses. Others say that these names applied to God signify His relationship towards creatures: thus in the words, "God is good," we mean, God is the cause of goodness in things; and the same rule applies to other names. Both of these opinions, however, seem to be untrue."[403] Thomas disagrees with this negative approach to divine names and attributes. He, after rejecting the above discussed interpretations, forwards his own explanation in the following words: "Therefore we must hold a different doctrine---viz. that these names signify the divine substance, and are predicated substantially of God, although they fall short of a full representation of Him [...] For these names express God, so far as our intellects know Him. Now since our intellect knows God from creatures, it knows Him as far as creatures represent Him. Now [...] God prepossesses in Himself all the perfections of creatures, being Himself simply and universally perfect. Hence every creature represents Him, and is like Him so far as it possesses some perfection; yet it represents Him not as something of the same species or genus, but as the excelling principle of whose form the effects fall short, although they derive some kind of likeness thereto, even as the forms of inferior bodies represent the power of the sun."[404] Divine attributes are eternal and perfect like God's eternity and perfection while creatures' attributes are imperfect and temporal. Therefore, affirmation of divine names and attribute does not cause any defect or plurality in God; they show the limitations and finitude of creatures rather than any shortcoming or flaw in the divinity. Therefore, the multiplicity of divine attributes within divine essence does not cause any multiplicity within Godhead.

As is evident, Thomas disagreed with Mu'atazilites and philosophers that the attributes are mostly negative, and agreed with the Ash'arites that divine names and attributes are positive. They do not cause any contingency, mutability or multiplicity in God, as they are his essence. Moreover, they do not reveal his true essence because "in this life we cannot see the essence of God; but we know God from creatures as their principle, and also by way of excellence and remotion. In this way therefore He can be named by us from creatures, yet not so that the name which signifies Him expresses the divine essence in itself. Thus the name "man" expresses the essence of man in himself, since it signifies the definition of man by manifesting his essence; for the idea expressed by the name is the definition."[405] But that is not the case with divine names. They do not express or demonstrate divine essence as it is totally ineffable.

Thomas also agreed with the Ash'arites that creatures share in some of these attributes, in a relative fashion; man can be kind and merciful like God, but God's kindness and mercy is absolute while man's attributes of kindness and mercy are relative. In God they are eternal, perfect and superlative while in man they are derivative, temporal, imperfect and relative. "The names which import relation to creatures are applied to God temporally, and not from eternity."[406] He further observes that "For the words, 'God is good,' or 'wise,' signify not only that He is the cause of wisdom or goodness, but that these exist in Him in a more excellent way. Hence as regards what the name signifies, these names are applied primarily to God rather than to creatures, because these perfections flow from God to creatures; but as regards the imposition of the names, they are primarily applied by us to creatures which we know first. Hence they have a mode of signification which belongs to creatures."[407] He asserted that God provides for all things in accordance with their nature and abilities. Human beings use senses to access the world of intelligence. Consequently, the Scriptures imply metaphors taken from bodily things to communicate spiritual truths. In addition, these words are used metaphorically of God. Thomas's metaphorical approach to divine names and attributes bears resemblance to the Muslim orthodoxy.

Concerning the metaphor, he states that "a name is communicable in two ways: properly, and by similitude. It is properly communicable in the sense that its whole signification can be given to many; by similitude it is communicable according to some part of the signification of the name. For instance this name "lion" is properly communicable to all things of the same nature as "lion"; by similitude it is communicable to those who participate in the nature of a lion, as for instance by courage, or strength, and those who thus participate are called lions metaphorically."[408] He also states that "our knowledge of God is derived from the perfections which flow from Him to creatures, which perfections are in God in a more eminent way than in creatures. Now our intellect apprehends them as they are in creatures, and as it apprehends them it signifies them by names. Therefore as to the names applied to God---viz. the perfections which they signify, such as goodness, life and the like, and their mode of signification. As regards what is signified by these names, they belong properly to God, and more properly than they belong to creatures, and are applied primarily to Him. But as regards their mode of signification, they do not properly and strictly apply to God; for their mode of signification applies to creatures."[409] Thomas uses analogy on two very different levels, i.e., horizontal and vertical. On the horizontal level "it may be addressed at the level of beings insofar as they are discovered through sense experience and fall under being as being or being in general, the subject of metaphysics. It is at this horizontal level that we may ask how 'being' can be meaningfully applied to substance and to the other categories. But this issue may also be addressed at what we may call the vertical level or [...] the transcendental level. On this level one is concerned with explaining how 'being' and like names may be meaningfully applied to different kinds of substance, including not only finite and created realities but even God himself."[410]

Thomas agreed with the Ash'arites on metaphorical interpretations of anthropomorphic texts of the scripture based on analogy. "In names predicated of many in an analogical sense, all are predicated because they have reference to some one thing; and this one thing must be placed in the definition of them all. And since that expressed by the name is the definition, as the Philosopher says (Metaph. iv), such a name must be applied primarily to that which is put in the definition of such other things, and secondarily to these others according as they approach more or less to that first. Thus, for instance, 'healthy' applied to animals comes into the definition of 'healthy' applied to medicine, which is called healthy as being the cause of health in the animal; and also into the definition of 'healthy' which is applied to urine, which is called healthy in so far as it is the sign of the animal's health. Thus all names applied metaphorically to God, are applied to creatures primarily rather than to God, because when said of God they mean only similitudes to such creatures."[411]

Thomas differentiates between analogical, univocal and equivocal meanings. "In his very early treatise *De principiis naturae* Aquinas explains that something is predicated univocally when it remains the same in name and in intelligible content or definition. In this way the name "animal" is predicated of a human being and of a donkey. Something is predicated equivocally of different things when the name remains the same but its meaning differs in different applications. In this way the name 'dog' may be said of a barking creature and of a heavenly body. Finally, something may be predicated analogically of different things that differ in definition but that are relevantly related to one and the same thing."[412] The above example of "health" is a good example of such an analogy. "The name 'health' is said of an animal's body, of urine, and of a medicinal potion, but not in the same way. It is said of urine insofar as it is a sign of health, of the potion as a cause of health, and of the living body as the subject in which health is present. And each of these usages is relevantly related to one and the same end - the animal's health."[413] Likewise "some things are said of God and creatures analogically, and not in a purely equivocal nor in a purely univocal sense. For we can name God only from creatures [...] Thus whatever is said of God and creatures, is said according to the relation of a creature to God as its principle and cause, wherein all perfections of things pre-exist excellently. Now this mode of community of idea is a mean between pure equivocation and simple univocation. For in analogies the idea is not, as it is in univocals, one and the same, yet it is not totally diverse as in equivocals; but a term which is thus used in a multiple sense signifies various proportions to some one thing; thus 'healthy' applied to urine signifies the sign of animal health, and applied to medicine signifies the cause of the same health."[414]

Ibn Rushd, following Aristotle, had already preceded Aquinas in distinguishing between the univocal, equivocal, and analogous predication.[415] "Guided by Averroes's Commentary on this same passage from Aristotle's *Metaphysics*, Aquinas distinguishes different causal orders that may ground analogical predication. Such predication may be based, first, on the fact that different secondary analogates are ordered to one and the same end, as in the example of health. Or, second, it may be based on the fact that the secondary analogates are ordered or related to one and the same agent (efficient cause) [...] Or, third, it may be that the analogical predication rests on the fact that different secondary analogates are ordered or related to one and the same subject."[416] God and creatures share the "being," but they possess two different kinds of being; God is the necessary being while the creatures have an existence that is contingent. "According to Aquinas being is intrinsically present in accidents as well as in substance, but in a different way."[417] Following Aristotle and the Muslim philosophers, Thomas categorises being into an established hierarchy; to him "weakest in their claim on being are those things that exist only in the order of thought: negations and privations. Somewhat stronger in their title to being are generation, corruption, and change or motion, because they are processes leading to substance or corruptions of substance. Higher in their claim upon being, but still with only a fragile degree of being since they exist only in something else, are quantity, qualities, and the properties of substance. Highest in its degree of being is substance, that which is most perfect because it enjoys being in itself."[418] God is the perfect being, who enjoys being in Himself. Creatures are analogical beings as their being is caused by God and not by themselves; therefore, only analogous predication is permitted between God and creatures. The Fourth Lateran Council (1215 AD) rejected the former two kinds of meanings whilst accepting the third, the analogous concept, which became a fundamental in Christian circles. Therefore, Aristotle's influence through the medium of Ibn Rushd and other Muslim philosophers was carried through Thomas to the subsequent Christian generations.

It is evident from the above discussion that Thomas was introduced to the Muslim debates about divine attributes through the "Guide" of Maimonides. He picked and chose ideas from Muslim theologians and philosophers in accordance with his project, creating a synthesis which received a wide circulation in the following centuries. His direct access to some works of al-Farabi, Ibn Sina, Ibn Rushd, al-Ghazali along with Maimonides's "Guide" enabled this synthesis. He was quite indebted to his Muslim and Jewish predecessors.

Ibn Sina's Metaphysical System and Aquinas

In addition to debates about divine names and attributes, the Muslim philosophers strove to bridge the gap between Muslim theology and Aristotelian metaphysics. Ibn Sina provided a unique window of opportunity to mitigate and narrow this gulf by devising a complete system of philosophical theology, which preserved the absolute divine transcendence and unity while relating God to man and cosmos through emanation of intermediary intellects. His was a unique metaphysical system, which simultaneously maintained both divine transcendence and imminence. It was this "kind of originality which rendered him unique not only in Islam but also in the medieval West where the reformulations of the Roman Catholic theology at the hands of Albert the Great, and, especially, of Thomas Aquinas, were fundamentally influenced by him."[419] The likes of al-Ghazali, Albert and Thomas disagreed with Ibn Sina in many points, but in the process absorbed many of his ideas and made them their own at times without recognition. This is the nature of transmission of ideas from person to person, place to place and cultures to cultures; conflict usually forces the opponents to clarify and explain their own positions, and meticulous opposition usually helps in expediting the process of identity formation. Muslim theologians were forced to establish demarcation lines for their orthodoxy and clarify their positions against the intellectual assault of the Muslim philosophers. Likewise, the Christian theologians were obliged to elucidate and refine their theological stances, in opposition to the Muslim views. Latin Christians absorbed a lot of Muslim ideas and strategies in this process of identity formation. It is pertinent here to quote Eby and Arrowood, who stated that "it is of particular interest that Moslem scholars contributed to the development of Christian thought by furnishing opposition to Christian theologians [...] In later centuries, the scholastic theologians of the Roman Catholic Church elaborated their own system in refuting the doctrines of Islam."[420]

Muslim early dominance in the Mediterranean, as well as Southern Europe, and their attacks upon the Christian dogmas as irrational and intelligible forced Christian theologians to deal with the challenges on rational grounds. They were obliged to think out of the box, imply logical arguments and in the process establish genuine demarcation lines for the Christian orthodoxy. Menocal elaborates the point very well. "The phenomenon of cultural interaction that leads to some kind of assimilation is bound to lead, in the same instance, to a demarcation, an identification, and an elaboration of the ways in which the cultures do differ and of the instances in which assimilation does not take place. What this means, however, is that in providing a vivid sense of a different culture, the Arab cultural presence in Europe in many instances played the critical formative role of an identity against which many other Europeans might define themselves. Thus, when we study a writer such as Dante, for example, it is incumbent upon us not to ignore the role of Arabic culture, because it was influenced not in the sense that he embraced it but in the sense that his work may have been a considered reaction against its encroaching presence in his intellectual milieu."[421] The same applies to Thomas's appropriation of Ibn Sina and others.

The important portions of Ibn Sina's philosophical encyclopedia (*al-Shifa*) were translated to Latin in the twelfth century, including works of great interest to twelfth and thirteenth-century thinkers such as *De anima, Metaphysics, Physics,* and a small part of the *Logic,* only the *Isagoge* of the logical parts. "Ibn Sina's influence in the West started penetrating palpably since the time of Albert the Great, the famous saint and teacher of St. Thomas Aquinas. Aquinas's own metaphysics (and theology) will be unintelligible without an understanding of the debt he owes to ibn Sina. No one can fail to observe ibn Sina's influence even in Aquinas's later and bigger works like the *Summa Theologiae* and the *Summa contra Gentiles.* But the influence of the Muslim philosopher in the earlier formative period of the Christian Saint is overwhelming; he is mentioned by the latter, e.g., on almost each page of his De *Ente et Essentia* which is, indeed, the foundation of Aquinas's metaphysics. No doubt, ibn Sina is also frequently criticised by Aquinas and others, but even the amount of criticism itself shows in what esteem he was held in the West."[422]

Ibn Sina was equally influential among the medieval Jewish and Christian philosophical circles. Jon McGinnis observes that "Avicenna became a profound influence not only on Islamic thinking but also on that of Jews (such as Maimonides) and Christians (such as Thomas Aquinas). If a great thinker is one whose thought can be assimilated and developed by people of very different intellectual traditions, then Avicenna was, without doubt, a great thinker."[423] It was his philosophical writings which impacted the Latin West more than any other of his works. "Avicenna's *Canon*, with its handy compendium format, proved to be immensely popular in Europe, and continued to be a medical textbook at universities into the eighteenth century. It was his philosophy, however, that would have the most enduring effect, for it would influence (sometimes negatively, other times positively) some of the great Catholic theologians and philosophers of that time, such as Albert the Great, Thomas Aquinas, and Duns Scotus."[424] Avicenna's thought "played an important role in the reinvigoration of philosophy in Europe, as well as the formulation of Christian theology by such notaries as Thomas Aquinas and others."[425]

Ibn Sina was well received by Thomas's teacher Albert the Great (c. 1200–1280). Albert quoted Ibn Sina extensively. He confessedly took even his famous question about motion "Is motion a flowing form (*forma fluens*) or the form of a flow (*fluxus formae*)?" from the *Physics* of Avicenna's *Cure*."[426] McGinnis notes that "the psychological work of Avicenna's *Cure*, was second only to Aristotle's in influencing Albert's own psychological works. Thus, as a notable example, in Albert's *De homine*, he cited Aristotle 280 times with Avicenna coming in close behind with some 230 citations. In fact, it would seem that Albert preferred the way that Avicenna structured the science of psychology over that of Aristotle, as well as giving Avicenna pride of place when discussing the vegetative soul—that is, the principle associated with the functions of self-nourishment, growth, and reproduction— as well as the internal senses, such as imagination and memory."[427]

The influence of Ibn Sina upon Thomas was even greater. As seen above, he widely quoted Ibn Sina and absorbed many of his metaphysical ideas. McGinnes notes that "perhaps of more importance in the long run was Avicenna's influence on Thomas Aquinas (1225–1274), whose system of thought still makes up much of the philosophical theology of the Catholic Church and Christian apologetics more generally. Here it is important to note that in Thomas's earlier works, he is much more willing to reference Avicenna by name in a positive way, whereas in his more mature works, such as the *Summa Theologiae* and commentaries on Aristotle, he prefers to mention Avicenna by name only when he is in disagreement with him. Such a seeming turn of opinion, I believe, is not so much because, as Thomas grew older, he came to reject the Avicennan elements that impressed him in his youth, but because by then he had so thoroughly incorporated those elements into his own system of thought that they genuinely became his own."[428] John Wippel observes that Ibn Sina's influence upon Thomas "is both positive and negative. That is to say, Thomas borrows and incorporates into his own philosophy various points already made by Avicenna, though frequently not without changing and adapting them to his own purposes. At the same time, Thomas is aware of a number of other Avicennian positions which he regards as incorrect and which he therefore rejects. Moreover, on many occasions Thomas cites Avicenna by name, thereby leaving no doubt concerning whom he has in mind. On many other occasions he does not explicitly identify Avicenna as his source even when he actually uses him. This is something Thomas's reader must discover for himself."[429]

Jean-Pierre Torrell pinpoints another reason which might have led Thomas to reduce dependence upon and quotations from Ibn Sina. He states that "first received favourably, he was (Ibn Sina) later criticised by William of Auvergne in 1230, but remained in favour among certain English Franciscans such as Roger Bacon and Duns Scotus. As for Thomas, he cites him about 450 times. Avicenna's influence is quite strong in the treatise *De ente et essential* (before 1256), and if Thomas cites him numerous times in the *Sentences* (more than 150 times in the first two books), in the two series of disputed questions *De veritate* and *De potentia,* and in several other older works, he becomes more rare as time goes on, eventually disappearing almost entirely."[430] This initial dependence was diluted in the later phase. "Now we have to point out a curious phenomenon: if the name of Avicenna disappears, his teaching is still recognisable in a number of places, and so we have to ask the reasons for this silence. The most likely reason, perhaps, would be that Thomas did not want to compromise a teaching that he deemed to be true with the name of a philosopher who was more and more under attack. George Anawati established a list of forty-seven instances of ideas, definitions, and distinctions from Avicenna approved by Thomas. But he also emphasises the fact that Thomas distances himself from him on decisive matters such as the existence of secondary causes, the theory of the separated agent intellect, the necessity of creation, the creation from all eternity, the denial of free will and of the resurrection of the body, and so on. Most importantly, we might add, Thomas's philosophy is before all else that of existent being, whereas Avicennism is a form of essentialism. In spite of the multiplicity of things that Thomas borrowed from Avicenna, we cannot qualify his synthesis as Avicennian."[431]

Let us look at some of the examples where Thomas integrated Ibn Sina's metaphysical ideas into his writing. For instance, he borrowed from Ibn Sina the definition of "truth", "creation" and differentiation between essence and existence, details about the nature and subject of metaphysics and discovery of being as being.

Thomas defined truth as 'the adequation of intellect and thing,' inasmuch as the intellect says that what it is and what is not is not, truth belongs to that in the intellect which the intellect says, not to the operation by which it says it."[432] E. Gilson notes that Thomas borrowed the definition of "truth" from Ibn Sina[433] who in Metaphysics 1, 9 defines truth in the following words: "If existence belongs to it necessarily, then it is the truth in itself and that whose existence is necessary from itself. This is the Independent Reality."[434] Gilson also notes that "Thomas's definition of creation is the very one given by Avicenna."[435]

The philosophical distinction between essence and existence goes back to Aristotle.[436] The Muslim theologians and philosophers of the ninth century Baghdad introduced it into religious discussions long before Ibn Sina.[437] Usually al-Farabi is credited with its introduction.[438] Jean Jolivet, on the other hand, argues against Ibn Sina's indebted to al-Farabi regarding this distinction. "The distinction between essence and existence is another feature of Ibn Sina's thought which is his own; he did not take it from al-Farabi, as was long thought because of the misattribution of a short treatise (*Fusus al-hikam,* which might be translated as *Precious Aphorisms*) which continues Ibn Sina's own formulation of the distinction."[439] David Burrell quotes Ibn Sina that the "nature which is proper to each thing (*haqiqa*: lit., its truth) is other than [its] existence (*al-wujud*), which is synonymous with affirming it to be the case (*al-ithbat*)" and observes that "this is the first clear formulation of a distinction between essence and existence, and it is this text of Avicenna's to which Aquinas has recourse in his early essay which has provided the framework for subsequent discussion in the West: *De ente et essential.*"[440]

Ibn Sina had the credit of introducing this doctrine to Latin West through Latin translation of his Metaphysics. He introduced the distinction in chapter 1.5 and V. 1-2 of his Metaphysics.[441] He used the essence-existence distinction in discussions related to primary concepts, of universals and of the necessary first being or cause, in addition to several other metaphysical contexts;[442] this distinction was subservient to another fundamental distinction between the necessary and contingent beings.[443] The necessary being is necessary through itself while the contingent being is necessary through another. Ibn Sina states that "Every being, if considered from the point of view of its essence and without consideration of other things, is found to be such that either existence necessarily belongs to it in itself or it does not. If existence belongs to it necessarily, then it is the truth in itself and that whose existence is necessary from itself. This is the Independent Reality. If, on the other hand, existence does not belong to it necessarily, it is not permissible to say that it is impossible in itself after it was supposed existing. But if, in relation to its essence, a condition is linked to it, such as the condition of the nonexistence of its cause, it becomes impossible or, such as the condition of the existence of its cause, it becomes necessary. If no condition is linked to its essence, neither existence nor nonexistence of a cause, then there remains for it in itself the third option, that is, possibility. Thus, with respect to its essence, it would be a thing that is neither necessary nor impossible. Therefore every existent either has necessary existence in essence or has possible existence in essence."[444] Shams Inati explains the concept in a simple fashion. "The existence of a thing is either necessary or possible (contingent). Necessary existence is such that if the thing to which it belongs is assumed to be non-existent, an impossibility arises. Possible existence is such that if the thing to which it belongs is assumed to be non-existent or existent, no impossibility arises. Ibn Sina mentions that in other contexts "possible existence" could also be used in the sense of "being in potentiality". Necessary existence is either that which always belongs to a thing through that thing itself, or that which always belongs to it through another."[445]

Causality is the main difference between the two categories of being; the necessary being is not caused, while the contingent is caused. "That to which possibility belongs in essence does not come into existence by its essence, for, inasmuch as it is possible, existence by its essence is not more appropriate than nonexistence. Thus, if its existence or non-existence becomes more appropriate [than the other], that is because of the presence or absence of a certain thing [respectively]. It follows that the existence of every possible thing is from another."[446] God, the First Mover, is the only necessary being, hence is not caused;[447] the creation is contingent and caused by God. "Every totality organised of causes and effects consecutively, including a noncaused cause, has this uncaused cause as an extremity; for if this cause were an intermediate, it would be caused."[448] Ibn Sina further states that "if this chain includes an un-caused thing, then this thing is an extremity and a limit. Therefore every chain terminates in that whose existence is necessary in itself."[449]

The existence of multiple necessary beings is logically incoherent;[450] the necessary being must be simple, unique and united without com-position, components or constituent elements in line with Islamic idea of al-Tawhid. "We also say it cannot be the case that the necessary ex-istent has principles that are gathered together and the necessary exist-ent is constituted of them."[451] Composition and constituency requires a priory existence of the constituent elements which is impossible when it comes to the necessary being. "If the essence of that whose existence is necessary is composed of two or more things that unite, it becomes necessary by them. One of these things or every one of them will be pri-or to it and a constituent of it ... Therefore that whose existence is nec-essary is indivisible, whether in concept or in quantity."[452] McGinnes explains that to Ibn Sina "what exists necessarily is not a body, nor any matter of a body, nor a form of a body, nor an intelligible matter of an intelligible form, nor an intelligible form in an intelligible matter, nor divisible—whether in quantity, principles, or account—and so it is one from these three perspectives."[453]

In Ibn Sina's philosophy, the essence is different from the existence. "Everything, the comprehension of whose essence does not include ex-istence [...] such that existence is not a constituent of its quiddity. Fur-ther, it is not permissible that existence be a concomitant of its essence [...] It remains, therefore, that existence is due to something other than

141

its essence."[454] The substance of a thing is its essence (form and matter) plus the existence. Burrell observes that "for Maimonides, as for Ibn-Sina, the distinction of existence from essence functions primarily to distinguish possible from necessary being, and as a way of affirming the uniqueness of the necessary existent. It does not, in their hands, allow us to say anything more about divinity than that, nor do they use it to delineate the *sui-generis* activity of creating. These steps will be taken by Aquinas."[455]

Thomas appropriated the very distinction between essence and existence to his metaphysical designs. McGinnis observes that "the most obvious case of such an appropriation is the real distinction between being (*ens*)—Avicenna would say existence—and essence (*essentia*). In fact, Thomas names one of his earlier *opuscula*, *On Being and Essence* (*De ente et essentia*), after the famous Avicennan distinction. In this work, if one sets aside the final chapter that discusses accidents, Avicenna is positively referenced more than any other philosopher, including Aristotle. Even if one includes the final chapter, where nearly half of the Aristotle references occur, Avicenna still ties Aristotle for the overall number of explicit positive references, thirteen in all. Even in Thomas's later works where the Aristotelian actuality-potentiality distinction comes to predominate, he never fully discards Avicenna's essence-existence distinction, as is clearly witnessed in Thomas's account of divine simplicity and divine perfection at *Summa Theologiae*, part I, question 3 and 4, respectively."[456]

Thomas developed the distinction to a higher level. Burrell argues that Thomas's work "moves the distinction beyond Ibn- Sina's initial formulations, and toward subsequent development of existence as *actus essendi* (the act of being). For it will be this latter formulation which offers a way of characterising divinity, and of delineating the properly divine activity of creation. What is more, for Aquinas the two will be related: a characterisation of divinity as that One whose essence is simply to-be will allow him to delineate creation as "producing to-be as such"[457] This is a clear example where Thomas inherits something from Ibn Sina and then develops it further in accordance with the demands of his theology and overall project. Burrell elaborates the point very well. "The candidate proposed the distinction between essence and existence finds its roots in Alfarabi, its first articulation in Ibn-Sina, is approved by Maimonides, and brought to a refined status by Aquinas.

What Aquinas clarifies is the logical (or categorical) status of this distinction. By transforming existence from 'something which happens to' an essence to that to which essence must be related as the primary ontological constituent of an existing thing, Aquinas proposed reshuffling the metaphysical schemata inherited from Aristotle and Plato through the Arabs."[458]

Thomas was also influenced by Ibn Sina on the nature and subject matter of metaphysics. The scholastics were well aware of the differing opinions of Ibn Sina and Ibn Rushd on the subject of metaphysics. Ibn Sina argued that God was not the subject of metaphysics, as no science can demonstrate the existence of its proper subject, while metaphysics does prove the existence of God. Ibn Sina, in the opening chapters of his *Metaphysics,* argued that the subject matter of metaphysics is being as being; we discuss God as the First Cause of being and not as the subject of metaphysics. Wipple notes that "concerning this issue, Avicenna's influence on thirteenth-century Latin thinkers is pronounced indeed. As they saw things, another and later Islamic thinker—Averroes—had in fact concluded that the subject of metaphysics is a special kind of being, i.e., separate or divine entity. While Averroes agreed with Avicenna that no science can establish the existence of its own subject, he emphatically denied that God's existence is proved in metaphysics. It is rather physics which demonstrates this by proving that there is a First Mover."[459] Ibn Rushd's argument was promulgated in his *Long Commentary on the Physics* (ch. I.83).[460] Both Albert and Thomas preferred Ibn Sina's argument over Ibn Rushd. "Aquinas agrees with Avicenna that God's existence can be demonstrated in metaphysics, and not (merely) in physics, as Averroes held. This forces Aquinas to eliminate God as the subject of metaphysics."[461] Thomas further developed the argument of "being as being" into God as the cause of all being. Therefore, God is the aim of metaphysics not the subject of it; to Thomas, God was the proper subject of theology, and not metaphysics. Wippel observes that this is "a case where Thomas borrows heavily from Avicenna, but also goes beyond his Islamic predecessor."[462] Thomas eliminated the chasm between metaphysics and theology in a way "that appears to be unique among thirteenth-century thinkers."[463] He clearly borrowed something from Ibn Sina and then developed it further in conformity with his project.

Thomas disagrees with Ibn Sina on the emanative scheme and procession of creation without divine will or action. He also disagreed with Ibn Sina on the eternity of world. Ibn Sina held that from the "Necessary Being, the rest of the existing things overflow through the process of emanation. The first things that emanate are the celestial intellects, followed by the celestial souls, the celestial bodies and finally terrestrial beings. All these things emanate from It in eternity; otherwise, a state would arise in It that was not there before. But this is impossible in a being whose existence is necessary in all respects. This emanation is a necessary outcome of God's Essence and cannot be linked to any intention external to His Essence."[464] Unlike Thomas, Ibn Sina preserved divine simplicity, unity and transcendence by employing the emanative hierarchical scheme of pure intellects, souls and bodies. The matter and other terrestrial bodies emanated from the last and least of all the celestial bodies. The changing, corruptible and imperfect matter had no direct contact with the immutable, perfect First Mover or God. The material world was an indirect production of God. Thomas would disagree with this preposition and argue that the material world was a direct and willed creation of God, as will be seen in the coming pages.

Ibn Sina argued that the world, creation or matter proceeded spontaneously and constantly from God and emanative intermediaries, and that God is the only necessary being with fullness of goodness and being; it essentially tends to diffuse and emanate its goodness and being, and hence creates necessarily. Ibn Sina entertained the notion of creation as the necessary overflow of nonessential contingent being from the one necessary being. God was the efficient cause of the heavenly and earthly bodies but not the creator in a traditional religious sense who creates and destroys at will, "whatever is more complete in existence than another cannot intend that other. God, therefore, cannot intend the world or anything in the world, since He is more complete in existence than the world. Even though neither God nor any other cause can be perfected essentially by its effects and therefore cannot intend its effects or anything for them, still it may lead accidentally to beneficial effects and, if it is divine, know and be pleased with these effects."[465] Therefore, the world was continuous and lasting; the creation of the eternal being must be eternal.

This eternity argument was a reflection of Aristotle's statement that "there never was a time when there was not motion, and there never will be a time when there will not be motion."[466] Aristotle also said that "it is clear that the first unmoved mover cannot have any magnitude. For if it has magnitude, this must be either finite or infinite. We have already proved that there cannot be an infinite magnitude, and we have now proved that it is impossible for a finite magnitude to have an infinite force, and also that it is impossible for a thing to be moved by a finite magnitude for an infinite time. But the first cause causes a motion that is eternal and causes it for an infinite time. It is clear therefore that it is indivisible and is without parts and without magnitude."[467] Ibn Rushd connected this Aristotelian theory with God as the prime mover of the physical phenomena and hence a possible subject of natural philosophy. The Latin world knew the Aristotelian arguments about world's eternity through the commentaries and lenses of Ibn Rushd. It was Ibn Rushd's understanding of Aristotle on this subject which became normative in the subsequent centuries. Dales notes that "Averroes, the Commentator, was so universally known and so frequently cited that we need only mention that he interpreted Aristotle as having definitely taught that the world was without a beginning. He agreed with this doctrine without qualification and devised a number of subsidiary arguments to strengthen this position, and in the process he also passed along the teachings of other philosophers. It was almost always his Aristotelian commentaries which were cited in connection with the eternity of the world, rather than his original treatise *De substantia orbis*."[468] This was one of the main reasons that Ibn Rushd was vehemently condemned by the Church in the thirteenth century.

The Church, like Muslim orthodoxy, strongly condemned both Ibn Sina and Ibn Rushd on the issue of world's eternity. Following the Church teachings, Thomas disagreed with both Ibn Rushd and Ibn Sina mostly on theological grounds; he toed the lines of Muslim orthodoxy and refuted the Muslim philosophers' arguments on faith and revelation. Thomas's arguments against the eternity of world were almost identical to those of al-Ghazali, al-Shahrastani and al-Razi with few divergences. He, like the Muslim theologians, argued that creation was the free act of God in time, and not an unintended eternal procession. He introduced an additional distinction, the "distinction between the world understood as possibly not having existed and God understood as possibly being all that there is with no diminution of goodness or greatness."[469] He argued that the things can be, but need not be. If it is possible for things to not be, then it is also possible that it did not exist at one time. It requires that the necessary being brought it into being from nothing. God, the eternal and essential being, brought the contingent being into existence. The existence of countless contingent beings was also used by Thomas to prove the existence of non-contingent necessary being. This cosmological argument of proving the existence of necessary first cause on the basis of multiple contingent beings was used in *Kalam* (Muslim speculative theology) centuries before Thomas. Aquinas was also preceded by al-Ghazali, al-Shahrastani and al-Razi in refuting the eternity of world on the so perceived philosophical grounds. Dales explains that al-Ghazali presented a philosophical argument "namely that if the world had existed for an infinite time, there would now be an actually infinite number of human souls departed from their bodies, and an actual infinity is impossible; therefore the world could not be without a beginning. Algazel himself did not accept the force of this argument and conceded that there could be an actually infinite number of departed human souls, 'since there is no natural ordering in them by the removal of which they might cease to be souls, because none of them is the cause of the others, but they are simultaneous, without before and after with respect to nature or position [...] but only according to the time of their creation.' The conservatives all used this argument, and insisted that it was demonstrative, ignoring or dismissing Algazel's rebuttal. And even so ardent a supporter of the possible perpetuity of the world as Aquinas found this a difficult argument to get around."[470]

Thomas, like al-Ghazali, Fakhr al-Din al-Razi (1149-1209) and Muhammad bin Abd al-Karim al-Shahrastani (1086–1153) before him, rejected the notion of world's eternity and argued for creation of the world in time *ex nihilo* but not on strong philosophical foundations. Alfred Guillaume, in his famous article *Christian and Muslim Theology as Represented by al-Shahrastani and St. Thomas Aquinas,* draws close parallels between al-Shahrastani and Thomas's treatment of the subject, concluding that "if we now turn to the *Summa* Philosophica the first thing that leaps to the eye is the extraordinary similarity between theme and treatment in the Christian and Muhammadan apologists. The problems are the same, the same solutions are reached, and the same opponents are in view, namely the Arabian philosophers."[471] He further observes that "in II, xv, St. Thomas makes much of the argument which constitutes the fundamental difference between Shahrastani and Avicenna, namely the difference between essential causation and bringing into being. God is the sole possessor of being essentially in the sense that nothing is the cause of His being. Everything other than God owes its being to something external to itself-a cause. But God is the first cause. Everything that can or cannot be must have a determining cause, and since that cannot be traced to infinity it follows that one necessary being is the cause that determines the actuality of the contingent."[472] Thomas did not differ much with al-Shahrastani except in some minor details. "Nothing that St. Thomas has said is in any sense *contra Mauros*. Unwittingly he makes common cause with Shahrastani in his opposition to the philosophers. The only considerable difference that I can find is in II, xxxviii, where Aquinas rejects the arguments which Shahrastani accepts in favour of the world's not being eternal. For him it is a dogma of revelation rather than an intellectual truth, while Shahrastani believed that it was also logically true."[473]

Muammer Eskenderoglu, in his *Fakhr al-Din al-Razi and Thomas Aquinas on the Question of the Eternity of the World,* shows close resemblance between al-Razi and Thomas's treatment of the subject.[474] In chapter 4, Muammer shows that the similarities far outweigh the minor differences between al-Razi and Thomas's arguments. Both agreed that that the doctrine of the eternity of the world cannot be conclusively proved or disproved using rational evidence.[475]

Thomas like al-Razi, al-Shahrastani and al-Ghazali rejected the argument on theological basis. He was mostly influenced by Maimonides, who in turn was indebted to al-Ghazali and other Asha'rite theologians, especially on this subject. Both Maimonides and Aquinas almost copied al-Ghazali's stance on eternity of the world. Herbert Davidson has concluded that "the threads out of which Maimonides wove his arguments for creation derive from the Islamic thinker Ghazali, and he conceded that the arguments fall short of being apodictic demonstrations. They nevertheless constitute the most original set of proofs for creation in medieval Jewish philosophy."[476] Frank Griffel observes that according to Ghazilian perspective "the world's pre-eternity can be seen as a false position simply because it cannot be demonstratively proven. The opposing position—that the world was created in time—takes its truth from a higher authority than reason."[477] Al-Ghazali and other orthodox

Muslim scholars argued that creation of world could not be demonstrated with authentic philosophical knowledge. Showing the lack of demonstrative knowledge regarding the eternity was easier than proving the non-eternity with it. Therefore, the scale was tipped by means of faith and revelation. Al-Ghazali, observes Griffel, "assumes that the world's temporal creation is established on an authority that transcends reason and that refuting all claims of demonstrating otherwise establishes this doctrine on religious grounds. Showing that there are no demonstrative arguments that prove the world's pre-eternity is, of course, easier than establishing creation in time with one's own demonstrative arguments. Given that there is a certain balance of arguments, of which none truly reaches the threshold of apodeixis, Al-Ghazali and many religious scholars after him assumed that, in this question, a religious authority—meaning revelation or the consensus of Muslims—tips the scale."[478]

Moreover, al-Ghazali refutes the eternity argument based upon divine volition, arguing that the divine will and intention are directly related to the creation at a time determined by God. He rejects the argument in two ways: "The first of them is to ask by what means would you [philosophers] censure one who says, "The world is temporally created by means of an eternal will that made necessary [the world's] existence at the moment at which it came to exist; [the world's] nonexistence continued to the limit up to which it continued, and the existence began from whence it began; before the existence it was not something willed and so owing to that was not created, but at the moment at which it was created, it was willed by the eternal will and so owing to that was created"? What precludes this belief and would render it absurd?"[479] He continues, arguing that "before the world's existence, the one who wills, the will, and its relation to the one who wills [all] existed, and neither did the one who wills, nor the will, nor some relation that did not belong to the will come to be anew, for all of that is to change. So [...] how did that which is willed come to be anew, and what prevented [its] coming to be anew earlier? The new state is no different from the previous state with respect to some factor, state of affairs, state or relation. In fact, the states of affairs were just the same as they were [before]. Therefore, what is willed would not have existed but would have remained the same as it was. But [on the present view] the willed object comes to exist! What is this, but the most extreme absurdity?!"[480]

Al-Ghazali combines divine will with divine intention to produce the argument of world's creation at an appointed time.[481]

We will see almost identical arguments against eternity in both Maimonides and Aquinas, and both will construct their arguments on faith as well as divine will and intention. I will give a detailed account of both Maimonides and Aquinas's positions on the topic to avoid any subjectivism. Before doing so I would give a brief account of Muslim influences upon the medieval Jewish philosophy especially Moses Maimonides. Thomas was greatly indebted to Maimonides who in turn was a sort of fine product of the thirteenth century Muslim culture.

Muslim Influences on Jewish Philosophy

Julius Guttmann has observed that "The Jewish people did not begin to philosophize because of an irresistible urge to do so. They received philosophy from outside sources, and the history of Jewish philosophy is a history of the successive absorptions of foreign ideas which were then transformed and adapted according to specific Jewish points of view."[482] Jews has mostly lived as minorities within various majorities, and assimilated the majority's philosophical views, with the intention of bridging the gap between their religious thought and the majority's world view. Philo of Alexandria is a good example of this assimilation process; he almost Hellenised Jewish theology, with the view of making it compatible with Roman philosophical outlook. Saadia Gaon and Maimonides did almost the same thing within the Islamic culture and civilisation. Both the ancient and medieval Jewish philosophy was predominantly a defence of Jewish religious tradition; as H. Wolfson has observed, the Jewish philosophy from Philo to Spinoza was mostly religious in nature. It was not pure philosophy but a sort of philosophical theology developed to defend Jewish religion.[483] Most medieval Muslim theologians and philosophers had almost the identical agenda. The problematic relationship between reason and revelation was discussed among the Jews since the times of Philos. The Jewish community did not produce the likes of Philo after the destruction of the Temple in the first century. There was not much of a philosophical tradition among the Jews for the next five to six centuries as most of the Talmudic academies focused upon law rather than philosophy. The Rabbinic tradition was legally oriented until the times it was challenged by the Muslim Kalam. The Karaites were the first to subject Judaism to Mu'atazili theology. There was a big gap between the times of Philo and reappearance of philosophical thought among the Jews of Muslim lands, and mostly under Muslim auspices. The Jews were granted the protected status of *ahl al-Zimmah*, which allowed them relative ease, freedom and autonomy (though not always); at times there were close personal friendships and business alliances between various individuals. The transmission of knowledge and information between the two communities, and even intercommunal theological debates initiated and patronised by the Muslim and Jewish elites, were a norm. This was the so-called "Golden Age" of Muslim civilisation, where ecumenical dialogues and interfaith relations were mostly cherished. The Jewish community benefitted from the countless possibilities of cultural exchanges, and contributed to the overall Muslim civilisation especially in the tenth century.

The Radhanites (medieval Jewish merchants) played a decisive role in facilitating the transition. Shlomo Pines notes that "philosophy and ideology reappeared among Jews, a phenomenon indicative of their accession to Islamic civilisation. There is undoubtedly a correlation between this rebirth of philosophy and theology and the social trends of that period, which produced Jewish financiers—some of whom were patrons of learning and who, in fact, although perhaps not in theory, were members of the ruling class of the Islamic state—and Jewish physicians who associated on equal terms with Muslim and Christian intellectuals."[484] Pines also notes that "approximately from the ninth to the thirteenth centuries, Jewish philosophical and theological thought participated in the evolution of Islamic philosophy and theology and manifested only in a limited sense a continuity of its own. Jewish philosophers showed no particular preference for philosophic texts written by Jewish authors over those composed by Muslims, and in many cases the significant works of Jewish thinkers constitute a reply or reaction to the ideas of a non-Jewish predecessor. Arabic was the language of Jewish philosophic and scientific writings."[485] One should not overlook the influence Islamic theology and philosophy had upon medieval Jewish thought, especially that of Karaites, Saadia Gaon, Jacob al-Qirqisani, Isaac Israeli, Solomon Ibn Gabirol, Bahya Ibn Paquda, Abraham bar Hiyya, Joseph Ibn Zaddik, Moses Ibn Ezra, Judah Halevi, Abraham Ibn Daud, Moses Maimonides, Samuel Ibn Tibbon, Shem Tov Ibn Falaquera, Levi ben Gershom (Gersonides), Moses Narboni, and Hasdai Crescas. E. Renan noted that the "Arabic philosophy was never really taken seriously except by the Jews [...] whose literary culture in the Middle Ages is merely a reflection of Muslim culture."[486] To Arthur Hyman, "by and large Jewish philosophy was a continuation of the philosophy which flourished in the Islamic world."[487]

Oliver Leaman notes that "It is difficult to overemphasise significance which Islamic philosophy had for Jewish thinkers who were working at the same time in the Islamic world, or who were influenced by such work. Many Jewish thinkers wrote in Arabic and their main philosophical authorities were Arabic authors, which is hardly surprising given the pervasiveness of Arabic culture within the Islamic Empire. It was possible then as now for Jews to maintain their religious identity while at the same time becoming an important part of the cultural exchange of ideas. A very rich corpus of science, mathematics, medical theory, astronomy and philosophy was available to any literate member of society, and it was not the sole preserve of Muslims. Jews were excited by the diversity of theoretical perspectives which existed, and enthusiastically threw themselves into contemporary intellectual life. They even adapted much of the theory connected with specifically Islamic areas of enquiry, such as law and theology, to their own legal and religious texts. This is hardly surprising. Minorities generally acquire the culture of the dominant community, or at least as much of the culture as they can adapt to their own needs and interests."[488]

Islam, like Judaism, was an ethical monotheistic tradition where law and theology were crowned as the highly prized sciences. There was so much common between the two faith traditions that theological insights, inquiries, concerns and even the legal theories and framework were almost identical. Both traditions were orthodoxies as well as orthopraxies. Jews had lived for centuries among the Muslim with relative ease. Unlike the majority of Christians with some exceptions[489], they were the likely allies of the Muslims in their struggles against the Christian world and enjoyed high official positions, especially in Muslim Baghdad, Cairo and Andalus. The dominant medieval Muslim culture and civilisation was a model for the Jewish community, and the Jews greatly contributed to that culture and civilisation.

Many of the theological questions raised by Muslim theologians and philosophers were closely related to the religious discussions prevalent among the medieval Jews. The Muslims lead on many such thorny questions was well appreciated by the Jewish scholars. Leaman states that "when we look at the works of thinkers such as Saadiah, Halevi, Maimonides and even Gersonides we can observe the curriculum of Islamic philosophy quite fully represented. They did not just take some of the leading ideas and try to see how far they could use them to make sense of their own philosophical concerns, as was very much the case with many of the major Christian philosophers. The Jewish philosophers went much further than this in their work, often working well within the tradition of Islamic philosophy itself, albeit just as often using it to develop points which were of specifically Jewish concern. Perhaps one of the reasons why Jewish philosophy came to rely so much on Islamic philosophy lies in the proximity of the religions."[490] Steven Wesserstrom agrees that "another reason for common cause on the part of Jewish and Muslim philosophers was their joint monotheistic opposition to a common pagan adversary. The ostensible impetus of this joint counterforce remains a leitmotif of scholarship on Jewish-Muslim symbiosis."[491]

Muslims absorbed multiple ideas from various philosophical traditions such as Greek, Egyptian, Persian and Indian. The impact of Greek philosophy was so great that at times the Muslim philosophical terms, phrases and ideas looked like mere reflection of Greek philosophy. But there was a subtle caveat that those terms and ideas were synthesised in such a fashion that they took a new Islamic shape as well as meaning. The Greeks were mostly pagan, while the Muslims were monotheists; therefore, Greek philosophy was synchronised with fundamental Islamic beliefs. Aristotle's First Cause was merged into Islamic concept of transcendent God- even though the terms were same, the agenda was totally different. This was not the case with the Jewish tradition. The Jews not only adopted Muslim terms, phrases, ideas and concepts, they adopted the whole scheme with similar agendas. Leaman rightly observes that "what we should look for is not so much the people who are quoted or the sort of language which is used but the ways in which the arguments are supposed to work. If they are supposed to work in a way which is very similar to the way in which they are taken to work in a previous cultural context, or in a different cultural atmosphere, then we can rightly say that the influence of that culture is very important for the framing of the arguments. We can say this about the links between much Islamic and Jewish philosophy. What is significant about these links is that the latter reproduces much of the agenda of the former, not just the language and the individual thinkers but the agenda itself."[492] Undoubtedly, the influence of Islamic culture and civilisation upon the medieval Jewish culture and civilisation was tremendous.

The identification and similarities between the two communities were so great that just like the Muslim community there were Jewish Kalam Mu'atazilites[493], Jewish philosophers, Jewish Aristotelians, Jewish Platonists, Jewish Neo-Platonists, Jewish Averroists, Jewish mystics, Jewish jurists just like their Muslim counterparts. Colette Sirat observes that "Jews in Islamic lands divided into the same philosophical schools as the Muslims: the *kalam,* Neoplatonism and Aristotelianism. Similarly, the questions which Jewish philosophers set themselves were, to a large extent, the same as those discussed by their Muslim counterparts."[494]

The medieval Jewry was a true reflection of the majority Muslim community in so many ways that it would not be wrong to call the resultant civilisation an Islamico-Hebraic civilisation, as Mauro Zonta states: "We might speak of 'Hebrew-Arabic' philosophy while considering the great influence of Islamic thought on much of the Jewish philosophical legacy written in the Hebrew language during the thirteenth, fourteenth and fifteenth centuries. The close relationship of late medieval Jewish philosophy to Islamic thought has been stressed by the editors of the recent two-volume Routledge History of Islamic Philosophy in their decision to devote several chapters of their work to medieval Jewish philosophy. The reasons that led to this choice may be discerned from Arthur Hyman's contribution to the book. Interestingly, these chapters are found in a lengthy section entitled *The Jewish Philosophical Tradition in the Islamic Cultural World,* even though one of the chapters is on the phenomenon of Jewish Averroism, which developed in Christian Spain and Provence (which surely do not belong to the Islamic world), and one on Gersonides, who lived always in a Christian milieu, and might have not even had a knowledge of Arabic. As a matter of fact, the work of most late medieval Jewish philosophers in Europe consisted mainly in interpreting Islamic philosophical texts (mostly Averroes, but also Alfarabi and, in some cases, Avicenna) in light of some general lines, some of which had been already traced by the Islamic philosophical tradition. Thus a significant part of their work looks like a continuation of the work of their Islamic counterparts, where the difference is marked only (or mostly) by the different religious context- a context which is marked, after1200, by the use of Hebrew instead of Arabic."[495]

Almost all of Ibn Rushd's "philosophical works were translated from Arabic into Hebrew in the period 1230–1330, sometimes even more than once (only one of them was later translated from Latin into Hebrew, around 1480); almost all of them were quoted, summarised, paraphrased, annotated and commented on by a number of philosophers during the 14th and 15th centuries. As a matter of fact, some of these texts are preserved only through these translations, due to the loss of their original versions, and their success among Jewish philosophers was surely wider than the success they gained among Arabic thinkers, and probably equal to the success they gained among Latin Christian ones."[496] Mauro Zonta has well illustrated this translation and transmission campaign.[497] Moses Maimonides (d. 1204), confessed in a letter addressed to his disciple, Joseph Ben Juda, written in Cairo in 1191, that "he had received lately everything Averroes had written on the works of Aristotle and found that he was extremely right."[498] Majid Fakhry states that "the two Aristotelians had so much in common, especially in their attitude to Ash'arite Kalim, that readers of Maimonides tended to find Averroes particularly intriguing and to look upon the former as the disciple of the latter."[499]

Maimonides set the tone of this enthusiastic Jewish approach to Ibn Rushd by affirming in his letter to Samuel Ibn Tibbon: "The works of Aristotle are the roots and foundations of works on the sciences, and cannot be understood except with the help of commentaries, those of Alexander of Aphrodisias, those of Themistius and those of Averroes. I tell you, as for works on logic, one should only study the writings of Abu Nasr al-Farabi. All his works are faultlessly excellent. One ought to study and understand them; for he was a great man."[500]

Jewish philosophers usually ignored both Alexander and Themistius but depended upon Ibn Rushd as a true sage and commentator on Aristotle. "The first Jewish translator or paraphrast of Averroes' physical and metaphysical writings was Samuel Ben Tibbon, who based his *Opinions of the Philosophers* almost exclusively on Averroes. Other Jewish scholars, such as Juda Ben Solomon Cohen of Toledo, in his book the *Search for Wisdom*, and Shem Tob Ben Joseph Falquera, relied completely on Averroes, quoting him sometimes word by word. The first Jewish translator of Averroes in the strict sense was Joseph Ben Abba Mari of Naples, who translated for Frederic I1 Averroes' commentaries on the *Organon* around 1232. Around 1260, Moses Ben Tibbon published an almost complete translation of Averroes' commentaries, as well as some of his medical writings. In 1259, Solomon Ben Joseph of Granada translated the commentary on *De Coelo et Mundo* and in 1284, Zerachia Ben Isaac of Barcelona translated the commentaries on the *Physics*, the *Metaphysics* and *De Coelo et Mundo*."[501]

Shem Tov Ibn Falaquera, in the introduction to his work *The Opinions of the Philosophers* (a detailed commentary on Aristotle's physics and metaphysics), affirms: "All that I have written here corresponds to Aristotle's words, as they are commented on by the sage Averroes. He was the last of the commentators (of Aristotle), and collected the cream of the works of the previous commentators, as well as of Aristotle's words."[502] Jewish Averroism, in the sense of a substantial agreement with Averroes' interpretation of Aristotle's works, continued in 15th-century Spain and Italy. "The Jewish translations paved the way for the Latin translations, sometimes collaterally, of Averroes' commentaries on Aristotle. Those translations which began early in the thirteenth century had a more durable impact on European thought and led at once to the rediscovery of Aristotle, who had been almost completely forgotten [...] in Western Europe, since the time of Boethius."[503]

The medieval Jewish philosophy was, in a sense, an extension and appropriation of Islamic philosophical thought. Wesserstrom succinctly elaborates the point by noting that "there is little dissent from the general agreement that Jewish philosophy from the tenth to the thirteenth centuries functioned in a social and cultural context which was thoroughly arabicised, if not islamicised. Of the eighteen philosophers listed in Husik's *A History of Mediaeval Jewish Philosophy*, thirteen lived in the Islamicate world; while the proportions are slightly different in Sirat's A History of Jewish Philosophy in the Middle Ages, the Islamicate character of medieval Jewish philosophy remains beyond dispute."[504] Both Muslims and Jews were actively engaged in civilisational endeavours. Muslim culture and civilisation were joint Muslim and Jewish ventures, though the Muslims had the fundamental leadership role. The modern civilisation owed much to that synthesis, as Alfred North Whitehead had long ago noticed: "The record of the Middle Ages, during the brilliant period of Mahometan ascendency, affords evidence of joint association of Mahometan and Jewish activity in the promotion of civilisation. The

culmination of the Middle Ages was largely dependent on that association […] The association of Jews with the Mahometan world is one of
the great facts of history from which modern civilisation is derived."[505]
Maimonides was a perfect example of this synthesis.

Maimonides: the Product of Islamicate

Maimonides was a fine product of the "Islamicate", to use Hodgson's
term. He was, in a sense, the pure creation of thirteenth-century Islamic cultural milieu. J. Kraemer says that "only when we read Arabic
sources can we have a true picture of this period, identify the actors in
this drama, and have reliable knowledge of circumstances and events."[506]
In the same spirit, Kraemer situates Maimonides right in the middle of
Islamic philosophical, theological, historical and literary context.

Maimonides was born and raised in the Muslim Cordoba of Ibn
Rushd and died in the Muslim Cairo. He worked for the Muslim rulers and elites, studying and absorbing many Muslim philosophers and
theologians alongside his studies of the Rabbinic corpus. Maimonides
to Alexander Brodie "was steeped in Islamic philosophy."[507] In his *Maimonides, The Disciple of Alfarabi*, L. V. Berman argues that Maimonides
was an avid disciple of al-Farabi.[508] A. Eran shows similarities between
al-Ghazali and Maimonides works on spirituality and soteriology.[509] S.
Harvey illustrates the influence of al-Farabi, Ibn Sina and al-Ghazali
upon the 14th century Jewish philosophers and theologians.[510] To Majid
Fakhry, Maimonides was a pure disciple of Ibn Rushd.

Herbert Davidson notes that Maimonides was an admirer of Abu
Nasr al-Farabi, and quoted him in his writings by name. He also quoted Ibn Bajja and was indebted to Ibn Sina, even though he considered
him an inferior authority on philosophy. He knew and read some of
al-Ghazali's work, and must have known Ibn Tufayl's philosophical
novel *Hayy bin Yaqzan*, as he quoted an example of an isolated child.
He was a contemporary Cordoban and knew Ibn Rushd's works, as is
clear from his letter to Ibn Tibban.[511] Colette Sirat notes that "after Aristotle, al-Farabi was Maimonides' real master. His influence is visible in
a youthful work, the *Milot-ha-Higayon*, 'A Logical Vocabulary', written
at the age of 16, and it remains in Maimonides' last work, the *Guide*."[512]
Davidson notes that "Maimonides evaluated previous philosophers for
Ibn Tibbon: he there offers brief assessments of the four leading figures
of the Arabic Aristotelian school, Alfarabi, Ibn Bajja (Avempace), Avi-

cenna, and Averroes. In the Arabic world, Alfarabi had the reputation of being the "second teacher," that is, the thinker who was second only to Aristotle in instructing mankind. Maimonides, in the same spirit, describes Alfarabi as "a great man," praises his books as flawless, and states that the only logical treatises one should consult are Alfarabi's. He specifically recommends a book of Alfarabi's called the *Principles of Existent Beings*. The book in question—better known under the title of *al-Siydsa al-Madaniyya*, or *Political Government*—opens by sketching the structure of the universe very much as Maimonides was to do, whereupon it turns to political theory. Ibn Bajja, Maimonides' letter to Ibn Tibbon continues, "was likewise a great philosopher" and his compositions are "correct." Maimonides rates Avicenna's writings as inferior to Alfarabi's, although he grants that they have "value" and are worthy of study. It is perhaps not pure coincidence that Averroes, a contemporary of Maimonides' and a fellow citizen of Cordova, also considered Avicenna to be inferior to Al-Farabi; the two Cordovans may have been echoing an evaluation of Avicenna that was current among intellectuals in the city. As for Averroes, Maimonides was already seen to list him among the commentators with whom Aristotle should be read."[513]

Al-Farabi had a lasting effect on Maimonides, especially his logic. Maimonides respected his writings, admired his insights, accepted most of his metaphysical opinions and directly quoted him with name. Davidson notes that "Alfarabi is the Arabic philosopher cited most frequently in Maimonides' writings, and to the extent that Maimonides was conscious of his sources, Alfarabi was undoubtedly the Arabic philosopher who had the strongest impact on his thought... Maimonides' Commentary on the Mishna quotes at length from an ethical work of Alfarabi's, without mentioning the author's name or the title of his composition, and it may allude to a book of his on the subject of the human intellect [...] Maimonides' *Book of Commandments* also quotes from a logical work of Alfarabi's without giving the author's name [...] In the *Guide for the Perplexed*, Maimonides refers to Alfarabi a half dozen times, naming four of his philosophic works, [...]and possible echoes of Alfarabi's logic have been discerned in passages of the *Guide* where he is not named [...] Alfarabi makes one more appearance in the final chapter of Maimonides' most comprehensive medical composition. In three places there, Maimonides cites Alfarabi and, in doing so, names two further philosophic works of Alfarabi's; he says explicitly that he is quoting directly from at least one of them. The books in question have been preserved and published, but I was not able to identify the pertinent passages, and we must therefore allow for the possibility that a mistake of some sort has crept in [...] All in all, there is good evidence, apart from the letter to Ibn Tibbon, that Maimonides knew, and at various times used, a half dozen of Alfarabi's philosophic compositions and weaker evidence that he used others as well."[514]

Ibn Bajja (d. 1139) was another Muslim philosopher who was cited by Maimonides by name. Abu Bakr Muhammad Ibn Bajja (Avempac) lived in Saragossa, not far from Miamonides' Cordoba. Like Maimonides, Ibn Bajja was a physician and a Farabian. He wrote nine medical treatises and many commentaries on Al-Farabi's works. He commented freely on Aristotle's works and wrote independent articles on a host of subjects. McGinnis observes that "Some thirty-odd treatises have come down to us by Ibn Bajja. These works may loosely be divided into three categories: (1) writings on music, astronomy, and logic, particularly commentaries on the logic of al-Farabı; (2) works on aspects of natural philosophy, which would include primarily his commentaries on Aristotle's *Physics* and *De anima*; and (3) treatises representative of Ibn Bajja's own philosophical thought, the most important of which are *The Governance of the Solitary*, the *Epistle of Farewell*, and the *Epistle of Conjunction of the Intellect with Man*."[515] Maimonides was quite impressed by Ibn Bajja's erudition. Davidson notes that "Maimonides refers to Ibn Bajja five times in the *Guide for the Perplexed* and cites two of his works [...] In addition, the distinction between four kinds of human perfection—the possession of property, physical health, ethical perfection, and intellectual perfection—around which the final chapter of the *Guide is* built, has been traced to Ibn Bajja."[516]

It is pertinent to mention here that Maimonides was not in the habit of identifying his sources; he seldom mentioned the names of his philosophers or teachers from whom he derived his philosophical knowledge. Therefore, quoting Ibn Bajja with name clearly indicates the level of respect Ibn Bajja carried with Maimonides. Arthur Hyman states that "In formulating his views he (Maimonides) drew upon the works of Aristotle and his Hellenistic commentators and upon the writings of Muslims such as al-Fārābī, Avicenna and Avempace."[517] Ibn Sina was a major influence over Maimonides' overall philosophy, even though

Maimonides seldom mentioned his name. I . Dobbs-Weinstein observed that as a fine product of the "Islamicate" and an enthusiastic philosopher Maimonides definitely read all works of Ibn Sina available in Andulus, Fez and Cairo.[518] "Ibn Sina's influence is most pronounced in investigation of questions that exceed the limits of demonstration, especially, questions on the origin of the universe."[519] Maimonides derived and understood most of the Aristotelian metaphysics from the writings of Ibn Sina. Even though he acknowledged and praised al-Farabi, Maimonides understanding of the universe was mostly depicted through the lenses of Ibn Sina. Davidson pinpoints that "Avicenna's name never appears in the *Guided* Nevertheless, and despite Maimonides' judging him inferior to Alfarabi, he contributed considerably to the formation of Maimonides' philosophic thinking: What Maimonides calls Aristotle's *Metaphysics* is [...] not Aristotelian but Avicennan, and Maimonides' picture of the structure of the universe, while it draws from both Alfarabi and Avicenna, owes more to the latter than to the former, although Maimonides was unconscious of the debt."[520]

Ibn Sina's influence can be identified in both Maimonides' philosophy as well as religious thought. I. Dobbs-Weinstein identifies "Ibn Sina's clearest influence upon Maimonides' thought evident in the latter's development of the following, closely related distinctions and problems: (1) the origin of the universe or, more precisely, the specific formulation of emanation in a manner that emanation could be reconciled with creation, (2) the distinction between the necessary and possible existence, (3) the nature of acquired, specifically prophetic human knowledge, in particular, the capacity for insight as a unique mark of the prophet."[521]

Sarah Pessin observes that "Rich and complex in their own right, Maimonides' writings must, however, be understood within their 12th-13th century Islamicate context, revealing, as they do, the imprint of earlier Greek and Islamic philosophical traditions."[522] She notes that "more scholars are finding the direct influence of Averroes and al-Ghazali in Maimonides' Guide."[523] Sirat notes that "Maimonides had seen no need to use texts written by other Jews, since Greek and Islamic works provided what was essential in disciplined knowledge."[524] Maimonides truly benefitted from the works of both Muslim philosophers and theologians. He toed the lines of Muslim philosophers wherever he felt that their arguments were based upon demonstrative knowledge. In other areas he followed the Muslim theologians. The eternity of world was such an area where Maimonides felt that the philosophers' arguments were not founded upon authentic demonstration. Therefore, he decided to stick to the Muslim theologians' lead.

Maimonides' overall project in the *Guide* was to reconcile reason with revelation, but as Eliezer Schweid notes: "The question of creation, as a formative, voluntary action of a sovereign, omnipotent God, the fulfilment of whose will is not conditioned or restricted by any external principle, was the most difficult test of the project to reconcile philosophical Aristotelianism with the truth of the revealed Torah [...] on the basis of this assumption Maimonides presented prophecy as a summit of intellectual achievement that took philosophy as its foundation. But when one examines this assumption against the difference between the Aristotelian conception of God as the final cause of the world and the Torah's view, one cannot help admitting an irreconcilable contradiction between the two."[525] Creation *ex nihilo* was an intrinsic and substantive part of the Torah and Prophets, but something secondary or non-essential from the philosophical standpoint. Here Maimonides diverted from his overall objective and preferred the revelation over philosophy.[526] Maimonides, in his *Guide for the Perplexed,* argued that from a philosophical vantage point both eternity and non-eternity of the world were possible.[527] Schweid observes that "Maimonides surprises us with the argument that it is a philosophical consideration from the Torah's perspective that necessitates his preference for the view that the world was created *ex nihilo.* He emphasises this point against the Kalamic sages, just as he had emphasised the superiority of Aristotelian physics as a basis for the proof of God."[528]

Maimonides notes that "although our theory includes points open to criticism, I will show that there are much stronger reasons for the rejection of the theory of our opponents."[529] He considered Neoplatonist Aristotelian arguments about eternity not convincing, as demonstration of instantaneous creation and eternity was rationally not possible. "As to the proofs of Aristotle and his followers for the Eternity of the Universe, they are [...] not conclusive; they are open to strong objections [...] the theory of the Creation, as taught in Scripture, contains nothing that is impossible; and that all those philosophical arguments which seem to disprove our view contain weak points which make them inconclusive, and render the attacks on our view untenable. Since

I am convinced of the correctness of my method, and consider either of the two theories—viz., the Eternity of the Universe, and the Creation—as admissible, I accept the latter on the authority of Prophecy, which can teach things beyond the reach of philosophical speculation. For the belief in prophecy is […] consistent even with the belief in the Eternity of the Universe."[530] Maimonides held that eternity of the world was not logically authenticated otherwise he would have allegorically interpreted the scriptural passages which contradicted it. His allegorisation of anthropomorphic scriptural passages was necessitated by reason and philosophy; such a necessity did not exist for eternity of the world. "WE do not reject the Eternity of the Universe, because certain passages in Scripture confirm the Creation; for such passages are not more numerous than those in which God is represented as a corporeal being; nor is it impossible or difficult to find for them a suitable interpretation. We might have explained them in the same manner as we did in respect to the Incorporeality of God. We should perhaps have had an easier task in showing that the Scriptural passages referred to are in harmony with the theory of the Eternity of the Universe if we accepted the latter, than we had in explaining the anthropomorphisms in the Bible when we rejected the idea that God is corporeal. For two reasons, however, we have not done so, and have not accepted the Eternity of the Universe. First, the Incorporeality of God has been demonstrated by proof; those passages in the Bible, which in their literal sense contain statements that can be refuted by proof, must and can be interpreted otherwise. But the Eternity of the Universe has not been proved; a mere argument in favour of a certain theory is not sufficient reason for rejecting the literal meaning of a Biblical text, and explaining it figuratively, when the opposite theory can be supported by an equally good argument."[531]

The second reason is far more important, as it relates to the foundation of Judaism. "Secondly, our belief in the Incorporeality of God is not contrary to any of the fundamental principles of our religion; it is not contrary to the words of any prophet. Only ignorant people believe that it is contrary to the teaching of Scripture; but we have shown that this is not the case; on the contrary, Scripture teaches the Incorporeality of God. If we were to accept the Eternity of the Universe as taught by Aristotle, that everything in the Universe is the result of fixed laws, that Nature does not change, and that there is nothing supernatural, we should necessarily be in opposition to the foundation of our religion, we should disbelieve all miracles and signs, and certainly reject all hopes and fears derived from Scripture, unless the miracles are also explained figuratively."[532] Hyman observes that "reviewing at length Aristotelian arguments for the eternity of world, Maimonides asserts that they are not conclusive demonstrations but only dialectical arguments designed to show that the eternity of the world is more plausible than its creation. Agreeing that the question whether the world is eternal or created has only a dialectical solution, Maimonides goes on to argue that creation is the more plausible alternative. His main support comes from a certain disorder in the hierarchy of the celestial spheres and in their motions which, in his opinion, point to creation by the divine will. He finds additional support for this opinion in scriptural teachings. While the world has a beginning in time, it does not have a temporal end."[533]

Maimonides contended that Aristotle himself was not absolutely convinced of his eternity arguments. "Aristotle was well aware that he had not proved the Eternity of the Universe. He was not mistaken in this respect. He knew that he could not prove his theory, and that his arguments and proofs were only apparent and plausible. They are the least objectionable, according to Alexander; but, according to the same authority, Aristotle could not have considered them conclusive, after having himself taught us the rules of logic, and the means by which arguments can be refuted or confirmed.[534] He further argued that 'I show that Aristotle himself did not claim to have proved the Eternity of the Universe. He says in his book *Physics* (viii., chap. i.) as follows: "All the Physicists before us believed that motion is eternal, except Plato, who holds that motion is transient; according to his opinion the heavens are likewise transient.' Now if Aristotle had conclusive proofs for his theory, he would not have considered it necessary to support it by citing the opinions of preceding Physicists, nor would he have found it necessary to point out the folly and absurdity of his opponents. For a truth, once established by proof, does neither gain force nor certainty by the consent of all scholars, nor lose by the general dissent."[535]

To Maimonides, creation both *de novo* and *ex nihilo* was more plausible due to multiplicity, purpose and design in the universe; the design needed a designer. Continuous creation is something philosophically demonstrable. This can be understood only by a cause which is God. The purposive nature of the cosmos inevitably leads to God's willed creation. This cosmological vision also accounts for multiplicity of creations from divine simplicity, the so-called main reason for Ibn Sina's emanative cosmology. To Maimonides, Ibn Sina also failed to explain multiplicity of creation without divine will, as emanation is just a mechanical necessity. His claims of eternal will that created eternally were also undercut by his assertion that at no time was nature other than what it is now, as Aristotle also presumed. Ibn Sina had argued that "before the world came to be, its creation was possible, necessary, or impossible. If it was necessary, the world always had to exist and is eternal. If it was impossible, it would not exist now. If it was possible, it had to have a substratum that accounts for its possibility. If there is a substratum that pre-exists creation, creation is absurd."[536] As the outcome of the necessary being the world is necessary and not mere possible and hence eternal.

Maimonides disagreed with Ibn Sina. He showed that he had properly understood Ibn Sina's arguments but rejected them due to lack of demonstration. Maimonides explained the philosophers' argument in the following words: "Similarly there is, according to them, no defect in the greatness of God, when He is unable to produce a thing from nothing, because they consider this as one of the impossibilities. They therefore assume that a certain substance has coexisted with God from eternity in such a manner that neither God existed without that substance nor the latter without God. But they do not hold that the existence of that substance equals in rank that of God; for God is the cause of that existence, and the substance is in the same relation to God as the clay is to the potter, or the iron to the smith; God can do with it what He pleases; at one time He forms of it heaven and earth, at another time He forms some other thing."[537] He further observed that "Aristotle maintains, like the adherents of the second theory, that a corporeal object cannot be produced without a corporeal substance. He goes, however, farther, and contends that the heavens are indestructible. For he holds that the Universe in its totality has never been different, nor will it ever change: the heavens, which form the permanent element in the Universe, and are not subject to genesis and destruction, have always been so; time and motion are eternal, permanent, and have neither beginning nor end; the sublunary world, which includes the transient elements, has always been the same, because the *materia prima* is itself eternal, and merely combines successively with different forms; when one form is removed, another is assumed. This whole arrangement, therefore, both above and here below, is never disturbed or interrupted, and nothing is produced contrary to the laws or the ordinary course of Nature. He further says—though not in the same terms—that he considers it impossible for God to change His will or conceive a new desire; that God produced this Universe in its totality by His will, but not from nothing. Aristotle finds it as impossible to assume that God changes His will or conceives a new desire, as to believe that He is non-existing, or that His essence is changeable. Hence it follows that this Universe has always been the same in the past, and will be the same eternally."[538]

Maimonides discusses eight arguments of the philosophers such as "motion *par excellence*, is eternal," that "The First Substance common to the four elements is eternal," "The substance of the spheres contains no opposite elements; for circular motion includes no such opposite directions as are found in rectilinear motion," "The actual production of a thing is preceded in time by its possibility. The actual change of a thing is likewise preceded in time by its possibility" and "If God produced the Universe from nothing, He must have been a potential agent before He was an actual one, and must have passed from a state of potentiality into that of actuality—a process that is merely possible, and requires an agent for effecting it."[539] Maimonides argues that all these arguments are founded on the same assumptions. "The Aristotelians oppose us, and found their objections on the properties which the things in the Universe possess when in actual existence and fully developed. We admit the existence of these properties, but hold that they are by no means the same as those which the things possessed in the moment of their production; and we hold that these properties themselves have come into existence from absolute non-existence. Their arguments are therefore no objection whatever to our theory; they have demonstrative force only against those who hold that the nature of things as at present in existence proves the Creation. But this is not my opinion."[540]

Kenneth Seeskin notes that "Maimonides' overall response is to point out that these arguments are based on the same assumption: the origin of the world is analogous to the origin of a natural thing within it. Put otherwise, they assume that the principles one would use to explain the world as it is now can also explain its origin."[541] Maimonides argues that "EVERYTHING produced comes into existence from non-existence; even when the substance of a thing has been in existence, and has only changed its form, the thing itself, which has gone through the process of genesis and development, and has arrived at its final state, has now different properties from those which it possessed at the commencement of the transition from potentiality to reality, or before that time. Take, e.g., the human ovum as contained in the female's blood when still included in its vessels; its nature is different from what it was in the moment of conception, when it is met by the semen of the male and begins to develop; the properties of the semen in that moment are different from the properties of the living being after its birth when fully developed. It is therefore quite impossible to infer from the nature which a thing possesses after having passed through all stages of its development, what the condition of the thing has been in the moment when this process commenced; nor does the condition of a thing in this moment show what its previous condition has been. If you make this mistake, and attempt to prove the nature of a thing in potential existence by its properties when actually existing, you will fall into great confusion; you will reject evident truths and admit false opinions."[542] The philosophers' argument is not valid because they project now to then (meaning before the creation of the world). As all things come to be now from some pre-existent matter and form, they argue that nothing can come to be from non-being. Maimonides states that "there is no necessity for this according to our plan; for we do not desire to prove the Creation, but only its possibility; and this possibility is not refuted by arguments based on the nature of the present Universe, which we do not dispute."[543]

Maimonides summarises his two main arguments in the following words: "Being convinced that the question whether the heavens are eternal or not cannot be decided by proof, neither in the affirmative nor in the negative, we have enumerated the objections raised to either view, and shown how the theory of the Eternity of the Universe is subject to stronger objections, and is more apt to corrupt the notions concerning God [than the other]. Another argument can be drawn from the fact that the theory of the Creation was held by our Father Abraham, and by our Teacher Moses."[544]

In conclusion, we can infer that Maimonides could have allegorically interpreted the biblical passages had he felt the need to do so. He did not feel the need because eternity of the world was not proved philosophically. He also believed that the creation was also not proved by reason though its plausibility was greater than eternity. He preferred the creation over eternity due to revelation, tradition and faith. The bottom line was "why should we not support our view by that which Moses and Abraham said, and that which follows from their words?[545] Thomas almost copied Maimonides' arguments.

Chapter 7

Thomas's Interactions with Muslim Philosophy

Thomas and Maimonides

Thomas argued that "one cannot demonstrate either eternity or noneternity of the world."[546] He contended that from the philosophical perspective the eternity thesis was more probable than non-eternity. This was a clear influence of Ibn Sina and Ibn Rushd rather than al-Ghazali or Maimonides.[547] Aquinas further argued that belief in the doctrine of world's eternity is against the revelation therefore false and heterodox, "we must simply concede, in accordance with faith, that a thing caused by God cannot have existed forever, because such a position would imply that a passive potentiality has always existed, which is heretical. However, this does not require the conclusion that God cannot bring it about that some being should exist forever."[548] Here he toed the lines of Maimonides. To Aquinas the eternity of the world like its creation was non-demonstrable and hence non-essential. His work *On the Eternity of the World*[549] was far closer to Ibn Sina and Ibn Rushd than his Christian colleagues. In it he defended the possibility of an eternal creation and hence an eternal world.[550] The scheme, methodology and even the phrases were almost identical to Ibn Sina's treatment of the subject. To Wippel "Thomas was once again influenced by Avicenna. This time the debt is not explicitly acknowledged by Aquinas."[551]

In his Commentary on the Sentences (II, d.1 q.1 a.5) he almost quotes Ibn Rushd and Ibn Sina verbatim in favour of possibility of the eternity of world. Moreover, he incorporates Ibn Sina's argument into his *Summa* even when refuting the eternity thesis based upon revelation. Just like Ibn Sina, he describes God as the necessary and intelligent being and creation as non-necessary contingent.[552] For instance he states that "no creature's existence is absolutely necessary; consequently we do not have to hold that some creature has always existed. Again, nothing that proceeds from the will is absolutely necessary, unless the will happens to be impelled by necessity to will something. But God brings creatures into existence, not by any necessity of His nature, but by His will [...] nor does He necessarily will creatures to be [...] Hence it is not absolutely necessary for any creature to be, and therefore it is not necessary that creatures should always have existed."[553]

In Book II, chapters 31 to 34 of *Summa Contra Gentiles*, Thomas presents the arguments of those who insist upon eternity of world.[554] Again the scheme, methodology and vocabulary are indebted to Ibn Sina. In chapters 35 and 37 he refutes some of these arguments. Many of these arguments were already reflected in al-Ghazali's *Tahafut al-Falasifah*.[555] H. A. Wolfson, after giving detailed accounts of the Mutakallimun's (Muslim speculative theologians) eighth main arguments against eternity and for creation, concludes that most or all of these arguments were absorbed, appropriated and used by Albert the Great and Thomas. They could have come to our Schoolmen through Maimonides and Ibn Rushd.[556]

Aquinas, al-Ghazali and Asha'rites

Let us look at some of the examples where Thomas's arguments closely resemble the arguments forwarded by al-Ghazali and other Asha'rites. For example, Aquinas states that "God's action existed from eternity, although its effect was not produced from eternity but occurred at the time eternally appointed for it. This consideration also makes it clear that, even though God is the sufficient cause producing the existence of things, we do not have to conclude that His effect is eternal just because He Himself exists eternally."[557] He focuses a great deal on divine volition and differentiates between eternal will and its contingent effect, as already seen in the case of al-Ghazali. He argues that "The proper effect of the will is the production of that which the will decides; if something else that what the will decrees were to result, the effect would not be proper to the cause but would be alien to it [...] just as the will determines that a thing should be of a definite nature, so it wills that the thing should exist at a particular time. In order that the will may be a sufficient cause, therefore, the effect need not exist when the will itself exists, but only at the time which the will appoints for it."[558]

Thomas pinpoints the unity of divine will and intention by stating

that "the will, however, acts in a way that is governed, not by its existence, but by its intention. And therefore, just as the effect of a natural
agent is determined by the agent's existence, if the latter is a sufficient
cause, so the effect of a voluntary agent is produced in accord with
the agent's purpose."[559]

Time, like everything other than God, is also the creation of God
and not eternal, "outside the totality of creation there is no time, since
time was produced simultaneously with the universe; hence we need
not go into the reason why it exists now and not earlier, and so we
will not be led to concede the infinity of time. We have only to ask
why it did not exist always, or why it came into being after non-being, or why it had a beginning at all."[560] God's actions are voluntary
(based upon will and intention) and full of wisdom and goodness.
He is under no constraint to create or effect change. The contingent
changes God causes are full of purpose and not random.[561] They do
not make the transcendent God mutable[562] or make the effects eternal, "all things outside of God have Him as the author of their being,
and that His power is under no necessity to produce such effects, as
nature is with regard to natural effects; and consequently that He is a
voluntary and intelligent agent. Some thinkers have entertained views
opposed to these truths, because they assume the eternity of creatures.
Accordingly there is nothing on the part of the agent that compels us
to hold the eternity of creation."[563] Regarding Aristotle and Ibn Sina's
above sketched argument about eternity of motion, Thomas argues
that "without any change in Himself, God the agent can accomplish
something new, something that is not eternal. But if something can be
done by Him anew, it is clear that something can also be put in motion
by Him anew, for newness of motion follows on the decision of the
eternal will that motion is not to be eternal."[564] He concludes observing that "Therefore it is quite evident that nothing prevents us from
maintaining that the world has not always existed. And this is what
the Catholic faith teaches: "In the beginning God created heaven and
earth" (Genesis 1:1); and in Proverbs 8:22 it is said of God: "Before He
made anything from the beginning," etc."[565]

As seen above, Aquinas's arguments against eternity of world are
mostly founded on divine volition, and are neither very strong nor demonstrable. Their strength lies in scripture and faith and not in philosophy; rationally they are plausible but spiritually superior. Faith is

founded on the creation of world, as the Bible states. Divine volition is the foundation of revelation, prophecy, miracles, Trinity, Incarnation, Resurrection and Soteriology. Accepting eternity of the world and denying creation is tantamount to rejecting Christianity. Therefore, it is of paramount significance to reject the eternity of material world and its mechanical emanation and evolution. Thomas is totally indebted to Maimonides in this line of argument.

The claims of creation do not necessarily mean that the world was created from nothingness. There were philosophers who maintained that God created the world from an existing matter. Unlike them Thomas argues for the creation of world from nothing. Both the Mu'atazilites and Asha'rites have tried to prove creation of the world from nothingness long before Aquinas who had access to their arguments.[566] Both Maimonides and Aquinas's faith-based arguments for creation *ex nihilo* reflect the Muslim theologians.[567] Aquinas argues "That God is the cause of all things [...] But a cause must precede in duration the things that are produced by its action [...] Again, since all being has been created by God, it cannot be said to have been made from some being, and so we conclude that it was made from nothing. Consequently its existence must be subsequent to non-existence."[568] Thomas does not claim that the arguments presented for creation *ex nihilo* are categorical or demonstrative. He confesses that they are probable, but their probability is substantiated by faith. "Since these arguments do not conclude with strict necessity, although they are not entirely devoid of probability, it is enough to touch on them briefly, so that the Catholic faith may not seem to rest on inept reasonings rather than on the unshakable basis of God's teaching."[569] He also confesses that refutation of world's eternity claims is necessitated by the Catholic Faith. "Reflections such as these enable us to avoid various errors into which pagan philosophers fell. Some of them asserted the eternity of the world. Others held that the matter of the world is eternal, and that the world began to be fashioned from it at a certain moment, either by chance, or at the direction of some intellect, or else by attraction and repulsion. But all of them take it for granted that something besides God is eternal; and this is incompatible with the Catholic faith."[570]

In Question 3 Article 17 of *On the Power of God* Thomas repeats 30 strong arguments in favour of world's eternity[571] but at the end he generically refutes them based upon divine volition, scripture and

Catholic faith. He states that "it is proper to goodness to bring things into existence through an act of the will, whose object is the good. Therefore things did not have to be brought into being in such a way as to be coeternal with the divine goodness; rather they were produced in the way that the divine will disposed for them.[572] Even in the *Summa Theologia* he does not refute the eternity with demonstrative force. He does not think that it is necessary or demonstrable.[573] Creation like Trinity is known through revelation and not demonstration, "articles of faith cannot be proved demonstratively, because faith is concerned with 'things that appear not,' according to Hebrews 11:1. But that God is the Creator of the world in such a way that the world began to exist, is an article of faith; for we say: "I believe in one God," etc. And likewise Gregory points out that Moses prophesied about the past when he said, "In the beginning God created heaven and earth." In these words the inception of the world is conveyed. Therefore the inception of the world is known exclusively by revelation. Accordingly it cannot be proved demonstratively."[574] His final conclusion is that "we must hold firmly that the world has not always existed, as the Catholic faith teaches. And this truth cannot be effectively attacked by any demonstration based on physics."[575]

It should be manifest by now that Thomas rejects the eternity arguments based upon revelation and not reason. He uses Ibn Sina and other philosophers' arguments to refute them. He uses their phrases, ideas and vocabulary to elucidate his points; his dependence upon and indebtedness to them is beyond any doubt. Thomas also benefits from the arguments of Asha'rites such as al-Ghazali for creation and against eternity; his indebtedness to both Muslim philosophers and theologians is manifest. It is noted with surprise that an authority like A. Kenny states that Thomas was unique in his treatment of the eternity and creation subjects. He claims that "his philosophical treatment of this issue had a sophistication unmatched before or since: by patient examination he refuted not only Aristotelian arguments for the eternity of the world, but also arguments put forward by Muslims and Christians to show that the world was created in time. Neither proposition, he maintained, could be proved by reason, and philosophy must be agnostic on the issue; we should believe that creation took place in time simply because the book of Genesis told us so."[576] This claim cannot be authenticated, as al-Ghazali and Maimonides had preceded him on this.

Kenny also argues that "Aquinas' most famous contribution to the philosophy of religion is the Five Ways or proofs of the existence of God to which he refers early in his *Summa Theologiae*."[577] Even these "five ways" of proving God's existence in the *Summa* are clearly imbued with Ibn Sina's thoughts as well as phrases[578] though the influence of Maimonides here is more marked, "the distinction Ibn Sina introduced in his theodicy, for example, between evil in itself and evil for another was borrowed by Aquinas [...] Furthermore, two of Aquinas's well-known proofs of God's existence, that from efficiency and that from contingency, as well as his distinction between essence and existence, were also borrowed from Ibn Sina. The numerous references Aquinas gives to Ibn Sina in Being and Essence and elsewhere are sufficient to show the influence Ibn Sina had on this prominent Christian philosopher and theologian whose ideas dominated Western thought for so long."[579] McGinnis observes that "thus, on the one hand, in a very positive way, Thomas consistently draws upon Avicenna when considering so-called demonstrations for the world's temporal createdness in order to criticise those proofs. On the other hand, when he considered the arguments for the world's eternity, Avicenna's proof from necessity and possibility always appeared in Thomas's catalogue of arguments. In fact, Avicenna's proof is the premier argument for that thesis considered by Thomas in the *Summa Theologiae* (part I, question 46), as well as framing the topic in his *On the Eternity of the World* (*De Aeternitate mundi*), which, as the title indicates is dedicated to this issue. While further examples of Avicennan influence on Thomas could certainly be multiplied, these instances at least suggest the role that Avicenna played in the development of two of the more distinctive doctrines in Aquinas's thought."[580] He further states that "Even when Thomas is clearly at odds with Avicenna, such as on the subject of the cosmos' past eternity, the former very much respects and even positively draws on his Muslim predecessor."[581]

It must be noted here again that Thomas did not just copy arguments from Muslim theologians and philosophers. He appropriated them to his Christian context. His project of reconciling the Christian faith with Aristotelian philosophy came later than his Muslim predecessors. Muslims were the medieval pioneers in the field of reconciliation of faith and reason, with multiple viable paradigms. Thomas benefitted from these endeavours and appropriated them to his Christian needs and designs with marvelous creativity. Ibn Sina was among the widely translated and read medieval figures. He had a complete system of metaphysics, as noted above; the wide circulation of his works in the medieval universities was among the main factors of his wider appeal. That is why his influence upon Thomas is more marked. "No doubt the following factors facilitated Ibn Sina's influence on Latin philosophical circles: first, the translation into Latin, and fast circulation in universities, of the most essential parts of al-Shifa as early as the twelfth and thirteenth Christian centuries; and, second, Ibn Sina's efforts to synthesise Greek and Islamic thought, an attempt in which the West found the seed for a synthesis between Greek philosophy and Christianity."[582] Therefore, Thomas, the medieval stalwart of this reconciliation project, was an heir to Ibn Sina.

Ibn Rushd and Aquinas

The tremendous impact of Spanish Ibn Rushd upon his Italian neighbor Thomas cannot be denied. Thomas, like other scholastics, was actively engaged with Aristotelianism. Ibn Rushd was the "Commentator" who had extensively studied Aristotle and explained the meanings and implications of his philosophy. Thomas did not refer to Ibn Rushd by name but simply as the "Commentator," expecting his readers to know who the "Commentator" was due to Ibn Rushd's popularity among the Latin Christians. Majid Fakhry, one of the leading authorities on Ibn Rushd, observes that "Averroes was a towering figure in the history of philosophy in general and Aristotelianism in particular, both in the East and West. Surpassing all of his predecessors, from Alexander of Aphrodisias in the second century, to Boethius in the fifth century and Avicenna in the eleventh, he was the most meticulous expositor of Aristotle's philosophy in any language or clime up to his own day. Despite his divergences from most of the early Greek or Arab commentators, whom he constantly refers to or criticises, his understanding of the Master is profound."[583] Ibn Rushd was the medieval Europe's gateway to Aristotle; as Aristotelianism served as the core of Latin Europe's intellectual foundations, the impact of Ibn Rushd upon the medieval Europe was tremendous. Fakhry notes that "Averroes' impact on Western-European thought, the translation of the whole Averroist corpus of commentaries on Aristotle into Hebrew and Latin, starting early in the thirteenth century, had a far-reaching effect on philosophical and theological developments [...] throughout the next three centuries and beyond."[584]

Latin Averroism, the philosophical school named after Ibn Rushd, became so pervasive especially in the universities such as Paris that it became the major concern for the Popes and Bishops starting from the end of the twelfth century all the way to fifteenth century. M. M. Sharif states that "By the end of the sixth/twelfth century Averroism, i.e., the philosophy of ibn Rushd, had become so popular, particularly among the whole school of philosophers represented first by the Faculty of Arts at Paris, and had become such a menace to Orthodox Christianity that in 607/1210 the Council of Paris forbade all teachings of Aristotle's Natural History and ibn Rushd's commentaries on it. This prohibition was confirmed by the Legate Robert of Courcon, Cardinal of Paris, in 612/1215, and renewed by the Popes in 629/1231 and 643/ 1245. The Physics and Metaphysics of Aristotle were forbidden at the University of Toulouse by Urban IV in 662/1263. In 668/1269 the Bishop of Paris condemned thirteen of ibn Rushd's basic doctrines, and in 676/1277 he condemned the prominent Averroist, Siger of Brabant. Yet the strength of Averroism was irresistible. No force could suppress it."[585]

Ibn Rushd was a pure rationalist, who believed that human intellect (reason) was a universal divine gift and the core of true knowledge and understanding. He believed in the unity and universality of human intellect, in the sense that reason was the aggregate of human knowledge and experience; it was a universal phenomenon stemming from the divine powers.[586] "This intellect is eternal and enters us from outside to unite with, or rather be received by the material intellect."[587] Demonstration is based upon this universal human phenomenon, and is the highest source of certitude because it implies the rational principles. Just like the human dignity, human collective reason constitutes the fundamental psychological make up of humanity.[588] To Ibn Rushd intellect is an intellectual mind shared by all human knowers.[589] The person who knows through demonstration and experimentation partakes the universal wisdom and is no more an individual but a specimen of the universal. Majid Fakhry notes that "in the summary of the *Analytica Postevtora*, Averroes begins by paraphrasing Aristotle's dictum that all instruction and 'intellectual learning' is rooted in pre-existing knowledge, which is shown to be evident by induction (*istiqra'*). Like Aristotle, he then instances reasoning in mathematics and other theoretical sciences to illustrate this point. Even inferior forms of reasoning, such as the dialectical and rhetorical, rest on pre-existing knowledge of particulars, unlike the former which rests on self-evident premises which are universal in character."[590]

Ibn Rushd's emphasis upon human reason as the universal divine gift and the highest source of certitude was close to the Mu'atazilites, even though Ibn Rushd had limited knowledge about their rational discourse. In case of conflict he, like the Mu'atazilites, would metaphorically interpret the religious texts based upon rational postulates.

Authentic religion and revelation cannot contradict rational demonstration as the source of both is the one and same, i.e., God (Active Intellect). The truth cannot contradict the truth as the source of truth is the One and Only God. Ibn Rushd categorises the arguments into three categories based upon their strength and certitude. They are rhetorical, dialectical and demonstrative.[591] "Now the methods available to men of [arriving at] judgments are three: demonstrative, dialectical, and rhetorical; and the methods of forming concepts are two: either [conceiving] the object itself or [conceiving] a similitude of it. But not everyone has the natural ability to take in demonstrations, or [even] dialectical arguments, let alone demonstrative arguments, which are so hard to learn and need so much time [even] for those who are qualified to learn them. Therefore, since it is the purpose of the Law simply to teach everyone, the Law has to contain every method of [bringing about] judgments of assent and every method of forming concepts."[592]

The rhetorical argument is founded on generic propositions, mostly accepted by the masses, and is persuasive in nature. The dialectical argument is based upon proposition, accepted by some learned people but not all of them. It has a higher degree of certainty than rhetorical but its conclusions are not without the shadow of doubt. The demonstrative, or necessary, argument yields certitude which is categorical. Such a precise and knowledge-based argument elucidates the premises as well as the reasons behind them. Demonstrative knowledge is the "deduction (*qiyas*) which imparts the knowledge of the thing as it actually is, through the cause whereby it is what it is."[593] The "why" part of such an argument is demonstrative therefore yielding the certain knowledge and categorical acceptability. Consequently, the demonstrative argument is the most certain and scientific of all the arguments. Only reason and philosophy can produce such a categorical and authentic argument. Religions are mostly based upon rhetorical arguments. "Now some of the methods of assent comprehend the majority of people, that is, the occurrence of assent as a result of them [is comprehensive]: these are the rhetorical and the dialectical [methods]-and the rhetorical is more comprehensive than the dialectical. Another method is peculiar to a smaller number of people: this is the demonstrative. Therefore, since the primary purpose of the Law is to take care of the majority (without neglecting to arouse the elect), the prevailing methods of exposition in the Law are the common methods by which the majority comes to form concepts and judgments."[594]

The founders of various religious traditions use persuasion to appeal to a wider crowd, who otherwise may not have the capacity or aptitude for demonstrative or rational inquiry. The religious arguments are mostly rhetorical due to the psychology of masses and not because of any deficiency in themselves; they are rhetorically constructed to garner the masses' acceptance and conformity. Richard C. Taylor states that "truth in the practical sphere of action is determined with a view to the end to be achieved, while truth in the speculative or theoretical sphere is absolute. If the end is moral excellence and proper moral practice for the people and an adherence to the dictates of right reason and sound and beneficial Religious Law, it makes little difference if the people attain that end by rhetorical persuasion or dialectical convincing. The weakness of the psychological characters and abilities of the people result in corresponding weaknesses in epistemological foundations for their beliefs, even if those beliefs are true beliefs."[595]

The dialectical arguments are usually implied by theologians, but the demonstrative or logical arguments are devised and comprehended by the minority blessed with true knowledge and understanding. Philosophers constitute that learned minority. "Thus people in relation to the Law fall into three classes: One class is those who are not people of interpretation at all: these are the rhetorical class. They are the overwhelming multitude, for no man of sound intellect is exempted from this kind of assent. Another class is the people of dialectical interpretation: these are the dialecticians, either by nature alone or by nature and habit. Another class is the people of certain interpretation: these are the demonstrative class, by nature and training, that is, in the art of philosophy. This interpretation ought not to be expressed to the dialectical class, let alone to the multitude."[596]

Ibn Rushd argues that the Quran not only encourages but mandates the Muslims to know the artisan through the work of creation.[597] Demonstration is the best mean of accomplishing such a task; therefore, philosophy and demonstrative knowledge is obligatory for those Muslims who have the capacity, skill and propensity for such a science. The masses are not obliged to go through such a vigorous endeavour; they are required to outwardly conform to the general religious norms. The masses should be prohibited from the demonstrative arguments, so as to protect them from confusion and disbelief. "When something of these interpretations is expressed to anyone unfit to receive them-especially demonstrative interpretations because of their remoteness from common knowledge-both he who expresses it and he to whom it is expressed are led into unbelief. The reason for that [in the ease of the latter] is that interpretation comprises two things, rejection of the apparent meaning and affirmation of the interpretation, so that if the apparent meaning is rejected in the mind of someone who can only grasp apparent meanings, without the interpretation being affirmed in his mind, the result is unbelief, if it [the statement in question] concerns the principles of the Law. Interpretations, then, ought not to be expressed to the multitude nor set down in rhetorical or dialectical books, that is, books containing arguments of these two sorts."[598]

The Prophets are those philosophers who have mastered the syllogistic skills and known the demonstrative arguments. Their overall approach is rhetorical in view of their larger audiences, the masses. Consequently, their poetical and rhetorical approach does not reflect badly upon their teachings.[599] It is based upon wisdom to accommodate and move the large number of masses for universal impact and reformation.

Ibn Rushd contends that philosophers are just like Muslim jurists who study legal reasoning to comprehend legal categories. The philosophers utilise logic to understand God and his creation. Undoubtedly the philosophy is better than theology and jurisprudence, as it yields more certitude by demonstrative knowledge. As the Greek philosophers preceded Muslims in logic and reasoning, their books must be studied by the Muslims. This will be nothing but fulfilling the divine commandment of studying the works of God with logic, reasoning and wisdom.[600] Not everyone is qualified to study philosophy and benefit from it; it needs a special sort of intelligence and capacity, as well as teachers. There is a possibility that the incapable individuals may go astray or get confused by studying philosophical works due to a number of factors unrelated to philosophy itself. That should not prevent the qualified to study philosophy. Therefore "a man who prevents a qualified person from studying books of philosophy, because some of the most vicious people may be thought to have gone astray through their study of them, is like a man who prevents a thirsty person from drinking cool, fresh water until he dies of thirst, because some people have choked to death on it."[601]

Ibn Rushd proposes that Islam is true and that it leads people to the knowledge of God and His creation and hence happiness, but different persons are led differently due to their dispositions. Consequently, assent to Islam is open to everyone except those who intentionally choose ignorance over knowledge. Islam, like other true religions, is fundamentally concerned with the eternal success in the life to come. "The chief merit of religion, as compared with philosophy, is that it addresses all classes of men and defines the actions which conduce to their happiness in the hereafter, unlike philosophy which addresses a small group of men and defines the conditions of "their intellectual happiness."[602] It brings Ibn Rushd to the logical conclusion that Islam and philosophy, revelation and reason are compatible. Islam encourages demonstrative study, which leads to conclusions consistent with Islam, or at least not contradictory to the essentials of Islam. The "truth does not oppose truth but accords with it and bears witness to it"[603] Majid Fakhry notes that "For Averroes [...] the primacy of reason is unquestioned and it is for this reason that Gilson regards him as the herald of rationalism long before the Renaissance. Averroes had in fact distinguished between three levels of assent (*tasdiq*), the philosophical, the dialectical and the rhetorical. The first, which ensues upon the 'demonstration' of the philosophers, is higher than that of the theologians, or people of dialectic (*jadaliyun*), or that of the masses at large, or the people of rhetoric (*khatabiyun*) [...] Averroes maintains a position which may be called the 'parity' of truth, philosophical and religious. According to this position, philosophical truth, although superior to religious truth, is not really incompatible with it, or even different from it. The only difference between the two types of truth is that they are addressed to three different classes of hearers (or readers), and are for that reason cast in different idioms."[604] The Islamic Law (meaning the Quran) has an outer as well as an inner meaning due to variety of capacities and intellectual dispositions of its recipients.

Consequently, if there appears to be a conflict between the Quran, revelation and established philosophical facts (science) one must look into overall intent of the Quran and overarching objectives of the revelation to amicably resolve such a conflict. The problem could be in the way the Quranic or Prophetic text is interpreted. The revelation must be metaphorically interpreted in case of a clear-cut conflict with philosophy, as the revelatory text is probable while the philosophical or demonstrative knowledge is categorical. The probable (both rhetorical and dialectical) will give a way to the categorical in light of the established linguistic rules and overall objectives of the Islamic canon. Ibn Rushd states that "[We] affirm definitely that whenever the conclusion of a demonstration is in conflict with the apparent meaning of Scripture [or Religious Law], that apparent meaning admits of allegorical interpretation according to the rules for such interpretation in Arabic. This proposition is questioned by no Muslim and doubted by no believer. But its certainty is immensely increased for those who have had close dealings with this idea and put it to the test, and made it their aim to reconcile the assertions of intellect and tradition. Indeed we may say that whenever a statement in Scripture [or Religious Law] conflicts in its apparent meaning with a conclusion of demonstration, if Scripture [or Religious Law] is considered carefully, and the rest of its contents searched page by page, there will invariably be found among the expressions of Scripture [or Religious Law] something which in its apparent meaning bears witness to that allegorical interpretation or comes close to bearing witness." (Hourani, 1967, p. 51.) In the ultimate sense, reason and revelation, philosophy and religion are absolutely compatible. Fakhry observes that "in the event of 'apparent' conflict between the religious texts (in this case the Quran) and philosophical texts, chiefly Aristotle's, it is the duty of the philosophers, whom the Quran calls 'those who are well grounded in knowledge' (3:5-6), according to Averroes' own reading, to resolve the conflict by recourse to the method of interpretation (*ta'wil*). This method had been consecrated by many accredited scholars. Properly understood and applied, the method of interpretation is bound to show that on all fundamental issues, philosophy (*hikmah*) is in agreement with religion (*shari'ah*)."[605] Therefore there is no issue of "Double Truth" as wrongly attributed to Ibn Rushd in the Latin West.[606] Richard Taylor shows that Ibn Rushd, following Aristotle, held the unity of truth. "The interpretation of the Religious Law and the enactment of its consequent practical dictates in religious and moral action indicate that right and truly understood Religious Law must not conflict with, but rather must be able to coincide with, the philosophically established principles of right moral action. There can be no 'Double Truth' in this regard, although there may be truth doubly attained."[607] H. Wolfson calls it a "Double Faith Theory" that faith can be attained through assent (*tasdiq*) which could be either primary or acquired.[608] "When therefore Averroes says that the methods of *tasdiq* in the sense of belief are 'demonstrative, dialectical and rhetorical,' he means thereby that belief may be either 'acquired,' such as are obtained syllogistically by arguments, or 'primary,' such as are learned not syllogistically but rather directly by 'maxims' and indirectly by 'examples.' Belief or faith, then, in its general epistemological sense of the term, is used by Averroes in its two Aristotelian senses. In the first place, it is the judgment of the truth of undemonstrated knowledge, such as the truth of ethical maxims or generally known primary premises. In the second place, it is the judgment of the truth of conclusions which have been arrived at by demonstration."[609] Each man will have the faith in accordance with his capacities, the philosopher with demonstrative knowledge and the common believer with rhetorical and persuasive method. That does not mean that there is a double truth. The truth is same and united but the people's capacities are divergent. This is the "Double Faith Theory". Wolfson states that "we have in Averroes a double faith theory [...] There is one truth underlying both forms of faith, the truth of the revealed teachings of the Koran. There is only a difference in the method by which different believers arrive at that truth. Some accept it implicitly and hence take the teachings of the Koran literally; others are supported in their acceptance of it by demonstration and hence understand some of those teachings as interpreted philosophically. To the former, the truth of the teachings of the Koran is like an indemonstrable primary premise or a maxim or an example; to the latter, it is like the conclusion of a syllogism."[610] Wolfson further notes that the "development of the problem of the relation of faith to reason in the Moslem branch of Arabic philosophy was the reverse of that of its Jewish branch. Arabic Jewish philosophy started with Saadia's double faith theory, then developed, in Hallevi, a single faith theory of the authoritarian type, and ended up with Maimonides' single faith theory of the rationalist type. Arabic Moslem philosophy, on the other hand, started with the Mu'tazilite view of a single faith theory of the rationalist type, then developed, in Algazali, a single faith theory of the authoritarian type, and ended up with Averroes, a contemporary of Maimonides, with a double faith theory like that of Saadia and Clement of Alexandria."[611] It is pertinent to emphasise here that the double faith theory of Ibn Rushd is in essence identical with the Mu'atazilite's single faith theory of rational type, as faith's double implications are based upon human capacities and not on the nature of faith itself or the truth of its content. The demonstrative aspect of truth may not be comprehended by the masses due to its abstract nature and the type of knowledge, experience and time required. Such an understanding and interpretation is the prerogative of the philosophers. The theologians or masses cannot take charge of such a demonstrative endeavour because "the philosopher in possession of a truth garnered through demonstration in the full and complete sense of demonstration does stand in a position to veto or deny certain possible interpretations of a text of the Religious Law. That is, while the philosopher cannot demonstrate the necessity and truth of understanding a text of the Religious Law in a certain way, he can certainly exclude any interpretation which contradicts the conclusion of a proper demonstration, i.e., demonstrated truth."[612]

To Ibn Rushd, philosophy takes precedent over theology in case of a conflict. Intellect or reason is universal and united- it is the divine gift to all humanity. Therefore, its collective demonstrations are categorical while the theological claims are mostly dialectical and hence probable. The categorical is superior to the probable. Resultantly, the philosophers and not the theologians would determine which verses to accept at the face value and which one to interpret metaphorically. Of course, the philosophers are bound to interpret the verses in accordance with the overarching principles of Islamic law and fundamental rules of the Arabic language, the language of the revelation. It is not philosophical free for all. Here Ibn Rushd is in conformity with the Mua'tazilites and earlier Muslim philosophers in opposition to the Asha'rites who prefer revelation over reason and philosophy.

Al-Fārābī had already articulated this position most fully in his *Kitāb al-Ḥurūf (Book of Letters)* which argued for the priority of philosophy to religion. Following Aristotle[613], he had also categorised the arguments into "Poetics-rhetorical" "sophistical-dialectical" and "demonstrative", the rhetorical being the least certain while demonstrative being the most certain.[614] "And whenever religion is made a human thing it is posterior in time to philosophy, and in general too, since through it one only seeks to teach the masses the theoretical and practical matters which have been discovered in philosophy in ways which make the understanding of these things easy for them, through persuasion or the evoking of images or by the two together."[615] Human reason is the key to understanding, and there is nothing impenetrable for unaided human reason. There is nothing so mysterious that human beings cannot understand it; man has the capacity to understand, comprehend and gain demonstrative and certain knowledge about both theoretical and practical matters. Now not all human beings are equally rational; rationality is distributed among mankind in accordance with their aptitudes and propensities. The philosophers are human elites, having the utmost share of rationality and demonstrative knowledge. Theologians are also elites but among the masses. They are not at par with the philosophers in terms of rationalism and logical demonstration. "It must be known that [the theologian] is also one of the elite, but in relation to the people of this religion only. For it is the philosopher who is elite in relation to all people and all nations."[616] As the theologians mostly depend upon the dialectical methods which lacks the certitude and demonstration of the philosophers, theologians often oppose the philosophers. Fārābī declares that "it is clear that in every religion there is opposition to philosophy, for in the art of theology there is opposition to philosophy."[617]

There was nothing comparable to the rationalism of al-Farabi and Ibn Rushd in the Latin Europe. The likes of Albert and Thomas gave precedent to theology over philosophy, and made philosophy the maiden of theology, as St. Thomas declared that "other sciences are called the handmaidens of this one." [618] In the Latin West the "Queen" was made servant; the philosophy was made subservient to theology serving as a propaedeutic to theology. Muslim philosophers were among the initiators and introducers of rationalism in the Latin West. "The classical rationalist philosophical tradition in Arabic, represented by thinkers such as al-Fārābī, Avicenna (Ibn Sīnā) and Averroes (Ibn Rushd), developed and expanded the rationalism of the Greek philosophical tradition into a powerful intellectual tool for seeking out truths concerning God, human beings and the world, independent of religious doctrines and Islamic teachings. Through the many scientific, medical and philosophical works translated in Toledo and in Sicily by Domingo Gundisalvi, Gerard of Cremona, Michael Scot and others, Christian thinkers in the Latin West learned of the power of human reason to attain truths without the aid of religion."[619] R. Taylor states that "arguably the most sophisticated rationalist tradition was that of Averroes, whose many commentaries on Aristotle's key works challenged Christian beliefs on God, human nature and reason and exercised a powerful and multifaceted impact on the methods and doctrines of Christian theologians and philosophers in the high Middle Ages."[620] In reality Ibn Rushd was the true medieval rationalist. "In those cases where certainty is established by demonstrative syllogism, the conclusion can be overturned neither by apparent contradictory statements in the religious law nor by community consensus (*al-ijmā'*). Consequently, in the case of religious law, Averroes asserts that, where there is difference between its apparent sense and the conclusion of a demonstrative syllogism, religious law must be interpreted to be in accord with the necessary truth achieved in demonstration."[621] Taylor further observes that "Averroes clearly asserts the primacy of philosophical consideration (*i'tibār*) through intellectual syllogistic *qiyās 'aqlī* of a demonstrative sort (*burhānī*) as the proper type of reflection (*al-naẓar*) for reaching the most perfect knowledge of God, the Artisan of all beings."[622] As only philosophers were truly equipped to attain the most authentic, certain and perfect knowledge of God through the study of nature, they were best suited to worship Him in the best possible manner. "The *sharīʿa* specific to the philosophers [*al-sharīʿatu 'l-khāṣatu bi 'l-ḥukamā'*] is the investigation of all beings, since the Creator is not worshipped by a worship more noble than the knowledge of those things that He produced which lead to the knowledge in truth of His essence—may He be exalted! That [investigation philosophers undertake] is the most noble of the works belonging to Him and the most favoured of them that we do in God's presence. How great is it to perform this service which is the most noble of services and to take it on with this compliant obedience which is the most sublime of obediences! (*Tafsīr mā baʿd aṭ-Ṭabīʿat* 1: 10.11-10.16)"[623] Ibn Rushd's both theological and philosophical works emphatically emphasised the above point. Taylor observed that "The rationalism of Averroes in the *Faṣl al-Maqāl* recognised a plurality of methods of assent to truths concerning both God as Artisan and all the beings formed by the Divine Artisan. There he found to be primary the truth to be garnered by assent through demonstrative syllogistic since, as demonstrative in the strict sense, this constituted the grasp of incontrovertible truth. In the face of conflict with the apparent meaning of the religious law, Averroes refused to assert the possibility of a double truth and instead insisted that the apparent meaning of religious law be recognised as incorrect and requiring interpretation of its inner meaning when in conflict with philosophical demonstration. Since this philosophical method yields truth in the fullest sense regarding God and all beings, the assertion here, while certainly bold if not shockingly blunt, follows in complete accord with the account in the *Faṣl al-Maqāl*: the most perfect form of worship is that which attains the most complete knowledge of God and his created works. This worship is most fully realised in the Aristotelian science which is devoted to the study of beings and their cause, God, namely the theoretical science of metaphysics."[624] In his last philosophical work he reiterated the same fact. The "primacy in the knowledge and worship of God lies with the philosopher who has access to proper scientific knowledge of the world and thereby also to the nature of its Artisan through natural human reasoning of a compelling demonstrative sort. It does not lie with the religious believer whose knowledge and worship come only from persuasive religious statements in the *Qur'ān* and other declared sacred sources, the truth of which is not immediately and *per se* evident. It is precisely this view that Averroes expresses boldly and without reservation in one of his last philosophical works, the *Long Commentary on the Metaphysics of Aristotle.*"[625]

Ibn Rushd's reconciliation of reason and revelation, religion and philosophy and his emphasis upon rational discourse in religion greatly threatened the core of Church teachings on a number of fundamental issues. The dogmas such as the Trinity, Incarnation, Original Sin, Intercession, Purgatory and Church's mediational role were all imperilled. None of these so-called paradoxes and mysteries was capable of demonstrative knowledge or rational analysis. They had neither strong foundation in the scripture nor in human logic, and were mostly based upon the Church tradition and Council's authorities. Ibn Rushd, by assigning central roles to inductive reasoning in theology and giving philosophy upper hand at times of conflict, juddered the very foundation of Catholic Church and its fundamental doctrines. It was not only the Christian clerical establishment which felt jolted by Ibn Rushd's rational, anti-tradition and anti-authority stance; Muslim clerical circles and orthodoxy were also shuddered by this purely rational synthesis. The orthodox Muslims accused Ibn Rushd of following Aristotle rather than the Prophet of Islam, Muhammad. Ibn Rushd vehemently denied such accusations and contended that there was no inherent conflict between Aristotle and Islam; if there was any conflict, that was due to orthodoxy's irrational interpretations of Islam. Any such conflict could be resolved by allegorical interpretations of the religious texts. Reason, rather than the literal meanings or orthodox tradition, was to be the arbiter in these situations. The overarching message of the scripture and higher objectives of the Islamic Shari'ah would define the true meanings of the apparently conflicting texts. The orthodoxy accused Ibn Rushd of placing philosophy, reason and Aristotle over faith, revelation and Prophet Muhammad.

The fact of the matter is that Ibn Rushd was not denying the authority of the Quran or Prophet Muhammad. He, like his predecessors, was challenging the traditional orthodox authority which in the name of religious purity and piety had at times mixed irrational, illogical and inauthentic ideas with the revelation. To Ibn Rushd, nature and authentic scripture or reason and true revelation would never contradict each other as both came from the same source i.e., God. Therefore, any apparent contradiction was either the result of wrong interpretations or mistaken philosophical perceptions. In an instance of such a conflict, reason, philosophy and demonstrative knowledge must take precedence over revelation and orthodox interpretations of it because reason brings categorically certain knowledge while certain areas of revelation provide only imprecise or non-demonstrable knowledge. Therefore, reason must be given precedence over revelation in case of conflict.[626] Reason gives the type of categorical certitude (*Burhan*) while the revelation gives a sort of relative certitude. Therefore, rationalism, philosophy, demonstrative knowledge, experience and logical discourse are the crowns of human understanding and knowledge. Rational discourse should not be given second fiddle in the name of tradition, authority or revelation. With this, Ibn Rushd brought Aristotle and Islamic revelation together in a comprehensive alliance against the established religious authorities. To him, natural science was not against the true revelation or religion- it was against the ignorance of religious authorities.

The orthodoxy could not digest this devastating blow, and in turn condemned Ibn Rushd for placing secular knowledge over and beyond the religious knowledge. He died in exile but not without the pursuing death of irrational, overly authoritative, anti-reformist, un-lightened and reactionary stance of orthodoxy especially in the West. Unfortunately, his writings were not very influential among the Muslims. His books and commentaries were taken over by the Jewish intelligentsia, translated into Hebrew and Latin and exacted a lasting effect upon the Latin Europe as Fakhry states that "the most important part of the Arab-Islamic philosophical legacy to find its way into Western Europe and to exert a lasting influence on Western-European thought, during the thirteenth century and beyond, was Averroes' corpus of Aristotelian commentaries."[627]

In addition to Jewish philosophers, Christian elites such as Emperor Frederick II played a major role in bringing Ibn Rushd to the Christian circles. The progressive and liberal emperor was at loggerheads with the Popes, and found Ibn Rushd's anti-clerical rational discourse handy in his battles against the Church. He facilitated, expedited and patronised the translation, assimilation and appropriation of Ibn Rushd's writings and commentaries. He was perhaps the first modern emperor who sowed the seeds of modernity through the writings of Aristotle, mediated through the commentaries, interpretations and additions of Ibn Rushd. Together they partially cleared the fog that had hampered the intellectual discourse of Latin Europe for centuries. Sharif notes that "In 612/1216, Frederick II became the Emperor of Rome. Having been educated at Palermo under Arab teachers and having come into close contact with the Muslims of Sicily and during the Crusades also with those of Syria, he had become a great admirer of Muslim thought in general, and of ibn Rushd in particular. In 621/1224 he established a university at Naples chiefly with the object of introducing Muslim philosophy and science to the people of the West. Thomas received his education at this university. Here both Christian and Jewish translators were engaged for rendering Arabic works into Latin and Hebrew. The works of Aristotle and ibn Rushd in their Latin translation were used not only in the curriculum of this university, but were sent also to the Universities of Paris and Bologna. Nowhere did Averroism strike deeper roots than in the Universities of Bologna and Padua. Of these two centres of learning Padua became the hot bed of Averroism."[a] No wonder that, later on in the sixteenth century, the same University of Padua became the centre of antitrinitarianism, anti-traditional and anti-clerical approach to Christianity.

Thomas, the product of Frederick's Southern Italy and University of Naples, closely interacted with the writings of Ibn Rushd. They shared the philosophical aptitude, reformist mind, religio-political concerns and overall cultural milieu though differing religious traditions. Their end goal was the same. They intended to reconcile reason with revelation, the secular knowledge with the religious as Fakhry states. "As the two greatest Aristotelians of the twelfth and thirteenth centuries, Averroes and Aquinas, had, despite their differences, a great deal in common. Apart from writing the most elaborate commentaries, prior to modern times, on the works of Aristotle, they were both genuinely interested in reconciling his metaphysical and ethical teaching with religious orthodoxy, Islamic in the first case and Christian in the second."[628] As mentioned earlier, the Muslims had been having this debate from the middle of the eighth century. Both the theological and philosophical traditions were well established in the Muslim East as well as West by the time Aquinas embarked upon his project. He undoubtedly benefitted from these established traditions and appropriated them in accordance with his needs and agendas.

While Aquinas's indebtedness to Islamic philosophical thought is emphasised by the majority, not many scholars active in the field openly emphasise his appreciation and appropriation of Muslim orthodox theological thought. Aquinas's project of reconciliation of theology with philosophy, and his overall goal of emancipating faith from the bondage of secular philosophical knowledge, was identical to Asha'rites like al-Ghazali, al-Shahristani and al-Razi. Though less accommodative of reason in the realms of faith than the Asha'rites, nonetheless Aquinas was still closer in his overall approach to the Asha'rites than the Muslim philosophers. He referred to al-Ghazali almost 33 times in his *Summa*, mostly to the philosopher Ghazali for less than his countless references to Ibn Sina and Ibn Rushd but still a considerable number. His teacher Albert Magnus's references to, and appropri-

---

[a] M. M. Sharif, A History of Muslim Philosophy, v. 2, p. 601.

ation of, al-Ghazali's ideas were far greater than Thomas's. His overall theological outlook was closer to al-Ghazali than Ibn Rushd, while in philosophical realms he towed the lines of Muslim philosophers more than that of Muslim theologians.

Scholars agree that Thomas was not a blind imitator or copier of Muslim philosophical or theological ideas. He picked and chose according to his needs and appropriated the material to his Christian context. Thomas was confronted with issues related to faith and reason similar to what Mu'atazilites, Asha'rites and Muslim philosophers faced centuries before him. Islamic scholastic and philosophical traditions were handy, as most of the related works were already translated from Arabic to Latin and Thomas had access to them. He acted and reacted to them, and in the process digested and absorbed whatever was useful to his project of reconciliation of faith with philosophy and discarded whatever he thought was in conflict with the Christian faith and tradition. There was quite a bit of absorption, appropriation and assimilation of Muslim ideas on the way. For example, even though Thomas disagreed with Ibn Rushd on a number of important points, he absorbed and utilised many of Ibn Rushd's philosophical ideas. His indebtedness to Ibn Rushd can be gauged from his frequent quotations from, assessments of, interactions with and reactions to Ibn Rushd's writings. He referred to Ibn Rushd, the Commentator, almost 503 times in his *Summa Theologiae,* as already mentioned. At times he seemed to be more receptive of and sympathetic to the Jewish philosopher Moses Maimonides' ideas than Ibn Rushd himself as Maimonides was less rational than Ibn Rushd.

As mentioned earlier also, Moses Maimonides' project was very similar to those of Ibn Rushd and Aquinas. There was a slight difference between their overall approaches and ultimate goals. Ibn Rushd was more rationalistic than Maimonides, who in turn was more rational than Aquinas. Joseph A. Buijs put the point succinctly when he noted that "Maimonides' position on religion and philosophy differs from that of both Averroes and Aquinas. For each of them reason is associated with the demonstrative knowledge of philosophy and faith with the acceptance of religious truths. For Aquinas, however, reason exercises no control over the content of faith; for Maimonides it does, albeit negatively. For Averroes, faith has no independent access to truth; for Maimonides it does, albeit imperfectly."[629] He further explains that philosophy and reason have no control over the content of faith in Aquinas's system. A revealed truth claim accepted on the basis of faith can neither be proved nor disproved on the basis of demonstrative knowledge. When the faith's claim contradicts reason then reason is subjected to faith, and not the other way around. The faith urges assent to revelatory claims without rational or intellectual understanding of those claims. Faith is sort of blind. "In Aquinas's view, the act of faith is subject to philosophic justification but its content is not. The acceptance of revelation as a source of truth is philosophically justified in terms of establishing the preconditions of faith, namely, the existence of God and the fact of divine communication. But what is thus revealed and believed extends beyond the scope of philosophical understanding. Hence faith extends beyond reason. Claims can be made on behalf of revelation that are contrary to rational considerations. In this sense, reason gives way to faith."[630] The dogmas of Trinity and Incarnation are good examples of these supra rational faith based superior claims. The validity of theological claims is solely dependent upon the faith. The will of the faithful directs one's intellect to assent to these truths presented by the revelation even though the intellect is at a loss to understand or comprehend them. These mysteries are beyond human rational discourse.

Ibn Rushd is on the opposite side of the spectrum. He, like Mu'atazilites, believes that faith and reason supplement each other and cannot contradict each other. Faith is substantiated by demonstrative facts but it cannot create those facts. In case of any apparent conflict, faith-based claims and sacred texts must be interpreted in light of reason, and the apparent contradiction must be resolved through allegorical interpretation. The true faith can never contradict reason as both come from the same source i.e., God; the truth does not contradict the truth. Buijs notes that "in Averroes' view, to the contrary, faith gives way to reason. For him, the act of faith is not philosophically justified; at best it has some pragmatic justification in that religious beliefs serve a useful purpose. However, the content of faith is fully subject to philosophical justification. Unless what is believed on faith is philosophically intelligible, its truth is questionable. Thus, either faith is replaced by reason or else it remains a dubious alternative to reason."[631] Ibn Rushd, like Mu'atazilites, gives reason and philosophy precedence over faith and revelation. This is pure rationalism.

Maimonides strikes the middle position. He "offers a third alternative, intermediate to both of the above positions. The act of faith is subject to philosophic justification and so is its content—in part. Prophecy and prophetic authority, the vehicles of revelation, need to be established in order to accept these as a source of truth. But what is thus believed is subject to the further condition that it is not demonstrably false. Only if it is not, does faith extend beyond reason. Hence, neither does reason fully give way to faith nor does faith fully give way to reason. Consequently, for Maimonides religious beliefs are less rational than they are for Averroes and more rational than they are for Aquinas."[632]

Aquinas was the first medieval Christian theologian who allowed even this much room to intellectual demonstrative knowledge in theological realms. He was the first Christian divine who tried to reconcile faith with philosophy, reason with revelation and Aristotle and Plato with Christ, albeit not succeeding fully like Ibn Rushd and Mu'atazilites. Aquinas followed Ibn Rushd's schemes, arguments, ideas and even methodology to at times absorb him but mostly to refute him. Randle Cloud observes that "Aquinas completes the philosophical circuit in that his work was closely influenced by that of Averroes, as both a protagonist and antagonist, but without doubt adopting the method of commentary modeled by Averroes."[633] Fletcher states that "St. Thomas Aquinas, whose achievement it was to show that reason and revelation could co-exist in a Christian philosophy, explicitly cited Averroes no less than 503 times in the course of his work."[634] M. M. Watt argues that "the whole range of [...] European philosophy was deeply indebted to the Arabic writers; and Thomas Aquinas owed just as much to the Aristotelianism of Averroes as did Siger of Brabant [the Latin Averroist and philosophical opponent of Aquinas]."[635] E. Renan then was not too radical in his assessment that Thomas Aquinas was "the first disciple of the Grand Commentator (i.e. Averroes). Albert Magnus owes everything to Avicenna, St. Thomas owes practically everything to Averroes."[636]

E. Gilson would pretty much agree with Renan. He qualified the oft-repeated claims that modern rationalism and scientific inquiry were the products of Italian intellectual revolution with his counter claim that the true rationalism was a product of Averroes' mind. He argued that the pure rationalistic revolution took place in the Muslim Spain long before the Italian Renaissance, stating that "When Averroes died, in 1198, he bequeathed to his successors the ideal of a purely rational philosophy, an ideal whose influence was to be such that, by it, even the evolution of Christian philosophy was to be deeply modified."[637] Gilson argued that Ibn Rushd was an heir to the 9th century Mu'atazilites who endeavoured to reconcile Aristotle with the Quran. The problem for them was "how to think as Aristotle if we believe as Mohammed?"[638] Ibn Rushd's predecessors, such as Ibn Sina, succeeded in solving this difficult problem by crowning natural theology and leaving the door open for supernatural light of revelation. Al-Ghazali used reason to authenticate and substantiate fundamental articles of the Muslim creed, but placed it under the yoke of revelation. The credit of pure rationalism goes to Ibn Rushd who crowned philosophical rationalism even at the expense of tradition or revelation, as seen above. He believed that there was no inherent conflict between true genuine philosophy and theology even though philosophy founded on demonstrative knowledge produced more certitude. Theology was based upon the authority of revelation while philosophy was based upon inductive reasoning. Revelation was directed to the masses while the philosophy was meant for rational thinkers. Though revelation and philosophy both lead to certitude, the philosophical certitude was of higher quality.

The book discussed above, *The Agreement of Religion and Philosophy* or *Decisive Treatise* to Gilson, was "a landmark in the history of western civilisation."[639] Thomas greatly benefitted from Ibn Rushd's overall arguments (not necessarily his arguments in "The Agreement of Religion and Philosophy or Decisive Treatise") and crafted his discussions and arguments accordingly. Gilson sees a parallel between Ibn Rushd and Thomas in that "nothing should enter the texture of metaphysical knowledge save only rational and necessary demonstration. For the same reason, he [Aquinas] even agreed with Averroes that the so-called necessary reasons of so many theologians were merely dialectical probabilities."[640] Majid Fakhry also noted the same similarities by stating that "Averroes wrote one of the most systematic treatises in Arabic on the relation of reason and revelation, or philosophy and religion, entitled the *Decisive Treatise on the Relation of Philosophy and Reason,* in which he dealt with this question in a manner thoroughly comparable to Aquinas's procedure in the opening parts of the *Summa Theologica* (Prima Pars) and his other works. More specifically, in the other theological treatise, the *Exposition of the Methods of Proof,* Averroes' discussion of God's existence, His attributes, His creation of the world, free will and predestination is reminiscent of Aquinas own discussion of these questions in his various scholastic writings. The striking correspondence between their two methods of dealing with this common cluster of questions was not purely coincidental."[641]

Ibn Rushd and Thomas were both heirs to Aristotelian tradition which had reached to Thomas and other Latin scholars, predominantly through the medium of Ibn Rushd. Even though Ibn Rushd's "Decisive Treatise" was not available to Thomas in Latin, his detailed commentaries on Aristotle and other philosophical works were. Ibn Rushd's overall philosophy and theological methodology was variegated throughout his works. Thomas digested Ibn Rushd's overall methodology and incorporated many of his ideas into his project and methodology. That is why the introductory chapters of both his *Summa Theologiae* as well as *Summa Contra Gentiles* bore close resemblance to Ibn Rushd's works. For instance he, like Ibn Rushd, argued for the unity of reason and revelation based upon divine authorship, "that which is introduced into the soul of the student by the teacher is contained in the knowledge of the teacher-unless his teaching is fictitious, which it is improper to say of God. Now, the knowledge of the principles that are known to us naturally has been implanted in us by God; for God is the Author of our nature. These principles, therefore, are also contained by the divine Wisdom. Hence, whatever is opposed to them is opposed to the divine Wisdom, and, therefore, cannot come from God. That which we hold by faith as divinely revealed, therefore, cannot be contrary to our natural knowledge."[642] He also noted that "what is natural cannot change as long as nature does not. Now, it is impossible that contrary opinions should exist in the same knowing subject at the same time. No opinion or belief, therefore, is implanted in man by God which is contrary to man's natural knowledge."[643] Thomas also held that the demonstrative rational arguments were the most authentic and certain of all the arguments; authentic faith could not contradict the rational facts. The "truth that the human reason is naturally endowed to know cannot be opposed to the truth of the Christian faith. For that with which the human reason is naturally endowed is clearly most true; so much so, that it is impossible for us to think of such truths as false. Nor is it permissible to believe as false that which we hold by faith, since this is confirmed in a way that is so clearly divine. Since, therefore, only the false is opposed to the true, as is clearly evident from an examination of their definitions, it is impossible that the truth of faith should be opposed to those principles that the human reason knows naturall."[644] Just like Ibn Rushd, Thomas also argued that the philosophy, wisdom and demonstrative knowledge was the prerogative of a few select people. It needed special aptitude, knowledge, training and was time consuming. That is why the revelation employed mostly rhetorical and dialectical arguments for wider appeal to the masses. "Hence it was necessary for the salvation of man that certain truths which exceed human reason should be made known to him by divine revelation. Even as regards those truths about God which human reason could have discovered, it was necessary that man should be taught by a divine revelation; because the truth about God such as reason could discover, would only be known by a few, and that after a long time, and with the admixture of many errors. Whereas man's whole salvation, which is in God, depends upon the knowledge of this truth. Therefore, in order that the salvation of men might be brought about more fitly and more surely, it was necessary that they should be taught divine truths by divine revelation. It was therefore necessary that besides philosophical science built up by reason, there should be a sacred science learned through revelation."[645]

In his *Summa Contra Gentiles* he elaborated the point in the following words: "Yet, if this truth were left solely as a matter of inquiry for the human reason, three awkward consequences would follow. The first is that few men would possess the knowledge of God. For there are three reasons why most men are cut off from the fruit of diligent inquiry which is the discovery of truth. Some do not have the physical disposition for such work. As a result, there are many who are naturally not fitted to pursue knowledge; and so, however much they tried, they would be unable to reach the highest level of human knowledge which consists in knowing God. Others are cut off from pursuing this truth by the necessities imposed upon them by their daily lives. For some men must devote themselves to taking care of temporal matters. Such men would not be able to give so much time to the leisure of contemplative inquiry as to reach the highest peak at which human investigation can arrive, namely, the knowledge of God. Finally, there are some who are cut off by indolence. In order to know the things that the reason can investigate concerning God, a knowledge of many things must already be possessed. For almost all of philosophy is directed towards the knowledge of God, and that is why metaphysics, which deals with divine things, is the last part of philosophy to be learned. This means that we are able to arrive at the inquiry concerning the aforementioned truth only on the basis of a great deal of labour spent in study. Now, those who wish to undergo such a labour for the mere love of knowledge are few, even though God has inserted into the minds of men a natural appetite for knowledge."[646] He continued, observing that "The second awkward effect is that those who would come to discover the abovementioned truth would barely reach it after a great deal of time. The reasons are several. There is the profundity of this truth, which the human intellect is made capable of grasping by natural inquiry only after a long training. Then, there are many things that must be presupposed, as we have said. There is also the fact that, in youth, when the soul is swayed by the various movements of the passions, it is not in a suitable state for the knowledge of such lofty truth. On the contrary, 'one becomes wise and knowing in repose,' [...] If the only way open to us for the knowledge of God were solely that of the reason, the human race would remain in the blackest shadows of ignorance. For then the knowledge of God, which especially renders men perfect and good, would come to be possessed only by a few, and these few would require a great deal of time in order to reach it."[647] That is why revelation was necessary for a wider appeal and benefit. "That is why it was necessary that the unshakeable certitude and pure truth concerning divine things should be presented to men by way of faith. Beneficially, therefore, did the divine Mercy provide that it should instruct us to hold by faith even those truths that the human reason is able to investigate. In this way, all men would easily be able to have a share in the knowledge of God, and this without uncertainty and error."[648] He also agreed with Ibn Rushd that God was an intellect, and that the highest knowledge and certitude is achieved through intellectual wisdom and truth, "the first author and mover of the universe is an intellect [...] The ultimate end of the universe must, therefore, be the good of an intellect. This good is truth. Truth must consequently be the ultimate end of the whole universe, and the consideration of the wise man aims principally at truth."[649] Pursuit of truth and wisdom granted a share in perfection and beatitude. "Among all human pursuits, the pursuit of wisdom is more perfect, more noble, more useful, and more full of joy. It is more perfect because, in so far as a man gives himself to the pursuit of wisdom, so far does he even now have some share in true beatitude."[650] People were categorised based upon their intellectual categories; philosophy was the climax of intellectual pursuits. "Consider the case of two persons of whom one has a more penetrating grasp of a thing by his intellect than does the other. He who has the superior intellect understands many things that the other cannot grasp at all. Such is the case with a very simple person who cannot at all grasp the subtle speculations of philosophy."[651]

Thomas also believed in a twofold truth theory based upon human intellectual capacities. He stated that "one kind of divine truth the investigation of the reason is competent to reach, whereas the other surpasses every effort of the reason. I am speaking of a 'twofold truth of divine things,' not on the part of God Himself, Who is truth one and simple, but from the point of view of our knowledge, which is variously related to the knowledge of divine things."[652] He also argued that theology was more speculative than philosophy and less demonstrative: "Since this science is partly speculative and partly practical, it transcends all others speculative and practical. Now one speculative science is said to be nobler than another, either by reason of its greater certitude, or by reason of the higher worth of its subject-matter. In both these respects this science surpasses other speculative sciences; in point of greater certitude, because other sciences derive their certitude from the natural light of human reason, which can err; whereas this derives its certitude from the light of divine knowledge, which cannot be misled: in point of the higher worth of its subject-matter because this science treats chiefly of those things which by their sublimity transcend human reason; while other sciences consider only those things which are within reason's grasp. Of the practical sciences, that one is nobler which is ordained to a further purpose, as political science is nobler than military science; for the good of the army is directed to the good of the State. But the purpose of this science, in so far as it is practical, is eternal bliss; to which as to an ultimate end the purposes of every practical science are directed. Hence it is clear that from every standpoint, it is nobler than other sciences."[653] Ibn Rushd had already preceded him in a sort of double truth theory, having argued: "Therefore interpretations ought to be set down only in demonstrative books, because if they are in demonstrative books they are encountered by no one but men of the demonstrative class. But if they are set down in other than demonstrative books and one deals with them by poetical, rhetorical, or dialectical methods, as Abu Hamid [Algazel] does, then he commits an offense against the Law and against philosophy, even though the fellow intended nothing but good. For by this procedure he wanted to increase the number of learned men. But this increased the number of the mischievous, although not without some increase in the number of the learned. As a result, one group came to slander philosophy, another to slander the Law, and another to reconcile the two [...] The imams of the Muslims ought to forbid those of his books which contain learned matter to all save the learned, just as they ought to forbid demonstrative books to those who are not capable of understanding them."[654]

In conclusion we quote Edward Booth, a contemporary authority on Aristotle, who reaffirms the debt of Thomas to Ibn Rushd in the following strong words: "The ontology of Ibn Rushd (Averroes) was, therefore, a greater tributary to the comprehensive ontological figure of Thomas than appears from explicit references, and the critical association of Avicennian and Averroan theses in the *De ente et essential* shows this to have been the case from his earliest writings."[655]

Al-Farabi and Aquinas

Rev. Robert Hammond demonstrates influence of al-Farabi[656] on medieval philosophical thought[657] especially the close resemblance and parallels between him and Thomas. Hammond observes that "St. Thomas describes Being in much the same way. Not only does he unfold the same ideas as those of Alfarabi [sic], but the surprising thing is that the ideas are couched in exactly the same words as those of Alfarabi. A glance at the writings of both Alfarabi and St. Thomas bears this out."[658] He further demonstrates that al-Farabi's division of being into necessary and contingent, along with its definition and vocabulary was taken over by Thomas, just like al-Farabi's division of the beings into potential and actual, and his definitions of potentiality and actuality.[659]

Hammond shows that St. Thomas copied not only the ideas but also the terms, phrases and words from al-Farabi. For instance, the proofs of God's existence through motion, efficient cause and contingency are identical in Al-Farabi and Thomas. Hammond brings the quotations from both al-Farabi and Thomas to show their close affinity. For example, the "Proof of Efficient Cause" in al-Farabi states that "in contemplating the changeable world, one sees that it is composed of beings which have a cause, and this cause, in turn, is the cause of another. Now, in the series of efficient causes it is not possible to proceed to infinity. For, if A were the cause of B, B of C, C of D, and so on, here A would be the cause of itself, which is not admissible. Therefore, outside the series of efficient causes, there must be an uncaused efficient cause, and this is God."[660] Thomas states that "in the world of sense we find there is an order of efficient causes. There is no case known (neither is possible) in which a thing is found to be the efficient cause of itself [...] Now, in efficient causes it is not possible to go on to infinity [...] Therefore, it is necessary to admit a first efficient cause, to which everyone gives the name of God."[661] The proof of contingency is also identical. The cosmological argument of al-Farabi is the same cosmological argument of Thomas.[662] "The proof of an immovable mover by Aristotle, which leads to the conclusion that God is a designer and not a creator, was improved and corrected by Alfarabi nearly three hundred years before St. Thomas was born."[663] Hammond notes that "the proofs of causality and contingence as given by St. Thomas are merely a repetition of Alfarabi's proofs. This is said, not because of any bias against St. Thomas, but rather because this is evident to anyone after studying the works of both Alfarabi and of St. Thomas."[664] Al-Farabi has proven the existence of God from causality. Every changing body has a cause which causes change. The series of causes has to end at an uncaused source of all causes, as the circle cannot go into infinity; that uncaused cause of all causality is God. "An analysis of the proofs adduced by Alfarabi shows how he was able to arrive at their formulation. In each of his three proofs he starts out from a fact, applies a principle, and arrives at the conclusion. The fact is *change, caused being* and *contingence*. The principle is: that which is moved, is moved by another; the effect implies a cause; the contingent implies the necessary. The conclusion is that God exists."[665] Thomas argues on the exact same lines.[666]

Al-Farabi and Thomas's arguments about divine simplicity are also identical. Al-Farabi states that "God is simple because He is free from every kind of composition physical or metaphysical. Physical composition may be either substantial or accidental. It is substantial if the composite substance consists of body and soul, of matter and form. Now, an infinite being cannot be a substantial composite of matter and form, because this would mean that God results from the union of finite parts which would exist before Him in time, and therefore be the cause of His being. Nor can an accidental composition be attributed to the infinite, because this would imply a capacity for an increase in perfection, which the very notion of the infinite excludes. Therefore, there is not and cannot be any physical composition."[667] Thomas says that "there is no composition in God. For, in every composite thing there must needs be act and potentiality [...] But in God there is no potentiality. Therefore, in Him there is no composition [...] Every composite is subsequent to its components. Therefore, the first being, namely God, has no component parts."[668]

Al-Farabi argues that "neither can there be that kind of composition known as metaphysical, which results from the union of two different concepts so referred to the same real thing that neither one by itself signifies the whole reality as meant by their union. Thus, every contingent being is a metaphysical composite of essence and existence. Essence, as such, in reference to a contingent being, implies its conceivableness or possibility, and abstracts from actual existence; while existence, as such, must be added to essence before we can speak of the being as actual. But the composite of essence and existence in a contingent being cannot be applied to the self-existent or infinite being in whom essence and existence are one. Therefore, there is no composition of essence and existence in God. Nor can the composition of genus and difference, implied in the definition of man as a rational animal, be attributed to Him. For, God cannot be classified or defined, as contingent beings can. The reason is because there is not a single aspect in which He is perfectly similar to the finite, and consequently no genus in which He can be included."[669] Thomas states that "existence denotes a kind of actuality [...] Now everything to which an act is becoming, and which is distinct from that act, is related thereto as potentiality to act [...] Accordingly if the divine essence is distinct from its existence, it follows that His essence and existence are mutually related as potentiality and act. Now it has been proved that in God there is nothing of potentiality, and that He is pure act. Therefore God's essence is not distinct from His existence. Wherefore it is likewise evident that God cannot be defined: since every definition is composed of genus and difference."[670]

Concerning divine infinity, al-Farabi observes that "the uncaused being is infinite. For, if He were not, He would be limited, and therefore, caused, since the limit of a thing is the cause of it. But God is uncaused. Hence, it follows that the first being is infinite."[671] Thomas's argument is very similar. "Being itself, considered absolutely, is infinite [...] Hence if we take a thing with finite being, this being must be limited by some other thing which is in some way the cause of that being. Now there can be no cause of God's being, since He is necessary of Himself. Therefore He has infinite being, and Himself is infinite."[672]

Al-Farabi argues that God is immutable because "God as the first cause is pure act, without the admixture of any potentiality, and for this reason He is not subject to any change."[673] Thomas states that "it is shown that God is altogether immutable. First, because it was shown above that there is some first being, whom we call God; and that this first being must be pure act, without the admixture of any potentiality, for the reason that, absolutely, potentiality is posterior to act. Now everything which is in any way changed, is in some way in potentiality. Hence it is evident that it is impossible for God to be in any way changeable."[674]

Al-Farabi argues about divine unity in the following words: "God is only one. For, if there were two gods, they would have to be partly alike and partly different: in which case, however, the simplicity of each would be destroyed. In other words, if there were two gods, there would necessarily have to be some difference and some identity between them; the differential and the common element would constitute the parts of the essence of each one, and these parts, in turn, would be the cause of all; and then, not God, but His parts, would be the first being."[675] Thomas writes that "if there be two things, both of which are of necessity, they must needs agree in the intention of the necessity of being. It follows, therefore, that they must be differentiated by something added either to one or to both of them; and consequently that either one is composite, or both. Now no composite exists necessarily per se. Therefore there cannot possibly be several things each of which exists necessarily; and consequently neither can there be several gods."[676] Al-Farabi further argues that "if there was anything equal to God, then He would cease to be the fullness of being, for fullness implies impossibility of finding anything of its kind. For instance, the fullness of power means inability of finding identical power anywhere else; the fullness of beauty means inability of finding identical beauty. Likewise if the first being possesses the fullness of being, this means that it is impossible to find anyone or anything identical with Him.

Therefore, there is one infinite being, only one God. God is one, because He is free from all quantitative divisions. One means undivided. He who is indivisible in substance is one in essence."[677] Thomas states that "God comprehends in Himself the whole perfection of being. If then many gods existed, they would necessarily differ from each other. Something therefore would belong to one, which did not belong to another [...] So it is impossible for many gods to exist. God is existence itself. Consequently He must contain within Himself the whole perfection of being [...] It follows therefore that the perfection of no one thing is wanting to God. Since one is an undivided being, if anything is supremely one it must be supremely being, and supremely undivided. Now both of these belong to God. Hence it is manifest that God is one in the supreme degree."[678]

Al-Farabi states that "God is intelligent. A thing is intelligent because it exists without matter. Now, God is absolutely immaterial. Therefore, He is intelligent. God knows Himself perfectly. If there is anything that would keep God from knowing Himself, that would certainly be matter. But God is absolutely immaterial. Hence it follows that He knows Himself fully, because His intellect is His essence."[679] Thomas says that "a thing is intelligent from the fact of its being without matter. Now it was shown above that God is absolutely immaterial. Therefore He is intelligent. That which by its nature is severed from matter and from material conditions, is by its very nature intelligible. Now every intelligible is understood according as it is actually one with the intelligent; and God is Himself intelligent, as we have proved. Therefore since He is altogether immaterial, and is absolutely one with Himself, He understands Himself most perfectly."[680]

Al-Farabi further argues "that which by its essence is intellect in act, is, too, by its very essence intelligible in act. Now, the divine intellect is always intellect in act, because if it were not so, then it would be in potentiality with respect to its object; and this is impossible. Just exactly the opposite occurs in man. The human intellect is not always in act. Man knows himself in act after knowing himself potentially. The reason for this is that man's intellect is not his essence. Hence, what he knows does not belong to him by essence."[681] Thomas says that "a thing is actually understood through the unification of the intellect in act and the intelligible in act. Now the divine intellect is always intellect in act [...] Since the divine intellect and the divine essence are one, it is evident that God understands Himself perfectly: for God is both His own intellect and His own essence."[682]

Al-Farabi argues that God knows all things through his knowledge of himself: "It must not be said that God derives His knowledge of things from the things themselves, but rather it must be said that He knows things through His essence. By looking at His essence, He sees everything. Hence, knowing His essence is the cause of His knowing other things."[683] Thomas almost repeats the same argument. "So we say that God sees Himself in Himself, because He sees Himself through His essence; and He sees other things, not in themselves, but in Himself; inasmuch as His essence contains the similitude of things other than Himself."[684]

To al-Farabi God is truth: "Truth follows being, namely, truth and being coincide. But God is the supreme being. Therefore, He is the supreme truth'. Truth is the conformity of the intellect and thing. But in God intellect and object of thought are one and the same."[685] To Thomas God is truth also. "Truth and being are mutually consequent upon one another; since the True is when that is said to be which is, and that not to be, which is not. Now God's being is first and most perfect. Therefore His truth is also first and supreme [...] Truth is in our intellect through the latter being equated to the thing understood. Now the cause of equality is unity. Since then in the divine intellect, intellect and thing understood are absolutely the same, His truth must be the first and supreme truth."[686]

Al-Farabi says that God is life. "Just as we call ourselves living beings, because we have a nature capable of sensation or understanding, in like manner God, whose intellect is His essence, must have life in the most perfect degree."[687] Thomas says the same thing. "Wherefore that being whose act of understanding is its very nature, must have life in the most perfect degree."[688]

It is evident that Thomas's theodicy bears close resemblance with that of al-Farabi; the arguments about God's existence, being and attributes are almost identical in them. There is only one possible explanation; that Thomas and other medieval thinkers must have studied al-Farabi's philosophy, and copied multiple arguments and ideas from him. He wrote his works three centuries before the birth of Thomas. "That Alfarabi's Theodicy exerted a great influence on Medieval thinkers is evident, because, upon comparing the teachings of Alfarabi with those of St. Thomas, we see without doubt the influence of the former on the latter, but not vice versa."[689]

Al-Farabi argues that senses are the transmitters of ideas to intellect. The mind is like tabula rasa. "Every idea comes from sense experience according to the adage: "There is nothing in the intellect that has not first been in the senses." The mind is like a smooth tablet on which nothing is written. It is the senses that do all the writing on it."[690] Thomas almost agrees. "Now, sense is a passive power, and is naturally changed by the exterior sensible. Wherefore the exterior cause of such change is what is directly perceived by the sense, and according to the diversity of that exterior cause are the sensitive powers diversified."[691] About tabula rasa he states that "The human intellect is in potentiality with regard to things intelligible, and is at first like a clean tablet on which nothing is written."[692]

After all these parallels, one is tempted to wonder about the originality of Thomas's metaphysical thought, "we might be tempted to wonder what is properly Aquinas's. As for the implicit citations, we have to acknowledge that all medieval writers did this. Copyright laws were not perceived as they are now. Many ideas were considered to be public property, and no one felt the need to reference his sources. Thomas's strength lies in the fact the he did not simply create a mosaic of all of these sources. What he wrote was his own; his teaching was not mere eclecticism, but an original synthesis."[693]

Thomas did not copy everything from al-Farabi; he picked and chose ideas in accordance with his philosophical needs and paradigms. For instance, he disagreed with al-Farabi on the eternal nature of the world, and agreed with Ibn Rushd and al-Ghazali that the world and matter was created *ex nihilo*. "The eternity of the world and of matter as held by Alfarabi and Avicenna was rejected by Averroes and Maimonides, who taught the 'creatio mundi ex nihilo.' From the latter St. Thomas borrowed the proposition that the world was created from nothing." [694] Thomas and his teacher were also influenced by al-Farabi.[695] "Alfarabi exerted a great influence on medieval thinkers. This is made clear by the fact that Albertus Magnus quotes Alfarabi, and evidently he could not quote him unless he had known his writings. Hence, the knowledge of the works of Alfarabi gave Albertus Magnus and his pupil, St. Thomas, an opportunity to do some sifting in the sense that they were enabled to throw out the theories that conflicted with Christian teaching and take in at the same time those that appeared to them as logically sound and reconcilable with Christianity."[696] In short, Thomas greatly depended upon al-Farabi in his philosophical theology. "In comparing the Theodicy of Alfarabi with that of St. Thomas, we found that the latter depends on the former for the first three arguments proving God's existence, and also for the way in which God's nature is known [...] Furthermore, Alfarabi, three hundred years before St. Thomas, taught in clear and distinct words, that the essence and existence in created things differ as different entities, while they are identical in God. This means that the Saint who came out with the same theory three hundred years later, must certainly have borrowed it from Alfarabi."[697]

Al-Ghazali and Aquinas

Imam al-Ghazali was perhaps the most pronounced Muslim theologian who not only thoroughly studied the Greek and Muslim philosophy, but refuted some of its fundamental concepts based upon its own grounds. For example, using the Avicennian definition of demonstrative logic he reinterpreted causality on occasionalist lines, and showed that there is no logical justification that cause and effect are necessarily always immediately and sequentially interconnected. He began his refutation by asking "whether the philosophers can demonstrate the impossibility of the contradictory of its conclusion, namely, the Ash'arite doctrine that the world is created at that moment of time which the eternal divine will has chosen and decreed for its creation (*Incoherence*, 17). He argues that they can do this neither syllogistically nor by an appeal to what is self-evidently necessary. If the denial of the conclusion cannot be proven to be untrue, then its premise that the divine essential cause necessitates its effect remains unproven."[698] He did not deny that the natural science depends upon the belief that the nature is uniform but he denied the logical, demonstrative underpinnings of such a belief.[699] He was not totally against philosophy, but was against total supremacy of philosophy especially against revelation and theology. He rebutted only those philosophical concepts which he considered incompatible with theology and conflicting authentic revelation; this is the area where he was most relevant and beneficial to Thomas. Al-Ghazali did for Islamic faith and theology what Thomas would do to the Christian faith and theology. Both reconciled theology with philosophy wherever reconciliation was possible but established superiority of revelation in areas of conflict where the conflicting philosophical principles were not categorical. For instance, if the imprecise non-categorical philosophical argument contradicted a faith based probable argument then they favoured the probable faith argument over the probable rational argument on the basis of revelation's divine origin. Their logic being that God's wisdom is higher than a human rational construct which is just possible and not definitive. In this specific area of reconciliation and rebuttal al-Ghazali was a good model to emulate and Thomas greatly benefitted from his endeavours. There are some striking parallels in the methods, arguments, sequences and even conclusions drawn by both philosophically oriented theologians.

Imam al-Ghazali had thoroughly studied Greco-Muslim philosophy and on the way digested, absorbed, embraced and incorporated many philosophical concepts into Islamic theology, jurisprudence and mysticism. His theologico-mystical instincts were a reflection of his re-oriented philosophy, to the extent that these seemingly contradictory sciences tend to complement each other in his scheme of thought. Michael Marmura observes that "this at first sight seems paradoxical, if not downright inconsistent. In fact, he adopted them after reinterpreting them [...] rendering them consistent with his theology. This reinterpretation is not without intrinsic philosophical interest."[700] The so-rationalised theology of al-Ghazali had lasting effects, not only upon the Muslim posterity but also upon the Latin West, as both the Muslim and Christian theologians were facing similar challenges. As seen above, the onslaught of Aristotelian logic and metaphysics along with pure rationalism of Ibn Rushd posed serious challenges to the traditional faith of Christendom. The deep probing of Latin Averroists and their rational inquiries left the biblical faith of the Church in a quandary forcing the Orthodox theologians to look for reconciling revelation with reason. This Latin struggle for intellectual dominion had its precedents in the eighth to ten centuries of Muslim Baghdad when the rational discourse of Muslim philosophers played havoc to the traditional dogmas of the orthodoxy. They forced the orthodoxy to defend its constructs by common-sense reason rather than faith-based miraculous claims. The result was Muslim *Kalam*, the speculative theologians' scholasticism or reconciliation of revelation with Aristotelian philosophy. As discussed in the previous pages, three main groups emerged among the Muslim theologians. The Mu'atazilites utterly rationalised the revelation and went to the extreme left, very close to Muslim philosophers in matters of interpretations. They metaphorically interpreted the Islamic texts whenever in clear conflict with rational premises. Hanbalites went to the extreme right by subjugating reason to the revelation in all its forms, including even the weak reports attributed to Prophet Muhammad. The Asha'rites, especially the later ones, adopted a middle position by reconciling authentic texts with categorical rational arguments, while giving texts with probable denotation preference over philosophical arguments which were not universally agreed upon, because their argumentative force was not scientifically demonstrative but plausible. They placed authentic revelation over and beyond human reason because the source of revelation i.e., God was absolute knowledge and wisdom while the human wisdom was relative. Al-Ghazali marked the climax of this philosophically oriented theological approach. His methodology was congenial to the Latin theologians who were faced with the mounting pressure of the Latin Averroists' rationalism. According to Eugene Myers, "since Al-Ghazali placed science, philosophy, and reason in position inferior to religion and theology, the Scholastics accepted his views, which became characteristic of most medieval philosophy"[701] Al-Ghazali was popular among the orthodox circles of both Muslim and Christian scholastics.

The later Muslim theologians benefitted from al-Ghazali's philosophical synthesis to fight against two extreme fronts; firstly, to resist the increased rationalisation and arbitrary allegorisation of scriptural sources by some Muslim philosophers and secondly, to thwart the ultra-literal anthropomorphic and corporeal tendencies of some orthodox theologians. This two-pronged strategy generated heated responses from both the philosophers and theologians giving al-Ghazali a wide readership among the two otherwise contending groups. While the centre right Asha'rites approved of and disseminated many of al-Ghazali's theological synthesis, the far right orthodox Hunbalites and Zahirites literalists refuted them with full force and religious zeal. The far-left philosophers/Ismailites and centre left philosophers, jurists and theologians such as Ibn Tufayl and Ibn Rushd countered them with equal philosophical, rational and textual vigour though absorbing some of his ideas and views on the way.

Al-Ghazali's ethico-mystical works also generated heated responses.

He, in his *Ihya Ulum al Din* (Revival of the Religious Sciences), insisted that the real spiritual essence of Islamic sciences was mortified due to worldly propensities of Muslim theologians and jurists. The theologians engaged in debates to put their opponents down for the sake of publicity. The jurists interpreted and twisted Islamic law to accommodate geo political realities and personal whims and group interests of the ruling regimes. The spiritual message and ethical contours of Islamic sciences were missing due to political designs of jurists and theologians. The sciences of theology and Islamic law were meant to be means to the ultimate goal of salvation in the life to come, but they became a distraction to the otherworldliness of the Islamic message. Therefore, the Islamic sciences needed real revival. He placed the spiritual sciences above and beyond the worldly sciences and incorporated certain aspects of Aristotelian ethics and Neoplatonic cosmology into his spiritual scheme, contending that these worldly Islamic sciences related to Muslim practices must be subjugated to the otherworldly mystical sciences of ethical dimensions. The daily prayers and outward practices must be used to purify inner intentions, reforming the ego and purging blameworthy traits, replacing them with praiseworthy habits. Al-Ghazali's shrill criticism of orthodox theologians and jurists was offensive to them, and they reacted with equal harshness. Consequently, al-Ghazali's philosophical, theological and ethical works were all discussed, debated, absorbed, accepted and rejected in his life time and soon after his death both in the Muslim East as well as the Muslim West.

Al-Ghazali was widely known and read in the Muslim West (North Africa and Spain) just 30 years after his death- so much so that the ultra-right Qadhi Abu Abdullah Muhammad ibn Hamdin of Cordova (d. 1114), along with a host of other Muslim leaders, had to issue a religious edict banning his books partly due to political reasons.[702] Orthodox theologians and jurists were the backbone of the Almoravid dynasty in North Africa and Spain. Their opponents adopted al-Ghazali's lines to critic the jurists' alliance with Almoravids' political agenda; his mystical ideas were used to create a new Sufi (mystical) identity and otherworldly group consciousness, in opposition to the worldly traits of semi-official jurists.[703] Al-Ghazali became the bone of contention between the pro regime jurists, theologians and philosophers and their Sufi opponents. He was especially embraced by Ibn Tumart (1080-1130), the Berber theologian of southern Morocco and the founder of Almohad dynasty, who fought the ruling Almoravids using al-Ghazali's ideas and books. Al-Ghazali's works were banned, confiscated, publicly burnt and destroyed all over Muslim Spain, with the threat of property confiscation and even death. The Almoravid Sultan of Morocco Ali ibn Yusuf ibn Tashifin (1084-1142) ordered burning and confiscation of al-Ghazali's books all over North Africa.[704] These drastic steps on the part of the highest religious and political authorities in the Muslim West indicate the level of popularity of his works among the Muslim populace and its perceived dangers. Later on, the Almoravids were forced to align themselves with al-Ghazali's mystical ideas and own him as a result of his sheer popularity. The later Almoravid caliphs tried to co-opt al-Ghazali and popularise his works to win mass approval, but it was too late.[705] The Almohad killed their Caliph Ishaq ibn Ali in 1147 and took control of both Morocco and Spain. Al-Ghazali's works and ideas travelled like a wildfire all over the Muslim West, including the Muslim community of Sicily. Throughout the life of Almohad dynasty (1121-1269) al-Ghazali remained the most popular Muslim figure in the Muslim West as he was already famous in the Muslim East. This complex love-hate relationship popularised al-Ghazali's works and ideas all over the Muslim world. Oriental Christians, Latin Christians in the Holy Lands, Spain and Sicily and the Jewish community from Spain to Jerusalem closely followed these debates, as they reflected the very real challenges they faced in their own traditions. Oriental Christians and Jewish philosophers, theologians and moralists assimilated many of al-Ghazali's ideas and works into their faith traditions. Ibn Rushd's refutation of al-Ghazali's "Incoherence of Philosophers" and Moses Maimonides' partial acceptance and partial rejection of his ideas resulted in increased publicity for al-Ghazali. That is why some of his works were among the very first translated in Toledo from Arabic to Latin. The Christian West was partially introduced to al-Ghazali especially the philosopher al-Ghazali through the Latin and Hebrew translations as well as through oral transmissions and the interactions of Oriental Christians, Jews and Latin Arabists with his works.

The thirteenth-century Christian West of Thomas got quite familiar with the works of al-Ghazali as most of his books were rendered into Latin as early as the 12th century. H. N. Rafiabadi notes that "now it has been established beyond any shade of doubt that Ghazali's original works on almost all subjects ranging from theology to philosophy were translated into Latin and Hebrew languages, starting from about forty years after Ghazali's death. In this way Sir Thomas Arnold, Gullaume, Rom Landau, W. Wolfson, Ben Ami Scharfstein, Nicholaus of Autrea-Court, W. J. Countary are of this opinion that Ghazali's books were available from Twelfth-Thirteenth-Century A. D. onwards."[706] Thomas Arnold and Alfred Guillaume noted that "His books on logic, physics, and metaphysics became known through the translators of Toledo in the twelfth century."[707] Frank Griffel notes that "The Doctrines of the Philosophers was translated into Latin in the third quarter of the 12th century and into Hebrew first in 1292 and at least another two times within the next fifty years. These translations enjoyed much more success than the Arabic original; in fact, in the Latin as well as in the Hebrew traditions they overshadowed all of al-Ghazâlî's other writings. The Latin translation, sometimes referred to as *Logica et philosophia Algazelis* [...] was translated by Dominicus Gundisalivi (Gundissalinus, d. *c.* 1190) of Toledo in collaboration with someone referred to as "Magister Iohannes" (d. 1215), also known as Iohannes Hispanus (or Hispalensis), probably an Arabised Christian (a Mozarab), who was dean at the cathedral of Toledo in the 1180s and 1190s"[708] S. Harvey explains that "The Maqasid was one of Alghazali's very first important works, written in Baghdad shortly before his famous departure from the city in 1095. The book was written to offer a clear exposition of the philosophy of Aristotle as it was explicated by the two philosophers Alghazali respected the most-Alfarabi and especially Avicenna. As is well known, Alghazali presented the teachings of his distinguished predecessors, and indeed endeavoured to improve upon them, only in order to refute them."[709] *Maqasid al Falasifah* found tremendous success in the medieval Europe both in the Jewish[710] and Christian circles and became an integral part of Latin canon of philosophy. It served as a primer to the Arabic philosophy which in turn was essential to understand Greek philosophy. It became Latin Christendom's doorway to the thirteen centuries of philosophical wisdom.[711]

In addition to Maqasid al-Falasifah, Ghazali's other works were also widely consumed through partial translations, assimilations, argumentations, refutations, appropriations and verbal transmissions. There were several channels through which Thomas could have had direct access to some of al-Ghazali's works which were not yet translated to Latin. Firstly, his contemporary Raymond Martini, a fellow

Dominican Friar and theologian, was an expert in Oriental languages, including Arabic.[712] As discussed above, he was a missionary in Spain and Tunis and spent long years in a monastery in Barcelona. Al-Ghazali was well-consumed in Tunis, Spain and Sicily from the 1130s onward. Marti compiled his main work *Pugio Fidei* (The Dagger of Faith) mainly to refute the philosophers' arguments against the Omniscience of God, creation ex-nihilo, immortality of the soul and resurrection of the dead. Al-Ghazali had already thoroughly exhausted these discussions in his Tahafut al-Falasifah which Raymond had access to. Raymond readily copied al-Ghazali's arguments for God's knowledge of particulars against the philosophers' claims that God knew only the universals, his arguments against the eternity of the world and for creation ex-nihilo, arguments for immortality of the soul and resurrection of the dead. Charles Burnett has noted that Raymond quoted from many other books of al-Ghazali in addition to his Tahafut, "in Barcelona, Ram'on Marti (ca. 1220–ca. 1285) was drawing on a wide range of Arabic philosophical texts: in his *Pugio Fidei* he cites (aside from those works already well known in the Latin) al- Farabi's commentary on the *Physics*, Avicenna's *Kitab al-isharat wa al-tanbiht* and *Kitab al-najat*, al-Razi's *Shukuk 'ala¯ Jalinus* (*Doubts about Galen*), al-Ghazali's *Tahafut*, *al-Munqidh min al-dalal*, *Mizan al-'amal*, *al-Mishkat al-anwar*, *Ihya' 'ulum al-din*, *Kitab al-tawba* and *al-maqsad al-asna fi asm 'Allah al-husna*, as well as Averroes' *Tahafut al-tahafut* and *al-damima*."[713] This comprehensive list shows that Marti was immersed in the main works of al-Ghazali, al-Razi and Ibn Rushd. He was well aware of al-Ghazali's refutations of the Muslim Aristotelians and Ibn Rushd's refutations of al-Ghazali's rebuffs. Rafiabadi showed how Raymond "reproduces all the arguments of al-Ghazali's Tahafut along with his own. In both of his books he freely quotes from Ihya, Mizan al Amal, and Tahafut and other works."[714] R. E. Abu Shanab highlighted "the manner in which Ghazali's works have played a role in the shaping of the philosophic ideas of Aquinas. As early as the twelfth century, Ghazali's books were translated chiefly in Toledo into Latin and from the outset exercised an influence on the Christian and Jewish thinkers of the Medieval period. Foremost among the Christian scholars who extensively studied the works of Ghazali was the Dominican Raymund Marti (d. 1285) of the Toledo school. According to one author, Raymund Marti was thoroughly familiar with a number of Ghazali's works such as Maqasid, Tahafut, Mizan al Amal ('The Criterion of Action'), Ihya Ulum ad-Din ('The Revival of the Religious Sciences'), and al-Munqidh min ad-Dalal ('Deliverance from Error'). Raymund Marti in his *Pugio Fidei* ('The Dagger of Faith') incorporates many of Ghazali's philosophic ideas into his book. For instance, Marti's views on the doctrines of creation *ex nihilo*, God's knowledge of the particulars and not just the universals, immortality of the soul, etc., are similar to those of Ghazali's. It has been attested by scholars that St. Thomas Aquinas, who was Raymund Martin's contemporary, borrowed a number of his ideas from the *Pugio Fidei*. "[715] George Sarton has long ago identified the parallels between Marti and Aquinas. "His (Marti's) best known work was the 'Dagger of Faith,' a dagger pointed against the hearts of Jews and Muslims; many parts of it have been identified with passages of St. Thomas's *Summa contra gentiles*."[716]

As discussed above, Marti is reported to have compiled the first part of his *Pugio* in 1250's when he was thoroughly engaged with Islam. His other two books against Islam were completed by 1267 long before completions of Thomas's two Summas. Marti and a host of other Dominican Arabists were the main sources of Thomas's access to the unpublished works of Muslim philosophers and theologians, including al-Ghazali. S. M. Gazanfer noted that Raymond's works "inspired St. Thomas's *Summa contra Gentiles*. Both of these treatises were written at the request of the Dominican order and were aimed at refuting the arguments of philosophers and sophists against faith."[717] M. M. Sharif explained that "Palacios traces the development of al-Ghazali's ideas in the West as follows. The Spanish Dominican monk Raymond Martini, who was Bar Hebraeus' contemporary, borrowed the same ideas from him and from al-Ghazali. Instead of profiting only by the books of Muslim 'philosophers,' he, unlike the scholastics, directly profited by al-Ghazali's texts in his books entitled *Pugio Fidei* and *Explanalio Symboli,* written in the field of religion. These texts were taken from *Tahafut, Maqasid, al-Munqidh. Mizan, Maqsad, Mishkal al-Anwar* and *Ihya'*. According to Palacios, the benefit derived here is more substantial than Bar Hebraeus' adaptations which he had made without mentioning any source, for the arguments have been taken exactly as they were in the original.[718] James W. Sweetman showed that Raymond Marti's views about God's knowledge of particulars, creation ex-nihilo, immortality of the soul and its ultimate felicity and beatitude run parallel to al-Ghazali.[719] Jules Janssens noted that "Marti introduces the titles of a few of al-Ghazali's works previously unknown in the Latin world. But that isn't all: Marti also presents new ideas absent in the *Maqāṣid al-falāsifa*, the only work with which the vast majority of the major Latin scholastics were familiar. Especially in the *Pugio* [...] Marti offers – in Latin translation – quotations and paraphrases of different Ghazalian texts, among which the *Munqidh* and, although to a lesser extent, the *Tahāfut*, figure pre-eminently. These translated fragments offer an intriguing picture of the 'critical' attitude (above all, towards philosophy) that is so typical of al-Ghazali."[720] The list of al-Ghazali's works consumed by Marti indicates that he was indebted to al-Ghazali, not only in philosophy but also in theology and mysticism. Margaret Smith notes al-Ghazali's spiritual influence upon Marti in the following words: "Among Christian writers who made a special study of Islamic teaching and made use of it in their own writings was the Dominican Raymond Martin (or Marti), a-Catalonian, who lived for a considerable time in Barcelona and died sometime after 1284. He was chosen out to study Oriental languages, for the purpose of missionary work among Muslims and Jews. In his *Explanatio Simboli* and his *Pugio Fidei* he quotes from al-Ghazali's Maqasid al-Falasifa, his Ihya and his Mizan al-'Amal, in each case to skew how al-Ghazali affirms that the joy of knowing God and of contemplating Him face to face is the most glorious and excellent of all joys. In his description of the ultimate Beatitude, he refers to the chapter in the Mizan, where al-Ghazali states that the true beatitude is the final state of the Blessed. Comparing it with other forms of happiness, al-Ghazali points out that wealth in the form of dirhams and dinars, even though they may serve to satisfy all needs, are but as pebbles beside it. The good, he writes, can be divided into the beneficial, the beautiful and the enjoyable, but these qualities, when related to earthly goods, are transient and shared with the lower creation, but the Beatitude of God's elect is a spiritual thing, abiding, unchangeable, a joy forever, for it consists in the Presence of the Eternal and the contemplation of His everlasting glory, Raymond Martin, therefore, takes al-Ghazali, among other Muslim writers, as his authority for the view that the joy of the Hereafter is a purely spiritual joy, and as such, above all sensual joys."[721] Jules Janssens shows close parallels between Ghazali and Marti in that they "identified eternal happiness with knowledge of God."[722] Later on we will see Aquinas incorporating the same into his treatment of the Beatitude. Janssens went on to show close resemblance, verbatim parallels and links between al-Ghazali and Marti's works.[723] Marti was truly indebted to al-Ghazali in philosophy, theology and ethics, and Thomas in turn was indebted to Marti in many aspects related to these very areas.

Sharif and Janssens observed that many passages of Thomas's *Summa Contra Gentiles* were identical to Raymond's *Pugio Fidei*.[724] Thomas, who did not hesitate to quote directly from al-Ghazali, on the other hand indirectly benefitted a great deal from works of al-Ghazali through the intermediary writings of Raymond Marti, especially in the areas of defending faith and revelation against the onslaught of Aristotelian sophists as well as genuine philosophers. The same can be said about al-Ghazali's ethical writings; there are clear parallels between al-Ghazali's ethico-spiritual teachings and Thomas's moral anthology. Detailed discussions of virtues and Beatitude are just one example of such a convergence.

The second channel of transmission was the Syriac Bishop Abu al Farj (Abulpharagius) Gregory Bar Hebraeus (1226 – 30 July 1286), an erudite Orthodox Bishop known for his encyclopaedic works in theology, philosophy, history, physics and metaphysics.[725] A. J. Wensinck in "Bar Hebraeus's Book of the Dove" has "demonstrated that Bar Hebraeus was a close student of al-Ghazali and modelled his mystical treatises on the Ihya, not only in arrangement but in ideas and expressions. He used, in fact, al-Ghazali for the mystical life as he had used Ibn Sina for Aristotle. It is not surprising that he should have accepted the philosophical and scientific guidance of a Moslem but that he should have extended his discipleship to the ruling and development of the religious life is almost startling and suggests how close must have been the contact between the intellectual minds of the time... Bar Hebraeus, who knew the Ihya so well, must surely have read the Munqidh, yet apparently, he never mentions its author who had died 167 years eariler."[726] M. Nesim Doru, in *The Influence of Islamic Philosophy on Bar Hebraeus*,[727] demonstrated that "Bar Hebraeus was greatly influenced by Avicenna's and Tusi's philosophical works. Yet, it was al-Ghazali's works that had more influence on him with respect to morality. This is well demonstrated in Bar Hebraeus' *Itiqon* (ܐܬܝܩܘܢ) and the *The Book of Dove* (ܝܘܢܐ ܟܬܒܐ)."[728] Hidemi Takahashi in his *The Influence of al-Ghazali on the Juridical, Theological and Philosophical Works of Bar-*

hebraeus,[729] has shown that the influence of al-Ghazali on Bar Hebraeus was far greater than morality. He elaborated "the not insignificant extent to which Barhebraeus depended on al-Ghazali in composing his works. One factor which Barhebraeus found attractive about al-Ghazalis writings was without doubt the clear, systematic presentation of the material he found in many of them. This would have been the case especially when he turned to the legal handbooks of al-Ghazali as the source for his *Book of Directions*; Barhebraeus' selection of al-Ghazali's *Maqāṣid al-falāsifa*, rather than the often more discursive works of Ibn Sīnā himself, as the principal source of his *Treatise of Treatises* may be explained in the same way. Similarly, it was no doubt the comprehensive and rational treatment of the material in the *Iḥyā' 'ulūm ad-dīn* that inspired and prompted Barhebraeus to use this work as the source in composing a new type of work which had no precedent in his own Syriac tradition."[730] He further noted that "Barhebraeus not only used al-Ghazali's works to provide a structure around which to build his writings, but also borrowed and transferred the contents of large portions of them into his works. For Barhebraeus to borrow as much as he did, he must have agreed with much of al-Ghazali had said, and found what he saw in al-Ghazali's writings congenial and convenient for his purposes. It is significant that Barhebraeus, as a learned leader of a Christian community, could borrow so much from a leading scholar of the Islamic sciences, not only in matters pertaining to the secular sciences but also in matters that lay at the core of his religious activities. This convergence tells us much about what the two religious traditions represented by these two men share in common."[731]

After a thorough comparison of al-Ghazali's Ihya Ulum al-Din and Bar Hebraeus's Itiqon, Doru concluded that "there is a similarity between Bar Hebraeus' and al-Ghazali's works in terms of structure. Although topics are examined under different titles, it is clear that Bar Hebraeus took al-Ghazali's *Ihya ' al-'ulu m al-din* as a model not only in structure and titles, but also in content. In this regard, it is possible to compare almost every title of the two books."[732] Bar Hebraeus garbed and transferred the Islamic concepts and contents into Christian vocabulary and images for the consumption of common Christian believers. His indebtedness to al-Ghazali's works is clear from minute details such as given examples, imagery, poetry and prayer formulas, but he never referenced al-Ghazali as his source. [733]

Bar Hebraeus's works were known to Latin monks especially in the Latin Levant. Raymond Marti, a contemporary of Bar Hebraeus, benefitted from his works, but Raymond's direct benefit from al-Ghazali's works was far greater as Asin Palacios has demonstrated. Thomas was the indirect beneficiary. Brian E. Cossell observed that Bar Hebraeus "reproduced the experience of Islam's AI-Ghazali (1058-1111), and anticipated that of Catholicism's Thomas Aquinas."[734] After analysing the fundamental contributions of Syrian Christians in transmission of Greek philosophy to Muslim Baghdad and transmission of Muslim sciences, including mysticism to the Latin West, Cossell stated that "when we recall the Arabic philosophic ideas and the erotic imagery of the Sufis reflected in the works of Dante, and the beatific vision shared by Al-Ghazali, Bar Hebraeus, and Thomas Aquinas, it is difficult to maintain that there was no mutual influence."[735] The influence could have been indirect. He concluded that "the ideas and features of Syrian, Muslim and Catholic mysticism touch one another so closely that it is difficult to deny any interaction among them."[736] These close interactions took place in the Holy Lands, North Africa and even in Latin West.[737]

The third channel was Moses Maimonides and other Jewish theologians and philosophers who greatly consumed al-Ghazali's both theologico-philosophical and ethical works. The tremendous Islamic influences upon Maimonides and in turn his influence upon Thomas are historical facts widely accepted by the scholarship active in the field.[738] Shlomo Pines,[739] Hava Lazarus-Yafeh,[740] Herbert Davidson,[741] Binyamin Abrahamov,[742] Amira Eran, Charles Manekin and Steven Harvey are just a few names to be mentioned.[743] They "have noted similarities between al-Ghazali's teachings and those of Maimonides in the *Guide*, or – in a few cases – argued for the direct influence of al-Ghazali upon the *Guide* with regard to particular points. Among the subjects of influence noted are the idea of particularization (*takhṣīṣ*), the treatment of knowledge of God, creation of the world, the World-to-Come and spiritual pleasures, the passionate love (*'ishq*) of God, and al-Ghazali's attempt to reconcile Islam and Sufism. The suggested texts of al-Ghazali are the *Tahāfut*, the *Maqāṣid*, and the *Ihyā*'"[744] Avner Giladi has "argued that the very title of the *Guide, Dalālat al-ḥā'irīn*, is borrowed from al-Ghazali's *Ihyā*', where the words *dalīl al-mutaḥayyirīn* ("the guide of the perplexed") occur at least twice, each time as an attribute of God."[745] Harvey noted that "although the evidence is mounting for al-Ghazali's influence on the *Guide*, little attempt has been made to investigate the extent of the parallels and similarities between al-Ghazali's philosophical thought and that of Maimonides. Some scholars are beginning to point at the direction such a study may take. Davidson, for example, has recently gone so far as to claim that ' virtually everything of a metaphysical character attributed by Maimonides to Aristotle but actually deriving from Avicenna can be found' in the *Maqāṣid*. The recent research on the influence of Avicenna on Maimonides has, I believe, prepared the way for an in-depth study of al-Ghazali's influence on the *Guide*."[746] Davidson has gone further than that in stating that "there are, moreover, striking similarities between what Maimonides writes, for example, in *Guide for the Perplexed* 2.4, and Ghazali's *Maqasid al-Falasifa* 209-21."[747]

Maimonides was particularly attracted to al-Ghazali's ethical works,[748] "Maimonides was also interested in al-Ghazali's *Iḥyā'*, that is in al-Ghazali, the religious scholar, in ways in which he was not interested in Avicenna."[749] Steven Harvey's "Al-Ghazali and Maimonides and Their Books of Knowledge" is a fantastic study of parallels between Ghazali and Maimmonides' treatment of knowledge. The "study followed the lead of Boaz Cohen and Franz Rosenthal. Cohen in a 1934 article had claimed Maimonides 'was able to produce such a remarkable Code because he brought to it a mind thoroughly trained in the law and theology of the Arabs.' For Rosenthal, most of the contents of Maimonides' *Book of Knowledge* "can be read as a summary in miniature of al-Ghazzālī's [*sic*] *Iḥyā*'" This influence of al-Ghazali on Maimonides' legal writings probably escaped the attention of the post-Maimonidean Jewish philosophers who did not read Arabic and who were not interested in al-Ghazali as a legal scholar, some of whom were quite convinced of al-Ghazali's influence on Maimonides' philosophical teachings. They were [...] for the most part, interested in al-Ghazali as a philosopher and/or as a critic of philosophy. Nonetheless, for a complete picture of the impact of al-Ghazali on Maimonides, further research on the influence of al-Ghazali's legal teachings upon Maimonides, such as that of Gideon Leibson over the past two decades, is needed."[750] Gideon has illustrated the tremendous influence Muslim legal tradition had upon Maimonides.[751]

Amira Eran, in *Al-Ghazali and Maimonides on the World to Come and Spiritual Pleasures*, shows that Maimonides closely followed and verbally copied many passages, examples, concepts and even words from al-Ghazali.[752] Al-Ghazali had "direct influence on Maimonides in this instance."[753] Eran's comprehensive study of striking parallels between al-Ghazali and Maimonides leaves no room to doubt that Maimonides was thoroughly influenced by al-Ghazali's ethical works. He amalgamated his Jewish religious tradition with the philsoph-ico-theological interpretations of al-Ghazali and Ibn Sina to create an aspired rational synthesis. Sarah Stroumsa has elaborated the type of manoeuvring Maimonides was able to do by imitating the Mus-lim scholars to camouflage his philosophical radicalism. He was no "longer focused on the Jewish tradition" and came remarkably close to Muslim Ibn Sina and al-Ghazali.[754] Maimonides' influence on Thomas is well documented.[755]

Lastly, Thomas's indebtedness to Ibn Rushd is amply demonstrated in the previous chapters. Ibn Rushd had directly read, discussed and refuted al-Ghazali in three of his works, namely Tahafut al-Tahafut, Fasl al-Maqal and Minhaj al-Adillah. He had quoted al-Ghazali verbatim in his *Tahafut al Tahafut al-Falasifah* (Incoherence of Incoherence of Philosophers) to refute him thoroughly. Therefore, all important as-pects of al-Ghazali's theology, philosophy and ethics were present in the books of Ibn Rushd which were widely translated into Latin and Hebrew. Thomas had access to many of these works through full Latin translations, partial translations via Marti and other Dominican Ara-bists and through Maimonides. Thomas was also heir to an oral tra-dition which transmitted Ghazali's works to Latin Christendom. Asin Palacios, Harry Austryn Wolfson, Hans Daiber and others have noticed that there was a wide range oral tradition of Arabic Latin translations and transmission among the missionaries working in the Holy Land, North Africa, Spain and Sicily through which they supplied their Latin compatriots with Muslim knowledge, ideas and discussions especially for collective missionary and apologetic works. There was a good num-ber of Arabists among the active missionaries in the Muslim lands as well as their superiors in the Dominican and Franciscan orders. Daiber wrote: "Most studies discuss the echo of Ghazali's writings and thought in Thomas Aquinas. It has been remarked that they might become known to Thomas Aquinas partly also through Maimonides (1137/8–1204/5), whose 'Guide of the Perplexed'(*More Nevukim*) was translated into Latin about 1233 at the court of Frederick II. The same possibility must also be taken into account with regard to Albertus Magnus, whose recourse to Ghazali has been considered by Angel Cortabarria Beita, without, however, making a precise identification of the sources. H. A. Wolfson defended the thesis, that even before the Latin translation of Ibn Rushd's refutation the *Tahāfut al-falāsifa* by Ghazali was known from a Latin translation; this can be proven from a passage in Albertus Magnus and from the criticism of causality by Bernard of Arezzo and Nicolaus of Autrecourt [...] In single cases scholars have pointed here at the possibility of an oral transmission or at the phenomen of "convergence" because of "analogous preconditions".[756]

H. A. Wolfson, in his article *Nicolaus of Autrecourt and Ghazali's Argument against Causality*,[757] has shown that "a knowledge of Ghazali's *Tahafut al-Falasifah* was somehow available to Latin Schoolmen long before the Latin translation of Averroes' *Tahafut al-Tahafut* in 1328... that the example of the burning of flax mentioned by Bernard in his argument for causality and by Ghazali in his refutation of the argument is based upon passages in Ghazali's *Tahafut al-Falasifah*."[758] Wolfson further argued that "a knowledge of Ghazali's *Tahafut al Falasifah* had been available to the Schoolmen long before the 1328 Latin translation of Averroes' *Tahafut al- Tahafut* can be shown by a passage in Albertus Magnus's Commentary on Aristotle's *Physics* [...] Albertus could not have known that the anonymous Mutakallim referred to by Maimonides was Ghazali unless he had a knowledge of the *Tahafut al-Falasifah*. So also, we may assume, both Bernard and Nicolaus could have had a knowledge of the *Tahafut al-Falasifah*, even if the 1328 Latin translation of Averroes' work had not yet reached them."[759] Though it could be argued that similarities in doctrine do not automaticlly imply direct influence.

Scholars like Robert Chazan, Benjamin Kedar, Robert I. Burns and John Tolan's detailed accounts of Dominican and Franciscan missionary zeal,[760] Raymond of Penyafort, Raymond Marti and other Dominicans' missionary works, some Dominican and Franciscan friars' proficiency in Arabic, their international missions and interactions especially during Crusades, their pursuit of Islamic philosophy, theology and spirituality for conversionary purposes and their role in Papal and monarchical diplomacy and politics, all substantiate the fact that there were ample communications and interactions between the Muslims, Dominicans, Franciscans etc. on the one hand and between the Eastern Orthodox, Jacobite Syrians, Maronites, Coptics and Latin Christians on the other hand. There were exchanges of all sorts of ideas and materials during the productive thirteenth century. Therefore Wolfson, Daiber, Palacios and others' contention that there was an oral tradition transmitting many philosophical, theological, moral and legal ideas and works from the Muslim East and Spain to Latin West even before or alongside the translation renaissance of the twelfth century are substantiated by historical proofs. The presence of such an oral tradition very well illustrates the fact that some passages of Ghazali's Tahafut and Ibn Rushd's refutation *Tahafutal Tahafut* got to Albert Magnus and others even before its Latin translations. Same happened with al-Ghazali's *Ihya* and other works through Raymond Marti, Hebraeus, Maimonides and other Christian Arabists.

Therefore, Thomas had ample opportunities to directly and indirectly read, understand, absorb, digest, act and react to al-Ghazali's main works. Al-Ghazali was perhaps the most relevant figure to the synthetic project of Thomas, and he admittedly consumed him a great deal. Ghazali's overall influence upon the theologico-moral thought of Aquinas is as great, if not greater, as his philosophical explanatory treatise *Maqasid al- Falasifah.* Aquinas is highly indebted to al-Ghazali in philosophy, theology and ethics with the exception of pure Christian dogmatic theology. Rafiabadi maintains that "the greatest of the Christian writers who was influenced by Ghazali was St. Thomas Aquinas."[761] Asin Palacios and D. B. Macdonald have elaborated how deeply the overall system of Thomas was effected by al-Ghazali.[762] Sharif noted that "St. Thomas used some texts of al-Ghazali's in *Contra Gentiles* either directly or through the mediation of Raymond Martini. Al-Ghazali's arguments in favour of the *creatio ex nihilo,* his proof that God's knowledge comprises particulars, and his justification of the resurrection of the dead were adopted by many scholastics including St. Thomas. St. Thomas, who had received his education from the Dominican order in the University of Naples, had known al-Ghazali's philosophy well, and used his arguments in attacks on Aristotelianism. St. Thomas's *Summa Theologica* and al-Ghazali's treatise on the place of reason as applied to revelation and theology run parallel in many places in their arguments and conclusions. Both of them claimed to have found happiness in the beatific vision, and both stated the case of their opponents fairly before pronouncing their own judgments on it. The questions on which St. Thomas seems to have been deeply influenced by al-Ghazali are the ideas of contingency and necessity as proving the existence of God, divine knowledge, divine simplicity, divine names, and divine attributes, God's speech a *perbum mentis,* the miracles as a testimony to the truth of prophecies, and resurrection of the dead."[763]

Aquinas and Al-Ghazali's Moral Synthesis

In the previous pages, we had the opportunity to discuss some of the above sketched topics and Thomas's indebtedness to Muslim theologians, especially to al-Ghazali's synthesis. Here we will draw a few parallels to show the nature and extent of this indebtedness. For instance, al-Ghazali refutes, with multiple arguments, the philosophers' claims that God knows only the universals because knowledge of particulars will cause change in God and change is against divine transcendental perfection.[764] Al-Ghazali argues the opposite: "For His perfection consists in that He knows all the things. Should we have a knowledge of all temporal phenomena, it would be a sign of perfection, not of deficiency or subjugation, on our part. The same may be true of God."[765] Thomas uses the same argument with little modifications. "God knows singular things. For all perfections found in creatures pre-exist in God in a higher way [...] Now to know singular things is part of our perfection. Hence God must know singular things [...] Now the perfections which are divided among inferior beings, exist simply and unitedly in God; hence, although by one faculty we know the universal and immaterial, and by another we know singular and material things, nevertheless God knows both by His simple intellect."[766]

Many scholars have found parallels between al-Ghazali's moral anthology *Ihya Ulum al-Din* and Thomas's *Summa Theologiae.* Both were pious believers who reconciled faith teachings with philosophy to enhance piety. Their treatment of morality was primarily theological.[767] Ghazali thought about moral questions in light of God, revelation, grace, worship, man and salvation.[768] Aquinas did the same without resorting to resolving moral philosophical dilemmas through theological claims, as was common with some of his contemporaries. Both instead strove to provide a broader and more profound treatment of underlying theological contexts, meanings and foundations of the moral teachings. Both were interested in philosophy and theology as preludes to proper ethics. Ghazali clearly indicated this in the *Muqaddimah* or *Khutbah* of his *Ihya.*[769] "Knowledge by means of which one progresses toward the afterlife (*al-'ilm alladhī yutawajjahu bihī ilā l-ākhira*) is divided into *'ilm al-mu'āmala* and *'ilm al-mukāshafa*. I mean by *'ilm al-mukāsha-fa* [the kind of knowledge] that aims only at the disclosure of the object of knowledge (*kashf al-ma'lūm faqat.*). I mean by *'ilm al-mu'āmala* [the kind of knowledge] that in addition to disclosure [of the object of knowledge] seeks to put it into practice (*ma'a l-kashf al-'amal bi-hī*)."[770] Alexander Treiger notes that "this division is modeled after the Aristotelian division of philosophy (and consequently of the sciences) into practical and theoretical (contem plative). In Aristotelian terms, sciences that aim at the acquisition of knowledge for the sake of putting it into practice are called practical (*'ulūm 'amalīya*), while those that aim solely at the knowledge of truth are called theoretical (*'ulūm naz. arīya*). This is precisely the distinction between *'ilm al-mu'āmala* and *'ilm al-mukāshafa*."[771] Therefore al-Ghazali's book Ihya was essentially a book of Islamic ethics. "It can be seen that the science of practice is essentially a religious ethics with a pronounced element of *askesis* ("training" of the soul). It focuses on the ethical aspects of religious and social life (vols 1–2), and on combating one's vices, cultivating the virtues, and developing proper religious attitudes, such as renunciation of the world, patience and thankfulness to God, reliance on God (*tawak-kul*), and mindfulness of death and the afterlife (vols 3–4)."[772]

Stephen Pope noted the same about Aquinas. "The *Secunda pars*, then, is not, and was never intended to be, a self-contained moral theory of the sort constructed by modern moral philosophers. Aquinas was a theologian who thought about moral questions in light of God, grace, and sacraments; he was not a professional ethicist merely drawing upon theological claims to resolve moral dilemmas. Standard treatments of ethics in Thomas's day focused primarily on resolving specific practical moral problems."[773] Pim Vilkenberg noted that "Aquinas did not write his summary of theology in a manner unrelated to the systematic study of spirituality [...] such a doctrina according to divine revelation is necessary as a separate discipline alongside the philosophical disciplines because of the salvation of humankind. Theology, therefore, is related to matters pertaining to the spiritual welfare of human beings: God is their origin and their final destination."[774]

The structural affinities between Ghazali's *Ihya Ulum al-Din* and Aquinas's *Summa* were telling.[775] Both started with theologico-philosophical chapters and climaxed in ethical conclusions. "While the first twenty books (of Ihya) concentrate on the physical wellbeing of Muslims and the role of their religion, the last twenty books concentrate on their spiritual wellbeing."[776] Their division of religious sciences into inward and outward[777] and their further subdivisions into saving and destroying acts[778] were pretty much the same. "In his muqaddima, he (Ghazali) makes a distinction between an outward science dealing with the functions of the senses, and an inward science dealing with the functions of the heart. The outward science is subdivided into acts of worship – the first quarter of the Ihya' – and usages of life – the second quarter. The inward science is subdivided into objectionable and praiseworthy things."[779]

Ghazali divided his Ihya into four quarters, covering acts of worship (*al-Ibadat*), matters of daily interactions (*al-Adat*), destructive matters (*al-Muhlikat*) and saving matters (*al-Munjiyat*).[780] Each quarter was further divided into ten chapters, making for a total of forty chapters. These were the gradual stairways to love of God, a trajectory of deeper demands of faith,[781] an amalgamation and unification of "the traditional material of the science of jurisprudence (*fiqh*) and the experiential knowledge of Sufism."[782] Annemarie Schimmel pointed out that Ghazali's division of chapters into forty was quite meaningful. "Forty is the number of preparation and is used in this work to lead the reader through the works of the Law and the acts of mystical love to the final chapter, which is devoted to the meeting with the Lord at the moment of death. It seems important that the central, twentieth, chapter is devoted to the central figure in Islam, the prophet Muhammad."[783] The Ihya had human salvation and ultimate success in sight, and it culminated in human death and return to God. Schimmel observed that "the whole *Ihya* may be called a preparation for death: its last chapter is devoted to death in its terrible and its lovable aspects: terrible, because it brings man into the presence of the stern judge at Doomsday, which may be the beginning of everlasting punishment; lovable, since it brings the lover into the presence of his eternal beloved and thus fulfils the longing of the soul, which has finally found eternal peace. All that Ghazzali teaches in the preceding thirty-nine chapters is only to help man to live a life in accordance with the sacred law, not by clinging exclusively to its letter but by an understanding of its deeper meaning, by a sanctification of the whole life, so that he is ready for the meeting with his Lord at any moment."[784]

The Ihya, then, was a reflection of Neoplatonic scheme of coming from and going back to God. Aquinas's *Summa* also served the same purpose, and followed the same scheme. Wilkenberg stated that "Aquinas structures this book according to the neo-Platonic schema of *exitus* and *reditus*: all creatures have come forth from God as source of their being, and will go back to God as their final end. This basic metaphor determines Aquinas's idea of human beings as moral creatures on their final destination in the second part of his Summa: meeting God in eternal bliss."[785] The first part of the *Summa Theologiae* (*Prima pars*) explained God as the prime source of their being and *Secunda pars* examined "the human acts by which rational creatures return to God."[786] This overarching structure represented "Aquinas's creative adoption of the Neoplatonic emanation and return *(exitus-reditus)* motif within his Christian depiction of the emergence of all creatures from God the Creator and the return of creatures to God the Redeemer."[787] The correct knowledge of God led to friendship with God. The moral growth transformed it into God's love. The love and grace resulted in the ultimate happiness, *Sa'adat al-Akhirah* of al-Ghazali and Beatitude of Aquinas. Marianne Farina has shown this convergence in a detailed fashion noting that "Ghazali, as well as Thomas Aquinas, connects the stages of moral growth and the stages of spiritual growth to the basic metaphor of friendship with God."[788] Therefore, Ghazli's Ihya was a tool of moral preparedness for ultimate goal of eternal success and everlasting life. "We can now understand why al-Ghazali uses the word ihya' (revival) to characterise his work: it is a book of spiritual medicine that guides the senses of the faithful by indicating the proper behaviour in their religious and their daily lives, and guides their hearts by indicating what is damaging and what is beneficial to their spiritual well-being."[789] Thomas's *Summa* served almost the same goal with the same overall scheme, methodology and steps.[790]

Clearly their theological and philosophical anthropology had ethical implications. Their ethics had telos. They were founded upon a concrete, well knit teleological view of reality well saturated with finality and ultimate goals. Man was an intrinsic part of that telos and must understand, comprehend and react to that final purpose for ultimate happiness. The speculative reason and practical reason must go hand in hand; both the faith and action must coincide. The goal-directed and oriented teleological scheme was the essence of human intentions,

actions and life. Virtuous human actions were a series of steps necessary for man to take on his journey back to the source of his existence
and the ultimate end of his longings.[791] The ultimate happiness was
not to be found in the material or temporary perfections but in the
ultimate perfection, the universal good, God Almighty. Both agreed
with philosophers that man's ultimate goal was attainment of happiness, but they disagreed with the philosophers' identification of that
happiness in the terrestrial realms; they found it truly in the celestial
realms, in the heavens in the life to come and only with the ultimate
source of human existence i.e., God. Both agreed with the philosophers that human will, emotions, habits, passions and actions could
be trained, channelised and controlled by habituation. The stable dispositions to do good (virtues) and the stable disposition to do evil
(vices) were human conditions. Virtues could be achieved by proper
training and vices could be shunned by adequate discipline. Unlike
some other Christian theologians, Aquinas also agreed that sin was not
something superimposed upon man due to his fallen nature; rather, it
was a voluntary human act where a person intentionally deviated from
the rational or scriptural standards. The original sin tainted the human nature but it did not completely destroy it. Man was in a corrupt
state but not in an absolutely deprived state. Therefore, both Ghazali
and Aquinas emphasised the need for human moral participation in
the saga of salvation. They were philosophically oriented theologians
and not pure philosophers who philosophised for the sake of mere
contemplation. Joseph Owens, R.-A. Gauthier,[792] Mark Jordan, Denis
Bradley[793] and many others have noted that Aquinas's commentary on
Aristotelian ethics (*Sententia libri Ethicorum) was* not a philosophical
commentary. It was a theological enterprise. According to Mark Jordan, Aquinas "chose not to write philosophy,'" and the *Sententia* on the
Ethics is only a preparation for the "full" and "Christian" commentary
known as the *Pars secunda* of the *Summa theologiae*."[794] In fact, Jordan
claims that "no single work was written by Aquinas for the sake of setting forth a philosophy."[795] He always had ethico-theological designs.
"Any appropriate formulation must begin by recognizing that whatever philosophy there is in Aquinas can be approached only through
his theology if it is to be approached as he intended it. Indeed, it is
very difficult to separate out the philosophical passages in his works.
His writings are overwhelmingly on the topics and in the genres of

the medieval faculties of theology. He wrote almost always in what is self-evidently the voice of a theologian."[796]

Both agreed upon the significance of divine law in guiding, maintaining and preserving human morality.[797] The divine law guided man to what was good and bad.[798] Man used his will in accordance with the law to realise moral goals. Both agreed that divine grace in the end was the most important factor in human morality. The deficiency of human capacities was supplemented by the divine grace to assist a person in achieving the supernatural good. Here, both disagreed with the philosophers, who had no concept of infused divine grace[799] or *Fadl min Allah*, as Ghazali would call it.[800] Philosophers focused upon human will and habituation, while Ghazali and Aquinas more on divine determinism.

Thomas "envisions two quite different ways in which one might acquire the practical wisdom that will enable one to judge correctly about how to act in particular situations. One might acquire it according to the natural means of which Aristotle speaks: 'by experience and over time.' But one might also acquire it in a supernatural way of which Aristotle knew nothing: it might be 'infused' — literally, 'poured in' — by God."[801] Here Thomas departed from both the philosophical as well as theological tradition of his time. Thomas William noted that "Later theologians will question whether it is necessary, or even rational, to posit infused cardinal virtues. Aquinas, however, is emphatic that there must be such virtues. His insistence on this point is another illustration of his distinctive way of negotiating a middle position between integral Aristotelianism and rejectionism. Although he upholds the integrity of the natural order, allowing that human beings have a natural end and a set of virtues that dispose them to achieve that end, he also acknowledges a distinct and superior supernatural order, with its corresponding set of virtues."[802] Ghazali's *Ilm al-Mukashafah* (the Science of Unveiling)[803] was influential here.

Both were elitists, in the sense that they accepted the philosophical cardinal virtues as springboards for the grace infused supernatural gifts, qualities and powers by which a virtuous seeker acquired the eternal good or ultimate beatitude.[804] These illuminations were given only to the elites who achieved the unique spiritual/mystical virtues by perfecting the cardinal and theological virtues. The natural disposition was supplemented by the divine grace, to transform it into a supernatural level where the lover and the beloved were united into a whole. Ghazali and Aquinas even agreed at this highest level of spiritual unification. Unlike Albert the Great,[805] Bonaventure and other contemporaries who leaned towards illumination,[806]Aquinas followed Ghazali in maintaining the final demarcation line between God and Man, the Beloved and lover. In Beatitude the human intellect is capable of seeing God face to face in his essence because the intellect is enhanced by the grace of God and not dissolved in His essence. This enhancement is a gift of grace and not human accomplishment. This enhancement is still relative and not absolute like God. "It ought not to be understood as if the divine essence is the true form of our intellect or that out of this and our intellect simply one thing is made, as in natural things made from natural form and matter [...] Rather, [it should be understood to come about] because the relation of the divine essence to our intellect is as the relation of form to matter. For whenever there are any two things of which one is more perfect than the other and these are received in the same recipient, there is a relation of one of the two to the other, namely, of the more perfect to the less perfect, as is the relation of form to matter."[807] Ghazali indeed had significant impact upon Aquinas's moral anthology.

Both were heir to Greco Muslim ethical tradition and acted and reacted to it in conformity with their synthetical projects. Aristotelian Nicomachean Ethics along with Muslim Aristotelian philosophers' commentaries were studied, incorporated, re-oriented and re-moulded by Ghazali in accordance with the demands of his theologico-rationalist mysticism.[808] The same commentaries of al-Farabi, Ikhwan al-Safa and later Aristotelians such as Ibn Rushd were available to Aquinas.[809] Thomas frequently referred to these Muslim philosophers' interpretations of morality in his treatment of ethics. Thomas had an additional source i.e., Ghazali who used the philosophico-ethical concepts wherever they conformed to the religious axioms but modified, appropriated, rejected and replaced them with more religious ones wherever considered incompatible with revelation and its corollaries. Ghazali was most helpful to Aquinas in these very specifically religious areas. Thomas followed Ghazali in his minute modifications, alterations and appropriations. For instance, Aristotelian ethics were geared to attaining excellence and perfection in this life[810], especially the highest possible happiness, was considered in the realms of politics. Aristotle was emphatic about it. "Since politics uses the rest of the sciences, and since, again, it legislates as to what we are to do and what we are to abstain from, the end of this science must include those of the others, so that this end must be the human good. For even if the end is the same for an individual and for a State, that of the State seems at all events something greater and more complete both to attain and to preserve; for though we should be content to attain the end for a single individual, it is more noble and more divine to attain it for a nation or for States. These, then, are the ends at which our inquiry, being a sort of political science, aims."[811] Ghazali replaced it with the ultimate happiness in the life to come. Aquinas followed the suit. With this in mind let us look at the overall structure of Ghazali and Thomas's ethical system.

Both accepted that the Aristotelian ethical virtues could serve as the foundations of religious virtues. Servais-Theodore Pinckaers, O.P., the leading authority on Aquinas's ethics states that "For Thomas, the chief philosophical source is obviously Aristotle, 'the Philosopher,' whom he uses throughout his work, even when treating specifically Christian questions. St. Thomas considers Aristotle an expert on human nature and borrows from him the basic structure of his morality: the ordering to happiness as our final end, the organisation of the moral virtues, and the analysis of friendship that serves him in defining charity. In Thomas's project of constructing a morality of virtues, he also exploits authors such as Cicero and Seneca in dealing with the virtues, Bocthius for the treatise on happiness, and Nemesius for the analysis of human acts [...] Furthermore, one must not forget the Arab (Averroes and Avicenna) and Jewish (Maimonides) philosophers. These commentators on Aristotle are for St. Thomas both adversaries and collaborators in researching the truth about God and the human person."[812] Thomas quoted Aristotle 1546 times in *Secunda pars* of the Summa, the part discussing ethics.[813] Ghazali almost depended upon the same philosophical sources.[814]

Both used Aristotle's cardinal virtues (wisdom, courage, temperance and justice) as the springboard of their moral systems.[815] Both accepted philosophical definitions of virtues, their psychological basis, their main division into four and then multiple subdivisions, equating virtues with good habits and identifying it as a balanced mean between two vices. Ghazali identified these cardinal virtues with the fundamentals of Islamic religion (*Usul al-Din*), and found ample religious justifications for their use. Aquinas followed suit.[816]

Ghazali did differ with the philosophers in couching their virtues into his specific religious mould. For instance, instead of just limiting the virtues to human training and habituation, Ghazali introduced the concept of natural righteousness and supernatural grace. A person could be righteous by nature or with the grace of God, a possibility denied by the philosophers.[817] Aquinas accepted that modification.[818]

Ghazali made certain modifications in the philosophical virtues by emphasising a few at the expense of others, or adding spiritual nuances totally missing in the philosophers' treatment of them. For instance, wisdom or prudence to Aristotle was the highest level of knowledge given in a certain situation enabling one to discern the appropriate course of action in timely fashion. Ghazali developed it to the spiritual level by modifying the genuine knowledge to the emotion it created i.e., the love of God and good action.[819] Genuine knowledge of God created bondage of love between God and believer. Love (a mixture of positive emotion of closeness and negative fear of distance) translated into sheer dependence, trust and submission. Prudence or wisdom was a combination of that knowledge and the ensuing emotional attitude not mere knowledge as Aristotle held. Genuine knowledge without ensuing emotional attachment to the source of knowledge was useless. Therefore, true prudence was a combination of genuine knowledge, divine love and sharing of that love with God's creatures. Thomas almost agreed. In "parallel with Thomistic ethics [...] a good character wisdom is considered as the highest of all the virtues, as it is confirmed by the Quranic verse: "whoever is granted wisdom he indeed is given a great good". However, Al-Ghazali does not give wisdom only a speculative or religious sense—knowledge of God—but also very practical subdivisions such as: sagacity, sound judgment, perspicuity and right opinion [...] Aquinas' account follows on very similar lines."[820] Thomas's interpretations of prudence went through gradual transformations.[821] In his final analysis he turned away from both Aristotle and his teacher Albert the Great[822] and got much closer to Ghazalian understanding. Thomas also shared Ghazali's concerns for sharing that wisdom. "If for Aristotle the ability to teach is a sign of the presence of wisdom, for Aquinas the wise not only can but must teach, in an act of pious gratitude for what they received through hearing the Word of the divine teacher. Thus do the wise take on a public role of proclamation and instruction unknown to Aristotle."[823] To Thomas "the function of prudence or right moral reasoning is to determine, intend, and choose actions that will lead to the right realization of those appetites. The mutual dependency of prudence and the moral virtues (this is an evolving spiral, not a vicious circle) incorporates and integrates moral reasoning into an evolving vision of the human person."[824] Thomas, like Ghazali, has a more integrated understanding of prudence in which the final ends are intrinsic to right knowledge and right living, "prudence is "about things ordained to the end."[825] When discussing "the priority of an intellectual virtue over a moral virtue, he adds that prudence directs the moral virtues not only in the choice of the means, "but also in appointing the end."[826] Prudence is more than good deliberation and sound judgment. It involves performance of right action.[827] Aquinas's prudence is not as Aristotelian as is sometimes assumed. "Aquinas's stress on the commanding of action as the chief act of prudence might seem to be in conflict with Aristotle's stress on deliberation and decision."[828] Joseph Pieper also noted that "Prudence […] is not only cognition, not only knowing what is what. The prime thing is that this knowledge of reality must be transformed into the prudent decision which takes effect directly in its execution. Prudence is immediately directed toward concrete realization; hence the difference between knowledge as viewed by moral science, including 'casuistic' moral science, and knowledge as viewed by prudence. It is important not to mistake these two forms of ethical knowledge for one another."[829] Finally, Thomas connects prudence with love and charity: "Clearly, through prudence, one can attain our natural ends, but prudence needs charity to be disposed to the supernatural end. Just as the natural inclinations are the ends or principles for prudence in the active life, so charity becomes the end or principle for the prudent person in the pursuit of supernatural happiness."[830] This combination is the hallmark of Christian faith, as Pieper states "the highest and most fruitful achievements of Christian life depend upon the felicitous collaboration of prudence and charity. This collaboration is linked to the pre-eminence of charity over prudence. Prudence is the mold of the moral virtues; but charity molds even prudence itself."[831] The divine love transforms prudence to the highest levels of inward sincerity, "all our works and being are elevated by charity to a plane which is otherwise unattainable and utterly inaccessible. For that reason, too, supernatural divine love which molds the decisions of the Christian indubitably means something far more than and far different from a mere additional "higher motivation" in the psychological sense. The divine love conferred by grace shapes from the ground up and throughout the innermost core of the most commonplace moral action of a Christian, even though that action may be "outwardly" without special distinguishing characteristics."[832]

Thomas's mixture of prudence and charity is close to Ghazali's emotion of loving God (*Hubbullah*), the final end of all human aspirations. The prudence (*Hikmah*) so derived from divine love and grace diverts one's eyes from the creatures solely to the creator, from the world to the God of this cosmos rendering the world naught and the God Almighty all in all. Aquinas's grace-filled prudence also leads to a complete naught of the material existence in the aught of divine presence. Pieper states that "in the *Summa Theologica* we learn that upon a higher plane of perfection, that is the plane of charity, there is also a higher and extraordinary prudence which holds as nought all the things of this world. Does this not run completely counter to all that the 'universal teacher' has said elsewhere about the nature of the first cardinal virtue? Is holding created things as nought not the exact opposite of that reverent objectivity which in the concrete situation of concrete action must attempt to recognise the 'measure' of that action? Things are nought only before God, who created them and in whose hand they are as clay in the hand of the potter. By the superhuman force of grace-given love, however, man may become one with God to such an extent that he receives, so to speak, the capacity and the right to see created things from God's point of view and to 'relativise' them and see them as nought from God's point of view, without at the same time repudiating them or doing injustice to their nature. Growth in love is the legitimate avenue and the one and only justification for 'contempt for the world.'[833]

The other examples that could be considered include the "relationship between prudence and the theological virtues caused by grace, the distinction between acquired prudence and infused prudence, and the link between prudence and God's providence. It is in the discussion of these theological issues, which go beyond Aristotle's philosophical scope, that it becomes clear that Aquinas's understanding of prudence involves an added dimension. This added dimension makes quite a significant difference."[834] Just like Ghazali, Aquinas moulded the most fundamental philosophical virtue, the mother and root of all virtues, into a spiritual and mystical virtue. "The relationship of charity to this acquired prudence as its formal cause distinguishes it quite sharply from Aristotle's *phronesis*. For Aquinas, the overriding concern was to develop a teaching on practical reasoning and its perfecting in the virtue of prudence that would be consistent with both the truth he saw in Aristotle and the truth Christian theology provides in helping the person to ascend to God."[835]

Both did the same theological modification to the virtue of courage. Aristotle's notion of courage in the *Nicomachean Ethics* was that "in the strict sense of the word the courageous man will be one who is fearless in the face of an honourable death, or of some sudden threat of death; and it is in war that such situations chiefly occur."[836] This Aristotelian mundane courage in the battlefield[837] was transformed by Ghazali into a spiritual virtue, the individual's struggles against one's own base desires and passions for the pleasure of God. This courage was required to prefer spiritual over material and divine over personal whims and desires. Thomas also expanded the Aristotelian concept of civil courage to include physical and spiritual sacrifices for higher goals. "First, the object of the special virtue of courage is wider than Aristotle had thought. Aristotle had limited true courage to the battlefield and had gone out of his way to show that being fearless in 'emergencies that involve death,' such as shipwrecks and disease, is the same as courage. Sailors and physicians do not face death directly because they hope their respective skills will save them. For his part, Aquinas turned Aristotle around and refused to narrow courage to the battlefield."[838] He interpreted "Aristotle's account of courage with further theological purposes in mind."[839] Aquinas added a special "Christian form of courage, one that is found in the first Christian ideal: the courage of the martyrs, who 'undergo personal battles for the sake of the highest good, who is God. Therefore, their courage is especially praised and is not outside the type of courage which concerns warfare.'[840] Martyrdom "renounces the most highly valued and loved good of one's own life in favour of God, it is the perfect expression of *caritas*."[841] Aquinas transformed a purely military virtue of Aristotle into a spiritual virtue of the highest degree. "In this way the ancient ideal of the 'beautiful death' (*bona mors*) is reformulated in Christian terms. At the same time, the expansion of true courage from the military background of the ancient world to the religious sphere of Christianity affects the interpretation of Aristotle's text on a subtle level."[842]Aquinas' virtue of courage combined both civic and spiritual realms, just like Ghazali.

The same can be said about Aristotelian interpretations of pride and magnanimity. To Aristotle "the proud man [...] is extreme in respect of greatness, but midway in respect of what he should be; for he claims what is in accordance with his worth, while the others are excessive or deficient."[843] The pride is connected with honour. "If, then, he is worthy of great things and claims them (and above all the greatest things), he will be concerned with one thing in particular. Worth is relative to external goods; and the greatest of these, we should say, is that which we render to the gods, and which people of prestige most aim at, and which is the prize appointed for the noblest deeds; and this is honour: that is the greatest of external goods. Honours and dishonours, therefore, are the objects with respect to which the proud man is as he should be. And even apart from argument it is evident that proud men are concerned with honour; for it is honour that they chiefly claim—but in accordance with their worth."[844] The proud man did not care much about even honour because he was too big for it. "It is chiefly with honours and dishonours, then, that the proud man is concerned; and at honours that are great and conferred by virtuous men he will be moderately pleased, thinking that he is coming by his own or even less than his own. For there can be no honour that is worthy of perfect virtue, yet he will at any rate accept it since they have nothing greater to bestow on him. Honour from all and sundry and on trifling grounds he will utterly disdain, since it is not this of which he is worthy, and dishonour too, since in his case it cannot be just. In the first place, then, as has been said, the proud man is concerned with honours; yet he will also bear himself appropriately towards riches and power and all good or bad fortune, whatever may befall him, and will be neither over-joyed by good fortune nor over-pained by bad. For not even about honour does he care much, although it is the greatest thing (for power and riches are desirable for the sake of honour—at least those who have them want to get honour by means of them); and for him to whom even honour is a little thing the other things must be so too. Hence proud men are thought to be supercilious."[845] The proud man was also haughty. "It is a mark of the proud man also to ask for nothing or scarcely anything, but to give help eagerly, and to be haughty towards people who enjoy prestige and good fortune, and unassuming towards those of the middle class—for it is a difficult and dignified thing to be superior to the former, but easy to be so to the latter, and a dignified bearing over the former is no mark of ill-breeding, but among humble people it is as vulgar as a display of strength against the weak."[846] He did not care much about his wrongs due to pragmatic reasons. "Nor is he given to admiration; for nothing to him is great. Nor is he mindful of wrongs; for it is not the part of a proud man to have a long memory, especially for wrongs, but rather to overlook them."[847] Aristotle's proud man even taunted some people and looked down upon them. "Vain people [...] are fools and ignorant of themselves, and that manifestly; for, not being worthy of them, they attempt honourable undertakings, and then are found out; and they adorn themselves with clothing and outward show and such things, and want their strokes of good fortune to be evident, and speak about them as if they would be honoured for them. Diffidence is more opposed to pride than vanity is; for it is both commoner and worse."[848]

Ghazali made a fundamental modification to Aristotelian concept of pride by directly connecting it with humility before God and before people for the sake of God.[849] To Ghazali pride was self-conceit. "Self conceit is self-contentment in thinking that one is superior to others. There are three elements in it- (1) one who is proud, (2) one on whom it is shown, (3) and the object for which it is felt. Self praise has got only one element, namely the person who takes pride, while the self-conceit has got these three elements."[850] Devil is the best "instance of this pride."[851] The medicin of pride is humility and modesty before God as well as people for the sake of God.[852] Aquinas agreed. "Differently from Aristotle, these two theologians do not consider one's sense of greatness or pride as a positive aspect of character but rather as a vice. Pride takes place when one considers his own worth better than that of others and he has contempt for others."[853] Therefore the Aristotelian puffed up, indifferent to others, ingrateful and seemingly arrogant magnanimous character was moulded by Ghazali into the Qura'nic servant of God[854] with humbleness to God and meekness towards God's creatures for the pleasure of God. Aquinas, unlike his contemporaries, moulded the Aristotelian "sinful and vicious"[855] character into a biblically-humble person, in line with Christ's docility. He acknowledged that Aristotelian ethics were mainly concerned with political realms and must be tamed to accommodate Christian motives. "He says that Aristotle intended to discuss the virtues in as much as they belong to the political domain (*secundum quod ordinantur ad vitam civilem*). Humility is not part of the political domain, for it is not concerned with the subordination of human persons to each other, but to God."[856] Looking into one's own shortcomings and other's virtues is integral to magnanimity. A "magnanimous person does not have contempt for other persons as such, but only insofar as they are deficient with regard to the gifts of God. Humility, by contrast, leads one to honour the others and to consider them superior with regard to the gifts received from God. Humble persons think lowly of themselves when considering their own defects."[857] Tobias Hoffmann rightly observes that "This doctrine is of course not meant to be an interpretation of Aristotle. It is evidence, however, that Aquinas does not hesitate to integrate the virtue of magnanimity into his taxonomy of virtues, where humility plays an important role."[858] Aristotle was transformed to the spiritual levels both by Ghazali and Aquinas in accordance with their moral projects.

Ghazali also adopted some of the extremes of certain philosophical virtues rather than the middleway emphasised by Aristotle. For instance, Humility,[859] modesty,[860] poverty and shyness are taken to the extremes which for the philosophers are not even virtuous.[861] Aristotle clearly stated that "modesty should not be described as a virtue; for it is more like an emotion than a state of character. It is defined, at any rate, as a kind of fear of disrepute and produces an effect similar to that produced by fear of danger; for people who feel disgraced blush, and those who fear death turn pale. Both seem to be in a way bodily conditions, which is thought to be characteristic of emotions rather than of states of character."[862] Humility was a vice.[863] Every man was daunted by poverty.[864] Ghazali made these modifications based upon Islamic tradition. Modesty which was not even a philosophical virtue was raised by Ghazali to the level of virtue by equating it with spiritual restrained out of fear of committing shameless acts.[865] To Ghazali, true modesty was shame before God, an aspect totally missing in Aristotle. Ghazali based these modifications, alterations, insinuations and emphasis upon religious texts and axioms. Aquinas did the same with some of these insignificant philosophical virtues or traits. "Humility thus receives an overly modest position, which is understandable among pagan authors, but St. Thomas knows perfectly well its importance in Christian tradition."[866] Christ's passion, humility, poverty and modesty were not moderate but extreme; Christ was an absolute model of these Islamic moral virtues looked down upon by the philosophers. Ghazali referred to Christ's model more often than Aristotle. Jesus like Muhammad was the pinnacle of morality in the Islamic teachings especially in poverty and humility. Ghazali frequently quoted from the Gospels especially the Gospel of Matthew, referred to the Sermon on the Mount and alluded to Church Fathers treatment of mystical topics.[867] The Ghazalian modifications resonated very well with Aquinas as they did with Abu al-Farj Bar Hebraeus before him. Aquinas was more Ghazalian than Aristotelian in these specific areas of Christian ethics. Just like Ghazali, Thomas subjected philosophical virtues to the yardstick of faith and "in each instance philosophical analysis rises toward Christian experience and places itself at the service of revelation."[868]

Another good example is the virtue of liberality. To Aristotle "the liberal man is praised not in respect of military matters, nor of those in respect of which the temperate man is praised, nor of assessments, but with regard to the giving and taking of wealth, and especially in respect of giving. Now by wealth we mean all the things whose worth is measured by money."[869] The "riches, therefore, will be used best by the man who has the virtue concerned with wealth, and this is the liberal man. Spending and giving seem to be the using of wealth; taking and keeping rather the possessing of it. That is why it is more the mark of the liberal man to give to whom he should to than to take whence he should and not to take whence he should not."[870] A liberal man gives to receive praise and honour and to avoid being called "miserly, close, stingy."[871] Ghazali conceded that a generous man gave liberally partially for the sake of praise, honour, gratitude and helping the needy but Ghazali brought love of God in the equation. The truly liberal and generous was the man who gave for the sake of God and not for the sake of praise or fame.[872] These modifications were based upon the Quranic and Prophetic texts.[873] Ghazali appropriated the philosophical virtues to serve a special religious purpose in his ethical scheme; they served as a natural springboard for higher spiritual designs. Aquinas pretty much followed the suit.[874] Ghazali found the climax of these philosophical cardinal virtues in Prophet Muhammad while Aquinas replaced Muhammad with Christ. Ghazali imported Quranic verses, prophetic traditions and mystics' interpretations to Islamise the philosophical virtues and Aquinas used Bible, Church Fathers[875] and various *Summas* to Christianise the Ghazalian and Rusdian modifications. The outcome was quite similar ethico-moral systems with some variances. Aquinas's system bore some striking similarities with his Muslim counterparts.

John Renard noted that "Thomas is perhaps best known for his global theological synthesis, the *Summa Theologiae,* founded on his interpretation of Aristotelian logic. He structured his magnum opus upon the classical two-part metaphor of 'going forth' from and 'return' to God, a construction well known to his Muslim contemporaries, such as Jalal ad-Din Rumi."[876] F. G. Moore observed that "Al-Ghazali (d. 1111) stands to Moslem theology in this respect in somewhat the same position that Thomas Aquinas does to Christian theology. His great work, *The Revival of the Religious Sciences*, may fairly be compared to the *Summa* of Thomas Aquinas, but his personal contribution to theology was more considerable than that of the Christian theologian."[877] Renard further notes that "Ghazali's *Revitalization* is one of the great synthetic works of the ethical and spiritual life from a Muslim perspective. Like Thomas Aquinas, Ghazali believes that human beings are made for felicity. The eleventh-century Muslim also builds his ethical treatise on a discussion of the optimal way of performing a host of often mundane deeds and proceeds to analyse in great detail "acts that lead to perdition," before building to a grand and lofty treatment of "acts that assure salvation." This last section, like that pertaining to Thomas's theological ethics, is virtually an essay on the path to spiritual perfection. Beginning with repentance, the journey leads through patience and gratitude, fear and hope, and poverty and asceticism. Acknowledging the unity of God, one proceeds to perfect trust, love and desire for God, purity of intention and sincerity. Achieving the states of mindfulness of God, self-examination, and meditation, the ascent culminates in a rich contemplation of death and the hereafter.[878] He continues observing that "Catholic moral theology blossomed into a distinct subdiscipline of the sacred sciences when Thomas Aquinas devoted a large segment of his grand synthesis, *The Summa of Theology,* to the subject. He opens the 'second part' of the work with a discussion of happiness as the ultimate goal of humankind, thus situating himself in the tradition of Aristotelian ethics, but with a very different analysis of means to the end. Thomas divides human actions into involuntary and voluntary, inward and outward, all capable of good or ill. In that context, he analyses human proclivities, or 'passions,' and the more enduring characteristics or 'habits' of the soul, with particular attention to virtue and vice. Thomas roots his discussion of sin in the concept of original sin, with its pernicious influence through the ages; he explains sin as a violation of the divine law, but goes on to insist that the heart of the matter remains dependent on human volition. In that context, he comes round to describing the eternal law as the standard against which one must assess the moral valence of all actions. At this juncture, Thomas introduces the element of divinely bestowed grace as the prime impetus to good action."[879] He notes the parallels between the works of al-Ghazali and Thomas in the following words. "Against the backdrop of these general principles, Thomas moves into a more detailed discussion of moral theology in light of more concrete characteristics and implications of the various virtues and vices, beginning with the 'theological virtues': faith, hope, and love. He expands on this by exploring the specific results of the 'four cardinal virtues': prudence, justice, fortitude, and temperance. His analysis culminates in an exploration of the relationship between virtue enacted and the requirements of the various 'states of life' to which believing Christians might devote themselves. In a manner reminiscent of the master work of earlier Muslim theologian Abū Hāmid al-Ghazali [...] Thomas associates the life of advanced virtue with lofty spiritual (even perhaps mystical) attainment."[880]

Margaret Smith observed that "It has now been fully realised that Christian scholasticism and mediaeval Christian mysticism derived certain conceptions from Muslim writers, among whom al-Ghazali was included. The greatest of these Christian writers who was influenced by al-Ghazali was St. Thomas Aquinas (1225-1274), who made a study of the Arabic writers and admitted his indebtedness to them."[881] She highlights the parallels by observing that "in reference to the inability of the creature to realise the Majesty of the Creator, St. Thomas uses the very words of al-Ghazali in saying that 'the sun, though supremely visible, cannot be seen by the bat, because of its excess of light.' Again, in dealing with the spiritual aspiration of the human soul, due to its affinity with the Divine, St. Thomas states that the ultimate perfection of the rational creature is to be found in that which is the principle of its being, since a thing is perfect in so far as it attains to that principle. God is the greatest of all goods and He alone is true perfection, and St. Thomas holds that He is the end towards which all things move, in order to achieve the perfection which can be given by Him alone, which is to become like Him. Man must find out wherein his own perfection consists and then seek to pursue it. He was not created simply for sensual satisfaction, for this is common to both man and the brutes, nor for the pursuit of material ends, for man shares the nature of the angels as well as the brutes. This argument is set forth by al-Ghazali, in almost the same terms, in his Kimiya al-Sa'ada and elsewhere."[882] She further states that "St. Thomas teaches that in this life God can be seen mirrored in His works, by consideration of which we can in the first place see something of the Divine wisdom. Then, in the second place, this consideration leads to a recognition of God's power and so the human heart is led to reverence before Him. Thirdly, it leads man to a love of God's goodness. His conclusion is that the goodness and perfection found in individual things is all united in the One Who is the Fountain of all goodness. If, therefore, man loves goodness, beauty and attraction in created things, then the very Fountain of goodness, their Creator, must influence men's minds and draw them to Himself. This is the theme of al-Ghazali's Hikmat fi Makhlugal Allah and is emphasised again in the Ihya, where he shews that all the causes of love are found in God, the Giver of every good and perfect gift."[883] Finally she illustrates the crystal-clear resemblance between Ghazali and Aquinas's concepts of Beatific Vision. "But it is in his teaching on the Beatific Vision and the gnosis which leads to it that St. Thomas seems to have derived most from the teaching of the Muslim mystics and especially al-Ghazali. The goal which man seeks, St, Thomas states, is the contemplation of Truth, for this is appropriate to his nature and no other earthly creature shares it with him. There is no end beyond it, for such contemplation is an end in itself." It is impossible for any created intellect to comprehend God," writes Thomas, and again: "We have a more perfect knowledge of God by grace than by natural reason." This grace, by which man understands God, is the gnosis which al-Ghazali calls "knowledge from on high" (*al-'ilm al-laduni*). In order to see the Vision of God, St. Thomas holds that the created intellect needs to be raised "by some kind of outpouring of the Divine grace," the disposition by which the created intellect is raised to the Beatific Vision is rightly called the light of glory (*lumengloriae*), and those who are raised to this rank know all things and the whole order of the universe, for this light is a likeness of the Divine intellect [...] This is the *Nur Allah*, which God casts "into the heart, "that which is attained without mediation between the soul and its Creator," wrote al-Ghazali, "the radiance from the Lamp of the Invisible shed upon the heart which is pure and at leisure."[884] Binyamin Abrahamove well explains this point in his "Divine Love in Islamic Mysticism".[885]

The perfect happiness in its entire can never be achieved in this temporal, imperfect, material life. It can be attained only in the eternal, spiritual, perfect and everlasting life. A partial beatitude is possible in this life by means of contemplation upon God's creation. "The contemplation of the Divine Vision, St. Thomas believes, will be perfected in the life to come, but even now, that contemplation gives us a foretaste of beatitude which begins here and will be continued in the life to come. The Vision is only for those who love and know God. 'He who possesses more love will see God the more perfectly and will be the more beatified.' So, the bliss of Paradise will be in proportion to the intensity of the love for God, as this love will be in proportion to the knowledge of God gained by His saints on earth and called, by Revelation, faith. The joy of contemplation consists not only in the contemplation itself, but in the love of Him who is contemplated. 'In both respects,' writes Thomas, 'the delight thereof surpasses all human delight, both because spiritual delight is greater than sensual pleasure [...] and because the love of God surpasses all other love.' It is the ultimate perfection of contemplation that the Truth be not only seen, but loved. It is by the Vision that man is made a partaker of Eternal life. This is the doctrine of al-Ghazali concerning the Vision, and is given almost in his words, for he writes: 'The joy of Paradise is in proportion to the love of God and the love of God is proportionate to the knowledge of Him, and so the source of that joy is the gnosis revealed through Faith,' and he, too states that the joy of the Vision surpasses all sensual joys."[886]

Marianne Farina, though denying any direct influence of Ghazali upon Aquinas, agrees to the close parallels and absolute convergence.[887] She notes that "each of these thinkers is paradigmatic for their respective traditions; though little direct influence can be traced from the earlier (Ghazali) to the later, their articulation of the final end for human beings, together with the paths to reach that end, show remarkable parallels."[888] Farina shows close parallels between al-Ghazali's state of real blessedness and Aquinas state of perfect happiness and Beatitude.[889] She examines the moral theories of Thomas and al-Ghazali, which describe the connection between moral goodness and friendship with God, and concludes that "Aquinas and Ghazali are appropriate partners for this exploration because in viewing human excellence as response to God's providence and grace, they wove sacred revelation, religious doctrine, and moral teachings into a unique synthesis revitalising moral education in their day. Although Aquinas and Ghazali vary in their methods of theological investigations they share ideas concerning God's friendship with human beings as the essence of knowledge and moral guidance. Both theologians maintain that friendship with God gives human existence its ultimate value and truest authority. They claim that divine guidance befriends human persons in such ways that they can lead lives full of meaning as they strive for perfect happiness with God in the hereafter."[890] Ghazali states that: "Know beloved that you were not created in jest or at random but marvellously made for some great end. Although you are not from everlasting, yet you will live forever; and though this body is finite, your spirit is made for the divine [...] Attaining that state is finding heaven and the contemplation of Eternal Beauty."[891] Aquinas almost says the same: "Final and perfect happiness can consist in nothing else than the vision of the Divine Essence. [This] happiness implies two things, the last end itself, i.e., the Sovereign Good [God]; and the attainment or enjoyment of that same Good."[892] It is pertinent to mention here that variance in theological method between Ghazali and Aquinas, alluded to by Farina, is the difference between Islamic ethical monotheism and Christian incarnational triune monotheism. For Ghazali the perfect human model is Prophet Muhammad, while for Aquinas it is the God-Man Christ. Aquinas just replaces Perfect Muhammad with Perfect Christ otherwise the overall moral scheme is very much the same.

Muslim mystics have always treated the ethics as a part of natural realms. The burst of supernatural divine grace always complemented the ethical preparedness. A righteous believer travelled through various phases of moral development and ethical growth by curbing passions, whims and vices while increasing virtues. This process of self-purification (internal as well as external) mitigated human self-assertions, egos, self-centeredness to the extent that in the end only the love of God, the absolute goal of human longing and endeavours, the Face of God remained all in all. Al-Ghazali systematised this natural moral scheme with the help of Neoplatonism, Aristotelianism and Muslim thought.

Thomas perhaps was the first scholastic to bring Christian ethics to the natural realms of passions, habits and norms. Supernatural divine interventions were the outcome of natural ethical preparedness. and not independent of it. The Pauline and Augustinian overemphasise upon divine grace was balanced by human participation and preparedness paving the way for combination of faith and actions. Aquinas in this specific area of ethics was closer to Muslim moralists than Augustinian tradition of grace. The Franciscan Bonaventure went on the other extreme far into Augustinianism. Thomas's introduction of natural law into ethical equation and man's conformity with the law for purposes of salvation and felicity were quite similar to al-Ghazali's insistence upon conformity to the Islamic law. Both Ghazali and Aquinas introduced a gradual moral scheme with specific natural benchmarks, phases and goals. "Aquinas's theological ethics addresses moral development as a dynamic movement from God-originating goodness to God-oriented goodness." Throughout this process, God is glorified because created realities are led to their perfection as ordained by God. Human beings who are made in the divine image, glorify God as they live according to the order and goal of their nature: to be united with God, through Christ and in the Holy Spirit. To understand more completely this theological anthropology, humans must contemplate the reality of God's existence and God's activity in creation (ST I, 1.7). The moral life celebrates knowledge of God's activity directed toward human beings, and is a commitment to cooperate with God's plan in the seeking of perfect happiness with God in heaven (ST III, 63.1). God's presence to the human soul is sanctifying grace disposing the soul to a "special mode belonging to the rational creature" necessary for attaining this goal (ST, I 43.3). The image of the Trinity in the soul facilitates a human response to know and love God now and in the vision of God in heaven (ST I, 92 .3, 93.3)."[893] Similarly, "Ghazali's exposition in *Ihya ulum al-din* examines ways humans develop greater trust in God *(tawakkul)* through realizing that God, the Only Existent *(tawhid)*, made humans in the 'best of molds [because they are] recipients of God's spirit' (Quran 95: 4 and 15:29). Nearness to God, as 'likeness to God' *(qurb)*, must be cultivated through belief in the fundamental principles of Islam *(usul-ud-Din)*, and putting faith into practice *(furud- Din)*. Muslims are urged to acquire greater certitude *(yaqin)* in the belief that God breathes the divine spirit into the human soul (Quran 15:29). God's presence, closer to them their own 'jugular vein' (Quran

50:16), is a divine mercy, enabling a person to choose the straight pathway to paradise."[894] Both agree that morality is a two-way traffic. God initiates the process by scriptural guidance and man responds to that initiative by good intentions, actions and virtues. Revelation, faith and law are intrinsic to human understandings of divine will and a proper moral response to that. The love is culmination of that process involving understanding, contemplation and submission. "Both Aquinas and Ghazali maintain that humans come to know God only when they open themselves to God's grace and mercy. Aquinas and Ghazali acknowledge that revelation is necessary for humans to understand God's relationship to creation, its true nature, and its authentic fulfilment. These truths reveal a God who is 'first grasped as an infinite and wise knower whose choices are fired by love' and whose guidance leads to each creature's fulfilment, which for humans is happiness with God."[895]

Farina shows close parallels between Ghazali's scheme of moral life, voluntary, inward and outward acts, definition, classification and developmental stages of virtues and finally love and friendship with God and Aquinas' treatment of the same in almost the same sequence with similar concepts, vocabulary and conclusions.[896]

Thomas exerted tremendous influence upon the Latin Christendom. His theologico-philosophical hybrid was a leading voice in many aspects of the later Christian centuries. Sarton noted that "it is remarkable enough that a philosopher of the second half of the thirteenth century should be the guide of a great part of Western Christendom to this day, but such is the fact, and the historian of science must bear it in mind."[897] The Christian civilisation accessed Aristotelian and Islamic philosophy and theology through the interactions, reactions, appropriations and rejections of Thomas.

In view of the above discussion, it is appropriate to state that Thomas owed much to the Muslim theologico-philosophical tradition and was, in a sense, product of it. His theological philosophy was a reflection of Muslim philosophico-theological thought. He was what he became partly due to Muslim precursors. He was an original thinker whose peculiar Christian synthetic works became a novelty in the Latin Christianity. Thomas stirred countless impulses, ideas and discussions which had ripple effects upon Christianity of later centuries all the way to our modern times. Thomas is perhaps the most discussed, followed and revered Christian philosopher, theologian and moralist in the twenty-first century. The Muslim contributions to his thought and works are tremendous and should be acknowledged, as Thomas did in many of his works.

Endnotes

1   See Fergus Kerr, *Thomas Aquinas: A Very Short Introduction*, Oxford, Oxford University Press, 2009

2   See Charles Burnett, *Arabic into Latin in the Middle Ages; The Translators and their Intellectual and Social Context,* Burlington, VT, Ashgate, 2009; Dimitri Gutas, *Greek Thought Arabic Culture: The Greco Arabic Translation Movement in Baghdad and Early Abbasid Society,* London, Routledge, 1999

3   Gordon Leff, *Medieval Thought: St.Augustine to Occam,* Quadrangle Books, Chicago, 1958, p. 141

4   See Abu Hamid al-Ghazali, *Tahafut al- Falasifah, Incoherence of the Philosophers,* Baltimore, Adam Publishers, 2007; *The Incoherence of the Philosophers* translated by Michael E. Marmura, Utah, Brigam Young University, 2002

5   See Zulfiqar Ali Shah, *Anthropomorphic Depictions of God: The Concept of God in Judaic, Christian and Islamic Traditions, Representing the Unrepresentable,* Washington, International Institute of Islamic Thought, 2012

6   See R. J. Hoffman (trans.), *Porphyry's Against the Christians,* New York, Prometheus Books, 1994; R. J. Hoffman (trans.), *Celsus: On the True Doctrine,* New York, Oxford University Press, 1987; Michael Martin, *The Case Against Christianity,* Philadelphia, Temple University Press, 1991

7   Alfred Guillaume, (1950). *Christian and Muslim Theology as Represented by Al-Shahrastāni and St. Thomas Aquinas.* Bulletin of the School of Oriental and African Studies, 13(3), 551-580. doi:10.1017/S0041977X00140005, p. 551

8   Guillaume, *Christian and Muslim Theology*, p. 552

9   Guillaume, *Christian and Muslim Theology*, p. 552-553

10   Guillaume, *Christian and Muslim Theology*, p. 580

11   David B. Burrell, *Thomas Aquinas and Islam*, Modern Theology, 20:1, Oxford, Blackwell, January 2004, p. 71

12   Mauro Zonta, *The Relationship of European Jewish Philosophy to Islamic and Christian Philosophies in the Late Middle Ages*, Jewish Studies Quarterly, Vol. 7, No. 2 (2000), pp. 127-140; Zonta, Mauro, "Influence of Arabic and Islamic Philosophy on Judaic Thought", *The Stanford Encyclopedia of Philosophy* (Spring 2011 Edition), Edward N. Zalta (ed.), URL = <http://plato.stanford.edu/archives/spr2011/entries/arabic-islamic-judaic/>.

13   David B. Burrell, *Thomas Aquinas and Islam*, p. 72

14   Burrell, *Thomas Aquinas and Islam*, p. 72

15   Christopher Tyerman, *The Invention of the Crusades*. London: Palgrave, 1998.

16   "It was the religion of a region, and not a very large one. Its people were all of one race, belonging to a limited number of interrelated ethnic groups with a strong common culture. In other words, it was rather like Hindu India, but smaller and poorer. Compared with Islam, Christendom was indeed poor, small, backward, and monochromatic. Split into squabbling, petty kingdoms, its churches divided by schism and heresy, with constant quarrels between the churches of Rome and the East, it was disputed between two emperors and for a while even two popes. After the loss of the Christian shores of the eastern and southern Mediterranean to the Muslim advance, Christendom seemed even more local, confined in effect to a small peninsula on the western edge of Asia which became—and was by this confinement defined as—Europe. For a time—indeed, for a very long time—it seemed that nothing could prevent the ultimate triumph of Islam and the extension of the Islamic faith and Muslim power to Europe." Bernard Lewis, *Islam and the West*, Oxford, Oxford University Press, 1994, p. 9

17   See Tholomeus Lucensis, *Historia Ecclesiastica Nova*, MGH SS, 29 (Hannover, 2009) 570; Andrew W. Jones, "A Most Christian Kingdom: Saint Louis Ix, Pope Clement Iv, And The Construction Of France In The Thirteenth Century" Ph.D. dissertation, Saint Louis University, 2012

18   See Michael Lower, Conversion and St Louis's Last Crusade, *Journal of Ecclesiastical History,* Vol. 58, No. 2, April 2007. *(*Cambridge University Press), doi:10.1017/S0022046906009006

19   See William Jordan, *Louis IX and the Challenge of the Crusade: A Study in Rulership.* Princeton: Princeton University Press, 1979; Jean Richard, *Saint Louis: Crusader King of France.* Ed. Simon Lloyd. Trans. Jean Birrell. Cambridge: Cambridge University Press, 1992; Caroline Smith, *Crusading in the Age of Joinville.* Aldershot: Ashgate, 2006

20   See Amanda *Power, Going among the infidels: the mendicant orders and Louis IX's first Mediterranean campaign,* Mediterranean Historical Review, (Routledge), Vol. 25, No. 2, December 2010, 187–202

21   See Lester K. Little, *Frater Ludovicus: A Study of Saint Louis's Involvement in Evangelical Christianity,* Ph. D. dissertation, Princeton University, 1962; Le Goff, Jacques. Saint Louis. Trans. Gareth Evan Gollrad. Notre Dame: University of Notre Dame Press, 2009; 'Saint Louis and the Mediterranean'. Mediterranean Historical Review 5, no. 1 (1990): 21–53; Lester K Little,. 'Saint Louis' Involvement with the Friars'. Church History 33, no. 2 (1964): 125–48; Lower, Michael. 'Conversion and St Louis's Last Crusade'. *Journal of Ecclesiastical History* 58 (2007): 211-31

22   See Lower, *Conversion and St. Louis's Last Crusade,* p. 229

23   Christoph T. Maier, *Crusade Propaganda and Ideology: Model Sermons for the Preaching of the Cross.* Cambridge: Cambridge University Press, 2000, p. 3

24   See Peter Jackson, ed. and trans., *The Seventh Crusade,* 1244–1254: Sources and Documents. Aldershot: Ashgate, 2007

25   R. Rist, *"The Medieval papacy, crusading, and heresy,* 1095-1291" in Keith Sisson and Atria L. Larson eds., *A Companion to the Medieval Papacy: Growth of an Ideology and Institution,* Leiden, Brills, 2016, p. 325-26

26   See P. J. Cole, *The Preaching of the Crusades to the Holy Lands,* 1095-1270, Cambridge, Mass., Medieval Academy Books, 1991

27   See Christoph T. Maier, *Crusade Propaganda and Ideology and also his Preaching the Crusades: Mendicant Friars and the Cross in the Thirteenth Century.* Cambridge: Cambridge University Press, 1994

28   See Richard W. Southern, *Western Views of Islam in the Middle Ages.* Cambridge, MA: Harvard University Press, 1962

29   See Anthony Cutler, *'Everywhere and Nowhere: The Invisible Muslim*

and Christian Self-Fashioning in the Culture of Outremer' in France and the Holy Land: Frankish Culture at the End of the Crusades, ed. Daniel H. Weiss and Lisa Mahoney, Baltimore: Johns Hopkins University Press, 2004, p. 253–81

30   See Peter Jackson, ed. and trans, *The Mission of Friar William of Rubruck: His Journey to the Court of the Great Khan Mongke, 1253–1255.* London: The Hackluyt Society, 1990; David Abulafia, *'Mediterraneans'.* In Rethinking the Mediterranean, ed. W.V. Harris, Oxford: Oxford University Press, 2006; Roxanne L. Euben, *Journeys to the Other Shore: Muslim and Western Travellers in Search of Knowledge.* Princeton: Princeton University Press, 2006

31   See David Carpenter, *The Struggle for Mastery: The Penguin History of Britain 1066–1284.* London, UK: Penguin, (2004); Henry Mayr-Harting, *Religion, Politics and Society in Britain, 1066–1272.* Harlow, UK: Longman, (2011); Peter Spufford, *Money and its Use in Medieval Europe.* Cambridge, Cambridge University Press, (1989); Christopher Tyerman, *England and the Crusades, 1095–1588.* Chicago, University of Chicago Press, (1996).

32   See details in William Chester Jordan, *Louis IX and the challenge of the crusade,* Princeton, Princeton University Press, 1979; Benjamin Z. Kedar, *Crusade and mission: European approaches toward the Muslims,* Princeton, Princeton University Press, 1984; Jean Richard, *Saint Louis, roi de France fe´odale, soutien de la Terre Sainte,* Paris 1983; Peter M. Holt, *The age of the crusades : the near east from the eleventh century to 1517,* London, Longman, 1986

33   See Sophia Menache, *When Jesus met Mohammed in the Holy Land: Attitudes toward the "Other" in the Crusader Kingdom,* Medieval Encounters 15 (2009) 66-85

34   Menache, *When Jesus met Mohammed in the Holy Land,* p. 70;

35   Stephen Howarth, *The Knights Templar,* New York, Barns & Noble, 1993, p. 223

36   See Jonathan Riley-Smith, *The Crusades: A History,* New Haven, Connecticut: Yale University Press, 2005

37   Robin Vose, *Dominican, Muslims and Jews in the Medieval Crown of Aragon,* Cambridge, Cambridge University Press, 2009, p. 6

38   Robin Vose, *Dominican, Muslims and Jews in the Medieval Crown of Aragon,* p. 6

39   See details in Eamon Duffy, *Saints and Sinners: A History of the Popes,* New Haven, Yale University Press, 2014, p. 150 onward

40   See Duffy, *Saints and Sinners,* p. 153

41   See Duffy, *Saints and Sinners,* p. 155

42   See Duffy, *Saints and Sinners,* p. 155

43   See A. E. Kennan, *"Innocent III and the First Political Crusade: A Comment on the Limitations of Papal Power",* Traditio 27 (1971), pp. 231-249; *Id., "Innocent III, Gregory IX and Political Crusades: A Study in the Disintegration of Papal Power",* in *Reform and Authority in the Medieval and Reformation Church,* ed. G. F. Lytle (Washington, DC, 1981), pp. 17-32; Norman Housley, *The Italian Crusades: Th e Papal- Angevin Alliance and the Crusades against Christian Lay Powers, 1254-1343* (Oxford, Oxford University Press,1982), pp. 75-110

44   See Ian P. Wei, *Intellectual Culture in Medieval Paris: Theologians and the University,* c. 1100-1330, Cambridge, Cambrdige University Press, 2012, p. 8 onward

45   See Wei, *Intellectual Culture of Medieval Paris,* p. 95

46   Hasse, Dag Nikolaus, "Influence of Arabic and Islamic Philosophy on the Latin West", *The Stanford Encyclopedia of Philosophy* (Winter 2018 Edition), Edward N. Zalta (ed.), URL =<https://plato.stanford.edu/archives/win2018/entries/arabic-islamic-influence/>.

47   See John B. Freed, *The Friars and German Society In the Thirteenth Century.* Cambridge, Mass.: Mediaeval Academy of America, 1977.

48   See Irving L. Horowitz, "Averroism and the Politics of Philosophy", *The Journal of Politics,* Vol. 22, No. 4 (Nov., 1960), pp. 698-727, p. 714 onward

49   See Paul 0. Kristeller, "Paduan Averroism and Alexandrism in the Light of Recent Studies," in *The Journal of Philosophy,* LIV (November 21, 1957) 774-775.

50   Horowitz, *"Averroism and the Politics of Philosophy",* p. 720

51   Ghazanfar ed., *Medieval Islamic Economic Thought: Filling the "Great Gap" in European Economics,* New York, Routledge Curzon, 2003, p. 18

52   See Wei, *Intellectual Culture of Medieval Paris,* p. 117

53   See Malcolm Lambert, *Franciscan Poverty: the Doctrine of the Absolute Poverty of Christ and the Apostles in the Franciscan Order, 1210-1323* (St. Bonaventure, NY: Franciscan Institute, 1998).; Bonaventure,

Disputed Questions on Evangelical Perfection, translated by Robert J. Karris (Saint Bonaventure, NY: Saint Bonaventure University, 2008); Bonaventure, *Defense of the Mendicants*, introduction and notes by Robert J. Karris, translation by Jose de Vinck and Robert J. Karris (Saint Bonaventure, NY: Franciscan Institute, 2010); and Bonaventure, *The Major Legend of Saint Francis*, translated by Regis J. Armstrong, in *Francis of Assisi: The Founder*, vol. 2 (New York: City Press, 2000).

54   See Wei, *Intellectual Culture of Medieval Paris*, p. 125

55   See Jan G. J. van den Eijnden, *Poverty on the Way to God: Thomas Aquinas on Evangelical Perfection* (Leuven: Peeters, 1994): 20 onward; David Burr, *The Spiritual Franciscans: from Protest to Persecution in the Century after St. Francis*,University Park, PA: Pennsylvania State University, 2001

56   Alex Metcalfe, *The Muslims of Medieval Italy*, p. 284

57   *Die Chronik von Saba Malaspina*, ed. Walter Koller and August Nitschke (MGH SS 35, Hanover 1999), p.170

58   GA Loud, *Communities, Cultures and Conflict in Southern Italy,* from the Byzantines to the Angevins. Al-Masāq, 28 (2). 2016, pp. 132-152. ISSN 0950-3110 https://doi., p. 24

59   David Abulafia, Frederick !!, p. 146

60   Julie Ann Taylor, *Muslim Christian Relations in Medieval Southern Italy, The Muslim World,* 2007, Vol. 97, Iss. 2, p. 194

61   Abulafia, *Frederick !!,* p. 147

62   Karen Armstrong, *Holy War: The Crusades and Their Impact on Today's World,* New York, Anchor Books, 2001, p, 418-419

63   Matthew Paris, *Chronica Majora* Trans. Henry Richards Luard (London: Longman & Co, 1877), V, p. 190. 'The wonder of the world, and the marvelous changer of the world.'

64   See Marjorie Reeves, *Influence of Prophecy in the later Middle Ages,* Oxford: Oxford University Press. 1969, p. 60.

65   See details John P. Lomax: *Frederick II, His Saracens, and the Papacy, in Medieval Christian Perceptions of Islam,* Edited by J.V. Tolan; London, Routledge, p. 178

66   Julie Ann Taylor, *Muslim Christian Relations in Medieval Southern Italy,* p. 191; Taylor Julie *Muslims in Medieval Italy: The Colony at Lucera,*

Lanham, Md., Lexington Books, 2003

67   Alax Metcalfe, *The Muslims of Medieval Italy,* Edinburgh, Edinburgh University Press, 2009, p. 287

68   Metcalfe, *The Muslims of Medieval Italy,* p. 288

69   Taylor, *Christian Muslim Relations,* p. 195

70   Taylor, *Christian Muslim Relations,* p. 192

71   Metcalfe, *The Muslims of Medieval Italy,* p. 290

72   Metcalfe, *The Muslims of Medieval Italy,* p. 288-289

73   Abulafia, *Frederick !!,* p. 303

74   Fergus Kerr, *Thomas Aquinas, A Very Short Introduction,* p. 10

75   Metcalfe, *The Muslims of Medieval Italy,* p. 289

76   Taylor, *Christian Muslim Relations,* p. 191

77   Lomax: *Frederick II,* p. 175

78   See details in Christoph T. Maier (1995) Crusade and rhetoric against the Muslim colony of Lucera: Eudes of Châteauroux's Sermones de Rebellione Sarracenorum Lucherie in Apulia, *Journal of Medieval History,* 21:4,343-385, DOI: 10.1016/0304-4181(95)00769-5

79   Lomax: *Frederick II,* p. 176

80   Lomax: *Frederick II,* p. 179

81   Lomax: *Frederick II,* p. 176

82   Lomax: *Frederick II,* p. 180

83   See Maier, *Crusade and rhetoric against the Muslim colony of Lucera,* p. 353

84   See Maier, *Crusade Preaching,* p. 27

85   Abulafia, *Frederick !!,* p. 148

86   E. Kantorowicz, *Frederick II.* New York: Ungar Publishing, 1931, *171*

87   Einstein, David, *Emperor Frederick II,* New York: Philosophical Library, 1949, p. 213.

88   Michaud, Joseph Francois, *Histoire des Croisades* ed. W. Robinson, London, George Routledge & Co, 1852, p. 50.

89   Thomas Van Cleve, *The Emperor Frederick II of Hohenstaufen.* Oxford:

Oxford University Press, 1972, p. 202

90   See Michele Amari, *Storia dei Musulmani di Sicilia* (Rome: Catani, 1938), iii p. 701.

91   Abulafia, *Frederick !!*, p. 147-148

92   See details in Maier, *Crusade and rhetoric against the Muslim colony of Lucera*, p. 358 onward

93   James Weisheipl, O.P., *Friar Thomas D'Aquino: His Life, Thought and Works*, Washington D.C., The Catholic University of America Press, 1983, p. 7

94   Weisheipl, O.P., *Friar Thomas D'Aquino*, p. 7

95   Weisheipl, O.P., *Friar Thomas D'Aquino*, P. 10

96   Weisheipl, O.P., *Friar Thomas D'Aquino*, P. 12

97   Weisheipl, O.P., *Friar Thomas D'Aquino*, P. 12

98   Weisheipl, O.P., *Friar Thomas D'Aquino*, P. 8

99   Weisheipl, O.P., *Friar Thomas D'Aquino*, P. 13

100   Weisheipl, O.P., *Friar Thomas D'Aquino*, P. 14

101   Weisheipl, O.P., *Friar Thomas D'Aquino*, P. 15

102   Weisheipl, O.P., *Friar Thomas D'Aquino*, P. 16

103   C. H. Haskins, *The Renaissance of the Twelfth Century*, London, Harvard University Press, 1955, p. 7

104   Haskins, *The Renaissance of the Twelfth Century*, p. 7

105   Haskins, *The Renaissance of the Twelfth Century*, p. 278

106   A. S. McGrade (ed.), *The Cambridge Companion to Medieval Philosophy*, Cambridge, Cambridge University Press, 2006, p. 21

107   Eric John Holmyard (ed.), *The Works of Geber*, translated by Richard Russel, London, Dent, 1928, digitalized by the University of Michigan on July 13, 2007, p. xv

108   Dorothee Metlitzki, *The Matter of Araby in Medieval England*, New Haven, Yale University Press, 1977, p.54

109   Haskins, *The Renaissance of the Twelfth Century*, p. 281

110   See Simon Barton and Peter Linehan (eds.), *Cross, Crescent and Conversion: Studies on Medieval Spain and Christendom in Memory of*

Richard Fletcher, Leiden, Brill, 2008, p. 53ff;

111 Haskins, *The Renaissance of the Twelfth Century,* p. 11

112 Haskins, *The Renaissance of the Twelfth Century,* p. 285; also see Eva R. Hoffman, *Pathways of Portability: Islamic and Christian interchange from the tenth to the twelfth century,* Oxford, Blackwell Publishers, Art History ISSN 0141-6790 Vol. 24 No. 1 February 2001 pp. 17-50

113 See Charles Burnett, *"Arabic into Latin: the Reception of Arabic Philosophy into Western Europe"* in Peter Adamson and Richard C. Taylor (eds.), The Cambridge Companion to Arabic Philosophy, Cambridge, Cambridge University Press, 2006, p. 370ff

114 Haskins, *The Renaissance of the Twelfth Century,* p. 290

115 See Jeremy Johns, *Arabic Administration in Norman Sicily,* Cambridge, Cambridge University Press, 2002

116 Haskins, *The Renaissance of the Twelfth Century,* p. 283

117 Haskins, *The Renaissance of the Twelfth Century,* p. 284

118 See George Saliba, *Islamic Science and the Making of European Renaissance,* London, MIT Press, 2007, p. viiiff especially chapter 6 "Islamic Science and the Renaissance Europe: The Copernican Connection".

119 Haskins, *The Renaissance of the Twelfth Century,* p. 290-291

120 Marvin Perry, Myrna Chase, James Jacob (Eds.), *Western Civilization, Ideas, Politics and Society,* Boston, Houghton Mifflin Company, sixth edition, 2004, p. 250

121 Alax Metcalfe, *The Muslims of Medieval Italy,* p. 106

122 Metcalfe, *The Muslims of Medieval Italy,* p. 106

123 Metcalfe, *The Muslims of Medieval Italy,* p. 141

124 Metcalfe, *The Muslims of Medieval Italy,* p. 106

125 See detail at http://en.wikisource.org/wiki/1911_Encyclop%C3%A6dia_Britannica/Frederick_II.,_Roman_Emperor

126 Donald S. Detwiler, *Germany: A Short History,* Carbondale, IL, Southern Illinois University Press. (1999), p. 43.

127 Joseph Schacht and C. E. Bosworth (Eds.), *The Legacy of Islam,* Oxford, Oxford University Press, Second Edition, 1979, p. 24.

128 See David Abulafia, *Frederick II, A Medieval Emperor,* Oxford, Oxford

University Press, 1988, p. 10

129   Abulafia, *Frederick II*, p. 12

130   See http://www.khm.at/en/

131   Abulafia, *Frederick II*, p. 186

132   Karen Armstrong, *Holy War*, p. 416

133   See Armstrong, *Holy War*, p. 418

134   Dorothea Weltecke, *Emperor Frederick II, "Sultan of Lucera", "Friend of the Muslims", Promoter of Cultural Transfer: Controversies and Suggestions, in Cultural Transfers in Dispute: Representations in Asia, Europe and the Arab World since the Middle Ages,* Edited by Jorg Feuchter, Friedhelm Hoffmann and Bee Yun, Campus Verlag, Frankfurt, 2011, p. 88

135   Armstrong, *Holy War*, 423

136   See Armstrong, *Holy War*, 424

137   Abulafia, *Frederick II*, p. 184

138   Armstrong, *Holy War*, p. 426

139   Abulafia, *Frederick II*, p. 318-319

140   Dorothea Weltecke, *Emperor Frederick II*, p. 85

141   Abulafia, *Frederick II*, p. 318

142   Abulafia, *Frederick II*, p. 368

143   Abulafia, *Frederick II*, p. 320

144   Abulafia, *Frederick II*, p. 369

145   Abulafia, *Frederick II*, p. 375

146   See Asma Afsaruddin (ed.), *Islam, the State, and Political Authority: Medieval Issues and Modern Concerns,* New York, NY: Palgrave McMillan, 2011; M. Galston, *Politics and Excellence: The Political Philosophy of Alfarabi,* Princeton, Princeton University Press, 1990

147   See John Finnis, *Aquinas: Moral, Political and Legal Theory. Oxford,* Oxford University Press, 1998; Thomas Gilby, *The Political Thought of Thomas Aquinas.* Chicago: University of Chicago Press, 1958; James Blythe, 1986. "The Mixed Constitution and the Distinction between Regal and Political Power in the Work of Thomas Aquinas," *Journal of the History of Ideas* 47, 198, p. 547-565.

148   Jacob Burkhardt, *The Civilization of the Renaissance in Italy,* translated by S. G. C. Middlemore, New York, Macmillan, 1904, p. 5

149   Burkhardt, *The Civilization of the Renaissance,* p. 5

150   Burkhardt, *The Civilization of the Renaissance,* p. 5, 6

151   Burkhardt, *The Civilization of the Renaissance,* p. 7

152   Burkhardt, *The Civilization of the Renaissance,* P. 18

153   Weisheipl, O.P., *Friar Thomas D'Aquino,* p. 27

154   J. Rubin, Theological Exchanges with Oriental Christians. In *Learning in a Crusader City: Intellectual Activity and Intercultural Exchanges in Acre, 1191–1291* (Cambridge Studies in Medieval Life and Thought, Cambridge: Cambridge University Press, 2018, p. 148

155   Rubin, *Learning in a Crusader City, p.155; see also* S. P. Cowe, 'The Armenians in the Era of the Crusades 1050–1350', in M. Angold (ed.), The Cambridge History of Christianity, 9 vols. (Cambridge, 2006), vol. V, pp. 418–19; J. D. Ryan, 'Toleration Denied', in M. Gervers and J. M. Powell (eds.), *Tolerance and Intolerance: Social Conflict in the Age of the Crusades* (Syracuse, NY, Syracuse University Press, 2001), p. 59; B. *Hamilton, 'The Armenian Church and the Papacy at the Time of the Crusades',* Eastern Churches Review 10 (1978), p. 82.

156   Rubin, *Learning in a Crusader City, p.160; also see* A. J. Novikoff, *The Medieval Culture of Disputation: Pedagogy, Practice and Performance* (Philadelphia, PA, 2013

157   See Amos Bertolecci, "Albert's Use of *Avicenna* and Islamic Philosophy" in Irven B. Resnick ed., *A Companion to Albert the Great: Theology,* Philosophy and the Sciences, Leiden, Brill, 2013, p. 551

158   Amos Bertolecci, *"Albert's Use of Avicenna and Islamic Philosophy",* p. 601

159   Amos Bertolecci, *"Albert's Use of Avicenna and Islamic Philosophy",* p. 602

160   Weisheipl, O.P., *Friar Thomas D'Aquino,* p. 47

161   Ian P. Wei, *Intellectual Culture in Medieval Paris: Theologians and the University,* c. 1100-1330, Cambridge, Cambrdige University Press, 2012, p. 167

162   Bonaventure, *Conferences on the Hexameron,* vision 3, discussion 7, in Arthur Hyman, James J. Walsh, and Thomas Williams eds., *Philosophy in the Middle Ages: The Christian, Islamic, and Jewish Traditions,* Cambridge, Hackett Publishing Company, 2010, p. 418

163   Bonaventure, *Conferences on the Hexameron, p. 419*

164   Bonaventure, *Conferences on the Hexameron, p. 419*

165   Will Durant, *The Story of Civilization: The Age of Faith,* New York, Simon and Schuster, 1950, v. 4 , p. 949

166   George Sarton, *Introduction to the History of Science,* Baltimore, The Williams and Wilkens Company, 1962, v. II, p. 358

167   George Sarton, *Introduction to the History of Science,* Baltimore, The Williams and Wilkens Company, 1962, v. II, p. 358

168   Marcia I. Colish, *Medieval Foundations of the Western Intellectual Tradition:* 400-1400 , Yale University Press, London, 1998, p. 291

169   Wei, *Intellectual Culture in Medieval Paris,* p. 162

170   Wei, *Intellectual Culture in Medieval Paris,* p. 163

171   Sarton, *Introduction to the History of Science,* v. II.2, p. 734

172   Wei, *Intellectual Culture in Medieval Paris,* p. 163

173   Horowitz, *Averroism and the Politics of Philosophy,* p. 711

174   See Sarton, *Introduction to the History of Science,* v. II.2, p. 543 onward

175   See Maier, *Crusade Preaching,* p. 12-31

176   William Hinnebusch, *History of the Dominican Order,* Alba House, Staten Island, New York, 1966, v. I, p. 401

177   Vose, Dominicans, *Muslims and Jews in the Medieval Crown of Aragon,* p. 35

178   See Simon Tugwell, ed. *Early Dominicans: selected writings.* Classics of Western Spirituality. London: SPCK, 1982

179   See Lester Little, *Frater Ludovicus,* chapters III and IV

180   See Lester Little, *Frater Ludovicus,* p. 90

181   R. F. Bennet, *The Early Dominicans: Studies in Thirteenth-Century Dominican History,* New York, Russel and Russel, 1971, p. 75

182   W. A. Hinnebusch, Origins and Growth to 1500, vol. 1 of *The History of the Dominican Order.* Staten Island: Alba House, 1965 p. 280; William A. Hinnebusch, *Intellectual and Cultural Life to 1500,* vol 2. of *The History of the Dominican Order,* (Staten Island: Alba House, 1965), 37; *Primitive Constitutions of the Order of Friars Preachers,* p. II. Sec .23, in Lehner, *Saint Dominic, Biographical Documents,* Washington DC:

Thomist Press, 1964, 244

183 Bennet, *The Early Dominicans, p. 75*

184 Hinnebusch, *Origins and Growth to 1500,* p. 330-331

185 See William A. Hinnebusch, "How the Dominican Order Faced its Crises," http://www.domcentral.org/ trad/crises.htm.,

186 See details in Lester Little, *Frater Ludovicus,* p. 139 onward

187 See Mark Johnson ed., *St. Thomas Aquinas and the Mendicant Controversies,* Three Translations, Leesburg, Virginia, Alethes Press, 2007

188 See details in Bert Roest, *Franciscan Learning,* Preaching and Mission c. 1220–1650, Leiden, Brill, 2015, p. 9 onward

189 See details at https://web.archive.org/web/20101229185458/http://www.domcentral.org/study/opstudy.htm

190 Rubin, p. 49

191 See M. Michele Mulchahey, *First the Bow is Bent in Study.* Dominican Education before *1350,* Toronto: Pontifical Institute of Mediaeval Studies, 1998.

192 Kerr, *Thomas Aquinas,* p. 15

193 Jordan, *The Encyclical Letter of Jordan of Saxony,* in Lehner, *Saint Dominic, Biographical Documents,* p. 206

194 See Mulchahey, *First the Bow is Bent in Study*, p. 75

195 See details in Mulchahey, *First the Bow is Bent in Study*, p. 86 onward

196 See details in Mulchahey, *First the Bow is Bent in Study*, p. 189 onward

197 Bennet, *The Early Dominicans*, p. 56

198 Robin Vose, Dominicans, *Muslims and Jews in the Medieval Crown of Aragon,* p. 7

199 Vose, Dominicans, *Muslims and Jews in the Medieval Crown of Aragon,* p. 23

200 John V. Tolan, *Saracens: Islam in the Medieval European Imagination,* New York, Columbia University Press, 2002, p. 225

201 Robert I. Burns, S.J, *Christian-Islamic Confrontation in the West: The Thirteenth-Century Dream of Conversion,* The American Historical Review, Vol. 76, No. 5 (Dec., 1971), pp. 1386-1434, p. 1387

202   See James Kritzeck, *Peter the Venerable and Islam* (Princeton, Princeton University Press, 1964

203   See T. Burman, *"Tafsir and Translation: Traditional Arabic Quranic Exegesis* and the Latin Qurans of Robert of Ketton and Mark of Toledo" in *Speculum* 73 (1998), 703–32.

204   Anna Sapir Abulafia, *Christians and Jews in the Twelfth-Century Renaissance* (London, 1995), p. 87.

205   Vose, Dominicans, *Muslims and Jews in the Medieval Crown of Aragon*, p. 28

206   Burns, S.J, *Christian-Islamic Confrontation in the West*, pp. 1389-90

207   Syds Wiersma, *Pearls in a dunghill: The anti-Jewish writings of Raymond Martin O.P.* (ca. 1220 - ca. 1285), Doctoral Thesis, Tilburg University, (2015), p. 17; https://research.tilburguniversity.edu/en/publications/pearls-in-a-dunghill-the-anti-jewish-writings-of-raymond-martin-o

208   BENJAMIN Z. KEDAR, *Crusade and Mission: European Approaches Toward the Muslims*, Princeton, Princeton University Press, 1984, p. 136

209   Kedar, *Crusade and Mission, p. 136*

210   Wiersma, *Pearls in a dunghill*, p. 19

211   Kedar, *Crusade and Mission*, p. 137

212   Kedar, *Crusade and Mission*, p. 137

213   Wiersma, *Pearls in a dunghill*, p. 22

214   Wiersma, *Pearls in a dunghill*, p. 22

215   Specialist research on the person and life of King James I of Aragon was done by Robert Burns. See especially: 'The Spiritual Life of James the Conqueror, King of Arago-Catalonia, 1208-1276. Portrait and Self-Portrait', *TCHR* 62 (1976), 1-35 [repr. in R. Burns, *Moors and Crusaders in Mediterranean Spain. Collected Studies*, London, Variorum, 1978; 'Castle of Intellect, Castle of Force. The Worlds of Alfonso the Learned and James the Conqueror', in: R. Burns (ed.), *The Worlds of Alfonso the Learned and James the Conqueror*, Princeton, Princeton University Press, 1985, 3-22.

216   Wiersma, *Pearls in a dunghill*, p. 23

217   Burns, S.J, *Christian-Islamic Confrontation in the West*, p. 1401

218   Vose, Dominicans, *Muslims and Jews in the Medieval Crown of Aragon*,

p. 136-139

219   See Rubin, *Learning in a Crusader City*, p. 49

220   Burns, S.J, *Christian-Islamic Confrontation in the West*, p. 1402

221   Wiersma, *Pearls in a dunghill*, p. 25. Wiersma and other scholars consider it an exaggeration.

222   Vose, Dominicans, *Muslims and Jews in the Medieval Crown of Aragon*, p. 96

223   See Maier, *Crusade Preaching*, chapter 2

224   See Maier, *Crusade Preaching*, chapters 3 to 6

225   John Tolan, *Saint Francis and the Sultan: The Curious History of a Christian-Muslim Encounter,* Oxford, Oxford University Press, 2009, p. 13; see more details about Franciscan mission strategy in Tolan, *Saracens*, chapter 9, p. 214 onward.

226   Amanda Power, *Roger Bacon and the Defense of Christendom,* Cambridge, Cambridge University Press, 2013, p. 2

227   Vose, Dominicans, *Muslims and Jews in the Medieval Crown of Aragon*, p. 30

228   *Opus maius* VII:1, ed. Bridges, vol. II, 373

229   John V. Tolan, *Saracens: Islam in the Medieval European Imagination,* p. 226

230   Burns, S.J, *Christian-Islamic Confrontation in the West*, p. 1400

231   See Tolan, *Saracens*, p. 227 onward

232   Burns, S.J, *Christian-Islamic Confrontation in the West*, p. 1400

233   See Amanda Power, *Roger Bacon,* p. 36; also see C. Burnett, *The Introduction of Arabic Learning into England,* London, British Library, 1997

234   Vose, Dominicans, *Muslims and Jews in the Medieval Crown of Aragon*, p. 30

235   Tolan, *Saracens*, p 229

236   Vose, Dominicans, *Muslims and Jews in the Medieval Crown of Aragon*, p. 31

237   Llull, *Vita coaetana* ¶7; Bonner, *Selected Works*, vol. i, 16.

238   Vose, Dominicans, *Muslims and Jews in the Medieval Crown of Aragon*,

p. 32

239 Vose, Dominicans, *Muslims and Jews in the Medieval Crown of Aragon*, p. 68

240 Burns, S.J, *Christian-Islamic Confrontation in the West*, p. 1402

241 Wiersma, *Pearls in a dunghill*, p. 20; see also Amanda *Power, Going Among the Infidels*, p. 192

242 Burns, S.J, *Christian-Islamic Confrontation in the West*, p. 1408

243 Burns, S.J, *Christian-Islamic Confrontation in the West*, p. 1403-04

244 Burns, S.J, *Christian-Islamic Confrontation in the West*, p. 1405

245 Robert Burns, "Stupor Mundi: Alfonso X of Castile, the Learned", in *Burns, Emperor of Culture: Alfonso X the Learned of Castile and His Thirteenth-Century Renaissance,* Philadelphia: University of Pennsylvania Press, 1990; F. O'Callaghan, *The Learned King: The Reign of Alfonso X of Castile,* Philadelphia, PA: University of Pennsylvania Press, 1993

246 Burns, S.J, *Christian-Islamic Confrontation in the West*, p. 1405-08

247 See Burns, S.J, *Christian-Islamic Confrontation in the West*, p. 1410

248 See E. R. Daniel, "Apocalyptic Conversion: The Joachite Alternative to the Crusades," *Traditio* 25 (1969):127–54; Brett Edward Whalen, *Dominion of God: Christendom and Apocalypse in the Middle Ages.* Cambridge, MA: Harvard University Press, 2009.

249 See details in Philip Schaff, *History of Christian Church*, The Middle Ages. A D. 1049-1292, Grand Rapids, MI: Christian CLassics Ethereal Library, 2002, v. 5, p. 198 onward

250 Majorie Reeves, *The Influence of Prophecy in the Later Middle Ages: A Study in Joachimism.* New ed. Notre Dame: University of Notre Dame Press, 1993.

251 Tolan, *Saracens*, p. 195

252 See E. Randolph Daniel, *Abbot Joachim of Fiore and Joachimism*, Variorum Collected Studies Series, Burlington, VT, Ashgate Publishing Ltd., 2011.

253 See Bernard McGinn, *The Abbot and the Doctors: Scholastic Reactions to the Radical Eschatology of Joachim of Fiore*, Church History, Vol. 40, No. 1 (Mar., 1971), pp. 30-47

254 Burns, S.J, *Christian-Islamic Confrontation in the West*, p. 1390; also see

Andrew Jotischky, *Penance and Reconciliation in the Crusader States: Matthew Paris,* Jacques de Vitry and the Eastern Christians, Studies in Church History, 2004, vol. 4

255   Burns, S.J, *Christian-Islamic Confrontation in the West*, p. 1391

256   Vose, Dominicans, *Muslims and Jews in the Medieval Crown of Aragon*, p. 43

257   See details in Chapter Three in R. Burns, *Muslims, Christians, and Jews in the Crusader Kingdom of Valencia, p.*80-108

258   Wiersma, *Pearls in a dunghill*, p. 19

259   See Farhad Daftary, *The Assassin Legends: Myths of the Ismai'lis,* London, I. B. Tauris, 1994, p. 80

260   Vose, Dominicans, *Muslims and Jews in the Medieval Crown of Aragon*, p. 44-45

261   Vose, Dominicans, *Muslims and Jews in the Medieval Crown of Aragon*, p. 45

262   E. Tracy Brett, *Humbert of Romans. His Life and View of Thirteenth-Century Society*, Toronto, Pontifical Institute of Mediaeval Studies, 1984, p. 132

263   Wiersma, *Pearls in a dunghill*, p. 19

264   Wiersma, *Pearls in a dunghill*, p. 21

265   Vose, Dominicans, *Muslims and Jews in the Medieval Crown of Aragon*, p. 47

266   Vose, Dominicans, *Muslims and Jews in the Medieval Crown of Aragon*, p. 47

267   Wiersma, *Pearls in a dunghill*, p. 21

268   Vose, Dominicans, *Muslims and Jews in the Medieval Crown of Aragon*, p. 49

269   See Tolan, *Saracens*, chapter 10, p. 233 onward

270   Tolan, *Saracens*, p. 234

271   See Jules Janssens "R. Marti and His Reference to al-Ghazali" in Georges Tamer, *Islam and Rationality: The Impact of al-Ghazali,* Papers Collected on His 900th Anniversary, Leiden, Brill, 2015, v. 1, p. 326-344; See its translation by R. Chazan, *Daggers of Faith. Thirteenth-Century Christian Missionizing and Jewish Response*, Berkeley, University of California Press, 1989 and his *Barcelona and Beyond. The Disputation*

of 1263 and its Aftermath, Berkeley, University of California Press, 1992.

272   Wiersma, *Pearls in a dunghill*, p. 12

273   See Wiersma, *Pearls in a dunghill*, p. 47-77

274   Wiersma, *Pearls in a dunghill*, p. 14

275   Wiersma, *Pearls in a dunghill*, pp. 14 -16

276   Tolan, *Saracens*, p. 242

277   Wiersma, *Pearls in a dunghill*, p 36

278   See Wiersma, *Pearls in a dunghill*, p. 42

279   Wiersma, *Pearls in a dunghill*, p 42-43

280   Wiersma, *Pearls in a dunghill*, p. 89

281   See R.-A. Gauthier, *Somme contre les gentils. Introduction*, Paris 1993, p. 115

282   Wiersma, *Pearls in a dunghill*, p. 90

283   See Jules Janssens, "R. Marti and His Reference to al-Ghazali" in Georges Tamer, p. 326

284   Wiersma, *Pearls in a dunghill*, p. 83

285   See Wiersma, *Pearls in a dunghill*, p. 83-84

286   Wiersma, *Pearls in a dunghill*, p. 84

287   Wiersma, *Pearls in a dunghill*, p. 85

288   Wiersma, *Pearls in a dunghill*, p. 94

289   See details in Rubin, chapter 2 "Acre's Christian And Jewish Centres Of Teaching And Learning", p. 48 onward

290   David Steward Bachrach, "The Friars Go to War: Mendicant Military Chaplains, 1216-c. 1300." *The Catholic Historical Review*, vol. 90 no. 4, 2004, pp. 617-633. *Project MUSE*, doi:10.1353/cat.2005.0003

291   See Damian J. Smith, *Crusade, Heresy and Inquisition in the Lands of the Crown of Aragon* (1167-1276), Leiden, Brill, 2010

292   Christine Caldwell Ames, *Righteous persecution inquisition, Dominicans, and Christianity in the Middle Ages*, Philadelphia : University of Pennsylvania Press, 2009

293   D. J. Smith, *Crusade, Heresy and Inquisition*, p. 2

294   Smith, *Crusade, Heresy and Inquisition*, p. 5; R. Kieckhefer, 'The Office of Inquisition and Medieval Heresy: The Transition from Personal to Institutional Jurisdiction', *Journal of Ecclesiastical History*, 46 (1995); E. Peters, *Inquisition,* Berkeley, University of California Press, 1989); B. Hamilton, *Th e Medieval Inquisition,* London, 1981

295   Ames, *Righteous Persecution*, p. 6

296   Ames, *Righteous Persecution*, p. 7

297   Walter Ullmann, *Short History of the Papacy in the Middle Ages*, New York, Routledge, 2003, p. 172

298   See details in D. C. Chambers, *Popes, Cardinals and War: The Military Church in Renaissance and Early Modern Europe,* London, I. B. Tauris, 2006, pp. 20-21

299   John W. O' Malley S. J., *A History of Popes: From Peter to the Present,* New York, Rowman and Littlefield Publishers, 2010, p. 130

300   Philip Schaff, *History of Christian Church*, v. 5, p. 111

301   Chambers, *Popes, Cardinals and War*, p. 21

302   Ullmann, *Short History of Papacy*, p. 172

303   William Hinnebusch, *The Dominicans: A Short History,* Staten Island, N.Y.: Alba House, 1975, p. 51

304   O' Malley S. J., *History of Popes*, p. 131

305   See details in Tolan, *Saracens*, p. 233 onward

306   See Amanda *Power, Going among the Infidels*, p. 195

307   Armstrong, *Holy War*, p. 445

308   Thomas F. O'Meara O.P., *The Theology and the Times of William of Tripoli O. P.: A Different View of Islam,* Theological Studies, 69, 2008, pp. 81-82

309   O'Meara O.P., *The Theology and the Times of William of Tripoli*, pp. 82-83

310   Christopher MacEvitt, *The Crusades and the Christian World of East,* Pennsylvania, University of Pennsylvania Press, 2008, p. 12

311   MacEvitt, *The Crusades and the Christian World of East,* p. 135; also see B. Kedar, Franks, *Muslims and Oriental Christians in the Latin Levant: Studies in Frontier Acculturation.* Aldershot: Ashgate, 2006 and *The Majlis: Interreglious Encounters in Medieval Islam,* ed. Hava Lazarus-Yafeh, *et al.,* 162–83. Wiesbaden: Harrassowitz, 1999

312 Kenneth M. Setton general editor, *A History of the Crusades,* v. 5 "The Impact of the Crusades on the Near East" edited by Norman P. Zacour and Harry W. Hazard, Madison, University of Wisconsin Press, 1985, p. 455

313 See Setton, *A History of the Crusades,* v. 5, pp. 455-470

314 George-Tvrtkovic, Rita. *A Christian Pilgrim in Medieval Iraq: Riccoldo da Montecroce's Encounter with Islam.* Turnhout, Belgium, Brepols Press, 2012

315 See Setton, *A History of the Crusades,* v. 5, p. 463

316 David Thomas and Alex Mallett eds., *Christian Muslim Relations: A Biographical History* Volume 4 (1200-1350), Leiden, Brill, 2012, p. 515-520

317 Some scholars doubt his proficiency in Arabic.

318 O'Meara O.P., *The Theology and the Times of William of Tripoli,* pp. 86-87

319 O'Meara O.P., *The Theology and the Times of William of Tripoli,* pp. 87

320 Tolan, *Saracens,* p. 203

321 David Thomas and Alex Mallett eds., *Christian Muslim Relations,* p. 386

322 David·Thomas and Alex Mallett eds., *Christian Muslim Relations,* p. 389

323 See C. Maier, Gilbert Of Tournai. In *Crusade Propaganda and Ideology: Model Sermons for the Preaching of the Cross* (pp. 176-209). Cambridge: Cambridge University Press, 2000

324 See J. F. Verbruggen, *The Art of Warfare in Western Europe During the Middle Ages,* translated by Sumner Willard, Woodbridge, Boydell Press, 2002, p. 279-302

325 O'Meara O.P., *The Theology and the Times of William of Tripoli,* p. 89

326 Rubin, *Learning in a Crusader City,* p. 1

327 Rubin, *Learning in a Crusader City,* p. 3

328 See Rubin, *Learning in a Crusader City,* p. 5

329 Rubin, *Learning in a Crusader City,* p. 5

330 See C. T. Maier, "Crusade and rhetoric against the Muslim colony of Lucera: Eudes of Chateauroux's Sermones de Rebellione Sarracenorum Lucherie in Apulia". *Journal of Medieval History.* 21 (4): 1995, p. 343–385. doi:10.1016/0304-4181(95)00769-5. Also Charles H. Haskins, *The University of Paris in the Sermons of the Thirteenth Century,* The American Historical Review, Vol. 10, No. 1 (Oct., 1904), pp. 1-27

331   See Kedar, *Crusades and Mission*, p. 139 onward

332   See Kedar, *Crusades and Mission*, p. 139

333   Rubin, *Learning in a Crusader City*, p. 19

334   Rubin, *Learning in a Crusader City*, p. 20

335   Rubin, *Learning in a Crusader City*, p. 21-22

336   Rubin, *Learning in a Crusader City*, p. 22

337   Rubin, *Learning in a Crusader City*, p. 45

338   Rubin, *Learning in a Crusader City*, 45-46

339   John Renard, *Islam and Christianity: Theological Themes in Comparative Perspective*, Berkeley, University of California Press, 2011, p. xxii

340   Quoted in Hamid Naseem Rafiabadai and Aadil Amin Kak, *The Attitude of Islam Towards Science and Philosophy*, New Delhi, Sarup and Sons, 2003, P. 43

341   See details https://academic.mu.edu/taylorr/Aquinas_and_the_Arabs/Aquinas_&_the_Arabs.html

342   Quoted by Haider Bammate, *Muslim contribution to Civilization*, Indiana: American Trust Publications, 1976, p. 23

343   M. M. Sharif (Ed.), *A History of Muslim Philosophy*, Wiesbadden, Otto Harrassowitz, 1963, v. 1, p. 480

344   Binyamin Abrahamov, *Anthropomorphism and Interpretation of the Quran in the Theology of al-Qasim ibn Ibrahim*, Boston: Brill, 1996, p.4.

345   Abrahamov, *Anthrpomorphism*, p.3.

346   Ian Richard Netton, *Allah Transcendent: Studies in the Structure and Semiotics of Islamic Philosophy*, Theology and Cosmology, New York, Routledge, 1995, p.2.

347   See Zahdi Hasan Jarallah, *al-Mu`tazilah* (Cairo: al-Mu'assasah al-`Arabiyyah li al-Dirāsāt wa al-Nashr, 1947), pp.33, 256; William M. Watt, *The Formative Period of Islamic Thought* (Edinburgh: Edinburgh University Press, 1973), pp.249-50.

348   Andrew Rippin, *Muslims: Their Religious Beliefs & Practices*, New York: Routledge, 1990, vol.1, p.65.

349   Rippin, *Muslims*, p.69.

350   See Qāāī `Abd al-Jabbār, *Sharh al-Uåūl al-Khamsah*, `Abd al-Karim

`Uthman, ed., 1ˢᵗ edn. (Cairo: Maktabah Wahabah, 1965); Al-Faruqi, *Cultural Atlas*, pp.287-91.

351   Ismail R. al-Faruqi, Lois L. al-Faruqi, *The Cultural Atlas of Islam* (New York: MacMillan Publishing Company, 1986), p.287.

352   Duncan B. Macdonald, *Development of Muslim Theology, Jurisprudence and Constitutional Theory*, Beirut: Khayats, 1965, p.136.

353   Macdonald, *Development of Muslim Theology*, pp.136-37.

354   A. K. Kazi, J. G. Flynn, trans., *Muslim Sects and Divisions: The Section on Muslim Sects in Kitab al-Milal wa al-Nihal by Shahrastani*, London, Kegan Paul International, 1984, p.46

355   Qāāī `Abd al-Jabbār, *Sharh al-Uåūl al-Khamsah*, `Abd al-Karim `Uthman, ed., 1ˢᵗ edn., Cairo: Maktabah Wahabah, 1965, pp.151-75.

356   Al-Faruqi, *Cultural Atlas*, p.288.

357   Netton, *Allah Transcendent*, pp.4-5.

358   Abū al-Ḥasan `Alī al-Ash`arī, *Maqālāt al-Islāmiyyīn wa Ikhtilāf al-Muåallīn*, M. `Abd al-Hamid, ed. (Beirut: Al-Ḥikmah, 1994). p.74.

359   al-Ash`arī, *Maqālāt*,Ibid.

360   See a detailed discussion of these interpretations in J. M. S. Baljon, "Quranic Anthropomorphism," *Islamic Studies* (Islamabad: Islamic Research Institute, 1988), vol.27; also al-Jabbār, *Sharh Uåūl al-Khamsah*, pp.227 ff.

361   Watt, *The Formative Period of Islamic Thought*, pp.248-49.

362   Macdonald, *Development of Muslim Theology*, p.145.

363   Fazlur Rahman, *Islam*, Chicago: University of Chicago Press, 1979, p.89.

364   Netton, *Allah Transcendent*, p.5.

365   William M. Watt, "Early Discussions about the Quran," *Muslim World* (1950), vol. XL, p.31.

366   Watt, *The Formative Period of Islamic Thought*, p.250.

367   Fakhr al-Dīn al-Rāzī, *Asās al-Taqdīs*, Cairo: Maæba`ah Muåæafà al-Bàbī, 1935, p.180.

368   See details of their philosophical positions in Seyyed H.., *History of Islamic Philosophy*, London; New York: Routledge, 1996, vol.1, pp.178-97.

369   See for a detailed study Netton, *Allah Transcendent*, pp.106 ff.

370 Abâ Naår al-Farabá, *al-Thamaràt al-Maràiyyah,* Leiden: Brills, 1895, pp.57 f.

371 Netton, *Allah Transcendent,* p.104.

372 Ibrahim Madkur, *Fī al-Falsafah al-Islāmiyyah,* Cairo: Dār al-Ma`ārif, 1976, vol.2, p.82.

373 Netton, *Allah Transcendent,* p.109.

374 See Arthur J. Arberry, *Avicenna on Theology,* Connecticut: Hyperion Press, 1979, p.25; Netton, *Allah Transcendent,* pp.150-53.

375 Netton, *Allah Transcendent,* p.154.

376 Arberry, *Avicenna on Theology,* p.32.

377 Quoted from Netton, *Allah Transcendent,* p. 154.

378 Arberry, *Avicenna on Theology,* p.36; also see Netton, *Allah Transcendent,* pp.162 f.

379 Madkur, *Fī al-Falsafah al-Islāmiyyah,* vol.2, p.82.

380 Kenny, *Illustrated History,* p. 153

381 H. A. Wolfson, *The Philosophy of the Kalam,* Cambridge, Mass., Harvard University Press, 1976, p. 352-354

382 Wolfson, *The Philosophy of the Kalam,* p. 353-354

383 Fakhr al-Dīn al-Rāzī, *Asās al-Taqdīs* (Cairo: Maktabah Mustafa al-Bàbī, 1935), p.180.

384 William M. Watt, *Early Islam: Collected Articles* (Edinburgh: Edinburgh University Press, 1990), p.91.

385 Abu Hamid Al-Ghazali, *Kitāb Iljam al-`Awām `an `Ilm al-Kalām* (Cairo: Maktabah al-Munīriyyah, 1933), p.7 where he gives example of "Surah" in connection with God.

386 See Ian R. Netton, *Text and Trauma: An East-West Primer* (Richmond: Curzon Press, 1996), p.91 onward; Richard P. C. Hanson, *Allegory and Event,* (London: S.C.M Press, 1959); Robert McQueen Grant, *The Letter and the Spirit,* London: SPCK, 1957; Frederic W. Farrar, *History of Interpretation,* [Bampton Lectures] (New York: E. P. Dutton & Co., 1886), [reprinted by Baker Book House, Michigan, 1961

387 See for definition of *'ta'wil'* in ibn Rushd, *Faål al-Maqàl,* http://shamela.ws/browse.php/book-12727#page-21; Fakhr al-Dīn al-Rāzī, *Asās al-Taqdīs* (Cairo: Maæba`ah Muåæafà al-Bàbī, 1935), p.182.

388   Watt, *Early Islam*, pp.91-92.

389   Watt, *Early Islam*, p.93.

390   See Ahmad Essa and Othman Ali, *Studies in Islamic Civilization: The Muslim Contribution to the Renaissance*, (Herndon, Virginia: International Institute of Islamic Thought, 2010), p. 250

391   Thomas Aquinas, *Summa Contra Gentiles*, translated by Anton C. Pegis, New York, Image Books, 1955, Book One, p. 63

392   Thomas Aquinas, *Summa Theologica*, http://www.ccel.org/ccel/aquinas/summa.html, p. 3

393   Aquinas, *Summa Theologica*, p. 3

394   Aquinas, *Summa Theologica*, p. 6

395   Aquinas, *Summa Theologica*, p. 7

396   Macdonald, *Development of Muslim Theology*, p.136-37

397   Al-Faruqi, *Cultural Atlas*, p.288

398   Fakhry, *al-Farabi*, p. 81-82

399   See Abu Hamid al-Ghazali, a*l-Iqtisad fi al-I'atiqad* translated by Alaadin M. Yaqub as *Moderation in Belief,* Chicago, University of Chicago Press, 2013, p. 79 onward

400   Aquinas, *Summa Theologica*, p. 101-102

401   Aquinas, *Summa Theologica*, p. 101

402   Aquinas, *Summa Theologica*, p. 99

403   Aquinas, *Summa Theologica*, p. 82-83

404   Aquinas, *Summa Theologica*, p. 82

405   Aquinas, *Summa Theologica*, p. 80

406   Aquinas, *Summa Theologica*, p. 88

407   Aquinas, *Summa Theologica*, p. 87

408   Aquinas, *Summa Theologica*, 91

409   Aquinas, *Summa Theologica*, p. 83

410   Norman Kretzmann and Eleonore Stump eds., *The Cambridge Companion to Aquinas,* Cambridge, Cambridge University Press, 1999, p. 89-90

411   Aquinas, *Summa Theologica*, p. 87

412   *Cambridge Companion to Aquinas*, p. 90

413   *Cambridge Companion to Aquinas*, p. 90

414   Aquinas, *Summa Theologica*, p. 86

415   See Abu al-Walïd Muhammad ibn Ahmad ibn Rushd, *Fasl al-Maqa'l fï m¥ bayn al-¤ikmah wa al-Sharï¢ah min al-Itti|¥l*, 2nd edn. (Cairo: Dar al-Ma'arif, 1983); see its translation in Hamid Naseem Rafiabadi, *The Attitude of Islam Towards Science and Philosophy,* A Translation of Ibn Rushd's Faslul al-Maqal, New Delhi, Sarup and Sons, 2003; for additional English source see Majid Fakhry, *A History of Islamic Philosophy* (New York; London: Columbia University Press, 1970), pp.302ff; and Fakhry, *Averroes*, p. 32-33; also see Ibn Rushd, *Tahafut al-Tahafut*, translated by Simon Van Den Bergh as "Incoherence of Incoherence", Cambridge, EJW Gibb Memorial Trust, 1987, v. 1, p. 175 onward

416   *Cambridge Companion to Aquinas*, p. 90

417   *Cambridge Companion to Aquinas*, p. 91

418   *Cambridge Companion to Aquinas*, p. 91

419   Sharif, *A History of Muslim Philosophy*, v. 1, p. 480

420   Frederick Eby, and Charles Flinn Arrowood. *The History and Philosophy of Education: Ancient and Medieval,* Englewood Cliffs, NJ: Prentice-Hall, Inc., 1940, p 698

421   Maria Rosa Menocal, *The Arabic Role in Medieval Literary History: A Forgotten Heritage,* Philadelphia: University of Pennsylvania Press, 1987, p. 52.

422   Sharif, *A History of Muslim Philosophy*, v. 1, p. 505

423   Jon McGinnis, *Avicenna*, Oxford, Oxford University Press, 2010, p. ix

424   McGinnis, *Avicenna*, p. 251

425   McGinnis, *Avicenna*, p. 244

426   McGinnis, *Avicenna*, p. 251

427   McGinnis, *Avicenna*, p. 251

428   McGinnis, *Avicenna*, p. 252

429   John F. Wippel, *Metaphysical Themes in Thomas Aquinas II*, Washington D. C., The Catholic University of America Press, 2007, p. 32

430   Jean-Pierre Torrell, *Aquinas's Summa, Background, Structure and*

Reception, translated by Benedict M.Guevin, Washington D. C., The Catholic University of America Press, 2005, p. 82

431 Jean-Pierre, *Aquinas's Summa,* P. 82-83

432 Thomas Aquinas, *Contra,* p. 101-102

433 E. Gilson, *History of Christian Philosophy in the Middle Ages,* New York, Random House,1955, p. 646 (note 2 6)

434 Shams Inati, *Ibn Sina's Remarks and Admonitions, Physics and Metaphysics,* An Analysis and Annotated Translation, New York, Columbia University Press, 2014, p. 122

435 Etienne Gilson, *Thomism: The Philosophy of Thomas Aquinas, A translation of* LE THOMISME *Sixth and final edition By* Laurence K. Shook and Armand Maurer, Toronto, Pontifical Institute of Mediaeval Studies, 2002, P. 139

436 Anthony Kenny says that "In a famous passage of Posterior Analytics (11. 7. 92b14) Aristotle says 'to be is not part of the substance (ousia) of anything, because what is (to on) is not a genus'. This can be taken as saying that existence is not part of the essence of anything: i.e. that there is such a thing is not what anything is. If that is what it means, then it deserves the compliment paid by Schopenhauer when he said that with prophetic insight Aristotle forestalled the Ontological Argument." *A New History of Western Philosophy: Ancient Philosophy,* Oxford, Clarendon Press, 2006, P. 224

437 See David Burrell, *Knowing the Unknowable God: Ibn-Sina, Maimonides, Aquinas,* Notre Dame, IN: University of Notre Dame Press, 1986, p. 19 onward.

438 See Robert Hammond, *The Philosophy of al-Farabi and Its Influence on Medieval Thought,* New York, Hobson Book Press, 1947, p. 13-14

439 Jean Jolivet, "From the Beginning to *Avicenna*" in John Marenbon (Ed), Medieval Philosophy, P. 44

440 Burrell, *Knowing the Unknowable God,* p. 19

441 See Inati, *Ibn Sina's Remarks and Admonitions,* p. 121

442 See A. Bertolacci, "On the Latin Reception of *Avicenna*'s Metaphysics before Albertus Magnus: An Attempt at Periodization", in D. N. Hasse and A. Bertolacci, eds, *The Arabic, Hebrew and Latin Reception of Avicenna's Metaphysics,* Berlin/Boston: deGruyter, 2012, p. 197–223.

443   See details in Frank Griffel, *Al-Ghazali's Philosophical Theology*, Oxford, Oxford University Press, 2009, p. 141 onward

444   Inati, *Ibn Sina's Remarks*, p. 122

445   H. Nasr and O. Leaman, eds., *History of Islamic Philosophy*, New York, Routledge, 1996, P. 446

446   Inati, *Ibn Sina's Remarks*, p. 123

447   See details in Nasr and Leaman, eds., *History of Islamic Philosophy*, p. 446 onward

448   Inati, *Ibn Sina's Remarks*, p. 124

449   Inati, *Ibn Sina's Remarks*, p. 124

450   See Inati, *Ibn Sina's Remarks*, p. 125-126

451   Jon McGinnis and David C. Reisman, *Classical Arabic Philosophy, An Anthology of Sources,* Cambridge, Hackett Publishing Company, 2007, p. 214

452   Inati, *Ibn Sina's Remarks*, p. 127

453   McGinnes, *Classical Arabic Philosophy*, p. 214

454   Inati, *Ibn Sina's Remarks*, p. 127

455   Burrell, *Knowing the Unknowable*, p. 26

456   McGinnis, *Classical Arabic Philosophy*, p. 252

457   Burrell, *Knowing the Unknowable*, p. 28

458   Burrell, , *Knowing the Unknowable*, p. 34-35

459   Wippel, *Metaphysical Themes in Thomas Aquinas*, p. 36

460   See A. Bertolacci, "*Avicenna* and *Averroes* on the Proof of God's Existence and the Subject-Matter of Metaphysics", *Medioevo*, 32: 61, 2007, p.97

461   Wippel, "Metaphysics" in *Cambridge Companion to Aquinas*, p. 85-86

462   Wippel, *Metaphysical Themes in Thomas Aquinas*, p. 39

463   Wipple, "Metaphysics" in *Cambridge Companion to Aquinas*, p. 86

464   Nasr and Leaman, eds., *History of Islamic Philosophy*, p. 448

465   Nasr and Leaman, eds., *History of Islamic Philosophy*, p. 448

466   Quotd from Richard C. Dales, *Medieval Discussions of the Eternity of the World,* Leiden, Brills, 1990, p. 40

467   Dales, *Medieval Discussions of the Eternity of the World*, p. 41

468   Dales, *Medieval Discussions of the Eternity of the World*, p. 44

469   Robert Sokolowsky, *The God of Faith and Reason, Foundations of Christian Theology,* Washington D.C., Catholic University of America Press, 1995, p. 23

470   Dale, *Medieval Discussions of the Eternity of the World*, p. 44; See St. Thomas Aquinas, Siger of Brabant and St. Bonaventure, *On the Eternity of the World,* translated from Latin by Cyril Vollert, Milwaukee, Marquette University Press, 1984, p. 24

471   Guillaume, *Christian and Muslim Theology*, p. 555

472   Guillaume, *Christian and Muslim Theology*, p. 555

473   Guillaume, *Christian and Muslim Theology*, p. 556

474   Muammer Eskenderoglu, *Fakhr al-Din al-Razi and Thomas Aquinas on the Question of the Eternity of the World,* Leiden, Brills, 2002

475   See Eskenderoglu, *Fakhr al-Din al-Razi and Thomas Aquinas,* p. 174 onward

476   Hebert Davidson, *Moses Maimonides: The Man and His Works,* Oxford, Oxford University Press, 2010, p. 399

477   Frank Griffel, *Al-Ghazali's Philosophical Theology*, p. 119

478   Griffel, *Al-Ghazali's Philosophical Theology,*   P. 119-120

479   McGinnis, *Classical*, p. 243

480   McGinnis, *Classical*, p. 243

481   See details in Al-Ghazali, *The Incoherence of the Philosophers,* translated by Michael E. Marmura, Provo, Utah, Brigham Young University Press, 2002, p. 13 onward

482   Guttmann in Schweid, E., "Religion and Philosophy: The Scholarly-Theological Debate Between Julius Guttmann and Leo Strauss," *Maimonidean Studies* 1:163–97. 1990, p. 172

483   H. A. Wolfson, *Religious Philosophy: A Group of Essays,* New York: Atheneum, 1965

484   S. Pines, "Jewish Philosophy," in *The Encyclopedia of Philosophy,* edited by P. Edwards, New York: Macmillan,1967, v.4, p.262–3.

485   Pines, *Jewish Philosophy*, p. 262–3

486   Majid Fakhry, *Averroes*, p. 132

487   Arthur Hyman, "Jewish Philosophy in the Islamic World," in Nasr and Leaman eds., *History of Islamic Philosophy*, p. 1200

488   Nasr and Leaman eds., *History of Islamic Philosophy*, p. 1191

489   See Sarah Stroums, Andalus and Sefarad. *On Philosophy and Its History in Islamic Spain,* (Princeton: Princeton University Press, 2019), p. 169

490   Nasr and Leaman eds., *History of Islamic Philosophy*, P. 1193

491   Steven M. Wesserstrom, "The Islamic Social and Cultural Context" in *History of Jewish Philosophy,* edited by Daniel H. Frank and O. Leaman, New York, Routledge, p. 73

492   Nasr and Leaman eds., *History of Islamic Philosophy*, p. 1195

493   See Harry A. Wolfson, *The Jewish Kalam,* The Jewish Quarterly Review, Vol. 57, The Seventy-Fifth Anniversary Volume of the Jewish Quarterly Review (1967), pp. 544-573; also his *Repercussions of the Kalam in Jewish Philosophy,* Cambridge, Mass., and London: Harvard University Press, 1979

494   Colette Sirat, "Jewish Philosophy" in John Marenbon ed., Medieval Philosophy, p. 66

495   Mauro Zonta, *The Relationship of European Jewish Philosophy to Islamic and Christian Philosophies in the Late Middle Ages,* Jewish Studies Quarterly, Vol. 7, No. 2 (2000), pp. 127-140

496   Zonta, Mauro, "Influence of Arabic and Islamic Philosophy on Judaic Thought", *The Stanford Encyclopedia of Philosophy* (Spring 2011 Edition), Edward N. Zalta (ed.), URL = <http://plato.stanford.edu/archives/spr2011/entries/arabic-islamic-judaic/>.

497   See Mauro Zonta, *The Relationship of European Jewish Philosophy to Islamic and Christian Philosophies in the Late Middle Ages,* Jewish Studies Quarterly, Vol. 7, No. 2 (2000), pp. 127-140

498   Fakhry, *Averroes*, p. 132

499   Fakhry, *Averroes*, p. 132

500   Majid Fakhry, *Al-Farabi', Founder of Islamic Neoplatonism: His Life, Works and Influence,* Oxford, Oneworld, 2002, p. 148

501   Fakhry, *Averroes*, p. 132

502   Zonta, Mauro, "Influence of Arabic and Islamic Philosophy on Judaic

Thought", *The Stanford Encyclopedia of Philosophy* (Winter 2016 Edition), Edward N. Zalta (ed.), URL = <https://plato.stanford.edu/archives/win2016/entries/arabic-islamic-judaic/>.

503   Fakhry, *Averroes*, p. 133

504   *Wessrstrom in Jewish Philosophy*, p. 75

505   A. N. Whitehead, "An Appeal to Sanity," in *Science and Philosophy*, New York: Philosophical Library, 1948, p. 79

506   Joel L. Kraemer, *Maimonides: The Life and World of One of Civilization's Greatest Minds*, New York, Doubleday Religion, 2010, p. 15

507   Nasr and Leaman, *History of Islamic Philosophy*, 1298

508   Zonta, Mauro, "Influence of Arabic and Islamic Philosophy on Judaic Thought", *The Stanford Encyclopedia of Philosophy* (Spring 2011 Edition), Edward N. Zalta (ed.), URL = <http://plato.stanford.edu/archives/spr2011/entries/arabic-islamic-judaic/>.

509   Zonta, Mauro, "Influence of Arabic and Islamic Philosophy on Judaic Thought", *The Stanford Encyclopedia of Philosophy* (Spring 2011 Edition), Edward N. Zalta (ed.), URL = <http://plato.stanford.edu/archives/spr2011/entries/arabic-islamic-judaic/>.

510   Zonta, Mauro, "Influence of Arabic and Islamic Philosophy on Judaic Thought", *The Stanford Encyclopedia of Philosophy* (Spring 2011 Edition), Edward N. Zalta (ed.), URL = <http://plato.stanford.edu/archives/spr2011/entries/arabic-islamic-judaic/>.

511   See https://plato.stanford.edu/entries/tibbon/

512   Colette Sirat, "Jewish Philosophy" in Marenbon ed., Medieval Philosophy, p. 77

513   Davidson, *Maimonides*, p. 113

514   Davidson, *Maimonides*, p. 114

515   McGinnis, *Classic*, p. 266

516   Davidson, *Maimonides*, p. 114-115

517   Nasr and Leaman eds., *History of Islamic Philosophy*, p. 1214

518   Jules Janssens and Daniel De Smet (Eds), *Avicenna and His Heritage*, Leuven, Leuven University Press, 2002, P. 283

519   Jules Janssens and Daniel De Smet (Eds), *Avicenna and His Heritage*, P. 285

520   Jules Janssens and Daniel De Smet (Eds), Davidson, *Maimonides*, p. 115

521   Jules Janssens and Daniel De Smet (Eds), *Avicenna and His Heritage*, P. 287

522   Sarah Pessin, "The Influence of Islamic Thought on Maimonides", *The Stanford Encyclopedia of Philosophy* (Summer 2014 Edition), Edward N. Zalta (ed.), URL <http://plato.stanford.edu/archives/sum2014/entries/maimonides-islamic/>.

523   Pessin, "The Influence of Islamic Thought on Maimonides"

524   Sirat, "Jewish Philosophy" in Marenbon ed., Medieval Philosophy, p. 84

525   Eliezer Schweid, *The Classic Jewish Philosophers: From Saadia through the Renaissance,* translated by Leonard Levin, Leiden, Brill, 2008, p. 266

526   Leo Strauss and following him many academicians believed in esoteric meanings of the Guide and argued that in reality Maimonides did not believe in the creation but in eternity but he did not argue for it to avoid persecution. Herbert Davidson rejects these claims. Schweid argues that "We should emphasize here that in *contra*st to the Kalamic sages, particularly Saadia, who based their affirmation of creation on a plain sense reading of Genesis, Maimonides argues vociferously not only that there is no problem interpreting the Torah in accord with an "eternal world" outlook, but that even the plain sense of the text of Genesis is indeterminate. Nowhere in Genesis does it say that the creation is *ex nihilo.* One can easily interpret it as depicting the impression of form on pre-existent matter." Davidson, Moses Maimonides, p. 267

527   See Dales, *Medieval Discussions of the Eternity of the World*, 45 onward

528   Schweid, *The Classic Jewish Philosophers,* p. 267

529   Moses Maimonides, *The Guide for the Perplexed,* translated by M. Friedlander, Skokie, Illinois, Varda Books, 2002, p. 178

530   Maimonides, *Guide*, p. 178

531   Maimonides, *Guide*, p. 199

532   Maimonides, *Guide*, p. 199

533   Nasr and Leaman eds., *History of Islamic Philosophy*, p. 1216

534   Maimonides, *Guide*, p. 176

535   Maimonides, *Guide*, p. 176

536   Kenneth Seeskin, *Maimonides on the Origin of the World,* Cambridge,

Cambridge University Press, 2006, p. 70

537   Maimonides, *Guide,* p. 172

538   Maimonides, *Guide,* 173

539   Maimonides, *Guide* p. 180

540   Maimonides, *Guide,* p. 180; see also *Seeskin,* p. 72 "Maimonides' reply is that the nature of a thing after it achieves stability may be different from the nature it has when it is generated, and that in turn may be different from the nature it has before it is generated."

541   Seeskin, *Maimonides on Origin,* p. 71

542   Maimonides, *Guide,* 178-179

543   Maimonides, *Guide,* p. 181

544   Maimonides, *Guide,* p. 195; also See Herbert Davidson, "Maimonides' Secret Position on Creation," *Studies in Medieval Jewish History and Literature* 1, 1979: 16-40 and William Dunphy, "Maimonides' Not-So-Secret Position on Creation," In *Moses Maimonides and His Time,* edited by Eric L. Ormsby. Washington, DC: Catholic University of America Press, 1989: 151-72.

545   Maimonides, *Guide,* p. 195; also see Daniel Davies, *Method and Metaphysics in Maimonides' Guide for the Perplexed,* (New York: Oxford University Press, 2011), 39 onward

546   Wippel, Did Thomas Aquinas Defend the Possibility of an Eternally Created World? (The De aeternitate mundi Revisited), *Journal of the History of Philosophy,* Volume 19, Number 1, January 1981, p. 21

547   See Herbert A. Davidson, *Proofs for Eternity, Creation, and the Existence of God, in Medieval Islamic and Jewish Philosophy,* New York, Oxford University press, 1987, p. 378-388

548   St. Thomas Aquinas, Siger of Brabant and St. Bonaventure, *On the Eternity of the World,* translated from Latin by Cyril Vollert, Milwaukee, Marquette University Press, 1984, p. 18

549   See Davidson, *On Eternity*

550   See Davidson, *On Eternity,* p. 18 onward

551   Wippel, *Did Thomas Aquinas Defend the Possibility of an Eternally Created World?* p. 41

552   See Davidson, *On Eternity,* p. 25 onward

553   Davidson, *On Eternity,* p. 26

554   See Davidson, *On Eternity,* p. 25-34

555   See Al-Ghazali, *The Incoherence of Philosophers,* Translated, Introduces and Annotated by Michael E. Marmura, Provo, Utah, Brigham Young University Press, 2000, p. 13 onward; also Marmura, *The Conflict over the World's Pre-Eternity in the Tahafuts of al-Ghazali and Ibn Rushd,* thesis submitted to University of Michigan, 1959; see also Muammer İskenderoğlu, *Fakhr-al-Dīn al-Rāzī and Thomas Aquinas on the Question of the Eternity of the World,* Leiden, Brill, 2002

556   Wolfson, *Philosophy,* p. 465

557   Davidson, *On Eternity,* p. 34

558   Davidson, *On Eternity,* p. 35

559   Davidson, *On Eternity,* p. 35; "All this makes it manifest that the effect of the divine will is not unduly retarded, as the fourth argument suggested, even though it did not always exist, notwithstanding the fact that it was willed. Not only the existence of the effect, but the time of its existence, is subject to the divine will. Therefore the thing willed, that is, the existence of a creature at a definite time, is not retarded, because the creature began to exist at the moment appointed by God from eternity." P. 35

560   Davidson, *On Eternity,* p. 36

561   See Kathryn Tanner, *God and Creation in Christian Theology: Tyranny or Empowerment?* , Oxford: Basil Blackwell, 1988; and William Placher, *The Domestication of Transcendence* , Louisville, KY: Westminster Press, 1996

562   See Brian J. Shanley, O.P., "Divine Causation and Human Freedom in Aquinas," *American Catholic Philosophical Quarterly* 72:1 (1998), pp. 100 and 108; Michael Miller, "Transcendence and Divine Causality," *American Catholic Philosophical Quarterly* 73:4 (Autumn 1999), pp. 537-554; David Burrell, *Freedom and Causation in Three Traditions,* Notre Dame, IN: University of Notre Dame Press, 1993, p. 97 onward; William E. Carroll, "Aquinas and the Metaphysical Foundations of Science," Sapientia 54:1 (1999), pp. 69-91.

563   Davidson, *On Eternity,* p. 37

564   Davidson, *On Eternity,* p. 38

565   Davidson, *On Eternity,* p. 41

566   See Ayman Shihadeh, From Al-Ghazali To Al-Ra'zi': 6th/12th Century *Developments In Muslim Philosophical Theology, Arabic Sciences and Philosophy*, Cambridge, Cambridge University Press, 2005, vol. 15, P. 144

567   "In the three questions first mentioned they were opposed to (the belief of) all Muslims, viz. in their affirming (1) that men's bodies will not be assembled on the Last Day, but only disembodied spirits will be rewarded and punished, and the rewards and punishments will be spiritual, not corporal. They were indeed right in affirming the spiritual rewards and punishments, for these also are certain; but they falsely denied the corporal rewards and punishments and blasphemed the revealed Law in their stated views. (2) The second question is their declaration: "God Most High knows universals, but not particulars." This also is out-and-out unbelief. On the *contra*ry, the truth is that "there does not escape Him the weight of an atom in the heavens or in the earth." (34.3; cf. 10.62/61). (3) The third question is their maintaining the eternity of the world, past and future." AL-Ghazali, *Deliverance from Error* (*al-Munqidh min al-Dalal*) Translated, with related works, by Richard J. MCCARTHY, S.J., as *Freedom and Fulfillment,* Boston, Twayne, 1980, P. 10-11

568   Davidson, *On Eternity,* P. 41

569   Davidson, *On Eternity,* P. 42

570   Davidson, *On Eternity,* p. 44

571   See Davidson, *On Eternity,* p. 45-50

572   Davidson, *On Eternity,* p. 53

573   Davidson, *On Eternity,* p. 61

574   Davidson, *On Eternity,* P. 65

575   Davidson, *On Eternity,* p.50

576   Kenny, *An Illustrated Brief History of Western Philosophy,* New Jersey, Wiley-Blackwell, 2006, p. 153-154

577   A. Kenny, *An Illustrated Brief History of Western Philosophy,* p. 152

578   See Majid Fakhry, *al-Farabi,* p. 133

579   Nasr and Leaman eds., *History of Islamic Philosophy,* p. 450-451; see also Carlos Steel, "*Avicenna* and Thomas Aquinas on Evil" in *Avicenna and His Heritage,* P. 171 onward

580   McGinnis, *Classic,* p. 253

581   McGinnis, *Classic,* p. 252

582   Nasr and Leaman eds., *History of Islamic Philosophy*, p. 451

583   Majid Fakhry, *Averroes (Ibn Rshd), His Life, Works and Influence*, Oxford, Oneworld, 2008, p. 165

584   Fakhry, *Averroes*, p. 167

585   Sharif, *A History of Muslim Philosophy*, v. 2, p. 1381

586   "The human material intellect is, then, an eternal substance, the lowest rung in the incorporeal hierarchy." H. Davidson, al-Farabi, *Avicenna and Averroes on Intellect*, New York, Oxford University Press, 1992, p. 292

587   Charles Genequand, *Ibn Rushd's metaphysics*, Leiden, Brills, 1986, p. 50

588   See detail in H. Davidson, al-Farabi, *Avicenna and Averroes on Intellect*, p. 292-93

589   See details in Hubert Dethier, *Averroes's Dialectic of Enlightenment. Some Difficulties in the Concept of Reason*, Sartonia 15 (2002) (Sarton-Chair Lectures), p. 59-63; "Our speculative intellect is thus, in a certain sense, transient (but it is everlasting in the sense that humankind, when it is viewed as the total of all individuals at one time, actually thinks all intelligibilia at one time)." P. 60

590   Majid Fakhry, *Averroes*, p. 34

591   See Ibn Rushd, *Decisive Treatise* translated by C. Butterworth, Utah, B. Young University Press, 2001, p. 10 onward

592   George F. Hourani (translator), *Decisive Treatise*, London, Luzac, 1967, p. 179

593   Fakhry, *Averroes*, p. 35

594   Hurani, *Decisive Treatise*, p. 180

595   Richard C. Taylor, "Truth Does Not Contradict Truth": *Averroes and the Unity of Truth*, Topoi 19: 3–16, 2000, Netherlands , Kluwer Academic Publishers, p. 8

596   Hurani, *Decisive Treatise*, p. 181

597   Hurani, *Decisive Treatise*, p. 166

598   Hurani, *Decisive Treatise*, p. 181

599   See Hurani, *Decisive Treatise*, p. 182

600   See Hurani, *Decisive Treatise*, p. 167

601   Hourani (translator), *Decisive Treatise*, p. 49 and p. 168

602   Fakhry, *Averroes*, p. 24

603   Hurani, *Decisive Treatise*, p. 169

604   Fakhry, *Averroes*, p. 161-62

605   Fakhry, *Averroes*, p. 162

606   See details in Taylor, *Truth Does Not Contradict Truth*

607   Taylor, *Truth Does Not Contradict Truth*, p. 11

608   Harry Austryn Wolfson, *The Double Faith Theory in Clement, Saadia, Averroes and St. Thomas, and Its Origin in Aristotle and the Stoics*, The Jewish Quarterly Review, New Series, Vol. 33, No. 2 (Oct., 1942), University of Pennsylvania Press, p. 246

609   Wolfson, *Double Faith Theory*, p. 247

610   Wolfson, *Double Faith Theory*, p. 250

611   Wolfson, *Double Faith Theory*, p. 243

612   Taylor, *Truth Does Not Contradict Truth*, p. 8

613   See C. Butterworth (editor and translator), *Averroes' Three Short Commentaries on Aristotle's "Topics," "Rhetoric," and "Poetics"*, Albany, State University of New York's Press, 1977

614   Al-Fārābī, *Kitāb al-Ḥurūf (Book of Letters)*, ed. Muhsin Mahdi (Beirut: Dar el-Machreq, 1969), Part II, chap. 19, n. 110, 132: –For philosophy in general precedes religion in the same way as the user of tools precedes the tools in time…. And religion precedes theology and jurisprudence in the same way as the master employing the servant precedes the servant, and the user of the tool, the tool ‖ (unless otherwise indicated, all translations are my own). See more details in Deborah Black, *Logic and Aristotle's "Rhetoric" and "Poetics" in Medieval Arabic Philosophy* (Leiden: Brill, 1990).

615   Fārābī, *Book of Letters*, II, 19, n.108, 131.

616   Fārābī, *Book of Letters*, II, 19, n.112, 133

617   Fārābī, *Book of Letters*, II, 24, n.153, 157

618   Aquinas, *Summa Contra Gentiles*, p. 5

619   R. Taylor, Ibn Rushd/Averroes and "Islamic" Rationalism, *Journal of Medieval Encounters*, 15, 2009, p. 225

620   Taylor, *Ibn Rushd/Averroes and "Islamic" Rationalism*, p. 225-226

621   Taylor, *Ibn Rushd/Averroes and "Islamic" Rationalism,* p. 230

622   Taylor, *Ibn Rushd/Averroes and "Islamic" Rationalism,* p. 231

623   Taylor, *Ibn Rushd/Averroes and "Islamic" Rationalism,* p. 232

624   Taylor, *Ibn Rushd/Averroes and "Islamic" Rationalism,* p. 232

625   Taylor, *Ibn Rushd/Averroes and "Islamic" Rationalism,* p. 231

626   See Rafiabadai and Amin Kak, *The Attitude of Islam Towards Science and Philosophy,* p. 145-146

627   Fakhry, *Averoes,* p. 131

628   Fakhry, *Averoes,* p. 139

629   Joseph A. Buijs, *Religions and Philosophy in Maimonides, Averroes, and Aquinas,* Medieval Encounters, 8, 2-3, Leiden, Brill, 2002, p. 181

630   Buijs, *Religions and Philosophy,* P. 181-82

631   Buijs, *Religions and Philosophy,* p. 182

632   Buijs, *Religions and Philosophy,* p 182

633   Randle Cloud, "Aristotle's Journey to Europe: A Historical Examination of the Role Played by the Islamic Empire in the Transmission of Western Philosophy of Education Sources to Europe from the Fall of Rome to the Medieval Period", Ph.D. thesis University of Kansas, 2007, p. 329

634   Richard Fletcher, Moorish Spain, Berkeley, University of California Press, 2006, p.134

635   Montgomery W. Watt, *The Influence of Islam on Medieval Europe,* Islamic Studies 9, Edinburgh: Edinburgh University Press, 1972, p. 71

636   Quoted in Rafiabadai and Amin Kak, *The Attitude of Islam Towards Science,* P. 43

637   Etienne Gilson, *Reason and Revelation in the Middle Ages,* New York: Charles Scribner's Sons, 1938, 38

638   Gilson, *Reason and Revelation,* p. 38

639   Gilson, *Reason and Revelation,* p. 40

640   Gilson, *Reason and Revelation,* p. 79

641   Fakhry, *Averroes,* p. 139-40

642   Aquinas, *Summa Contra Gentiles,* p. 74

643   Aquinas, *Summa Contra Gentiles,* p. 75

644   Aquinas, *Summa Contra Gentiles*, p. 74

645   Aquinas, *Summa Theologica*, p. 2-3

646   Aquinas, *Summa Contra Gentiles*, p. 66-67

647   Aquinas, *Summa Contra Gentiles*, p. 67-68

648   Aquinas, *Summa Contra Gentiles*, p. 68

649   Aquinas, *Summa Contra Gentiles*, p. 60

650   Aquinas, *Summa Contra Gentiles*, p. 61

651   Aquinas, *Summa Contra Gentiles*, p. 64

652   Aquinas, *Summa Contra Gentiles*, p. 77

653   Aquinas, *Summa Theologica*, p. 5

654   Hurani, *Decisive Treatise*, p. 178

655   Edward Booth, *Aristotelian Aporetic Ontology in Islamic and Christian Thinkers*, Cambridge, Cambridge University Press, 1983, p. 254

656   See Majid Fakhry, *al-Farabi: Founder of Islamic Neoplatonism, His Life, Works and Influence*, Oxford, Oneworld, 2002 and I. R. Netton, Al-Farabi and His School, New York, Routledge, 1992

657   Fakhry, *al-Farabi*, p. 148 onward

658   Hammond, *The Philosophy of al-Farabi*, p. 12

659   Hammond, *The Philosophy of al-Farabi*, p. 13-15 (in reality it could have been taken directly from Ibn Sina and Ibn Rushd and indirectly from al-Farabi).

660   Hammond, *The Philosophy of al-Farabi*, p. 20; see also Damien Janos, Method, Structure and Development in al-Farabi's Cosmology, Leiden, Brill, 2012

661   Hammond, *The Philosophy of al-Farabi*, p. 20; Aquinas, *Summa theological*, http://www.ccel.org/ccel/aquinas/summa.html, p. 15

662   See Hammond, *The Philosophy of al-Farabi*, p. 20-21

663   Hammond, *The Philosophy of al-Farabi*, p. 21

664   Hammond, *The Philosophy of al-Farabi*, p. 21-22

665   Hammond, *The Philosophy of al-Farabi*, p. 22

666   See details in Mary T. Clark (Ed), *An Aquinas Reader*, New York, Fordham University Press, 1999, p. 122 onward

667   Hammond, *The Philosophy of al-Farabi*, p. 23-24

668   Hammond, *The Philosophy of al-Farabi*, p. 23-24

669   Hammond, *The Philosophy of al-Farabi*, p. 24-25

670   Hammond, *The Philosophy of al-Farabi*, p. 24; see details in Summa, p. 17 onward

671   Hammond, *The Philosophy of al-Farabi*, p. 25; see more details in Herbert H. Davidson, *Alfarabi, Avicenna and Averroes on Intellect, Their Cosmologies, Theories of the Active Intellect and Theories of Human Intellect*, Oxford, Oxford University Press, 1992, p. 44 onward

672   Hammond, *The Philosophy of al-Farabi*, p. 25; see details in Summa, p. 40 onward

673   Hammond, *The Philosophy of al-Farabi*, p. 25

674   Hammond, The Philosophy of al-Farabi , p. 25; see more details in Summa, p. 50 onward

675   Hammond, *The Philosophy of al-Farabi*, p. 26

676   Hammond, *The Philosophy of al-Farabi*, p. 26

677   Hammond, *The Philosophy of al-Farabi*, p. 26

678   Hammond, *The Philosophy of al-Farabi*, p. 26; Summa, p. 63

679   Hammond, *The Philosophy of al-Farabi*, p. 27; see details in Fakhry, al-Farabi, p. 79 onwrd

680   Hammond, *The Philosophy of al-Farabi* p. 27; see Summa, p. 617

681   Hammond, *The Philosophy of al-Farabi*, p. 27

682   Hammond, *The Philosophy of al-Farabi*, p. 27; see Summa, p. 104

683   Hammond, *The Philosophy of al-Farabi*, p. 28

684   Hammond, *The Philosophy of al-Farabi*, p. 28; Summa, p. 102

685   Hammond, *The Philosophy of al-Farabi*, p. 28

686   Hammond, *The Philosophy of al-Farabi*, p. 28

687   Hammond, *The Philosophy of al-Farabi*, p. 28

688   Hammond, *The Philosophy of al-Farabi*, p. 28; Summa, p. 137

689   Hammond, *The Philosophy of al-Farabi*, p. 29

690   Hammond, *The Philosophy of al-Farabi*, p. 38

691   Hammond, *The Philosophy of al-Farabi*, p. 38; Summa, p. 521

692   Hammond, *The Philosophy of al-Farabi*, p. 42; Summa, p. 528

693   Torrell, *Aquinas's Summa*, P. 85

694   Hammond, *The Philosophy of al-Farabi*, p. 32

695   See Herbert Davidson, *Alfarabi, Avicenna and Averroes*, p. 215 onward

696   Hammond, *The Philosophy of al-Farabi*, p. 54

697   Hammond, *The Philosophy of al-Farabi*, p. 55

698   Michael E. Marmura, *"Al-Ghazali"* in the *Cambridge Companion to Arabic Philosophy* edited by Peter Adamson and Richard Taylor, Cambridge, Cambridge University Press, 2005, p. 145

699   See details in Marmura, *"Al-Ghazali"*, p. 153

700   Marmura, *"Al-Ghazali"*, p. 137

701   Eugene A. Myers, *Arabic Thought and the Western World*, New York, Frederick Ungar Publishing Co., 1964, p. 39-40

702   See a detailed study Kenneth Garden, *Al-Ghazali's Contested Revival: Ihya Ulum al-Din and its Critics in Khorasan and the Maghrib*, Ph. D. Dissertation, University of Chicago, 2005, p. 162ff

703   See details in Kenneth Garden, *Al-Ghazali's Contested Revival*, chapters III and IV

704   D. B. Macdonald, "The Life of al-Ghazali, with special reference to his religious experiences and opinions", in *Journal of the American Oriental Society* edited by George F. Moore, New Haven, July, 1899, vol. 20, p. 99-100; N. Hanif, *Biographical Encyclopaedia of Sufis: Central Asia and Middle East*, New Delhi, Sarup & Sons, 2002, p. 178

705   See Garden, *Al-Ghazali's Contested Revival*, chapter IV

706   Hamid Naseem Rafiabadi, *Emerging From Darkness: Ghazali's Impact on the Western Philosophers*, New Delhi, Sarup & Sons, 2002, p. 170-171

707   Thomas Arnold and Alfred Guillaume eds., The Legacy of Islam, Oxford, Clarendon Press, 1931, P. 270

708   https://plato.stanford.edu/entries/al-ghazali/

709   Steven Harvey, *Why Did Fourteenth-Century Jews Turn to Alghazali's Account of Natural Science?*, The Jewish Quarterly Review, New Series, Vol. 91, No. 3/4 (Jan. - Apr., 2001), pp.359-376, p. 361

710   "Indeed, *Maqāṣid al-falāsifa* survives in its various Hebrew versions, under the title *Kavvanot ha- Filosofim*, in over seventy-five manuscripts, which makes it one of the most popular Hebrew books of the medieval period." Steven Harvey, "The Changing Image of al-Ghazali in Medieval Jewish Thought" in Tamer, *Islam and Rationality,* p. 289

711   See a detailed study in Anthony H. Minnema, *The Latin Readers of Al-Ghazel,* 1150-1600, Ph. D. dissertation, University of Tennessee, Knoxville, 2013

712   See details in Richard Harvey, *Raymundus Martini and the Pugio Fidei: The Life and Work of a Medieval Controversialist* (London, 1991, available at lulu.com/content/1385305)

713   Charles Burnett, "Arabic into Latin: the reception of the Arabic Philosophy into Western Europe" in the Cambridge Companion to Arabic Philosophy, P. 382

714   Rafiabadi, *Emerging From Darkness,* p. 175

715   R . E. Abu Shanab, *Ghazali and Aquinas on Causation,* Monist 58, 1974,pp. 140–150, p.148-149

716   Georg Sarton, *Introduction to the History of Science,* Baltimore, The Williams and Wilkens Company, v. II.2, p. 734

717   S. M. Ghazanfer ed., *Medieval Islamic Economic Thought,* Filing the "Great Gap" in European economics, New York, Routledge, 2003, p. 21-22

718   Sharif, *Philosophy,* v. 2, p. 1361

719   See James Sweetman, *Islam and Christian Theology: A Study of the Interpretation of Theological Ideas in the Two Religions,* Cambridge, James Clark and Company, 2002, Part Two, V. 1, p. 89-93

720   Janssens in Tamer, *Islam and Rationality,* p. 326

721   Margaret Smith, *Al-Ghazali the Mystic: A Study of the Life and Personality of Abu Hamid Muhammad al-Tusi al-Ghazali, together with an account of his Mystical Teaching and an estimate of his place in the History of Islamic Mysticism,* Lahore, al-Hijra Publishers, 1940, p. 222

722   See Janssens in Tamer, *Islam and Rationality,* p. 329

723   See Janssens in Tamer, *Islam and Rationality,* p. 327-344

724   Sharif, v.2, p. 1362; Janssens, in Tamer, *Islam and Rationality,* p. 327

725   See Hidemi Takahashi, *Barhebraeus: A Bio-Bibliography.* Piscataway, NJ: Gorgias Press, (2005).

726   Samuel M. Zwemer ed., *The Muslim World,* New York, Missionary Review Publishing Co., 1919, v. 9, P. 433

727   M. Nesim Doru "The Influence of Islamic Philosophy on Bar Hebraeus" *Cumhuriyet İlahiyat Dergisi - Cumhuriyet Theology Journal,* ISSN: 2528-9861 e-ISSN: 2528-987X, CUID, December 2017, 21 (2): 913-946

728   Doru in "The Influence of Islamic Philosophy on Bar Hebraeus", p. 934

729   In Tamer, *Islamic Rationality,* p. 303-324

730   In Tamer, *Islamic Rationality,* p. 324

731   In Tamer, *Islamic Rationality,* p. 324

732   Doru in "The Influence of Islamic Philosophy on Bar Hebraeus", p. 937

733   See A. J. Wensinck trans., *Bar Hebraeus's Book of the Dove, Together With Some Chapters of His Ethikon,* Leyden, E. J. Brill, 1919, p. XVII onward; Weitz, Lev. "Al-Ghazali, Bar Hebraeus, and the 'Good Wife.'" *Journal of the American Oriental Society,* vol. 134, no. 2, 2014, pp. 203–223. *JSTOR,* JSTOR, www.jstor.org/stable/10.7817/jameroriesoci.134.2.203.

734   Brian E. Cossell, "The Legacy Of The Ancient Syrian Church", https://biblicalstudies.org.uk/pdf/eq/1968-2_083.pdf, p. 87-88

735   https://biblicalstudies.org.uk/pdf/eq/1968-2_083.pdf, p. 94

736   https://biblicalstudies.org.uk/pdf/eq/1968-2_083.pdf, p. 95

737   See https://biblicalstudies.org.uk/pdf/eq/1968-2_083.pdf, p. 90 onward

738   See Sarah Pessin, "The Influence of Islamic Thought on Maimonides", https://plato.stanford.edu/entries/maimonides-islamic/; see "Chales H. Manekin, "Divine Will in Maimonides' Later Writings," *Maimonidean Studies* 5 (2008): 207–209. Manekin focuses on certain parallels between the discussion of creation/eternity in the *Guide* II, 25 and al-Ghazali's *Faḍā'ih al-bāṭiniyya.* He notes the similarity between the two texts regarding the rules of interpretation of Scripture when the plain meaning is demonstrated to be false. What is more striking is his suggestion that Maimonides' statement there – that belief in the eternity of the world as Aristotle conceives it "destroys the law in its principle, necessarily gives the lie to every miracle, and reduces to inanity all the hopes and threats that the Law has held out, unless – by God! – one interprets the miracles figuratively also, as was done by the Islamic internalists [*ahl al-bāṭin*]; this, however, would result in some sort of crazy imaginings [*hadhayān*]" (*Guide,* II, 25, 328) – may have been influenced by *Faḍā'ih*

al-bāṭiniyya. In that work, al-Ghazali also refers to the crazy imaginings or *hadhayān* of the *bāṭiniyya*, precisely in connection with their allegorical interpretations of the miracles of the Qur'ān. Now Maimonides, in his various writings, does not refer only to the *hadhayān* of the internalists, but as Sarah Stroumsa has showed in several studies, uses the term to describe several different people and groups of people (see, e.g., Sarah Stroumsa, *Maimonides in His World: Portrait of a Mediterranean Thinker*, Princeton: Princeton University Press, 2009, 138–152). But in this passage from the *Guide*, the term appears, as in al-Ghazali, in connection with the interpretation of miracles of the internalists." S. Harvey, *Changing Image of al-Ghazali*, note 15, p. 293

739 See Maimonides, *Guide of the Perplexed*, trans. Shlomo Pines, Chicago: The University of Chicago Press, 1963

740 See Hava Lazarus-Yafeh, "Was Maimonides Influenced by Alghazali?" (Hebrew), in *Tehillah le-Moshe: Biblical and Judaic Studies in Honor of Moshe Greenberg*, ed. Mordechai Cogan, Barry L. Eichler, and Jeffrey H. Tigay, Winona Lake, Indiana: Eisenbrauns, 1997, 163–169. Some general similarities between al-Ghazali's *Deliverance from Error* and the *Guide* were discussed by Vincenzo M. Poggi in his study of the *Deliverance, Un classico della spiritualità Musulmana*, Rome: Libreria dell'Universita Gregoriana, 1967, chap. 6, 103–136. See McCarthy's summary of this discussion in his *Freedom and Fulfillment*, xliii–v.

741 Herbert A. Davidson, *Moses Maimonide: the Man and His Works*, p. 104.

742 See Tribute to Michael – *Studies in Jewish and Muslim Thought Presented to Professor Michael Schwarz*, (in Hebrew and English) eds. Sara Klein-Braslavy, Binyamin Abrahamov, Joseph Sadan, Tel Aviv 2009.

743 See S. Harvey, *Changing Image of al-Ghazali*, note 15, p. 293

744 Harvey, *Changing Image of al-Ghazali*, p. 293-294

745 Harvey, *Changing Image of al-Ghazali*, p. 294; Avner Gil'adi, "A Short Note on the Possible Origin of the Title *Moreh ha-Nevukhim*" (Hebrew), *Tarbiz* 48 (1979): 346–347. "According to Gil'adi, al-Ghazali uses the term *dalīl al-mutaḥayyirīn* (the guide of the perplexed) at least twice in the *Revival*, each time as an attribute of God. He suggests that Maimonides may have intentionally slightly modified this phrase in his title to *Dalālat al-ḥā'irīn* (literally, *The Instruction of the Perplexed*) to avoid exact identification with the divine attribute. See further Michael Schwarz's Hebrew trans. of the *Guide of the Perplexed*, Tel-Aviv: Tel-Aviv University Press, 2002, 11, n. 19; cf. R. J. McCarthy, *Freedom and Fulfill-*

ment, Boston: Twayne, 1980, xliv." Harvey, Changing Image, p. 294

746   Harvey, *Changing Image of al-Ghazali,* note 15, p. 293-294

747   Davidson, *Moses Maimonide: the Man and His Works,* p. 104

748   See Rom Landau, *Islam and the Arabs,* New York, Routledge, 2008, p. 153; see S. Harvey, "Al-Ghazali and Maimonides and Their Books of Knowledge" in J. M. Harris ed., Be'orot Yitzhak: *Studies in Memory of Isadore Twersky,* London, Harvard University Press, 2005, p. 99-118

749   Harvey, *Changing Image of al-Ghazali,* p. 295

750   Harvey, *Changing Image of al-Ghazali,* p. 295-296

751   On the influence of Islamic law on Maimonides, see, e.g., Gideon Leibson, "Parallels Between Maimonides and Islamic Law," in *The Thought of Moses Maimonides,* ed. Ira Robinson, Lawrence. Kaplan, Julien Bauer, Lewiston, New York: Edwin Mellen Press, 1990, 209–48, and Joel Kraemer, "The Influence of Islamic Law on Maimonides: The Case of the Five Qualifications," *Te'udah* 10 (1996): 225–44.

752   Amira Eran, "Al-Ghazali and Maimonides on the World to Come and Spiritual Pleasures", Jewish Studies Quarterly, Vol. 8, No. 2 (2001), pp. 137-166

753   Eran, "Al-Ghazali and Maimonides on the World to Come and Spiritual Pleasures", p. 143

754   Sarah Stroumsa, *True Felicity: Paradise in the Thought of Avicenna and Maimonides,* Medieval Encounters 4, 1, Leiden, Brill, 1998, p. 71

755   See Idit Dobbs-Weinstein, *Maimonides and St. Thomas on the Limits of Reason,* Albany, SUNY Press, 1995; Luis Cortest, Philo's Heirs: *Moses Maimonides and Thomas Aquinas,* Brighton, MA, Academic Studies Press, 2017

756   Hans Daiber, *Islamic Thought in the Dialogue of Cultures,* Leiden, Brills, 2012, p. 135-136

757   H. A. Wolfson, *Nicolaus of Autrecourt and Ghazali's Argument against Causality,* Speculum 44, 1969, pp. 234–238

758   Wolfson, *Nicolaus of Autrecourt and Ghazali's Argument against Causality,* p. 234

759   Wolfson, *Nicolaus of Autrecourt and Ghazali's Argument against Causality,* p. 234-235

760   Daniel, E. Randolph. 'The Desire for Martyrdom: A Leitmotiv of St.

Bonaventure'. Franciscan Studies 32 (1972): 74–87 and *The Franciscan Concept of Mission in the High Middle Ages.* Kentucky: University Press of Kentucky, 1975; Duuane V. Lapsanski, *Evangelical Perfection: An Historical Examination of the Concept in the Early Franciscan Sources.* New York: Franciscan Institute of St Bonaventure University, 1977; C. H. Lawrence, *The Friars: The Impact of the Early Mendicant Movement on Western Society.* London: Longman, 1994.

761   Rafiabadi, *Emerging From Darkness,* p. 184

762   See Zwemer ed., *The Muslim World,* v. 9, p. 432-433

763   Sharif, *Philosophy,* v. 2, p. 1362

764   Al-Ghazali, *Tahafut al-Falasifah,* Problem XIII, p. 153 onward

765   Al-Ghazali, *Tahafut al-Falasifah,* p. 162

766   Aquinas, *Summa Theologica,* p. 109

767   See Stephen J. Pope ed., *The Ethics of Aquinas,* Washington D. C., Georgetown University Press, 2002, p. 30

768   See Frank Griffle, *Al-Ghazali's Philosophical Theology,* Oxford, Oxford University Press, 2009, p. 48 onward

769   See Abu Hamid Muhammad al-Ghazali, *Ihya Ulum al-Din* translated by Fazl-ul Karim as "Revival of Religious Learnings", Karachi, Darul Ishaat, 1993, v. 1, p. 14; Alexander Treiger, *Inspired Knowledge in Islamic Thought,* p. 36-37

770   Qouted from Treiger, *Inspired Knowledge in Islamic Thought,* p. 37

771   Treiger, *Inspired Knowledge in Islamic Thought,* p. 37

772   Treiger, *Inspired Knowledge in Islamic Thought,* p. 38

773   Pope, ed., *The Ethics of Aquinas,* p. 31

774   Pim Valkenberg, *Being Found While Seeking: In Search of a Basic Structure of Root Metaphors in Muslim Spirituality,* Studies in Spirituality 16, 39-58, 2006, p. 40

775   See Marianne Farina c.s.c., 'God's Presence and the moral life: Shared resources from the writings of Thomas Aquinas and Abu Hamid Muhammad al-Ghazali', in: Jaarboek 2004 Thomas Instituut te Utrecht, Utrecht, 2005, p. 33-65.

776   Valkenberg, *Being Found While Seeking,* p. 53

777   See Jeffery Hause ed., *Aquinas' Summa Theologiae: A Critical Guide,* Cam-

bridge, Cambridge University Press, 2018, p. 160 and for Ghazali, M. A. J. Sharif, *Ghazali's Theory of Virtue,* Albany, Suny Press, 1975, p. 163

778   See al-Ghazali, *Ihya,* v. 3 and 4

779   Valkenberg, *Being Found While Seeking,* p. 54

780   See Annemarie Schimmel, *Mystical Dimentions of Islam,* Chapel Hill, University of North Carolina Press, 1975, p. 94

781   See details in Garden, *Ghazali's Contested Revival,* p. 17 onward;

782   Valkenberg, *Being Found While Seeking,* p. 54

783   Annemarrie Schimmel, *The Mystery of Numbers,* Oxford, Oxford University Press, 1993, p. 20-21

784   Schimmel, *Mystical Dimentions of Islam,* p. 95

785   Valkenberg, *Being Found While Seeking,* p. 40

786   Pope ed., *The Ethics of Aquinas,* p. 30

787   Pope ed., *The Ethics of Aquinas,* p. 30

788   Valkenberg, *Being Found While Seeking,* p. 55

789   Valkenberg, *Being Found While Seeking,* p. 55

790   See Michele Mangini, *Rationality and Ethics between Western and Islamic Tradition,* Religions 2018, 9, 302; doi:10.3390/rel9100302, p. 13; also Servais Pinckaers O.P. The Sources of Christan Ethics, translated by Mary Thomas Noble O. P., Edinburgh, T & T Clark, 1995

791   See details in Thomas Williams & E. M. Atkins (eds.), *Disputed Questions on the Virtues.* Cambridge, Cambridge University Press, 2005, p. 10

792   See Joseph Owens: "Aquinas as Aristotelian Commentator," in *St. Thomas Aquinas. 1274-1974.* Commemorative Studies (Toronto: Pont. Ins!. Med. Stud., 1974) V. 1, pp. 213-38. R.-A. Gauthier: *Introduction. Somme contre les gentiles* (paris: Editions Universitaires, 1993) pp. 150, 180. "St. Thomas et l'Ethique a Nicomaque," in Th. Aquinas: *Opera omnia* (Rome: Leonine Comm., 1971) T. 48, pp. xxiv-xxv.

793   Denis 1. M. Bradley: *Aquinas on the Twofold Human Good. Reason and Human Happiness in Aquinas's Moral Science* (Wash., D.C.: Catholic U. of America Press, 1997) pp. 514-34; especially pp. 528-30.

794   James C. Doig, *Aquinas' Philosophical Commentary on the Ethics: A Historical Perspective,* London, Kluwer Academic Publishers, 2001, p. XI

795   Mark D. Jordan, "Theology and Philosophy" in *Cambridge Companion to Aquinas*, p. 233

796   Jordan, "Theology and Philosophy" in *Cambridge Companion to Aquinas*, p. 232

797   Mangini, *Rationality and Ethics between Western and Islamic Tradition*, p. 10 onward

798   See Richard J. Regan, *Thomas Aquinas Treatise on Law*, Cambridge, Hackett Publishing, 2000

799   See Pieper, *Four Cardinal Virtues*, p. 14

800   See Sharif, *Ghazali's Theory of Virtue*, p. 79 onward

801   Thomas Williams & E. M. Atkins (eds.), *Disputed Questions on the Virtues*, p. 25

802   Thomas Williams & E. M. Atkins (eds.), *Disputed Questions on the Virtues*, p.26

803   See Timothy J. Gianotti, *Al-Ghazali's Unspeakable Doctrine of the Soul: Unveiling the Esoteric Psychology and Eschatology of the Iḥyāʾ*. Leiden: E. J. Brill, 2001; also see Alexander Treiger, *Inspired Knowledge in Islamic Thought: al-Ghazali's Theory of Mystical Cognition and its Avecinnian Foundations*, New Yourk, Routledge, 2012, chapter 2, p. 35 onward

804   See Pope ed., *The Ethics of Aquinas*, p. 23

805   See Geffrey P. Hergan, *St. Albert the Great's Theory of the Beatific Vision*, New York, Peter Lang, 2002 especially chapter 5, p. 73 onward

806   See Edward Jabra JurJi, *Illumination in Islamic Mysticism*, Princeton, Princeton University Press, 1938

807   Quoted from Richard C. Taylor, *Arabic / Islamic Philosophy In Thomas Aquinas's Conception Of The Beatific Vision In Iv Sent.*, D. 49, Q. 2, A. 11, The Thomist 76 (2012): 509-50, p. 540-541

808   I am indebted to Mohamed Ahmed Sharif for this valuable discussion. See his *Ghazali's Theory of Virtue*, Albany, SUNY Press, 1975

809   Averroes's Middle Commentary and apparently the *Summa Alexandrinorum* were both translated by *Hermannus Alemannus*, in 1240 and 1243/44.

810   Jonathan Barnes and Anthony Kenny eds., *Aristotle's Ethics: Writings from the Complete Works*, Princeton, Princeton University Press, 2014, p. 361

811   Barnes and Anthony Kenny eds., *Aristotle's Ethics*, p. 216

812   "The Sources of the Ethics of St. Thomas Aquinas" in Stephen J. Pope ed., *The Ethics of Aquinas*, p. 20

813   Pope ed., *The Ethics of Aquinas*, p. 17

814   See Sharif, *Ghazli's Theory of Virtue*, chapter 2

815   See Joseph Pieper, *The Four Cardinal Virtues*, New York, Pantheon Books, 1959

816   See Pope, ed., *The Ethics of Aquinas*, p. 22

817   See Sharif, *Ghazli's Theory of Virtue*, p. 74

818   See Donal Roche O. P., *Prudence in Aristotle and St. Thomas Aquinas*, Master Dissertation, National University of Ireland, Maynooth, 2005, p. 80 onward

819   See Sharif, *Ghazli's Theory of Virtue*, p. 74

820   Mangini, *Rationality and Ethics between Western and Islamic Tradition*, p. 14

821   See Doig, *Aquinas' Philosophical Commentary*, p. 48 onward

822   See Roche O. P., *Prudence in Aristotle and St. Thomas Aquinas*, p. 95

823   Thomas S. Gibbs, *Aquinas, Ethics and Philosophy of Religion: Metaphysics and Practice*, Bloomington, India University Press, 2007, p. 11

824   Pope ed., *The Ethics of Aquinas*, p. 259

825   See Pope ed., *The Ethics of Aquinas*, p. 259

826   Pope ed., *The Ethics of Aquinas*, p. 259

827   See details Jean Porter, *The Recovery of Virtue: The Relevance of Aquinas for Christian Ethics*, Louisville, Westminster/John Knox, 1990, p. 163

828   Roche O. P., *Prudence in Aristotle and St. Thomas Aquinas*, p. 95

829   Pieper, *Four Cardinal Virtues*, p. 12

830   Pope ed., *The Ethics of Aquinas*, p. 266; see details in Peiper, *Four Cardinal Virtue*, p. 32 onward

831   Pieper, *Four Cardinal Virtue*, p. 37

832   Pieper, *Four Cardinal Virtue*, p. 37

833   Pieper, *Four Cardinal Virtue*, p. 38-39

834   Roche O. P., *Prudence in Aristotle and St. Thomas Aquinas,* p. 96

835   Roche O. P., *Prudence in Aristotle and St. Thomas Aquinas,* p. 96; see more details in Josef Pieper, *Prudence,* trans. by Richard and Clara Winston, (London: Faber and Faber, 1959, p. 58 onward

836   Istvan P. Bejczy, *Virtue Ethics in the Middle Ages: Commentaries on Aristotle's Nicomachean Ethics,* 1200–1500, Leiden, Brill, 2008, p. 77; See Barnes and Anthony Kenny eds., *Aristotle's Ethics,* p. 268 onward

837   See Pope ed., *The Ethics of Aquinas,* p. 305

838   Pope ed., *The Ethics of Aquinas,* p. 309

839   Bejczy, *Virtue Ethics in the Middle Ages,* p. 99

840   Pope ed., *The Ethics of Aquinas,* p. 310

841   Bejczy, *Virtue Ethics in the Middle Ages,* p. 95

842   Bejczy, *Virtue Ethics in the Middle Ages,* p. 91

843   Barnes and Anthony Kenny eds., *Aristotle's Ethics,* p. 288-289

844   Barnes and Anthony Kenny eds., *Aristotle's Ethics,* p. 289

845   Barnes and Anthony Kenny eds., *Aristotle's Ethics,* p. 289-290

846   Barnes and Anthony Kenny eds., *Aristotle's Ethics,* p. 291

847   Barnes and Anthony Kenny eds., *Aristotle's Ethics,* p. 292

848   Barnes and Anthony Kenny eds., *Aristotle's Ethics,* p. 293

849   See Sharif, *Ghazali's Theory of Virtue,* p. 46 onward

850   Fazlul Karim trans., *Ihya,* v. III, p. 252

851   Fazlul Karim trans., *Ihya,* v. III, p. 257

852   Fazlul Karim trans., *Ihya,* v. III, p. 268 onward

853   Mangini, *Rationality and Ethics betweenWestern and Islamic Tradition,* p. 14

854   See Surah al-Furqan, 25:63-77

855   *Summa theologiae* II.II.130.1, *Opera omnia* 10: 71.

856   Bejczy, *Virtue Ethics in the Middle Ages,* p. 126

857   Bejczy, *Virtue Ethics in the Middle Ages,* p. 126-127

858   In Bejczy, *Virtue Ethics in the Middle Ages,* p. 127

859   See for Thomas, Pope ed., *The Ethics of Aquinas,* p. 45 onward

860   See Pope ed., *The Ethics of Aquinas,* p. 45 onward; for Ghazali see Fazlul Karim trans., *Ihya,* v. III, p. 272 onward

861   See Sharif, *Ghazli's Theory of Virtue,* p. 74

862   Barnes and Anthony Kenny eds., *Aristotle's Ethics,* p. 301

863   See Barnes and Anthony Kenny eds., *Aristotle's Ethics,* p. 11

864   See Barnes and Anthony Kenny eds., *Aristotle's Ethics,* p. 78

865   See Sharif, *Ghazli's Theory of Virtue,* p. 66

866   Pope, ed., *The Ethics of Aquinas,* p. 23

867   This has been noted by Tarif Khalidi, *The Muslim Jesus: Sayings and Stories in Islamic Literature* (Cambridge, MA: Harvard University Press, 2001), 33, and especially n. 43.

868   Pope, ed., *The Ethics of Aquinas,* p. 23

869   Barnes and Anthony Kenny eds., *Aristotle's Ethics,* p. 279

870   Barnes and Anthony Kenny eds., *Aristotle's Ethics,* p. 280

871   Barnes and Anthony Kenny eds., *Aristotle's Ethics,* p. 284

872   See Sharif, *Ghazli's Theory of Virtue,* p. 70

873   See Sharif, *Ghazli's Theory of Virtue,* p. 67

874   See Pope, ed., *The Ethics of Aquinas,* p. 313 onward

875   See Pope, ed., *The Ethics of Aquinas,* p. 17 onward

876   Renard, *Islam and Christianity,* p. 101

877   F. G. Moore, *History of Religions,* Edinburgh, T. & T. Clark, 1948, v. II, p. 457

878   John Renard, *Islam and Christianity: Theological Themes in Comparative Perspective,* Berkeley, University of California Press, 2011, p. 174

879   Renard, *Islam and Christianity,* p. 169

880   Renard, *Islam and Christianity,* p. 169

881   Margaret Smith, *Al-Ghazali the Mystic,* p. 220

882   Margaret Smith, *Al-Ghazali the Mystic,* p. 220-221

883   Margaret Smith, *Al-Ghazali the Mystic,* p. 221

884   Margaret Smith, *Al-Ghazali the Mystic,* p. 221-222

885   See Binyamin Abrahamov, *Divine Love in Islamic Mysticism: The Teachings of al-Ghazali and al-Dabbagh,* New York, Routledge, 2003, p. 84 onward

886   Margaret Smith, *Al-Ghazali the Mystic,* p.222

887   Jules Janssens does not deny any direct influence, as Farina does, but makes mention of a limited direct influence, agreeing, as she does, the existence of close parallells, and even, on occasion, of absolute convergences.)

888   Marianne Farina, *Moral Goodness And Friendship With God: The Moral Teachings Of Thomas Aquinas And Hamid Al-Ghazali,* Ph. D. Dissertation, Boston College, 2004, p. iii (abstract)

889   See Farina, *Moral Goodness And Friendship With God,* chapter two, p. 108-199

890   Farina, *Moral Goodness And Friendship With God,* p. 5-6

891   Ghazali, *The Alchemy of Happiness* translated by Claude Field, (Lahore: Ashraf Press, 1947) p.17

892   Thomas Aquinas, *Summa Theologica* Translated by the Dominican Friars. (New York: Benziger Brothers, 1947) I-II, 3.8 and 5.2.

893   Farina, *Moral Goodness And Friendship With God,* p. 15-16

894   Farina, *Moral Goodness And Friendship With God,* p.16

895   Farina, *Moral Goodness And Friendship With God,* p.16

896   See Farina, *Moral Goodness And Friendship With God,* chapter 3, p. 206-343

897   George Sarton, *Introduction to the History of Science,* Baltimore, William and Wlkins Company, 1950, v. II.2, p. 73

Bibliography

Abrahamov, B., *Anthropomorphism and Interpretation of the Qur'an in the Theology of al-Qasim ibn Ibrahim*, (Boston: Brill,1996).

Abrahamov, B., *Divine Love in Islamic Mysticism: The Teachings of al-Ghazali and al-Dabbagh*, (New York: Routledge, 2003).

Abulafia, A. S., *Christians and Jews in the Twelfth-Century Renaissance* (London, Routledge, 1995).

Abulafia, D., *Frederick II, A Medieval Emperor*, (Oxford: Oxford University Press,1988).

Adamson, P. and Taylor, R. eds., *Cambridge Companion to Arabic Philosophy*, (Cambridge: Cambridge University Press, 2005).

Afsaruddin, A. ed., *Islam, the State, and Political Authority: Medieval Issues and Modern Concerns*, (New York: Palgrave McMillan, 2011).

Al-Ash`arī, Abū al-Ḥasan `Alī, *Maqālāt al-Islāmiyyīn wa Ikhtilāf al-Muâallīn*, M. `Abd al-Hamid, ed. (Beirut: Al-Ḥikmah, 1994).

Al-Fārābī, Abu Nasr, *al-Thamaràt al-Marāiyyah*, (Leiden: Brill, 1895).

Al-Fārābī, *Kitāb al-Ḥurūf (Book of Letters)*, ed. Muhsin Mahdi (Beirut: Dar el-Machreq, 1969).

Al-Faruqi, I. R. and al-Faruqi, L. L., *The Cultural Atlas of Islam* (New York: Macmillan Publishing Company, 1986).

Al-Ghazali, Abu Hamid, *al-Iqtisàd fi al-I'atiqàd* translated by Alaadin M. Yaqub as *Moderation in Belief*, Chicago, University of Chicago Press, 2013).

Al-Ghazali, *Ihya Ulum al-Din* translated by Fazl-ul Karim as *"Revival of Religious Learnings"*, (Karachi: Darul Ishaat, 1993).

Al-Ghazali, *Kitāb Iljam al-`Awām `an `Ilm al-Kalām* (Cairo: Maktabah al-Munīriyyah, 1933).

Al-Ghazali, *Tahafut al- Falasifah, Incoherence of the Philosophers*, translated by Michael E. Marmura, (Utah: Brigam Young University, 2002).

Al-Ghazali, *The Alchemy of Happiness* translated by Claude Field, (Lahore: Ashraf

Press, 1947).

Ames, C. C., *Righteous Persecution: Inquisition, Dominicans, and Christianity in the Middle Ages*, (Philadelphia: University of Pennsylvania Press, 2009).

Arberry, A. J., *Avicenna on Theology*, (Connecticut: Hyperion Press, 1979).

Armstrong, K., *Holy War: The Crusades and Their Impact on Today's World*, (New York: Anchor Books, 2001).

Arnold, T. and Guillaume, A. eds., *The Legacy of Islam*, (Oxford: Clarendon Press,1931).

Bammate, H., *Muslim Contribution to Civilization*, (Indiana: American Trust Publications,1976).

Barnes, J. and Kenny, A. eds., *Aristotle's Ethics: Writings from the Complete Works*, (Princeton: Princeton University Press, 2014).

Barton, S. and Linehan, P. eds., *Cross, Crescent and Conversion: Studies on Medieval Spain and Christendom in Memory of Richard Fletcher*, (Leiden: Brill, 2008).

Bejczy, I. P., *Virtue Ethics in the Middle Ages: Commentaries on Aristotle's Nicomachean Ethics*, 1200–1500, (Leiden: Brill, 2008).

Bennet, R. F., *The Early Dominicans: Studies in Thirteenth-Century Dominican History*, (New York: Russel and Russel, 1971).

Booth, E., *Aristotelian Aporetic Ontology in Islamic and Christian Thinkers*, (Cambridge: Cambridge University Press,1983).

Bradley, D. I. M., *Aquinas on the Twofold Human Good: Reason and Human Happiness in Aquinas's Moral Science* (Washington D.C.: Catholic University of America Press, 1997).

Brett, E. T., *Humbert of Romans. His Life and View of Thirteenth-Century Society*, (Toronto: Pontifical Institute of Mediaeval Studies,1984).

Burkhardt, J., *The Civilization of the Renaissance in Italy*, translated by S. G. C. Middlemore, (New York: Macmillan,1904).

Burnett, C., *Arabic into Latin in the Middle Ages; The Translators and their Intellectual and Social Context*, (Burlington, VT: Ashgate, 2009).

Burnett, C., *The Introduction of Arabic Learning into England*, (London: British Library, 1997).

Burns, R., *Emperor of Culture: Alfonso X the Learned of Castile and His Thirteenth-Century Renaissance*, (Philadelphia: University of Pennsylvania Press, 1990).

Burns, R., *Moors and Crusaders in Mediterranean Spain*. Collected Studies, (London: Variorum, 1978).

Burr, D., *The Spiritual Franciscans: from Protest to Persecution in the Century after St. Francis*, (University Park, PA: Pennsylvania State University, 2001).

Burrell, D. B., *Knowing the Unknowable God: Ibn-Sina, Maimonides, Aquinas*, (Notre Dame, IN: University of Notre Dame Press,1986).

Burrell, D., *Freedom and Causation in Three Traditions*, (Notre Dame, IN: University of Notre Dame Press, 1993).

Butterworth, C., (editor and translator), *Averroes' Three Short Commentaries on Aristotle's "Topics," "Rhetoric," and "Poetics"*, (Albany: State University of New York's Press,1977).

Carpenter, D., *The Struggle for Mastery: The Penguin History of Britain 1066–1284*, (London: Penguin, 2004).

Chazan, R., *Daggers of Faith. Thirteenth-Century Christian Missionizing and Jewish Response*, (Berkeley: University of California Press, 1989).

Cloud, R., *"Aristotle's Journey to Europe: A Historical Examination of the Role Played by the Islamic Empire in the Transmission of Western Philosophy of Education Sources to Europe from the Fall of Rome to the Medieval Period"*, Ph.D. thesis (University of Kansas, 2007).

Cole, P. J., *The Preaching of the Crusades to the Holy Lands*, 1095-1270, (Cambridge, Mass.: Medieval Academy Books, 1991).

Colish, M. I., *Medieval Foundations of the Western Intellectual Tradition: 400-1400*, (London: Yale University Press, 1998).

Cortest, L., *Philo's Heirs: Moses Maimonides and Thomas Aquinas*, (Brighton, MA: Academic Studies Press, 2017).

Daftary, F., *The Assassin Legends: Myths of the Ismai'lis*, (London: I. B. Tauris, 1994).

Daiber, H., *Islamic Thought in the Dialogue of Cultures*, (Leiden: Brill, 2012).

Dales, R. C., *Medieval Discussions of the Eternity of the World*, (Leiden: Brill, 1990).

Daniel, E. R., *Abbot Joachim of Fiore and Joachimism, Variorum Collected Studies Series*, (Burlington, VT: Ashgate Publishing Ltd., 2011).

Davidson, H. A., *Proofs for Eternity, Creation, and the Existence of God, in Medieval Islamic and Jewish Philosophy*, (New York: Oxford University press,1987).

Davidson, H., A., *Moses Maimonides: The Man and His Works*, (Oxford: Oxford University Press, 2010).

Davidson, H., *al-Farabi, Avicenna and Averroes on Intellect*, (New York: Oxford University Press, 1992).

Davies, D., *Method and Metaphysics in Maimonides' Guide for the Perplexed*, (New York: Oxford University Press, 2011).

Dobbs-Weinstein, I., *Maimonides and St. Thomas on the Limits of Reason*, (Albany: SUNY Press, 1995).

Doig, J. C., *Aquinas' Philosophical Commentary on the Ethics: A Historical Perspective*, (London: Kluwer Academic Publishers, 2001).

Donald S. Detwiler, *Germany: A Short History*, (Carbondale, IL: Southern Illinois University Press 1999).

Durant, W., *The Story of Civilization: The Age of Faith*, (New York: Simon and Schuster,1950).

Eby, F. and Arrowood, C. F., *The History and Philosophy of Education: Ancient and Medieval*, (Englewood Cliffs, NJ: Prentice-Hall, Inc.,1940).

Edwards, P. ed., *The Encyclopedia of Philosophy*, (New York: Macmillan, 1967).

Eijnden, J. G. J., *Poverty on the Way to God: Thomas Aquinas on Evangelical Perfection* (Leuven: Peeters, 1994).

Einstein, David, *Emperor Frederick II*, (New York: Philosophical Library,1949).

Eran, Amira, *"Al-Ghazali and Maimonides on the World to Come and Spiritual Pleasures"*, Jewish Studies Quarterly, Vol. 8, No. 2 (2001).

Eskenderoglu, M., *Fakhr al-Din al-Razi and Thomas Aquinas on the Question of the Eternity of the World*, (Leiden: Brill, 2002).

Euben, R. L., *Journeys to the Other Shore: Muslim and Western Travellers in Search of Knowledge*, (Princeton: Princeton University Press, 2006).

Fakhar al-Dīn al-Rāzī, *Asās al-Taqdīs* (Cairo: Maktabah Mustafa al-Bàbī, 1935).

Fakhry, M., *A History of Islamic Philosophy* (New York, London: Columbia University Press, 1970).

Fakhry, M., *al-Farabi: Founder of Islamic Neoplatonism, His Life, Works and Influence*, (Oxford: Oneworld, 2002).

Fakhry, M., *Averroes (Ibn Rshd), His Life, Works and Influence,* (Oxford: Oneworld, 2008).

Farina, M., *Moral goodness and Friendship with God: The Moral Teachings of Thomas Aquinas and Hamid al-ghazali*, Ph. D. Dissertation, (Boston College, 2004).

Finnis, J., *Aquinas: Moral, Political and Legal Theory*, (Oxford: Oxford University Press, 1998).

Fletcher, R., *Moorish Spain*, (Berkeley: University of California Press, 2006).

Frank, D. H. and Leaman, O. eds., *History of Jewish Philosophy*, (New York: Routledge, 2004).

Freed, J. B., *The Friars and German Society In the Thirteenth Century*. (Cambridge, Mass.: Mediaeval Academy of America,1977).

Friedlander, M. trans., Moses Maimonides, *The Guide for the Perplexed,* (Skokie, Illinois, Varda Books, 2016).

Galston, M., *Politics and Excellence: The Political Philosophy of Alfarabi*, (Princeton: Princeton University Press,1990).

Garden, K., *Al-Ghazali's Contested Revival: Ihya Ulum al-Din and its Critics in Khorasan and the Maghrib*, Ph. D. Dissertation, (University of Chicago, 2005).

Genequand, C., *Ibn Rushd's Metaphysics*, (Leiden: Brill, 1986).

Ghazanfer S. M. ed., *Medieval Islamic Economic Thought, Filing the "Great Gap" in European economics*, (New York: Routledge, 2003).

Gianotti, T, J., *Al-Ghazali's Unspeakable Doctrine of the Soul: Unveiling the Esoteric Psychology and Eschatology of the Iḥyāʾ*, (Leiden: E. J. Brill, 2001).

Gibbs, T. S., *Aquinas, Ethics and Philosophy of Religion: Metaphysics and Practice*, (Bloomington: India University Press, 2007).

Gilby, T., *The Political Thought of Thomas Aquinas*, (Chicago: University of Chicago Press, 1958).

Gilson, E., *History of Christian Philosophy in the Middle Ages*, (New York: Random House, 1955).

Gilson, E., *Reason and Revelation in the Middle Ages*, (New York: Charles Scribner's Sons, 1938).

Gilson, E., *Thomism: The Philosophy of Thomas Aquinas, A translation of LE THOMISME Sixth and final edition By Laurence K. Shook and Armand Maurer*, (Toronto: Pontifical Institute of Mediaeval Studies, 2002).

Grant, R. M., *The Letter and the Spirit*, (London: SPCK, 1957).

Griffle, F., *Al-Ghazali's Philosophical Theology*, (Oxford: Oxford University Press, 2009).

Gutas, D., *Greek Thought Arabic Culture: The Greco Arabic Translation Movement in Baghdad and Early Abbasid Society*, (London: Routledge, 1999).

Hammond, R., *The Philosophy of al-Farabi and Its Influence on Medieval Thought*, (New York: Hobson Book Press,1947).

Hanson, R. P. C., *Allegory and Event*, (London: S.C.M Press, 1959).

Harris, J. M. ed., *Beʾorot Yitzhak: Studies in Memory of Isadore Twersky*, (London: Harvard University Press, 2005).

Harris, W. V. ed., *Rethinking the Mediterranean*, (Oxford: Oxford University Press, 2006).

Haskins, C. H., *The Renaissance of the Twelfth Century*, (London: Harvard University Press, 1955).

Hasse, D. N. and Bertolacci, A. eds, *The Arabic, Hebrew and Latin Reception of Avicenna's Metaphysics*, (Berlin/Boston: deGruyter, 2012).

Hause, J. ed., *Aquinas' Summa Theologiae: A Critical Guide*, (Cambridge: Cambridge University Press, 2018).

Hergan, G. P., *St. Albert the Great's Theory of the Beatific Vision*, (New York: Peter Lang, 2002).

Hinnebusch, W. A., *History of the Dominican Order*, (Staten Island, New York: Alba House, 1966).

Hinnebusch, W. A., *Origins and Growth to 1500, The History of the Dominican Order*, (Staten Island: Alba House, 1965).

Hinnebusch, W. A., *The Dominicans: A Short History*, (Staten Island, N.Y.: Alba House, 1975).

Hoffman, E. R., *Pathways of Portability: Islamic and Christian interchange from the tenth to the twelfth century*, (Oxford: Blackwell Publishers, 2001).

Hoffman, R. J. trans., *Celsus: On the True Doctrine*, (New York: Oxford University Press, 1987).

Hoffman, R. J. trans., *Porphyry's Against the Christians*, (New York: Prometheus Books, 1994).

Holmyard, E. J. ed., *The Works of Geber*, translated by Richard Russel, (London: Dent,1928) digitalized by the University of Michigan on July 13, 2007).

Howarth, S., *The Knights Templar*, (New York: Barns & Noble, 1993).

Hourani, G. F. trans., *Decisive Treatise*, (London: Luzac, 1967).

Hyman, Arthur, Walsh, J. A. and Williams, T. eds., *Philosophy in the Middle Ages: The Christian, Islamic, and Jewish Traditions*, (New York: Hackett Publishing Company, 2010).

Ibn Rushd, Abu al-Walïd Muhammad ibn Ahmad, *Fasl al-Maqa'l fï ma bayn al-Hikmah wa al-Shari'ah min al-I'attida'l*, 2nd edn. (Cairo: Dar al-Ma'arif, 1983)

Ibn Rushd, *Decisive Treatise* translated by C. Butterworth, (Utah: B. Young University Press, 2001).

Inati, S., *Ibn Sina's Remarks and Admonitions, Physics and Metaphysics*, An Analysis and Annotated Translation, (New York: Columbia University Press, 2014).

Jackson, P. ed. and trans, *The Mission of Friar William of Rubruck: His Journey to the Court of the Great Khan Mongke*, 1253–1255, (London: The Hackluyt Society, 1990).

Jackson, P. ed. and trans., *The Seventh Crusade*, 1244–1254: Sources and Documents, (Aldershot: Ashgate, 2007).

Janssens, J. and De Smet, D. eds., *Avicenna and His Heritage*, (Leuven: Leuven University Press, 2002).

Jarallah, Z. H., *al-Mu`tazilah* (Cairo: al-Mu'assasah al-`Arabiyyah li al-Dirāsāt wa al-Nashr, 1947).

Johns, J., *Arabic Administration in Norman Sicily*, (Cambridge: Cambridge University Press, 2002).

Jordan, W., *Louis IX and the Challenge of the Crusade: A Study in Rulership*, (Princeton: Princeton University Press, 1979).

JurJi, E. J., *Illumination in Islamic Mysticism*, (Princeton: Princeton University Press, 1938).

Kantorowicz, E., *Frederick II*, (New York: Ungar Publishing, 1931).

Karris, R. J. trans., *Bonaventure, Disputed Questions on Evangelical Perfection*, (Saint Bonaventure, NY: Saint Bonaventure University, 2008).

Kazi, K. and Flynn, J. G. trans., *Muslim Sects and Divisions: The Section on Muslim Sects in Kitab al-Milal wa al-Nihal by Shahrastani*, (London: Kegan Paul International, 1984).

Kedar, B., *Crusade and Mission: European Approaches Toward the Muslims*, (Princeton: Princeton University Press, 1984).

Kedar, B., *Franks, Muslims and Oriental Christians in the Latin Levant: Studies in Frontier Acculturation*, (Aldershot: Ashgate, 2006).

Kenny, A., *A New History of Western Philosophy: Ancient Philosophy*, (Oxford: Clarendon Press, 2006).

Kenny, A., *An Illustrated Brief History of Western Philosophy*, (New Jersey: Wiley-Blackwell, 2006).

Kerr, F., *Thomas Aquinas: A Very Short Introduction*, (Oxford: Oxford University Press, 2009).

Khalidi, T., *The Muslim Jesus: Sayings and Stories in Islamic Literature* (Cambridge, MA: Harvard University Press, 2001).

Klein-Braslavy, S., Abrahamov, B. and Sadan, J., *Tribute to Michael – Studies in Jewish and Muslim Thought Presented to Professor Michael Schwarz*, (in Hebrew and English), (Tel Aviv: Tel Aviv University, 2009).

Kraemer, J. L., *Maimonides: The Life and World of One of Civilization's Greatest Minds*, (New York: Doubleday Religion, 2010).

Kretzmann, N. and Stump, E. eds., *The Cambridge Companion to Aquinas*, (Cambridge: Cambridge University Press, 1999).

Kritzeck, J., *Peter the Venerable and Islam* (Princeton: Princeton University Press, 1964).

Lambert, M., *Franciscan Poverty: the Doctrine of the Absolute Poverty of Christ and the Apostles in the Franciscan Order*, 1210-1323 (St. Bonaventure, NY: Franciscan Institute, 1998).

Landau, R., *Islam and the Arabs*, (New York: Routledge, 2008).

Lapsanski, D. V., *Evangelical Perfection: An Historical Examination of the Concept in the Early Franciscan Sources*, (New York: Franciscan Institute of St Bonaventure University, 1977).

Lawrence, C. H., *The Friars: The Impact of the Early Mendicant Movement on Western Society*, (London: Longman, 1994).

Le Goff, Jacques, *Saint Louis*, trans. Gareth Evan Gollrad, (Notre Dame: University of Notre Dame Press, 2009).

Leff, G., *Medieval Thought: St.Augustine to Occam*, (Chicago: Quadrangle Books, 1958).

Lytle, G. F. ed., *Reform and Authority in the Medieval and Reformation Church*, (Washington, DC, Catholic University of America Press, 1981).

Macdonald, D. B., *Development of Muslim Theology, Jurisprudence and Constitutional Theory*, (Beirut: Khayats, 1965).

MacEvitt, C., *The Crusades and the Christian World of East*, (Pennsylvania: University of Pennsylvania Press, 2008).

Madkur,I., *Fī al-Falsafah al-Islāmiyyah*, (Cairo: Dār al-Ma`ārif, 1976).

Maier, C. T., *Crusade Propaganda and Ideology: Model Sermons for the Preaching of the Cross*, (Cambridge: Cambridge University Press, 2000).

Maier, C. T., *Preaching the Crusades: Mendicant Friars and the Cross in the Thirteenth Century*, (Cambridge: Cambridge University Press, 1994).

Maimonides, M., *Guide of the Perplexed*, trans. Shlomo Pines, (Chicago: The University of Chicago Press, 1963).

Marenbon, J. ed., *Medieval Philosophy*, (New York: Routledge, 2006).

Margaret Smith, *Al-Ghazali the Mystic: A Study of the Life and Personality*, (Lahore: al-Hijra Publishers, 1940).

Mark Johnson, M. ed., *St. Thomas Aquinas and the Mendicant Controversies*, Three Translations, (Leesburg, Virginia: Alethes Press, 2007).

Mayr-Harting, H., *Religion, Politics and Society in Britain*, 1066–1272, (Harlow, UK: Longman, 2011).

McGinnis, J. and Reisman, D. C., *Classical Arabic Philosophy, An Anthology of Sources*, (Cambridge: Hackett Publishing Company, 2007).

McGinnis, J., *Avicenna*, (Oxford: Oxford University Press, 2010).

McGrade, S. ed., *The Cambridge Companion to Medieval Philosophy*, (Cambridge: Cambridge University Press, 2006).

Menocal, M. R., *The Arabic Role in Medieval Literary History: A Forgotten Heritage*, (Philadelphia: University of Pennsylvania Press, 1987).

Metcalfe, A., *The Muslims of Medieval Italy*, (Edinburgh: Edinburgh University Press, 2009).

Metlitzki, D., *The Matter of Araby in Medieval England*, (New Haven: Yale University Press, 1977).

Michael Schwarz's Hebrew trans., *Guide of the Perplexed*, (Tel-Aviv: Tel-Aviv University Press, 2002).

Minnema, A. H., *The Latin Readers of Al-Ghazel*, 1150-1600, Ph. D. dissertation, University of Tennessee, Knoxville, 2013).

Moore, F. G., *History of Religions*, (Edinburgh: T. & T. Clark, 1948).

Mulchahey, M. M., *First the Bow is Bent in Study: Dominican Education before 1350*, (Toronto: Pontifical Institute of Mediaeval Studies, 1998).

Myers, E. A., *Arabic Thought and the Western World*, (New York: Frederick Ungar Publishing Co., 1964).

Nasr, H. and Leaman, O. eds., *History of Islamic Philosophy*, (New York: Routledge, 1996).

Netton, I. R., *Al-Farabi and His School*, (New York: Routledge, 1992).

Netton, I. R., *Allah Transcendent: Studies in the Structure and Semiotics of Islamic Phi-*

losophy, Theology and Cosmology, (New York: Routledge, 1995).

Netton, I. R., *Text and Trauma: An East-West Primer* (Richmond: Curzon Press, 1996).

Novikoff, A. J., *The Medieval Culture of Disputation: Pedagogy, Practice and Performance* (Philadelphia: University of Pennsylvania Press, 2013).

O' Malley S. J., J. W., *A History of Popes: From Peter to the Present*, (New York: Rowman and Littlefield Publishers, 2010).

O'Callaghan, F., *The Learned King: The Reign of Alfonso X of Castile*, (Philadelphia, PA: University of Pennsylvania Press, 1993).

Ormsby, E. L., *Moses Maimonides and His Time*, (Washington, DC: Catholic University of America Press, 1989).

Perry, M., Chase, M. and Jacob, J. eds., *Western Civilization, Ideas, Politics and Society*, (Boston, Houghton Mifflin Company, sixth edition, 2004).

Peters, E., *Inquisition*, (Berkeley: University of California Press, 1989).

Pieper, J., *The Four Cardinal Virtues*, (New York: Pantheon Books, 1959).

Pinckaers, S., *The Sources of Christan Ethics*, translated by Mary Thomas Noble O. P., (Edinburgh: T & T Clark, 1995).

Placher, W., *The Domestication of Transcendence*, (Louisville, KY: Westminster Press, 1996).

Pope, S. J. ed., *The Ethics of Aquinas*, (Washington D. C.: Georgetown University Press, 2002).

Power, Amanda, *Roger Bacon and the Defense of Christendom*, (Cambridge: Cambridge University Press, 2013).

Qādi, ʿAbd al-Jabbār, *Sharh al-Uåūl al-Khamsah*, ʿAbd al-Karim ʿUthman, ed., 1st edn., (Cairo: Maktabah Wahabah, 1965).

Rafiabadai, Hamid Naseem, *The Attitude of Islam Towards Science and Philosophy*, A Translation of Ibn Rushd's Faslul al-Maqal, (New Delhi: Sarup and Sons, 2003).

Rafiabadi, H. N., *Emerging From Darkness: Ghazali's Impact on the Western Philosophers*, (New Delhi, Sarup & Sons, 2002).

Rahman, F., *Islam*, (Chicago: University of Chicago Press, 1979).

Randolph, D. E., *The Franciscan Concept of Mission in the High Middle Ages*, (Kentucky: University Press of Kentucky, 1975).

Reeves, M., *The Influence of Prophecy in the Later Middle Ages: A Study in Joachimism*, (Notre Dame: University of Notre Dame Press, 1993).

Regan, R. J., *Thomas Aquinas Treatise on Law*, (Cambridge: Hackett Publishing, 2000).

Renard, J., *Islam and Christianity: Theological Themes in Comparative Perspective*, (Berkeley: University of California Press, 2011).

Resnick, I. B. ed., *A Companion to Albert the Great: Theology, Philosophy and the Sciences*, (Leiden: Brill, 2013).

Richard, J., *Saint Louis: Crusader King of France*, edited by Simon Lloyd, trans. Jean

Birrell, (Cambridge: Cambridge University Press, 1992).

Riley-Smith, J., *The Crusades: A History*, (New Haven, Connecticut: Yale University Press, 2005).

Rippin, A., *Muslims: Their Religious Beliefs & Practices*, (New York: Routledge, 1990).

Rita, George-Tvrtkovic, *A Christian Pilgrim in Medieval Iraq: Riccoldo da Montecroce's Encounter with Islam*, (Turnhout, Belgium: Brepols Press, 2012).

Robinson, I., Kaplan, L. and Bauer, J. eds., *The Thought of Moses Maimonides*, (Lewiston, New York: Edwin Mellen Press, 1991).

Roche, Donald O. P., *Prudence in Aristotle and St. Thomas Aquinas*, Master Dissertation, (National University of Ireland, Maynooth, 2005).

Rubin, J., *Learning in a Crusader City: Intellectual Activity and Intercultural Exchanges in Acre, 1191–1291* (Cambridge Studies in Medieval Life and Thought, Cambridge: Cambridge University Press, 2018).

Saliba, G., *Islamic Science and the Making of European Renaissance*, (London: MIT Press, 2007).

Sarton, G., *Introduction to the History of Science*, (Baltimore: The Williams and Wilkens Company, 1962).

Schacht, J. and Bosworth, C. E. eds., *The Legacy of Islam*, (Oxford: Oxford University Press, Second Edition, 1979).

Schimmel, A., *The Mystery of Numbers*, (Oxford: Oxford University Press, 1993).

Schimmel, A., *Mystical Dimentions of Islam*, (Chapel Hill: University of North Carolina Press, 1975).

Schweid, E., *The Classic Jewish Philosophers: From Saadia through the Renaissance*, translated by Leonard Levin, (Leiden: Brill, 2008).

Seeskin, K., *Maimonides on the Origin of the World*, (Cambridge: Cambridge University Press, 2006).

Shah, Z. A., *Anthropomorphic Depictions of God: The Concept of God in Judaic, Christian and Islamic Traditions*, Representing the Unrepresentable, (Washington: International Institute of Islamic Thought, 2012).

Sharif, M. M. ed., *A History of Muslim Philosophy*, (Wiesbadden: Otto Harrassowitz, 1963).

Sherif, M. A., *Ghazali's Theory of Virtue*, (Albany: SUNY Press, 1975).

Sisson, K. and Larson, A. L. eds., *A Companion to the Medieval Papacy: Growth of an Ideology and Institution*, (Leiden: Brill, 2016).

Smith, C., *Crusading in the Age of Joinville*, (Aldershot: Ashgate, 2006).

Smith, D. J., *Crusade, Heresy and Inquisition in the Lands of the Crown of Aragon (1167-1276)*, (Leiden: Brill, 2010).

Sokolowsky, R., *The God of Faith and Reason, Foundations of Christian Theology*,

(Washington D.C.: Catholic University of America Press, 1995).

Southern, R. W., *Western Views of Islam in the Middle Ages*, (Cambridge, MA: Harvard University Press, 1962).

Spufford, P., *Money and its Use in Medieval Europe*, (Cambridge: Cambridge University Press, 1988).

Sweetman, J., *Islam and Christian Theology: A Study of the Interpretation of Theological Ideas in the Two Religions*, (Cambridge: James Clark and Company, 2002)

Takahashi, H., *Barhebraeus: A Bio-Bibliography* (Piscataway, NJ: Gorgias Press, 2005).

Tamer, G., *Islam and Rationality: The Impact of al-Ghazali*, Papers Collected on His 900th Anniversary, (Leiden: Brill, 2015).

Tanner, K., *God and Creation in Christian Theology: Tyranny or Empowerment?*, (Oxford: Basil Blackwell, 1988).

Taylor, J. A., *Muslims in Medieval Italy: The Colony at Lucera*, (Lanham, Md: Lexington Books, 2003).

Thomas Aquinas, *Summa Contra Gentiles*, translated by Anton C. Pegis, (New York: Image Books, 1955).

Tolan, J. V., *Saracens: Islam in the Medieval European Imagination*, (New York: Columbia University Press, 2002).

Tolan, J., V., *Saint Francis and the Sultan: The Curious History of a Christian-Muslim Encounter*, (Oxford: Oxford University Press, 2009).

Torrell, Jean-Pierre, *Aquinas's Summa, Background, Structure and Reception*, translated by Benedict M.Guevin, (Washington D. C.: The Catholic University of America Press, 2005).

Treiger, A., *Inspired Knowledge in Islamic Thought: al-Ghazali's Theory of Mystical Cognition and its Avecinnian Foundations*, (New York: Routledge, 2012)

Tugwell, S. ed., *Early Dominicans: selected writings. Classics of Western Spirituality*, (London: SPCK, 1982).

Tyerman, C., *The Invention of the Crusades*, (London: Palgrave, 1998).

Van Cleve, T., *The Emperor Frederick II of Hohenstaufen*, (Oxford: Oxford University Press, 1972).

Verbruggen, J. F., *The Art of Warfare in Western Europe During the Middle Ages*, translated by Sumner Willard, (Woodbridge: Boydell Press, 2002).

Vollert, C. trans., *Medieval Discussions of the Eternity of the World*, St. Thomas Aquinas, Siger of Brabant and St. Bonaventure, On the Eternity of the World, (Milwaukee: Marquette University Press, 1984).

Vose, R., *Dominican, Muslims and Jews in the Medieval Crown of Aragon*, (Cambridge: Cambridge University Press, 2009).

Walter Ullmann, W., *Short History of the Papacy in the Middle Ages*, (New York: Routledge, 2003).

Watt, M. W., *The Influence of Islam on Medieval Europe*, (Edinburgh: Edinburgh University Press, 1972).

Watt, W. M., *Early Islam: Collected Articles* (Edinburgh: Edinburgh University Press, 1990).

Watt, W. M., *The Formative Period of Islamic Thought* (Edinburgh: Edinburgh University Press, 1973).

Wei, I. P., *Intellectual Culture in Medieval Paris: Theologians and the University*, c. 1100-1330, (Cambridge: Cambrdige University Press, 2012).

Weisheipl, James, O.P., *Friar Thomas D'Aquino: His Life, Thought and Works*, (Washington D.C.: The Catholic University of America Press, 1983).

Weiss, Daniel H. and Mahoney, L., *France and the Holy Land: Frankish Culture at the End of the Crusades*, (Baltimore: Johns Hopkins University Press, 2004).

Wensinck, A. J. trans., *Bar Hebraeus's Book of the Dove, Together With Some Chapters of His Ethikon Ethicon*, (Leiden, Brill, 1919).

Whalen, B. D., *Dominion of God: Christendom and Apocalypse in the Middle Ages*, (Cambridge, MA: Harvard University Press, 2009).

Whitehead, A. N., *Essays in Science and Philosophy*, (New York: Philosophical Library, 1947).

Wiersma, S., *Pearls in a dunghill: The anti-Jewish writings of Raymond Martin O.P.* (ca. 1220 - ca. 1285), Doctoral Thesis, (Tilburg University, 2015).

Wippel, J. F., *Metaphysical Themes in Thomas Aquinas II*, (Washington D. C.: The Catholic University of America Press, 2007).

Wolfson, H. A., *Religious Philosophy: A Group of Essays*, (New York: Atheneum, 1965).

Wolfson, H. A., *Repercussions of the Kalam in Jewish Philosophy*, (London: Harvard University Press, 1979).

Wolfson, H. A., *The Philosophy of the Kalam*, (Cambridge: Mass., Harvard University Press, 1976).

Zacour, N. P. and Hazard, H. W. eds., *The Impact of the Crusades on the Near East*, (A History of the Crusades v. V), (Madison: University of Wisconsin Press, 1985).

Zwemer, S. M. ed., *The Muslim World*, (New York: Missionary Review Publishing Co., 1919).

Index